Off The Beaten Track
GERMANY

GERMANY

Off the Beaten Track
GERMANY

Janet Aldridge · Grant Bourne
Sabine Körner-Bourne
George Speaight · George Wood

MOORLAND PUBLISHING

The Globe Pequot Press

Published by:
Moorland Publishing Co Ltd,
Moor Farm Road West, Ashbourne,
Derbyshire, DE6 1HD England

ISBN 0 86190 498 2 (UK)

The Globe Pequot Press
6 Business Park Road
PO Box 833, Old Saybrook,
Connecticut 06475-0833

ISBN 1-56440-301-7 (USA)

First published 1989. Reprinted 1989
Revised 2nd edition 1994
© Moorland Publishing Co Ltd 1994

Cover illustrations: *MPC Picture
Collection.*

Black and white illustrations have been
supplied by:
J. Aldridge; G. Bourne; Furth im Wald
Tourist Office; German National
Tourist Office; G. Holtl; MPC Picture
Collection; Oberbayern Tourist Office;
Regensburg Tourist Office; G. Speaight;
B. C. Walker; G. Wood; P. Wood.

Colour illustrations have been supplied
by:
J. Aldridge; G. Bourne; G. Holtl; Der
Senat der Hansestadt Lübeck; Oberbayern Tourist Office; G. Wood.

Quotations from *The German Lesson* by
Siegfried Lenz are reproduced with the
permission of Methuen, London.

Printed in Hong Kong by
Wing King Tong Co Ltd

British Library Cataloguing in Publication Data:
A catalogue record for this book is available from the British Library.

Library of Congress Cataloging-in-Publication Data
Off the beaten track. Germany/Janet Aldridge ... (et al.). — Rev. 2nd ed.
    p. cm.
  Includes Index.
  ISBN 1-56440-301-7 (USA). — ISBN 0-86190-498-2 (UK)
  1. Germany — Guidebooks.   I. Aldridge, Janet. II. Title: Germany.
DD16.035 1994
914.304'879 —dc20   93-10705
                                                                  CIP

Contents

Introduction 7

1 The Hanseatic Towns (*George Speaight*) 9

2 The East Friesland Islands (*George Speaight*) 21

3 The Sauerland (*George Wood*) 30

4 The Saar Valley (*George Wood*) 60

5 The Palatinate Forest Nature Park (*George Wood*) 84

6 Franconia (*George Speaight*) 101

7 The Tauber Valley (*George Wood*) 112

8 The Bayerischer Wald (*Janet Aldridge*) 132

9 The Bavarian Alps (Oberbayern) (*Janet Aldridge*) 184

10 The Upper Danube (*George Speaight*) 239

11 Eastern Germany — An Introduction 254
(*Grant Bourne & Sabine Körner-Bourne*)

12 The Baltic Coast (*Grant Bourne & Sabine Körner-Bourne*) 259

13 The Uckermark (*Grant Bourne & Sabine Körner-Bourne*) 284

14 The Altmark (*Grant Bourne & Sabine Körner-Bourne*) 298

15 The Harz (*Grant Bourne & Sabine Körner-Bourne*) 312

16 The Oberlausitz (*Grant Bourne & Sabine Körner-Bourne*) 334

Index 347

Accommodation and Eating Out 353

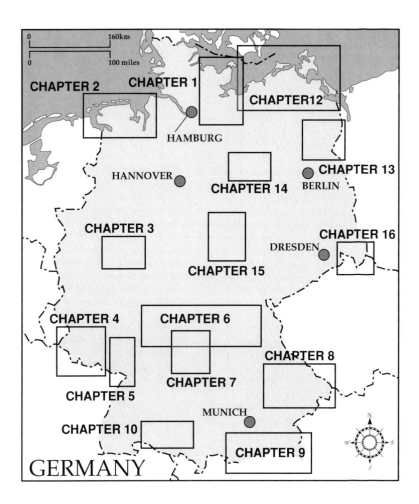

GERMANY

Museums and Other Places of Interest

Throughout Germany, State museums are often closed on Mondays and some times on public holidays. The tourist information bureaus listed at the end of each chapter can provide up-to-date lists of museums and other places of interest, with addresses and times of opening.

Note on Maps

The maps for each chapter, while comprehensive, are not designed to be used as route maps, but to locate the main towns, villages and places of interest.

Introduction

Western Europe is a continent of great diversity, well visited not just by travellers from other parts of the globe but by the inhabitants of its own member countries. Within the year-round processes of trade and commerce, but more particularly during the holiday season, there is a great surging interchange of nationalities as one country's familiar attractions are left behind for those of another.

It is true that frontiers are blurred by ever quicker travel and communications, and that the sharing of cultures, made possible by an increasingly sophisticated media network, brings us closer in all senses to our neighbours. Yet essential differences do exist, differences which lure us abroad on our annual migrations in search of new horizons, fresh sights, sounds and smells, discovery of unknown landscapes and people.

Countless resorts have evolved for those among us who simply crave sun, sea and the reassuring press of humanity. There are, too, established tourist 'sights' with which a country or region has become associated and to which clings, all too often, a suffocating shroud — the manifestations of mass tourism in the form of crowds and entrance charges, the destruction of authentic atmosphere, cynical exploitation. Whilst this is by no means typical of all well known tourist attractions, it is familiar enough to act as a disincentive for those of more independent spirit who value personal discovery above prescribed experience and who would rather avoid the human conveyor belt of queues, traffic jams and packed accommodation.

It is for such travellers that this guidebook has been written. In its pages, no more than passing mention is made of the famous, the well documented, the already glowingly described — other guidebooks will satisfy the appetite for such orthodox tourist information. Instead, the reader is taken if not to unknown then to relatively unvisited places — literally 'off the beaten track'. Through the specialist knowledge of the authors, visitors using this guidebook are assured of gaining insights into the country's heartland whose heritage lies largely untouched by the tourist industry. Occasionally the reader is urged simply to take a sideways step from a site of renowned tourist interest to find one perhaps less sensational, certainly less frequented but often of equivalent fascination.

From wild, scantily populated countryside whose footpaths and byways are best navigated by careful map reading, to negotiating the side streets of towns and cities, travelling 'off the beaten track' can be rather more demanding than following in the footsteps of countless thousands before you. The way may be less clear, more adventurous and individualistic, but opportunities do emerge for real discovery in an age of increasing dissatisfaction with the passive predictability of conventional holidaymaking. With greater emphasis on exploring 'off the beaten track', the essence of Germany is more likely to be unearthed and its true flavours relished to the full.

Martin Collins
Series Editor

1 • The Hanseatic Towns

The history of Germany is, until the nineteenth century, the story of separate kingdoms, dukedoms, and principalities, and even of individual self-governing towns. During the Middle Ages a number of these towns, mostly in the north of the country, joined together to protect their commercial interests in what was called the Hanseatic League. From the thirteenth to the fifteenth century this league, which was never more than a loose confederation, exercised a powerful influence in the north of Europe. It had a diet that met as and raised armed forces when its power was threatened. The cities upon which it was based expanded with docks and warehouses while the merchant families who directed its commerce grew rich.

Though the power of the league has long disappeared, the cities that built it up remain centres of commercial activity, with great civic treasures and a spirit of independence that, it seems, is somewhat different to anything found elsewhere in Germany. These towns are in no way off the beaten track, but they are largely unvisited by English speaking tourists and contain much that is well worth seeing. As a change from the lakes and mountains for which Germany is famous, the traveller with a feeling for the excitement of exploration might well consider a visit to a few of these historic towns.

Hamburg, the largest of these towns, lies at the end of the long estuary of the river Elbe. The best way to approach it is by the ship service from Harwich. As the ship moves up the estuary the dykes lining the banks, the marshy land and fields beyond them, the busy shipping, the multitude of small yachts on a summer weekend, the rows of fishermen's cottages that are now clearly gentrified for commuters to Hamburg, and the industrial developments that crowd increasingly along the shore, all prepare you for the great city that lies ahead. The ship berths at a quay right in the heart of the city.

It must be said at the start that one does not go to Hamburg to look at buildings. A large part of the town was burnt down in 1842 and the city suffered a terribly destructive air raid in 1943 which set a fire storm sweeping through the streets with a temperature of up to

1,000 °C (1,832 °F) killing in one night some 40,000 of its citizens. Everything is rebuilt now, and the six spires, which are the landmark of Hamburg, once more reach into the sky. Almost the only ruin still to survive is the remains of a U-boat bunker in the harbour, which all the high explosives of the Royal Air Force could not totally destroy! The most impressive building in the city, as one would expect, is not a cathedral or a palace but the town hall, the Rathaus, built in 1886 and boasts some fine rooms for civic ceremonies.

The docks of Hamburg have been affected by the growth of containers for commercial shipping and the dock area, like other dock areas, is seeking other uses for its vast warehouses. But if, in some respects, Hamburg seems run down, in other cases it is still vibrant with commercial life. In particular it is the chief city in the Federal Republic for journalism and contains the publishing offices of most of the picture magazines that decorate the news stands, and whose exposures of scandals (and inventions of scandals) have rocked society in recent years.

It is a very political city too, with a strong socialist tradition, and was one of the last cities in Germany to surrender to the Nazis. Chancellor Helmut Schmidt, who led the Social Democratic Party for so long is a Hamburger, and the type of cap which he always wore can be seen on the heads of many Hamburg citizens today.

But if one has an idea that this is just a bleak commercial city it will soon be dispelled if one was to make a tour from the river front, with its lively shipping activity, along a half ring of parks and gardens to the huge Alster lake whose edge lies only a few yards from the town hall. You can walk for 8½ miles (14km) round this lake by the Alster-wanderweg if you like. There are boat trips the lake and cafés and restaurants on its banks. In a few years time, when water purification measures are completed, bathing will be allowed in its waters.

As one would expect, the merchant princes of Hamburg were not going to be outdone by the royal princes of other German states and so they bought fine paintings and other works of art for the civic galleries and museums. The objects that are the most impressive in the museums of Hamburg are probably the nineteenth-century ones that would have appeared on the market after the affluent period of the great royal collectors in the German states had ended.

The Kunsthalle holds no less than eleven paintings by Caspar David Friedrich. Only the Nationalgalerie in Berlin has more. Friedrich was a pioneer of early nineteenth-century Romantic painting. His typical canvas depicts a man standing in a vast landscape of mountains brooding, it seems, upon the nature of the universe. It

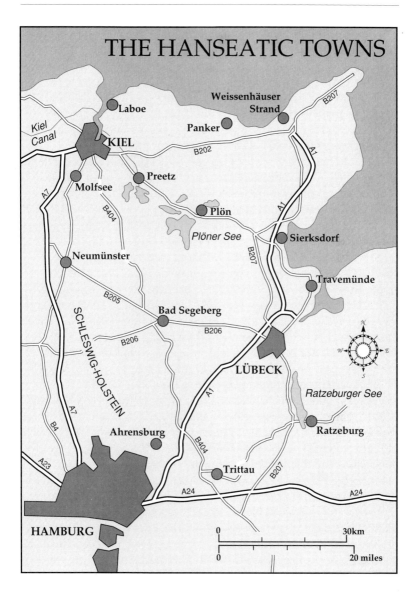

may be a man and woman gazing from the edge of a forest at the moon in a blood-red sky or a boat crew shipwrecked on a wide expanse of ice. He was fascinated by the landscapes of the Harz mountains and by the atmosphere of the Baltic coast but, by introducing a strange, unexplained human presence into his art, he lifts them into a realm beyond mere paintings of scenery and gives them a universal quality, a sense of man's smallness and helplessness against the forces of nature. The paintings of Friedrich were almost forgotten after his death, but have now been rediscovered and are widely appreciated as forecasting what has been called 'the existential isolation of the twentieth century'. Unless you go to Berlin or Dresden, the Kunsthalle in Hamburg is almost the only place where the visitor can study a number of his works together. These paintings alone make a visit worthwhile.

The other main gallery in Hamburg is the Museum für Kunst und Gewerbe, the art and craft museum. The chief attraction here is probably an extraordinarily rich collection of the style that the Germans call *Jugendstil* but which is also known as Art Nouveau. Much of this was purchased by the far-seeing museum director, Justus Brinkman, at the Paris exhibition of 1900. There is glass, pottery, carpets, furniture, books, and anything else one can think of displayed, not as individual items, but in entire rooms furnished in this style. This enables one to wander round them and really imagine those years when the fusty nineteenth century seemed to be blown away by the fresh, clean look of the new age, and with no warning of the horrors that this new age was to bring. In this collection the work of William Morris and other English designers of that school is well represented.

One other museum that may be missed as it is not well known is the Jenisch-Haus, reached from Klein-Flottbek on the *S-Bahn*. This was the home of a Hamburg banker and senator which he built as a summer residence in the 1830s. He gave receptions here for the high society of the day. The furnishings and decoration give a good idea of the taste and style of life of a successful, cultivated business man of the early nineteenth century. The house stands in a beautiful park that was laid out 'in the English style' as an ornamental farm. The Englischer Garten in Munich represents a similar taste. The garden architect was a Scotsman, William Booth.

If you have an interest in gardening you might well study the work not only of William Booth but of other members of his family who made a major contribution to the horticulture of the Hamburg area with the founding of a nursery in 1795. They introduced many foreign trees and shrubs to Germany, including rhododendrons, conifers and orchids. They were followed by another Scotsman, Peter Smith, who founded a business here in 1848. At the right season of the year every restaurant in Germany seems to offer asparagus specialities, *Spargel-Spezialitäten*.

One other excursion from the centre of Hamburg that is well

worth pursuing is to the Hagenbeck Zoo (*U-Bahn* Hagenbecks Tierpark). Carl Hagenbeck was a fish dealer who found that the net of one of his fishing boats had caught six seals. Rather than throw them back into the sea, he put them on show and found that they attracted much public interest. He went on from this to collect more animals and in 1907 his son opened a zoo in the suburb of Stellingen as the first in the world in which animals were displayed in natural surroundings and not behind bars. The zoo has been greatly extended, and is laid out with remarkably effective lakes, hills and landscape features, so that you really feel you might be on safari rather than a few miles from the centre of a city on the North Sea. The Hagenbeck family also started a circus that became one of the best known in Germany and led the way in the training of animals by kindness and rewards.

It is difficult to write about Hamburg without mentioning the Reeperbahn in the St Pauli district. For some visitors this is so far from being off the beaten track that it is the only object of their visit. But others may need some kind of guide.

Like all sea ports, there grew up in Hamburg the facilities that sailors are supposed to look for on shore: bars and brothels. St Pauli has always provided these, and the present administration of the city recognises that they will exist whether legally or not, and so sensibly provides some control over the way they are made available. There are said to be 3,000 licensed prostitutes in the area. If, between the river and the Reeperbahn, you chance upon a side street barricaded off with notices banning women and juveniles from entering, you will know that this is the street where the 'ladies' sit in the windows. It is believed that this is the only place in Germany where this custom, which is well established in Holland and Belgium, can be found.

Elsewhere there are bars for homosexuals and bars for transvestites and bars for other variations that could well qualify as off the beaten track, but one is assured that there are plenty of bars where one can take the wife or girlfriend without any problems. In 1962 The Beatles first made their reputation at one of these — the Star Club, at 39 Grosse Freiheit, which leads off the Reeperbahn.

One place of entertainment that is unique to Hamburg is the Hansa Theatre in Steindamm behind the railway station. This is a theatre offering a variety programme of singers, jugglers, comedians and acrobats of a type that unfortunately seems to have disappeared elsewhere. The audience sits in two- or five-seater well-upholstered benches, with a good view of the stage and a table in front, at which food and drink can be served. This theatre was originally opened in 1894, and the rather old-fashioned atmosphere is very attractive.

The Holstentor, Lübeck,

There is one further visit that the English speaking visitor may like to make. Near the Ohlsdorf Station is the largest cemetery in Europe, which provides a fine display of funerary art. But there are two things here that have a special involvement for British visitors. At B1-Bk59 are the graves of 2,500 British soldiers who died in the two world wars, which are looked after by the British War Graves Commission. At Bu-Bq66 is a mass grave and monument for the 55,000 citizens of Hamburg who were killed in British air raids on the city during World War II. No Briton of any sensitivity can visit Hamburg without some feeling of discomfort.

Lübeck and Kiel

Lübeck and Hamburg took it in turn to lead the Hanseatic League over the centuries with Hamburg commanding the North Sea and Lübeck the Baltic. In **Lübeck**, known as the Queen of the Hansa, there is plenty for the traveller to see.

From the fifteenth-century gateway, topped by twin turrets, you enter the old town, entirely encircled by water. Fine buildings, predominantly built in brick between the fifteenth and the eighteenth centuries, are on every side: the town hall, with its decorated Renaissance façade, churches, with their soaring spires, hospitals, ware-

The fraternity house of the Schiffergesellschaft in Lübeck, now a restaurant

houses and merchants' dwellings. Among these is the Buddenbrook House, owned in the nineteenth century by the ancestors of Thomas Mann, where he was born and the inspiration of his great novel, *Buddenbrooks*. There are museums, some in old churches, some in citizens' houses, and a particularly attractive and little-known museum of puppets adjoining the small puppet theatre in Kleine

Petersgrube. There are restaurants too: in the Rathaus cellar which, as everywhere else in Germany, provides food and drink; in the historic fraternity house of the Schiffergesellschaft, where the captains of the sailing ships used to meet and where models of their ships now hang over the tables; and in the rococo hall of the nineteenth-century Haus der Gesellschaft zur Beförderung gemeinsamer Tütigkeit (a typically Germanic mouthful which means the Public Welfare Work Society). There are also shops selling Lübeck marzipan, a speciality of the town. Everywhere one can see stepped gables and arched buttresses, narrow passageways and ostentatious façades witnessing to the pride, wealth and good taste of the city and its merchants. If the visitor has a feeling for architecture, days can be spent exploring this city with the aid of a detailed guide book, now available in English.

If you tire of architecture there is the idyllic fishing village of **Gothmund** nearby and the seaside resort of **Travemünde** offers bathing, sailing, a casino and a colourful night life. Beyond, on the other side of the estuary, lies the Federal State of Mecklenburg-Vorpommern (formerly part of East Germany).

Some 40 miles (64km) to the north is **Kiel**, the capital of Schleswig-Holstein. This was a small Hanseatic town but gained importance in 1895 with the building of the Kiel Canal, which the Germans call the Nord-Ostsee-Kanal. It used to be a major naval base but is now largely rebuilt and is a pleasant example of German post-war reconstruction, with its pedestrian precinct, university, parks, museums, theatres and concert hall, and above all the quays alongside which lie the liners that provide a service with Norway and Sweden. Unlike many major ports, where the harbour area is hidden away behind rows of warehouses, the ships here lie right beside the main street and bring the atmosphere of the sea to the centre of the town.

The canal itself lies a few miles up the Kieler Förde and cannot be seen from the town. It carries more traffic (though not a higher tonnage) than any other canal in the world. An interesting excursion is to watch the operation of the huge locks at Kiel-Holtenau. The new bridge here offers a good view of the canal and the Förde.

Kiel, on its sheltered Förde, is a great place for yachting. The high spot of the year is Kiel Week in June, when the town is full and regattas of every kind are held. What began in the nineteenth century as a society event has now developed into a hugely popular festival.

A few miles up the Förde, where it broadens out into the open sea, is the impressive Marine Memorial at **Laboe**, from the top of which one can see as far as the Danish islands. On the beach here a U-boat of World War II is preserved, and the interior can be visited. For any one of the now diminishing number of Englishmen who knew what it was for their ships to be sunk by one of these vessels, such a visit can be an uncanny experience.

In the other direction, to the south at **Molfsee**, is the Freilicht-museum, the open-air museum for Schleswig-Holstein. Here some sixty-five buildings from all over the area have been re-erected: farmhouses, cottages, barns, windmills, a bakery, a forge, a weaving mill, a pottery, and so on. Bread, wool, pottery, iron work and other craft objects are made by local craftsmen, and farm animals are reared on the site. Since its foundation in 1961 this has grown into one of the most important open-air museums of its kind.

The Countryside

There are many more conventionally scenic areas of Europe than Schleswig-Holstein, but if you come here to look at the towns you might find that you stay to savour the country round them. It is a rich, fertile countryside, with brick-built, half-timbered thatched farm-houses and the occasional grand mansion. On the way from Ham-burg towards Lübeck, for instance, the visitor soon comes to **Ahrens-burg**, with its Renaissance Ahrensburg Schloss, open to the public and surrounded by a pleasant park. Further on there is a nature reserve, Naturschutzgebiet Forst Hahnheide, at **Trittau**, with wide forests, a lake, and many attractive walks. Ratzeburg lies on an island in an extensive lake. At one end of the island is the twelfth-century Romanesque cathedral, Ratzeburg Dom, with a fine medieval altar-piece and beautiful cloisters. In a corner of the cloisters is a striking sculpture of a crippled man by Ernst Barlach, the Expressionist artist, and the Ernst-Barlach-Haus a museum devoted to this work is in the town. From here you can take a boat to Lübeck, which would provide a suitable approach to this maritime city.

Between Lübeck and Kiel there are no less than eleven nature reserves along the coast with sands, dune grasses, and a rich bird life. But if the visitor seeks a different kind of pleasure, there are holiday resorts here with every kind of attraction: at **Weissenhäuser Strand** there is the longest water slide in Europe — all of 150yd, and the Hansapark at **Sierksdorf** boasts what looks like a truly terrifying switchback called the Loopingbahn 'Nessie'. A more direct route passes through the vast lake area at **Plön**, which does not need the ridiculous title of the Holsteiner Switzerland for its beauties to be appreciated. The Plöner Schloss here, which served first as a summer residence for the Danish kings and then as a training academy for

Prussian military cadets, recalls the long dispute between Denmark and Germany for the possession of Schleswig-Holstein; it is now a boarding school. At **Panker** the Landgrave of Hesse built a country house at the beginning of the eighteenth century which is still inhabited by his descendants. They have established here a stud for breeding Trakehner horses, whose gleaming bay coats may be admired in the paddocks surrounding the house. This is a traditional East Prussian breed, whose survival was ensured by its transferance here before the advancing Russian army in the last months of the war. Almost everywhere you will find Heimatmuseums illustrating the local history traditions and occasional unexpected special collections of the work of some enthusiastic collector which is itself like the Circus Museum at **Preetz**, the site of a thirteenth-century monastery, the Preetzer Kloster, and is charmingly situated on a river on which one can paddle a canoe all the way down to Kiel.

On the way back to Hamburg you might call at the open-air zoo, the Tierpark Neumünster, at **Neumünster**, where you can see animals that once roamed across Germany but are now no longer found here, like aurochs (European bison), bears, lynx, wild horse, and wolves. At **Bad Segeberg** there is an open-air theatre, Segeberg's Freilichttheater, in a rocky setting that is the site of unique performances of the 'Western' adventure stories of Karl May, with hundreds of Red Indians galloping in on their horses and the air reeking with the smell of gunpowder.

A special interest that might be profitably pursued in Schleswig-Holstein is that of organ music. The composer Buxtehude was the organist at the Mariankirche in Lübeck at the end of the seventeenth century and his reputation attracted visits from Bach and Handel. The present organ, built in 1968, is dedicated to his memory but while most of the older organs in the big cities were destroyed in the war, almost every village church can boast a fine instrument. All through north Germany, from the border with Holland to that with Denmark, a wide and truly popular appreciation of organ music developed in the baroque period, encouraged by the congregational participation of the Lutheran church liturgy. Today many organ concerts are given on these instruments and a visit could be built round attending them. The Amt für Kirchenmusik at 76 Uhlandstrasse, 22087 Hamburg, publishes a two-monthly programme for the Hamburg area and other concerts are advertised locally.

Further Information
— The Hanseatic Towns —

Places to Visit

Hamburg
Alstertalmuseum
Wellingsbüttler Weg 79g
Open: Saturday and Sunday, 11am-
1pm and 3-5pm.

Automuseum Hillers
Kurt-Schumacher-Allee 42
Open: daily 10am-5pm.

Ernst-Barlach-Haus
Baron-Voght-Strasse 50a
Open: daily 11am-5pm, except Monday

Bischofsburg
(in Gemeindehaus St Petri)
Speersort 10
Open: Monday to Saturday, 10am-1pm.

Johannes-Brahms-Gedenkräume
Peterstrasse 39
Open: Tuesday and Friday, 12noon-
1pm, Thursday, 4-6pm. Also 1st
Saturday of every month 10am-2pm.

Deutsches Maler- und Lackierer-Museum
Billwerder Billdeich 72
Open: Saturday and Sunday 10am-
1pm. In summer also open Wednesday.

Das Museum der Elektrizität (electrum)
Klinikweg 23
Open: Tuesday to Sunday, 9am-5pm.

Gedenkstätte Ernst Thälmann
Tarpenbekstrasse 66
Open: Tuesday to Friday, 10am-7pm,
and Saturday and Sunday 10am-1pm.

*Geologisch-Päläontologisches
    Museum, Universität Hamburg*
Bunderstrasse 55
Open: Monday to Friday, 9am-6pm and
in term time, Saturday, 9am-12noon.

*Hamburgisches Museum für
    Völkerkunde*
Rothenbaumchaussee 64
Open: daily 10am-5pm, except Monday

Heine-Haus
Elbchaussee 31
Open: Tuesday to Friday, 11am-7pm,
Saturday, 11am-4pm.
Closed summer.

Jenisch-Haus
50 Baron-Voght-Strasse
Open: summer, Tuesday to Saturday 2-
5pm. Sunday, 11am-5pm. Winter,
Tuesday to Saturday, 1-4pm, and
Sunday 11am-4pm.

Krameramtswohnungen
Krayenkamp 10-11
Open: Tuesday to Sunday, 10am-5pm

Kunsthalle
Glockengiersserwall
Open: daily, 10am-5pm except Monday

Kunsthaus
Ferdinandstor 1
Open: Tuesday to Sunday, 10am-6pm.

KZ-Gedenkstätte Neuengamme
(Concentration Camp Memorial)
80 Neuengammer Heerweg
Open: Tues to Sunday 10am-5pm.

Luftwaffenmuseum Uetersen
2081 Appen/Unterlinde
Hauptstrasse 140
Open: Tuesday to Friday, 3-5pm,
Saturday and Sunday, 10am-5pm in
summer. Winter, open Saturday and
Sunday 10am-3pm.

*Mineralogisches Museum der Universität
    Hamburg*
Grindelallee 48
Open: Wednesdays, 3-7pm. Also 1st
Sunday in every month 10am-1pm.

*Museum der Elbinsel Wihelmsburg mit
    Milchmuseum*
Kirchdorfer Strasse 163
Open: Sundays 4-6pm in summer.

Museum für Kunst and Gewerbe
Steintorplatz 1
Open: daily 10am-5pm, except Monday

Museum für Hamburgische Geschichte
Holstenwall 24
Open: daily 10am-5pm, except Monday

Museum Mana Kumaka (Assida Indio-Museum)
Kramerkoppel 42
Open: Saturday & Sunday 11am-5pm.

Museum Rade am Schloss Reinbek
Reinbek
Schlossstrasse 4
Open: May-October Wednesday-Sunday & holidays 10am-6pm, rest of year 10am-5pm.

Museumsdorf Volksdorf
Im Alten Dorfe 48
Open: daily, except Monday, 10am-5pm.

Panoptikum (waxworks)
Spielbudenplatz 3
Open: Monday to Friday 11am-9pm. Saturday, 11am-11pm, and Sunday, 11am-9pm.

Planetarium
Hindenburgstrasse
Open: Shows on Wednesday & Friday at 4pm, 6pm; Sunday at 11am, 2.30pm, 4pm.

Postmuseum
Stephansplatz 1-5
Open: Tuesday to Friday 10am-3pm, Thursday, 10am-6pm.

Tourist Information Offices

Ahrensburg
Ahrensburger Fremden-und Verkehrsverein
Rathaus
222926 Ahrensburg

Bad Segeberg
Tourist-Information
Oldesloer Strasse 20
23795 Bad Segeberg
℡(0 45 51) 57231

Hamburg and Schleswig-Holstein
Fremdenverkehrszentrale Hamburg
Bieberhaus am Hauptbahnhof
Hamburg
℡(040) 300500-244

Kiel
Verkehrsverein der Landeshauptstadt Kiel
Sophienblatt 30
24103 Kiel 1
℡(04 31) 6 22 30

Lübeck
Touristbüro des Lübecker Verkehrsvereins
Am Markt
23552 Lübeck
℡(04 51) 1228106

Neumünster
Verkehrspavillon Grossflecken
24534 Neumünster
℡(0 43 21) 4 32 80

Plön
Kurverwaltung
Schwentinehaus
Am Lübschen Tor 1
24306 Plön
℡(0 45 22) 27 17

Preetz
Fremdenverkehrsverein
Mühlenstrasse 14
24211 Preetz
℡(0 43 42) 22 07

Ratzeburg
Amt für Fremdenverkehr und Kultur
Am Markt 9
Alte Wache
23909 Ratzeburg
℡(0 45 41) 80 00 81

Trittau
Gemeinde Trittau
Europaplatz 5
22946 Trittau
℡(0 41 54) 20 61

Weissenhäuser Strand
Kurverwaltung
Seestrasse
Weissenhäuser Strand
23758 Wangels
℡(0 43 61) 49 07 31

2 • The East Friesland Islands

This group of islands lying off the coast of north Germany, west of Denmark, was immortalised in a book called *The Riddle of the Sands* by an Anglo-Irish writer, Erskine Childers, published in 1903. It is a classic sea story, with a spying background, describing how a pair of English yachtsmen, sailing a boat for pleasure in these waters, discovered preparations for the invasion of England by flat-bottomed troop-carrying barges to be concealed under cover on these islands until the time for invasion came.

Whether such a plan was militarily feasible in the Kaiser's Germany is doubtful; it was certainly not considered in the vastly different conditions of Hitler's Germany in 1940. But the attraction of the book, which still exercises a powerful appeal, lies in its description of the islands, of the seas round them, and of the maze of sandbanks and mudbanks that lie between them and the coast.

These islands are known to discriminating Germans, who appreciate their remoteness from the busy mainland, their quietness (cars are forbidden), the invigoration of the air which is recommended for sufferers from coughs and catarrh, and their natural beauty. But to English speaking visitors they are indeed, off the beaten track.

These are, of course, not places to go to if one's wish is to lie in Mediterranean heat on a sun-baked beach. But if there is a feeling for subtler pleasures where the sea meets the sky a great discovery can be made here. There are indeed many visitors during the high summer, but other seasons can offer their own special qualities when the place is much less crowded.

Why should the English, who have their own North Sea coast, bother to visit the North Sea coast of Germany? It is probably because the conditions there are totally different. The English east coast has, indeed, its own charms, but it lies sheltered from the prevailing west winds. The German north-west coast has received the full force of the west winds for thousands of years, sweeping from the Atlantic up the Channel and piling the seas up on the stretch of coast between the mouths of the Ems and the Elbe. The land here has been ribboned and

21

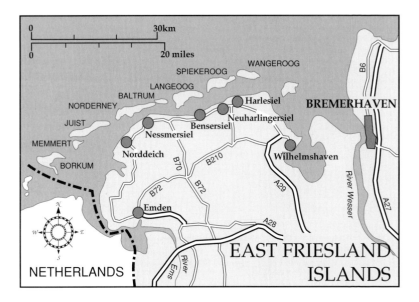

lacerated by gale and storm, leaving a line of what are really little more than sandbanks a few miles offshore which were rescued, by the fourteenth century, from the encroaching sea and have supported a cluster of houses and a church each ever since.

Between the islands and the mainland lies the area of part mud, part sand for which the German name is *Watt*. It is necessary to recognise this word if one is ever to go here and to give a general description of the area there is no better way than to quote the account in *The Riddle of the Sands.*:

> This singular region…is a low-lying country, containing great tracts of marsh and heath, and few towns of any size…. Seven islands lie off the coast. All, except Borkum, which is round, are attenuated strips, slightly crescent-shaped, rarely more than a mile broad, and tapering at the ends; in length averaging about 6 miles, from Norderney and Juist, which are seven and nine respectively, to little Baltrum, which is only two and a half. Of the shoal spaces which lie between them and the mainland, two-thirds dry at low-water, and the remaining third becomes a system of lagoons whose distribution is controlled by the natural drift of the North Sea as it forces its way through the intervals between the islands. Each of these intervals resembles the bar of a river, and is obstructed by danger-ous banks over which the sea pours at every tide scooping out a deep pool. This fans out and ramifies to east and west as the pent-up current frees itself, encircles the islands and spreads over the intervening flats. But the further it penetrates the less scouring force it has, and as a result no island is girt completely by a low-water channel. About midway at the

back of each of them is a 'watershed', only covered for five or six hours out of the twelve.

Erskine Childers and his friend (for his book is clearly based on a personal visit) explored the *Watt* in a boat with a draught of 4ft (1.2m), and a centre board to let down in deeper water. They were regularly stranded on the sand at low tide, but they chose sheltered places and came to no harm. A special type of flat-bottomed fishing boat, known as an Ewer, has been developed for use in the *Watt*, which abounds in crustaceans and shell fish. There are channels between the sandbanks which are marked — not always very accurately — by lines of saplings as booms, indicating somewhat deeper water, but it will be obvious that this is no place for normal yachting. The *Watt* can be explored on foot at low tide and its fascinating animal and vegetable life studied. There are some marked routes from one island to another, but the visitor must take care. The sea comes in very quickly, and the tide has a rise and fall of some 9ft (3m). Visitors should never venture unaccompanied for any distance from land. There are organised walks, guided by experienced locals, which are strongly recommended. A good experience is to take a ride in one of the high-wheeled horse-drawn wagons which make trips across the sands at low tide. A tide calendar is an indispensable reference for every islander.

For the visitor who looks for activity, the attractions that the islands can offer may be summed up as bathing, sports, camping, fishing and birdwatching. Bathing can be enjoyed on many beaches on the seaward side of the islands. The Germans still like to talk, in a rather Victorian way, of the health-cure that sea bathing offers, and the earliest popularity of these islands for visitors was, indeed, as health-cure resorts in the nineteenth century. The air temperature averages 19°C (69°F) at mid-day in July and August, and the sea temperature is only a degree or so lower. Nudist and topless bathing has not yet made much headway in these areas, but there are beaches on Borkum and Norderney that are reserved for this purpose. Rather more care than usual should be taken when swimming in these waters in view of the tides and the deeply scoured nature of the sea bed. Warning signs are displayed on the beaches when weather conditions render bathing not recommended. There are several enclosed swimming baths, with warmed sea water and artificial waves, which are always open.

Sports that can be practised on the islands include sailing at all times on the seaward side of the coast and in the lee of the islands at high tide; horse-riding on the sand, gymnastics on the beach, tennis, table tennis, and windsurfing can all be pursued here.

Camping sites are provided on several islands and reservation is essential. However caravan trailers are generally not permitted. As always in Germany, camping outside designated sites is only allowed with the permission of the owner, and non-existent as far as these islands are concerned.

Fishing is good. Plaice, sole, turbot, mackerel, smelt and cod are caught in the North Sea; flat fish, crab, mussels, cockles, shrimps and prawns are found in the *Watt*. All these will be served, fresh from the sea, at tables in local restaurants. A famous delicacy is Heligoland lobster, from the island far out in the North Sea. Be warned that *Ostfrieslands Krabben* in a local restaurant may not signify crabs but prawns — however none the less delicious for all that. The local name for crabs is *Granat*, which has led to the joke that this coast has been called the Costa Granata!

Substantial North Friesland dishes are *Eintopf aus Birnen, Bohnen und Speck* (hot-pot with pears, beans and bacon) and *Labskaus* (salt meat with herring and gherkins, served with fried egg). Beer is the local drink, often preceded by a *Schnaps* (strong liquor), and tea is drunk everywhere, usually with candy sugar and milk and sometimes with a spoonful of cream.

Birdwatching is the great speciality that these islands can offer. All the islands have bird sanctuaries and the whole area has been declared a National Park. Birds that may be seen include gulls of all kinds — black-headed, black-backed, herring, common, and occasionally the rare glaucous; terns and oyster catchers, sandpipers, plovers, pewits, moorhens, ducks and geese. When the colder weather begins great swarms of migratory birds settle on the *Watt* on their way from Scandinavia to warmer climes.

If a beginner would like to combine a little birdwatching with a foreign holiday, all that is needed is a pair of binoculars with 8x, 9x or 10x magnification, a pocket-sized guide to identifying birds (all the species that are seen on these islands are found in the British Isles as well) and some suitably drab weather-proof camouflage clothing. If you are an experienced birdwatcher you will know this already, but there is a book, *A Guide to Birdwatching in Europe* by J. Ferguson-Lees, which opens up the whole of the continent as an area for the observation of birds. Human intruders are, of course, barred from the bird sanctuaries, but tours of some of them are arranged. If you join one of these it is as well to remember that birds often use their droppings as bullets to deter invaders, and therefore a head covering and old clothes are recommended. It is not only birds that find sanctuary here. Seals, in particular, may be seen on a number of sandbanks. If a visitor encounters one he or she is asked not to try and touch or disturb it in any way.

But activities do not have to be pursued. It is enough merely to pace the dunes or sit in one of the basket chairs (*Strandkorb*) that are a feature of German beaches. You need to hire one for the length of your stay. There is a choice as to where it should be situated and it can be turned so that it acts as a shelter from the wind, or gives sun or shade. This is your private castle for as long as you desire.

All the islands are connected to the mainland by regular ship services, but the times of these are generally dependent on the tides. Motorists must usually leave their cars at car parks or garages at the ports of departure. There are air connections from the mainland to some of the islands, and light aircraft link all the islands (except Spiekeroog) together. Although some people may regret the noise of the aircraft, the view of the islands, from the air, lying between the sea and the *Watt* is a striking one.

The economy of the islands now depends mainly on their holiday visitors. The number of beds available for visitors is usually about double the number of permanent residents and every island has a choice of hotels. There is still a local community and the inhabitants are true Frieslanders — a race of quiet, self-reliant individuals whose motto indicates their character, 'God made the sea, the Frieslanders made the dykes'. They feel the influence of the sea in their bones, and according to local experience life comes and goes with the tides: babies are born as the tide comes in, and people die as it goes out.

The Islands

Visitors can travel to **Borkum** by car-ferry and ship from Emden. There is a limited access for cars on this island and a small airport provides a service for inter-island flights. One may be interested in visiting the dyke and aquarium museum of North Sea fish life, the Nordseeaquarium, and the *Heimatmuseum* of local fishing and sea-faring life, in the daytime; for evening entertainment there is a casino. For a totally relaxing holiday there are bathing beaches on the island and a nature reserve, the Landschaftsschutzgebiet Greune Stel.

No cars are permitted on the island of **Juist** but there is means of reaching it by ship from Norddeich; the island transport is by horse coaches. The coastal museum of marine biology, Küstenmuseum, is highly recommended, or one may wish to take a visit to Memmert, an uninhabited sandbank to the south-west which is the largest bird sanctuary in Germany, where thousands of herring-gull pairs breed.

*The island of Norderney from the air. The harbour is nearest the camera with a
deep-water channel dredged in the* Watt

The unbroken sandy beaches stretch along the entire north side of
Juist and the Hammersee is the only sweet-water lake to be found on
the islands.

   Norderney is the most developed of the islands but like Borkum
has a very limited access for visitors' cars. There is a car-ferry from
Norddeich and with the mainland, there is an airport which provides
a link. Unusually for these islands, Norderney has a fair amount of
deciduous and coniferous trees. This was a fashionable resort in the
nineteenth century with many eminent visitors, including European
royalty. Indeed, there is a variety of facilities to cater for the interests
of the visitors: a fishing and local history museum, the Fischerhaus-
Museum — the Kurtheater which stages varied performances
throughout the year and golf courses which can be found on the
dunes. For those wishing to relax under the sun there is a bathing
beach. A bird sanctuary is here and also a camping site.

   Baltrum, being the smallest of the islands, does not have much to
offer although there is an airport and bathing beach. Ships provide
a service from Nessmersiel and Norddeich. Yet again cars and bicycles are not permitted and so transport on the island is by horse
coaches.

Probably one of the most eye catching features of **Langeoog** is its dunes, the highest of all the islands, which tower to a peak of 30ft (9m)! There is a small airport, bathing beach and bird sanctuary here, not forgetting a large yacht harbour. Cars are not permitted but there is a shipping service from Bensersiel.

Spiekeroog, known as the 'Green Island' because of its small clumps of trees, was a refuge for pirates in the fifteenth century. In the Napoleonic period a military garrison was based here which, in 1812, repulsed an attempted British landing. A bus service was established here in 1949 but horse coaches still run. No cars are allowed but bicycles have limited access. The Inselkirche is a good Renaissance building of 1696 with a model of the flagship of the Spanish Armada (wrecked here in 1588) hanging in the nave and a medieval *pieta* that came from this ship. A place of interest on the island is the local natural history museum, the Inselmuseum. There is a ship from Neuharlingersiel to Spiekeroog and half of the island is a nature reserve.

Wangerooge is a highly developed health resort complex. A ship from Harlesiel gives access to the island for no cars are allowed. There is a small airport, bathing beach, seabird sanctuary and camping site here.

The Mainland

Attractive though the islands are, the coast of the mainland behind them should not be neglected. A long line of dykes stretches a hundred yards or so in from the shore all along the coast. These are some 25ft (8m) high, with a path along the top which provides a splendid walk, far more extensive than can be obtained on any island. Below, on one side, lies the *Watt* with the islands in the distance. On the other side the fields are intersected with draining ditches, with perhaps a row of alders or poplars, brick farmhouses here and there, and maybe an old windmill. Some black and white cattle may graze in the fields perhaps, while covered with tarpaulins to protect them from the cool night air. The security offered by the dykes has only been preserved by constant care and repair: as recently as 1962 and 1976 severe storms have breached the dykes and let the sea in.

Striding along the top of the dyke one feels, indeed, on top of the world. Whether it is a summer day, with swallows diving over the hot sand; or a clear day in spring, when the wind shifts to the northeast and burns the skin; or an autumn evening with the mist rising in banks, making the farmsteads seem to float off the ground like boats on a rising tide; or even winter, with the ditches frozen over and a north-westerly wind howling at the farms, bending the trees over and whipping up the seas, so that you are hard put to it to keep your feet, there is something special about this coast.

The Riddle of the Sands is not the only book which may arouse interest in this area, for there is another more recent book which conveys the atmosphere equally vividly from the standpoint of the land rather than the sea. This is *The German Lesson* by the contemporary German novelist, Siegfried Lenz. The story deals with the harassment of a distinguished impressionist painter by the Nazis during the last year of the war, and the deliverance of the district by the British troops. But the great thing about this book is not so much the story but the way it evokes the landscape. The story is actually located in the North Friesland islands, which lie somewhat to the north of the East Friesland islands, on the west coast of the Schleswig-Holstein peninsula. There is no better way to create an impression of the feel of this area than by quoting a few passages. The book really should be read and is beautifully translated by Ernst Kaiser and Eithne Wilkins. The atmosphere of the *Watt* is well caught:

> There is the murky sadness of the flats, low clouds in the west, gusts of wind curling the water in the runnels and pools, and causing the sea-birds feathers to bristle; in the distance there is the faint hum of a lonely airplane…. In these flats, here in this expanse of mud-grey wilderness, hollowed and dotted by shallow puddles, here the emergence of life is supposed to have begun…. The rushing noise out there in the flats was the incoming tide. It came foaming shorewards, across the sand, filling up the runnels and moving in bubbling tongues across the flats, filling all the pools and water-holes, bringing with it grass and shells and bits of wood, covering up the traces that the sea-birds had left, and our own tracks. It came in northward right up the shore, quickly covering an expanse of grey clay…. Every flood-tide carried in some other booty. One cast up on the beach masses of roots washed bone-white by the sea, another one pieces of cork and a battered rabbit-hutch; lumps of seaweed, shells, and torn nets were lying about, and iodine-coloured plants that looked like grotesque trains torn off dresses.

Above all, it is the particular quality of the light that gives to these islands their unique character:

> It is always rewarding here in our countryside to watch somebody moving into the distance under our sky: one simply stands still of one's own accord and turns all one's attention to the interplay of space and movement, and one always marvels at the oppressive dominance of the horizon.

Further Information
— The East Friesland Islands —

PlacesTo Visit

Borkum
Alter Leuchtturm
Old lighthouse, 1576, 213ft (65m) high.
Open: April-October daily.

Neuer Leuchtturm
Guided tours throughout the year.
New lighthouse, built 1879, commanding a good view.

Inselmuseum Dykhus
Open: May-September daily 10am-12noon, also Tuesday-Friday 3-6pm.
October-April Tuesday & Friday 3-6pm.
Collections on the island's history and local life, animal, bird and marine life.

Nordseeaquarium
Displays of North Sea underwater life.
Open: all year.

Juist
Küstenmuseum
Collections on marine biology, prehistory, fishing, wrecks, lifeboats, and the extraction of North Sea gas.

Naturschutzgebiet Bill mit Hammersee
Bird sanctuary near sweet-water lake.

Norderney
Inselmühle
Only windmill on the islands, built 1862.

Leuchtturm
Lighthouse, 213ft (60m) high, with good view.

Fischerhaus-Museum
Open: May-September Monday-Saturday 3-5pm, Sunday 10am-12noon.
Collections on the life of the islanders, history of fishing, and development of seawater bathing as a medical cure.

Spiekeroog
Inselmuseum
In 'Haus Hero', collections on history of the island, animals, plant life, development of shipping, fishing and bathing, as well as the sea rescue service.

Wangerooge
Inselmuseum
In old lighthouse, with collections on local life and shipping.
Open: mid-May to October daily 10am-12noon, 3-5pm.

Neuer Leuchtturm
New lighthouse, built in 1933, with adjoining youth hostel.

Tourist Information Offices

Fremdenverkehrsverband
Nordsee-Niedersachsen-
Bremen
Bahnhofstrasse 19-20
Postfach 1820
26122 Oldenburg
☎(0441) 92171-0

Baltrum
Kurverwaltung
26579 Baltrum
☎0 49 39/80-0

Borkum
Kurverwaltung
Goethestrasse 1

Postfach 1680
26757 Borkum
☎0 49 22/841

Juist
Kurverwaltung
Friesenstr 18
26571 Juist
☎0 49 35/805-0

Langeoog
Kurverwaltung
Hauptstrasse (Rathaus)
26465 Langeoog
☎0 49 72/6930

Norderney
Kurverwaltung
Postfach 240
26548 Norderney
☎0 49 32/89 10 or 502

Spiekeroog
Kurverwaltung
26474 Spiekeroog
☎0 49 76/170

Wangerooge
Kurverwaltung
26486 Wangerooge
☎044 69/890

3 • The Sauerland

A sk the average English-speaking person where the Sauerland is to be found and you will probably be met with a blank stare. They have heard of the Black Forest and of Bavaria but not the Sauerland, which is a marvellously picturesque area lying east of Cologne (Köln) and the industrial Ruhr in the Federal State of Nordrhein-Westfalen. In the rather flowery terms of the tourist organisations it is described as the Land of a Thousand Mountains and even though the visitor may be inclined to think of them as hills rather than mountains — the highest is just 2,765ft (843m) — this at least makes it clear that it is by no means a flat and uninteresting landscape. Little known to overseas visitors it may be, but it is a deservedly popular area with the Germans, especially those living in the Ruhr megalopolis who can reach it very quickly. The Dortmunder, for example, could be well into the Sauerland by car or train within half an hour. From further afield the Dutch or Belgian can reach here in 3-4 hours driving time and this makes it evident that for the traveller from Britain there is no excessive journey to be faced once he or she has crossed the Channel or North Sea. The Dutch have made the Sauerland particularly their own and come here in vast numbers during the summer holiday period.

International visitors arriving at Cologne or Frankfurt airports can be at their destination in 1½-2½ hours by public transport or can, of course, hire a car and complete the journey at their own pace. For the rail traveller from Britain the overnight crossing from Harwich to the Hook of Holland is ideal and will enable the visitor to reach the Sauerland around mid-day or if preferred one can travel via Ostend to arrive at about the same time.

There are several theories as to the origin of the name Sauerland. Unlike Schwarzwald (Black Forest), there is no English version. Some people say that the name stems from the fact that Karl der Grosse (Charlemagne) conducted particularly 'sour' campaigns against the Saxon inhabitants. Be that as it may, there is certainly

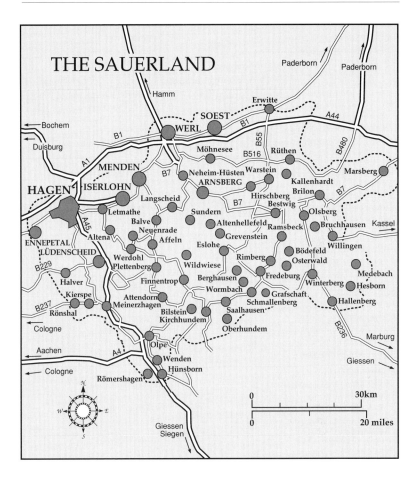

THE SAUERLAND

nothing sour about the welcome the visitor receives today. Because of its popularity with the locals and people 'in the know' there is an enormous amount and variety of holiday accommodation available. There are some well established and quite sophisticated resorts but in general it is a land of small towns and villages where farmhouse and self-catering holidays are widely available and offer excellent value for money.

There is no lack of opportunity for leisure activities either. The many lakes — they are mostly enormous reservoirs — dominate the landscape almost as much as the hills and water-orientated activities of every kind feature prominently in this area. It is possible to bathe either in the natural places or in the dozens of indoor and outdoor swimming pools. Sailing, windsurfing, boating and other activities can be enjoyed as well and in the summer there are steamer trips on a number of the lakes.

There are two German words which should be mastered. The first is *Talsperre* (*Tal* means valley, *Sperre* means barrier), the word for the mighty walls or dams which create the reservoirs. It is often combined with the name of the river which is dammed, thus Hennetalsperre, the dam across the valley of the river Henne. The word for reservoir is *Stausee* (*Stau* means dammed back water, *See* means lake); again it is often combined with the river name although the *Stau* bit is then often omitted, thus Möhne(stau)see, the lake created by the damming of the river Möhne. Incidentally, *Stau* is also the word used to describe a traffic jam on the *Autobahn* (motorway).

On land every other sporting activity is catered for with riding, cycling and tennis being especially favoured. There are many museums, caves, pleasure parks and theatres to be visited and the charming towns and villages with their black and white timbered houses will delight many a photographer. But it is for the simple pleasure of rambling in the countryside that many people come here and this activity is made all the more enjoyable by the many camp sites and youth hostels as well as plenty of simple bed and breakfast accommodation everywhere. The Sauerland visitor must not expect to find mighty cathedrals like those in Cologne or Freiburg, the towering Alps (although there is plenty of snow in winter), the fantastic palaces of King Ludwig II or the vineyard slopes of the Rhine or Mosel. The pleasures of this area are all its own and perhaps all the more approachable through being on a more modest scale.

There is no major river or designated tourist road to provide a logical pattern of exploration and therefore it is helpful to imagine the country divided into segments like a clock face with the centre point near Grevenstein in the Homert Nature Park and tour the area in a clock-wise direction. Begin in the south-west, for this is where the visitor from abroad is very likely to enter the Sauerland. The *Autobahn* (A4) from the Cologne direction joins the north-south A45 at Olpe south junction and the first stop should be made in the nearby town of **Olpe**. With its outlying district around the Biggesee reservoir this *Kreisstadt* (administrative centre of the district) lies in charming surroundings of woodland and water in the Ebbegebirge Naturpark and is an ideal place for outdoor activities. There are around 155 miles (250km) of waymarked footpaths and a number of long-distance trails cross here. North of the town things are dominated by the Biggesee, Westphalia's biggest reservoir. There are five

The Holstentor Lübeck, is the most famous town gate in Germany

The Glockenturm, Arnsberg, the Sauerland

The old town hall which now houses the local museum, Attendorn

recognised bathing beaches around the lake, rowing and sailing boats and pedalos to hire and also four steamers for lake cruises from Easter until the end of October. The visitor will find several open-air swimming pools (*Freibad*), and an indoor one (*Hallenbad*), with a giant chute in the town. Because there are well over eighty of them, not every public swimming pool in the Sauerland will be mentioned in the text but readers may be sure that they will never be far away from one. Here in Olpe there is a more than adequate selection of accommodation in hotels, inns (*Gasthöfe*) and *pensions*; there are numerous camp sites, a youth hostel in the part called Stade and also a hostel of the CVJM (equivalent to the YMCA). Olpe is certainly ideal for families; in 1986 in a national competition it achieved special mention for its welcome to family groups and the favourable offers made to them.

Imagining the clock-face in the segment between 25 and 20 minutes to the hour, continue in a north-easterly direction along the Biggesee and come, near the north end, to the little town of **Attendorn**. This is an old town of the Hanseatic League and a number of historic buildings remind one of its past. The old *Rathaus* now houses the district *Heimatmuseum* (museum devoted to local history, folklore, etc) and is the only secular Gothic building in southern Westphalia. The mighty Burg Schellenberg is open to the public and noted for its display of old weapons. The Catholic parish church (twelfth-fourteenth century) enjoys the honorary title of Sauerland Cathedral (*Dom*). The modern Civic Hall (*Stadthalle*) serves for exhibitions and conferences and the facilities available include a fully automatic bowling alley and a restaurant with wonderful views —

as well as excellent food, of course. The Attahöhle claim to be the biggest and most beautiful stalactite caves in Germany; certainly they are well worth a visit. As at Olpe, there is ample provision for leisure activities here and the accommodation available includes a youth hostel and camp sites. Accommodation prices generally appear to be very modest.

Continuing in the same direction reach, in another 5-6 miles (8-10km) the town of **Finnentrop**. Much of the population lives outside the town so it is by no means a big place. It lies between the Homert and Ebbegebirge Naturparks and its environs extend into both. In the summer months outdoor activities include sports and shooting contests and in the winter there is a varied programme of cultural events in the *Festhalle*. The indoor pool complex includes solarium, sauna and restaurant.

Administrative changes in recent years have created a situation in regard to addresses and locations which may well be confusing to the foreign visitor. Very large areas have been formed into a single unit and given a title such as Stadt Finnentrop, taking the name of the principle centre of population within the area. The areas are predominantly rural and the visitor arriving at Finnentrop, for instance by train, may well be surprised to find that the 'Finnentrop' address for which he or she is aiming is 9-12 miles (15-20km) away. In some cases, take Lennestadt for example, there is no place or railway station with that name which makes the matter even more confusing. The situation applies to a greater or lesser degree throughout Germany but for some reason appears to be particularly evident in the Sauerland.

As in Finnentrop, there is a youth hostel in **Plettenberg** about 6 miles (10km) to the north-west. Otherwise accommodation in the latter place is on a rather more limited scale and the tourist without an advance booking might have to go a little afield at busy seasons. However, the area should certainly not be overlooked and there are a number of sights to interest the visitor. A significant church building is the Protestant Christuskirche (about 1200) and the Böhler Kapelle, a little chapel endowed in 1422 which is noted for its glass painting. The village church in the part called Ohle dates from around 1050-1100 and has some early wall paintings; the ruins of the castle complex Schwarzenberg (about 1301) justify a little time. There is a well marked network of paths and a popular walk is that to the viewpoint on the Hohe Molmert (1,882ft, 574m) a few kilometres to the west. About 6 miles (10km) in the opposite direction the 1,791ft (546m) high Schomberg also has fine views.

The former domain of the Counts of the Mark — Märkisches Sauerland — was at one time noted for its many narrow-gauge railways, some of them passenger-carrying lines and others purely for freight. The Märkische Museums-Eisenbahn (museum railway) was founded in 1982 by enthusiasts anxious to record the history of these little lines. They have assembled a collection of historic locomotives and vehicles which runs on the metre-gauge line for 1½ mile (2km) line at between Plettenberg and **Hüinghausen**. The museum also has a workshop in the old boiler-house of Firma Graeka at **Eiringhausen** near Plettenberg. Due west of Finnentrop lies **Herscheid** at the foot of the highest point in the chain of the Ebbegebirge, the 2,175ft (663m) high Nordhelle. Several of the smaller lakes are within easy reach and there are many kilometres of footpaths providing rambling opportunities for every degree of effort. In winter the skiing area has facilities for beginners as well as for the more experienced skier. Before leaving this section, the town of **Meinerzhagen** deserves attention. It lies west of the A45 close to the western extremity of the Sauerland. The thick forests close to the town make it easy for the hiker to use this as a base and his or her walks could embrace visits to some of the smaller reservoirs. There is a Protestant church from the thirteenth century and Schloss Badinghausen which may be visited. In winter there are various theatrical productions and other entertainments; here close to the highest parts of the Ebbegebirge, there is ample opportunity for skiing although the activity is not highly organised. In and around the town there is a reasonable amount of accommodation including a youth hostel.

The most important town in the next segment of the clock-face is **Lüdenscheid**, one of the biggest Sauerland centres. It is the *Kreisstadt* of Märkisches Sauerland and lies on the forested ridge between the valleys of the rivers Lenne and Volme. It is not really the place to look for holiday accommodation, although there is a ninety-six-bed youth hostel here, but rather a place to be visited for shopping or sightseeing. There are frequent theatrical and musical productions, the latter no doubt influenced by the fact that there is a music school in the town. The *Stadtmuseum* is housed in a building of unusual style which was awarded the 'architectural prize for concrete' in 1983. The museum shows the history of the town and region and has an unusual collection of historic buttons. There is also a museum of fire-fighting with many interesting exhibits. The Bremecker Hammer is a museum of technological culture and the history of the iron industry. Schloss Neuenhof, 2 miles (3km) south of the town centre, is famed for its elaborate wrought-iron gateway. The present moated *Schloss* was built in 1643 and has not been altered since 1693. The Protestant parish church is a neo-classical hall building which replaced a twelfth-century basilica in 1826. The west tower is mainly Romanesque and the neo-classical pulpit-altar is worth seeing. There are two indoor pools in the town and an open-air *Wellenbad* (pool with artificial waves).

North-west of Lüdenscheid the little town of **Breckerfeld** has, in its Protestant parish church of St James (fourteenth century), an outstanding carved altar in oak depicting Mary, St James and St Christopher. The Catholic parish church dedicated to the same saint — confusing surely — is also worth seeing. Six miles (10km) south and close to the Sauerland border is **Halver**, a town which combines tourism and industry. It is surrounded by forests in which there are many waymarked paths but every kind of leisure activity can be indulged in here. There is a *Hallenbad* and a fine open-air pool while half a dozen man-made lakes are within each reach. A short distance to the south-east, is **Kierspe**, a health resort in the Ebbegebirge where the *Hallenbad* has a sauna and also medical baths. There are medieval churches in Kierspe and in nearby **Rönsahl**. In addition to the inevitable reservoirs there is the Wasserschloss Haus Rhade (a moated palace). Neither Halver nor Kierspe have very much holiday accommodation although there are a few *Ferienwohnungen* (holiday flats) mainly in the latter place. It has to be remembered that here in the west of the Sauerland, very close to the industrial Ruhr, these resorts probably cater more for day visitors than for long-stay guests.

East of Lüdenscheid and in this sector the neighbouring communities of **Werdohl** and **Neuenrade** can be considered. The former is mainly an industrial town in a charming setting and has the usual leisure facilities and a reasonable amount of accommodation. The Protestant Christuskirche (1868) and the Catholic St Michaelskirche (1901) are both built in neo-Gothic style and the latter has an old crucifixion group dating from the early sixteenth century. Neuenrade has more to offer the visitor but not a great deal of accommodation in the centre. Swimming instruction is available at the heated *Freibad* and there is also a *Hallenbad*. The surrounding woods have a nature trail and a keep fit circuit as well as many kilometres of marked paths and cross-country ski routes. There are many fine old trees in the town park including a reputedly 1,000-year-old *Lindenbaum* (lime tree).

The thirteenth-century village church in nearby **Affeln** contains a rare treasure in its colourful 'Antwerp' altarpiece. This was carved

Burg Altena

in Antwerp in 1525 and was intended for a church in Norway but the Reformation caused the cancellation of the order and the residents of Affeln were able to purchase this masterpiece at a bargain price.

Continuing the clock-wise circuit, come in 7 miles (12km) from Lüdenscheid to the old town of **Altena** straddling the river Lenne and a favourite excursion goal for the residents of the industrial areas to the west. The town is dominated by the romantic castle Burg Altena, the seat of the Counts of the Mark and now the home of the museum of that family. This is not the only museum here, however, for there is also the German Wire Museum to tell the history of that local industry with which is combined the Smithy Museum complete with the workplace of a medieval blacksmith. Burg Altena has another claim to fame for it was the first of the world's youth hostels and the complex includes a museum of youth hostelling and rambling. The old dormitories are of interest but today's hostellers are accommodated in a more modern building nearby. There is another youth hostel down in the town where the swimming pools and sporting facilities are to be found. There is a citizens' centre in Burg Holtzbrinck (seventeenth century) where concerts and theatrical productions take place. The town art gallery is in Haus-Köster-Emden at 93 Lennestrasse. In fairness it must be said that Altena itself is a rather scruffy industrial town with the wire works and other industries rather prominent along the valley road. There is, however, a pleasant pedestrian precinct.

The holiday area centred on **Balve** is about 10 miles (17km) east of Altena and lies in the picturesque and historically interesting Hönnetal between the Balver Forest and the Sorpesee, one of the large reservoirs which has steamer services between May and September. The caves near Balve have an area of 20,000ft^2 (2,000m^2) and are quite spectacular. They are called *Kulturhöhle* which means that they are prehistoric dwelling places as distinct from *Tropfsteinhöhle* which are stalactite caves such as those near Attendorn. The caves now provide the venue for various events including an annual jazz festival in June and a shooting contest in August. In Balve the Romanesque parish church of St Blasius has a rather striking interior and there are parts dating from the end of the twelfth century with frescoes from about the middle of the thirteenth century. The Museum für Vor- und Frühgeschichte has minerals and fossils of great antiquity together with finds from some of the caves in the area. Schloss Wocklum is a nobleman's two-winged moated house from around 1700 south of which is the 1,259ft (384m) high Burgberg which has remains of old fortifications with walls, gateways and the graves of early occupants. At the foot of this hill the Luisenhütte is a foundry and mining museum. The rambling possibilities of the area are considerable and there are numerous places of interest — castles, caves, dams and so on — creating goals to aim for. Balve and its neighbouring villages have a fair amount of guest accommodation including a good proportion of *Ferienwohnungen*. The indoor pool is called the *Schwimmhalle* and includes a sauna.

The iron industry established in the Middle Ages is still important in the economy of **Iserlohn** but let it not be thought that this in any way detracts from the many attractions there are for the visitor. It is a favoured residential town and has a worthwhile amount of accommodation mainly in hotels and *Gasthöfe*. Sights of interest in the town include the late Gothic upper town church of St Marien (fourteenth century) which contains a carved altar (around 1400), probably Dutch and is an important work of the period; there is also the Protestant Pankratius Church, originally a Romanesque pillared basilica but altered in late Gothic style. Nearby a patrician house (1763) with external staircase has become the Haus der Heimat with administrative offices and the interesting Heimatmuseum.

Just to the west of the town towards Letmathe between the A46 and B7 are the extensive stalactite caves called the Dechenhöhle which are well worth a visit. Iserlohn is surrounded by forests and provides well for sporting and leisure activities. It would be an ideal centre for a weekend break.

Hagen is the Sauerland's biggest city. With its suburbs it covers a large area which is crossed by four rivers. The Lenne flows north-wards along the east side of the city to add its waters to the Ruhr, a hitherto picturesque rural river which now continues westwards to give its name to Westphalia's huge industrial area. West of the city the Ennepe and Volme combine and after a short distance they too make their contribution to the Ruhr which, for practical purposes, forms the Sauerland boundary in this north-west corner. The visitor may be surprised to find that Hagen presents him or her with a townscape unusual in Germany for around the turn of the century this was a centre of early *Jugendstil*, largely due to the initiative and patronage of the industrialist Karl Ernst Osthaus.

Architects like Henry van der Velde and Peter Behrens and the painter Thorn Prikker lived and worked here and their thinking and artistic attitudes have had a marked influence. The *Hauptbahnhof* (main railway station) for example, has a monumental entrance hall with windows depicting *The Obeisance of the Crafts before the Artist*, Thorn Prikker's first work in glass. The Eduard Müller Crematorium is an important work by Behrens. The Hohenhof built by van der Velde after 1906 has been acquired by the town and restored to contain some of the surviving furnishings designed by the architect and contributions by other artists of the period including Matisse.

The oldest parts of Schloss Hohenlimburg date from 1230 but the palace has suffered many modifications over the centuries. The central feature is the inner courtyard which has a high wall with passages and turrets. The fine half-timbered oriel and wrought-iron fountain are attractive features. The Heimatmuseum is to be found here. The Karl-Ernst-Osthaus Museum has a collection of twentieth-century art. The entrance hall survives from van der Velde's interior. The Hagen Freilichtmuseum is an open-air museum tracing the history of technology and crafts, the working of metals, timber and paper with more than seventy early workshops and industrial plants. Various musical and other entertainments take place in the 'village' square of the museum, a visit to which can be recom-mended.

Needless to say, Hagen is not entirely composed of cultural attractions and leisure and sporting activities are not forgotten as is evidenced by the presence of four indoor and four heated outdoor swimming pools. The countryside with its forests, lakes and rivers is never far away. The railway enthusiast, finding him or herself in this area, could be forgiven for venturing a little over the Sauerland boundary to **Oberwengern** about 6 miles (10km) west of Hagen city centre to travel in the historic 'museum' train which runs west along a pleasant 13 miles (21km) stretch of line from Wengern Ost to Hattingen closely following the river Ruhr. The track is mostly a freight line of the Federal Railway (Deutsche Bundesbahn) and the train consists of carriages dating from 1893 onwards drawn by historic steam or diesel locomotive. The locomotive and vehicles belong to the big railway museum in Bochum not far away.

Another interesting excursion would be that to **Wuppertal** (about 20 minutes by train from Hagen) where the unique *Schwebebahn* is an elevated railway with suspended cars which serves the commuters of the Wupper valley. For much of its route the railway straddles the river Wupper and although modern vehicles have now been provided, the system, with its eighteen stations, is essentially that which has been operating safely and efficiently for more than 60 years. In Wuppertal there is a tramway museum and also a museum of historic timepieces. Hagen claims to have beds for 1,000 visitors and there is a large youth hostel.

About 6 miles (10km) south-west of Hagen the town of **Ennepetal** in the valley of the river Ennepe has many attractions but will be mentioned here only for its remarkable caves, the *Kluterthöhle*. Although the caves are millions of years old, little is known of them before the sixteenth century. They comprise an imposing system of caverns and passageways of which nearly 4 miles (6km) are so far accessible. They are a wonderful natural monument but more surprising is that in the last few decades they have been found to have a climate which is very beneficial to sufferers from asthma and similar complaints and since they are officially recognised by the leading authorities as a place of medical treatment, certain areas have been set aside for sufferers.

North of Iserlohn the countryside is noticeably less hilly but still quite well wooded as far as **Menden** 7 miles (12km) away. There is a youth hostel here and ample opportunity for rambling in the surrounding countryside in which there are a number of places of interest. In adjoining **Lendringsen** there is a big leisure centre with a heated *Freibad* and other facilities. In Menden itself there is a *Hallenbad* and three more open-air pools. The huge hostelry on the Wilhelmshöhe has seats for some 1,000 guests. There are churches from the fourteenth and seventeenth centuries in the town where there is a religious procession on Good Friday. There is also a Whitsun church fair here as there is in many other places. There is a museum of natural history and one dealing with the local and cultural history of the area. The river Hönne flows northwards through the town, shortly to join the Ruhr. Cross that river to reach the town of Werl 11 miles (18km) to the north-west and nearly on the northern fringe of the Sauerland. The route is through fairly flat, mostly agricultural, land. **Werl**, although by no means a holiday resort, has quite a lot to interest the sightseer who may join the 250,000 visitors who come each year to the Franciscan pilgrimage church to see the thirteenth-century *Gnadenbild* (miraculous image) of the Madonna and Child, gilded and enthroned. The Kapuzinerkirche is an eighteenth-century pilgrimage church. The priory church of St Walburga is a Gothic hall church which incorporates the late Romanesque tower from an earlier building. The altars are well worth seeing and include a fifteenth-century canopied one in the south aisle and a side altar (dated around 1560) representing the life of Our Lady. The contents of the *Heimatmuseum* include references to salt mining and pilgrimages while the *Missionsmuseum* has collections from areas visited by Franciscan missionaries.

While here, at the northern limit of the Sauerland, it is an easy journey of a few minutes to visit Soest 9 miles (14km) to the east along *Bundesstrasse* (Federal road) B1 or along the parallel *Autobahn* 44. **Soest** has a rather fine medieval town centre and is another place in which the visitor could well spend some interesting hours. The old *Rathaus* (1713-18) is well worth seeing. Also not to be missed is the church of St Maria zur Wiese and the three lofty aisles which make it one of the most beautiful hall churches in Germany. The building is mainly from the fourteenth century; there are fine windows from the end of that period and amongst these is the curiosity of the *Westphalian Last Supper* in which Jesus and his disciples are depicted as in a Westphalian tavern partaking of a meal with boar's head, ham and beer. The Madonna of Werl was once in this church. Parts of its Romanesque predecessor are incorporated in the church of Maria zur Höhe (around 1225) which is noted for its particularly fine wall paintings. Wall paintings are also a feature of the Protestant parish church of St Peter (twelfth to thirteenth century) and of the twelfth-century Nikolaikapelle. The cathedral is the collegiate church of St Patroklus: the present building corresponds in all essentials to the twelfth-century original, the opportunity having been taken to remove certain later disfiguring alterations in the course of repairs to damage sustained in World War II. The massive tower is considered to be the finest Romanesque tower in Germany. Nearly all the Romanesque wall paintings were destroyed in the war as was most of the original glass. The most important feature of the furnishings is the tall 7ft (2m) tall triumphal cross.

The old ring wall is largely intact and the massive Osterhofentor houses one of several museums concerned with local history and culture. The biggest inner town fair in West Germany takes place in the shadow of the cathedral from the first Wednesday in November after Allerheiligen (All Saints Day) until the following Sunday and this is followed in December by the annual Christmas fair. About another 10 miles (16km) eastwards along the B1 is *Erwitte* an unspoiled little town where a royal court was established by Heinrich I in 935. However the long two-storey moated *Burg* was only built in the seventeenth century; it was re-built in 1934 and is now owned by the town.

Also worth seeing are the sixteenth to eighteenth-century half-timbered houses around the *Marktplatz*, the former *Rathaus* (1716) and the former residence (1716) of the Droste family, which became the Marienhospital in 1859. The imposing thirteenth-century tower of St Laurentius' Catholic parish church vies in its impressiveness with that of St Patroklus in Soest while the interior decoration includes nine near life-size wooden apostles (1763), the *Madonna of the Seven Swords* and a thirteenth-century wooden crucifix.

Only about 5½ miles (9km) south of Soest along the B229 the community of **Möhnesee** is made up of fifteen little villages. The name is taken from that of the major man-made lake of 4sq miles (10km²) created by the damming of the river Möhne. This was the scene of the successful but costly war-time air attack by the British 'dam-busters' of 617 Squadron, RAF. Several other reservoirs in the Sauerland were also subjected to similar raids but it is the Möhne episode which has been most publicised in war stories and films. The raid resulted in the death of nearly 1,300 people, many of them foreign workers pressed into the service of German industry. All this is now part of local history and the souvenir kiosks at the lakes have books telling the stories of the raids and postcards with graphic pictures of the breached dam based on official photographs taken at the time. Today the Möhnesee is at the heart of one of the most popular outdoor holiday areas in Westphalia, the accent being on water-based activities of course. Steamers ply from April until October and there are many rowing and sailing boats for hire. There is a 220 bed youth hostel and many camp sites and car parks ring the water. There is a lot of holiday accommodation here including a high proportion of *Ferienwohnungen*.

The parish church in **Körbecke**, the biggest village in the group, has fine baroque furnishings while the Heilig-Geist-Kapelle (chapel of the Holy Ghost, dated around 1140) in **Druggelte** is a small, vaulted, twelve-sided rotunda with lavish architectural ornamenta-

Möhnesee from the dam wall

tion. Körbecke has a museum with a permanent exhibition of the works of local artists.

Here, in the Arnsberg Forest Nature Park, the B229 continues for 6 miles (10km) or so beyond the Möhne to **Arnsberg**. A great loop of the river Ruhr encloses much of the town including the charming old part with its many splendid timbered buildings and ruined *Schloss*. Do not miss the historic Maximiliansbrunnen (a fountain) of 1779. Only the priory church of St Laurentius remains of the Premonstratensian abbey of Wedinghausen which was founded here in 1173 and dissolved in 1803. The tower area is from the twelfth century, the early Gothic choir was consecrated in 1253 and building continued into the sixteenth century to create the church seen today. Of interest within are the early baroque high altar in marble and alabaster, the tomb of Friedrich von Fürstenberg (around 1680), the double high tomb of Count Heinrich and his wife Ermengard (fourteenth century), the pulpit and the pews (around 1740).

Near the priory church is the Hirschberg Gate of 1753 while the *Altes Rathaus* (1710) is also worthy of inspection. The imposing *Glockenturm* (bell tower), an old gateway, dominates this upper end of the old town and in its shadow the Stadtkapelle justifies a few minutes of the visitor's time. The Landberger Hof (1605) now houses the Sauerlandmuseum. Arnsberg is a very good shopping centre; there is plenty of accommodation of all types and prices are fairly

Historic iron postbox near the Glockenturm, Arnsberg

modest considering the popularity of the area.

About 3 miles (5km) north-west of Arnsberg at **Hüsten** is the Deutsches Vogelbauermuseum (Birdcage Museum) which traces the history of the keeping of birds as pets over the last five centuries; not only birdcages but paintings, etchings and literature. In addition to the comprehensive facilities at Arnsberg, the town of **Neheim-Hüsten** has its own attractions including a rather rare nine hole golf course. The *Wasserschloss* of **Herdringen** is considered to be the most significant neo-Gothic palace in Westphalia. There is open-air theatre here from June to September.

Six miles (10km) south-west of Arnsberg the eastern side of the Sorpesee mentioned earlier is reached. The central resort here is **Sundern** in the Röhrtal and it is surrounded by a host of large and small villages in a fine holiday area. Much of the community is within the Homert Nature Park, a wonderfully picturesque country-side with a wealth of facilities. Each village has its own particular attractions. For example, **Langscheid** is a *Luftkurort*, that is to say it is a health resort where the air (*Luft*) is considered to be especially beneficial; **Wildewiese** is noted for its winter sports activity with eight ski-tows and a floodlit slope; there are indoor pools in Sundern, Hagen (not to be confused with the city already described) and Langscheid, the latter having a sauna and massage facilities; Sundern has a tennis hall and there are courts in a number of other places.

To the east and south-east there is an area of great tranquility with the remarkable name of Altes Testament (Old Testament) which comprises the villages of **Hellefeld**, **Altenhellefeld** and **Grevenstein** right at the centre of the imaginary clock-face. There is quite a lot of farmhouse and self-catering accommodation here as well as more formal quarters in hotels and *Gasthöfe*. Well-tended parks and gardens provide for the visitor who does not wish to indulge in the more strenuous rambling along the many waymarked paths in the neighbourhood. This is a place for a pleasant stay at any time and all leisure activities are catered for according to season. There is a ski-tow for winter visitors.

To the north-east the old town of **Meschede** is another which is at the centre of a group of holiday resorts in an extremely popular location in the heart of the Sauerland. There is an enormous choice of accommodation scattered over a large area. Meschede itself is on the river Ruhr between the Homert and Arnsberg Forest Nature Parks. A fine example of modern church architecture is the church of the Königsmünster Abbey just north of the town centre. The monks are responsible for a large *Gymnasium* (grammar school) which provides a fine education for pupils of all denominations. South of the town the landscape and activity is dominated by the Hennetalsperre with its large man-made lake on which there are cruises from April to October. Rowing boats and pedalos can be hired and there is a windsurfing school. There is a camp site close to the lake and the bungalow village 'Hennesee' has twenty houses available for short-term letting. There is also a large youth hostel.

North of Meschede a picturesque secondary road leads to **Hirschberg** about 6 miles (9km) away. The Catholic church here has an altar worth stopping to see. Two miles (3km) from the village there is a forest nature trail and a woodland play area, together with a keep fit circuit. The forests around Hirschberg are particularly well provided with car parks making it very easy to get access to the splendid network of footpaths. At Hirschberg a visit can be made to the caves, the Bilsteinhöhle, which are in a *Wildgehege* (a forest enclosure for red deer, wild boars and other animals). The town of **Warstein** 3 miles (5km) east of Hirschberg is surrounded by forests with well-marked footpaths and provision is made for skiing in winter. There is a *Hallenbad* and a heated *Freibad* to serve the many visitors to this centre which is well provided with accommodation including a lot for self-caterers and prices are generally moderate.

The town museum of Warstein in Haus Kupferhammer is by no means the conventional small town collection of local relics. The house was the home of one Wilhelm Bergenthal (1805-93), the industrialist who was primarily responsible for the growth of the metal-working industry in Warstein and many other neighbouring places. The house was part of the Kupferhammer (copper works or foundry) property from which it derived its name. Bergenthal was a privy

Rüthen town hall

councillor with diverse industrial interests and he also sought the furtherance of agriculture and the public well-being in general. The competition from the rapidly growing Ruhr industrial area soon resulted in a decline in Warstein.

After his death, Bergenthal's grandson — also Wilhelm — took over the dwindling undertaking and this, and the family itself, finally died out with the death of his wife Ottilie in 1951. She had arranged that her home and the surrounding park should fall to the town to be used as a museum and cultural centre. It tells not only of the history of the family and the industry but also has many works of art including the so-called *Muttergottes von Warstein*, a sandstone Gothic madonna from the fourteenth century. From time to time concerts take place in the museum.

Still in the Arnsberg Forest Nature Park **Kallenhardt**, 3 miles (5km) east of Warstein, has a fifteenth-century Rathaus, a baroque style church from 1722, the Wasserschloss Körtlinghausen and caves called the Hohler Stein a little way to the south. Here too, there is no shortage of parking places in the forest. A picturesque but somewhat twisty road goes 4 miles (6km) northwards to **Rüthen** just outside the Arnsberg forest and close to the north-eastern boundary of the Sauerland. With its many outlying villages Rüthen is a scattered community. The town itself is a rather charming old place with ancient fortifications including the town wall which is a mile (2km) long. There is a baroque town hall with a splendid external double staircase, a number of timbered buildings and two churches worthy of inspection. The leisure area Bibertal has ample parking, a nature trail, play areas, minigolf, a heated outdoor pool and a youth hostel. Eastwards from Meschede on the B7, upstream along the river Ruhr in about 6 miles (10km), is the resort of Bestwig, but a stop should be made on the way to see the church and the little timbered Rathaus in Eversberg. **Bestwig,** and the numerous villages which contribute to its population, lies in the *Feriengebiet* (holiday area) Ruhr-Valme-Elpetal and offers its guests a wide variety of activities and interests. In addition to all the more usual attractions there are organised rambling events and tours on horse-back to local beauty spots. Accommodation is mainly in the *Gasthof* and pension categories with an ample selection of self-catering houses and flats, some of them on farms. Three or four miles (5 or 6km) to the south the *Erzbergbau-Museum* (Mining Museum) at **Ramsbeck** is well worth a visit but do not economise by paying only to visit the museum; make sure that the visit includes a tour of the vast underground workings. The visitor will be asked to don protective overalls and a 'hard hat' and will then take his or her seat in the diminutive carriages of the train which used to convey the miners to the workings to labour at the extraction of zinc, silver and lead, a journey of about 12 minutes in almost total darkness. In the heart of the mountain the visitor is taken on a comprehensive tour of the installations which were in production until just a few years ago. Inside the mine the visitor is actually far beneath one of the many family leisure parks which have sprung up in recent years. This one is called Fort Fun Abenteurland (Adventure Land) and it has the almost obligatory 'Western' town and modern mechanical contrivances galore as well as a genuine old roundabout. The giant *Rutschbahn* (chute or summer bob-run) is 2,493ft (760m) long and a favourite pastime for all age groups. From April until October the replica of a 'Wild West' railway is in operation.

Back in the Ruhr valley, leave Bestwig on the B7 but soon turn off to visit **Olsberg,** the principal resort in a scattered community located in an area of great charm. Olsberg is a year-round *Kneippkurort*, that is to say, it is a health resort at which treatment is available in accordance with the principles of the famous Sebastian Kneipp. Of course, a health problem is not necessary for enjoyment of the many splendid facilities. There are indoor and outdoor pools — as well as special bathing facilities for those taking the *Kur* — and a concert hall.

In the summer months, concerts also take place in the *Kurpark*. Some 186 miles (300km) of waymarked paths are accessible. Schloss Gevelinghausen is now a fifty-bed hotel and restaurant. To the south of the town, **Assingshausen** (4 miles, 6km) has the interesting ancient granary, the Riesenspeicher (1556), another timbered building to delight the photographer. Almost adjoining to the east is **Bruchhausen**, famous for its rocky out-crops called the Bruchhauser Steine on the Istenberg, reminding one slightly of the 'tors' on England's Dartmoor. Bruchhausen also claims the distinction of being an access point to the (2,765ft, 843m) Langenberg, the highest point in the Sauerland. This is a favourite winter sports area and there is a camp site which is open all year round.

Back on the B7, **Brilon** is by far the biggest place in the extensive group of habitations of which it is the centre. Of interest in the town are the sixteenth-century *Marktbrunnen* (fountain) and the baroque façade of the *Rathaus*. The unusual turreted tower of the Propsteikirche St Peter and Andrew dominates the skyline behind the Rathaus. The church has some fine stained glass windows. Brilon is a very lively *Luftkurort* with every amenity one could wish for. Those who are here for health reasons can enjoy modest exercise on 31 miles (50km) of easy footpaths but another 279 miles (450km) of way-marked paths provides for those desiring more ambitious activity. There is winter as well as summer recreation here with provision for floodlit skiing. There is a large youth hostel and the extensive catalogue of accommodation would make it appear unlikely that any person wishing to stay here would be disappointed. There is, however, a very heavy demand in the summer holiday months and again during the winter sports season so advance booking at those times is strongly recommended.

Space considerations preclude mention of the many more delightful little places along the final 17 miles (27km) of the B7 into **Marsberg** almost at the eastern extremity of the Sauerland in a sort of peninsular that sticks out rather like the head of a tortoise from the main body. The town actually comprises Niedermarsberg and Obermarsberg, both of which claim the title *Ferienort* — holiday place. The former lies in the valley of the river Diemel and is the 'modern' town with swimming pools, a sports hall, a riverside promenade, a music pavilion, the *Heimatmuseum* and so on. Obermarsberg is a historic town, once the Saxon fortress of Eresburg which was overthrown by Karl der Grosse in 772. The collegiate church of St Peter and St Paul was completed about 1410 on the remains of a thirteenth-century church which had been destroyed by lightning and fire. The crypt beneath the chancel with its dominant octagonal middle pillar is of special interest. Interior decoration and the organ are baroque, an unusual feature in this region. The small

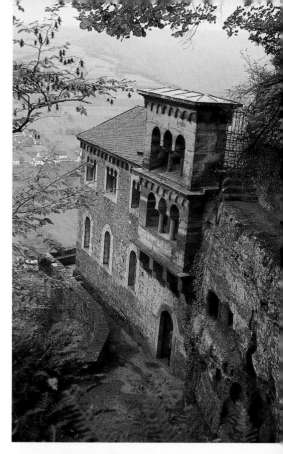

Roman remains near Kastel in the Saar Valley

Dörrenbach town hall, in the Palatinate Forest Nature Park

Siebeldingen near Landau, in the Palatinate Forest Nature Park

Deidesheim, in the Palatinate Forest Nature Park

Nicolai Chapel is first mentioned in the records in 1247 and is one of the most significant and charming early Gothic buildings in Westphalia. Inside there are tall round pillars topped by early Gothic leafwork capitals. Particularly to be noted are the surviving old windows and the Romanesque south portal.

Other things of interest in this part of the town are the Roland Column (1737), an old gateway and the Benediktusbogen with two towers and a sixteenth-century pillory. There are conducted tours round the old town: details from the information office at Bülberg 2. The Diemelsee about 7½ miles (12km) to the south-west is another man-made lake which is popular with anglers as is the river Diemel itself. Trout and pike are amongst the fish to be caught here: information and fishing permits can be obtained from the *Verkehrsbüro*.

If there is a need for a place to go on a wet day, note should be taken of the proximity of the city of **Kassel** to this end of the Sauerland. From Marsberg the B7 goes right into Kassel but by using the A44 the motorist could reach the city in about 30 minutes. It is a fine place and there are many sights of interest: museums include that devoted to the Grimm Brothers and one with the theme of wallpaper. There are many notable churches and other buildings to see and the railway enthusiast might enjoy a historic steam train trip between Kassel and Naumburg (20½ miles, 33km) in the Hessen Courier.

However, back to the Sauerland where the south-eastern corner will now be explored. If elsewhere the areas have been dominated by the lakes and their associated water activities, here the accent is on the mountains and, in particular, on their influence upon the winter sports scene. Indeed, in many of the resorts in this area, it is the winter which is the peak season with summer coming only a close second. There are, of course, the indigenous agricultural and forestry activities, but this is an area given over almost exclusively to the needs of those who come for relaxation in the beautiful countryside.

Willingen is a health resort with *Kneipp* — a type of treatment using the properties of water — and other facilities and is a winter sports centre. The climate is considered beneficial for sufferers of heart and circulatory conditions or with breathing and nervous disorders. For those unable to do more there are many level footpaths but the more active visitors are not forgotten with many high-level paths, indoor and outdoor tennis courts, an ice rink, riding stables and so on. There is a *Wald- und Heimatmuseum* and there are conducted tours of the Christine slate quarries. A vast amount of accommodation of all kinds is provided and no less than sixteen of the hotels have their own indoor pools. Visitors will always find a public swimming pool within easy distance, especially in the summer when the open-air facilities are available.

Medebach, right on this south-eastern fringe of the Sauerland, is yet another of those places encircled by its satellite villages, most of them very small. One of the latter, **Küstelberg**, has been a winner in Germany's 'Beautiful Village' competition many times. The refurbished church has a huge, modern stained glass window and outside a spring marks the Sauerland watershed. From here the streams flowing westwards eventually contribute to the river Rhine while those heading east find their way to the Weser. Everywhere are marked paths, those near the villages being generously provided with seats. Here too, the rambler will frequently come across that peculiarly German installation, the *Tretbecken*. There is no English word equivalent but this is a shallow basin or pool, usually fed by a natural stream, in which the passer-by may paddle to cool his or her feet. It is ideal after a warm and strenuous ramble although it often appears that the *Tretbecken* are even more popular with elderly ladies here for their health — indeed, some places claim that theirs are *Kneipp Tretbecken*, the worthy Sebastian having been convinced of the therapeutic qualities of water.

Nine miles (14km) west of Medebach **Winterberg** is at the centre of the biggest group of village resorts in the whole Sauerland. It is a health resort at the foot of the 2,758ft (841m) Kahler Asten and claims to be the highest 'town' in Western Germany. In fairness it must be noted that the same claim is made by several other places including Oberstdorf in Bavaria which, at 2,765ft (843m), lies higher than the summit of the Kahler Asten! It is entirely appropriate that the name of Winterberg should be primarily associated with winter sports but it is a delightful place at any time of year. In common with most Sauerland resorts there is no defined 'high season' here although there are acute peaks of activity in winter when skiing conditions are good and during the summer school holidays.

At all seasons the splendid vantage point of the Kahler Asten is a great attraction and another easy excursion is that to the source of the river Ruhr a few kilometres north of the town. Here, as elsewhere in the area, efforts are made to keep tracks clear for cross-country skiers and winter walkers.

The B236 runs south-east from Winterberg to **Hallenberg**, a distance of 9 miles (14km). From June to September the open-air theatre here is a great attraction with productions for children and adults. The picturesque old centre of Hallenberg is one of those places really worth visiting with its part-slated, timbered houses and

Oberkirchen

the fountain of 1756 in the market place. A pilgrimage chapel dates from the eleventh century and the parish church of St Heribert from the seventeenth century; both of them justify a visit as does the church in the village of **Hesborn** about 4 miles (6km) to the north which has altars from the former Kloster Glindfeld (a monastery). The church tower was built in 1127. Just to the west of Hesborn the 2,486ft (758m) Bollerberg has a tower which commands an extensive view of the countryside.

In a westerly direction from Winterberg, the B236 passes through a number of charming villages; Langwiese, Hoheleye, Albrechtsplatz (watch out for signs to the *Wildgehege*) and Oberkirchen on the little river Lenne. **Oberkirchen** is another previous winner of the 'Beautiful Village' competition. A little road to the south leads to **Grafschaft** (1 mile, 2km) where the former monastery is an extensive baroque complex (1729), now a hospital run by the nuns of the Benedictine Order. The small and mostly modern church of St George is attractive. Since Medebach the territory explored has been in the Rothaargebirge Nature Park which extends over the Sauerland boundary to cover a large part of the neighbouring Siegerland. The walker will find many historic remains in this old southern frontier land of the Saxons.

The B236 follows the Lenne to **Schmallenberg**, a bigger place than most in this area. It is a *Luftkurort* and unashamedly does all it can to provide every amenity and attraction for its many visitors. The large swimming pool complex includes a *Wellenbad*, sauna, sunbathing terrace, restaurant and café. The enormous network of footpaths radiating from the town make it easy to ascend to the viewing tower on the top of the Wilzenberg (2,158ft, 658m) or to several other worthwhile hilltops to survey the countryside below.

Neighbouring **Fredeburg** is a *Kneippkurort* and apart from the special facilities available to those taking the *Kur* it has a huge range of activity possibilities for the general holidaymaker. Some of the *Tretbecken* in the forest have an additional basin in which the arms may be cooled as well as the feet! There is a roller-skating rink, several bowling alleys, and adventure playgrounds, while concerts and folk evenings are regular events. In winter there are all types of skiing and instruction, including for children.

Visitors to Schmallenberg and Fredeburg should not fail to visit the little churches in nearby Berghausen and Wormbach. St Cyriacus in **Berghausen** is a Romanesque building from the end of the twelfth century. The date 1861 on the tower relates to major repairs carried out in that year. The church is notable for its fine ceiling and wall paintings dating from the early thirteenth century. These were cleaned and restored during renovations in 1961 when intruding baroque embellishments were removed, better to reveal the paintings. The old high altar completely concealed the marvellous paintings in the apse and was given to the church in Schönholthausen while two side altars were presented to the Jesuit church in Paderborn. A mile away (2km), the Romanesque church in **Wormbach** is considered to be the oldest church in the Sauerland. As was formerly the case in Berghausen, the baroque high altar conceals whatever may be of interest in the apse. The Wormbach organ recitals are a regular feature of the summer programme in this area. Four miles (6km) north-west of Fredeburg the tiny village of **Nierentrop** is of interest for its old rural bakehouse, disused now but still in good condition at the time of writing. There are numerous skiing possibilities at **Rimberg, Osterwald** and **Bödefeld** all of which lie to the north of Fredeburg and can be reached in a few minutes by car.

North-west in this segment is **Eslohe**, a *Luftkurort* in the Homert Nature Park with the holiday resort of **Reiste** within its orbit. This is a good central place with ready access to fine forest landscapes and to several lakes including the Sorpetalsperre and the Hennetalsperre already mentioned.

Lennestadt, taking the name from its river, is an administrative unit rather than a town in its own right. It was created in 1969 by the combination of eight closely related communities and, of course, a number of small villages. Of these constituent parts, **Saalhausen** to the east is a *Luftkurort*, Elspe to the north has a history going back more than a thousand years and **Bilstein** to the west stands at the foot of the historic *Burg* of the same name. The castle is now a youth hostel but is open to visitors. At **Oberhundem**, to the south-east, is another modern leisure complex, the Panorama Park Sauerland. There are mechanical amusements and extensive areas of fine countryside with enclosures for bison, deer, wild boar, elk and other animals. There is the inevitable 'Wild West' stockade, unusual power-driven bumper boats and a very long dry bob-run.

A rather different entertainment is provided by the Karl-May-Festival at **Elspe**. Here stories by the famous 'Western' writer are brought vividly to life. Almost daily from mid-June until September the battles between Red Indians and white men are re-enacted.

The visitor may bypass Olpe if this town has been visited earlier and complete his or her tour in the southernmost tip of the Sauerland at **Wenden**, a place of some interest and a peacefully situated holiday centre with surrounding villages. In Wenden the church of St Severinus should be inspected and the pilgrimage chapel in **Dörnschlade** is also worth a visit. Industrial archaeology in unusual form is to be found at the Wendenerhütte, the old iron-smelting furnace from 1728 which was fired by wood. In the village of **Römershagen** there is the source of the river Bigge which flows northwards to feed the huge reservoir which takes its name.

Sauerland is not a land with a large number of cultural monuments; there is nothing here to compare with the extravagent baroque churches of Bavaria but, all the same, a number of churches and chapels justify a visit if one is nearby. There is a certain amount of industrial archaeology but the outstanding civil engineering of the great reservoirs is likely to be of more interest to most of today's visitors, not only for the technical achievement but for the recreational facilities which these man-made lakes provide.

Natural attractions abound in the many caves, rivers, mountains and valleys. Lovers of outdoor life will certainly find plenty to occupy themselves. Visitors with young families will praise the leisure facilities, the swimming pools, the animal enclosures, the pleasure centres and so on.

Visitors are recommended to obtain the special map of the area, the 'Aral' *Tourenkarte Sauerland-Bergisches Land* (1:200,000), obtainable from Aral filling stations. Not only is it detailed but on the reverse is a comprehensive summary of places of interest.

Further Information
— The Sauerland —

Boating and Sailing

At many of the large artificial lakes boats or windsurfing equipment may be hired. The principal locations are Biggesee, Diemelsee, Harkortsee (Hagen), Hengsteysee (Hagen), Hennesee, Listersee (Meinerzhagen), Möhnesee, Seilersee (Iserlohn) and Sorpesee. There are pleasure cruises on: Biggesee — Easter until end October; Diemelsee — May to end October for groups of ten or more; Harkortsee (Hagen) — Easter to September; Hengsteysee (Hagen) — April to September; Hennesee — April to October; Möhnesee — April to October; Sorpesee — May to September. Outside the main holiday season sailings may be suspended during poor weather.

Cycling and Cycle Hire

A wide range of package cycling holidays is available, details from Touristikzentrale Sauerland. Cycles may also be hired from the DB railway station in Willingen. Cyclists arriving by train pay only half the normal hire charge.

Riding and Pony-Trekking

Numerous riding establishments offer a wide variety of facilities. They are listed in the *Unterkunftsverzeichnis* (catalogue of accommodation obtainable from Landesverkehrsverband Westfalen eV) or details from local tourist offices. All main centres provide excursions by horse-drawn coaches or covered wagons. For information on riding courses and adventure holidays contact Frau Kühn, Reiterverein, 5880 Lüdenscheid ☎ (02351) 437321.

Places to Visit

Altena
Museum Grafschaft Mark
Märkisches Schmiedemuseum
Deutsches Drahtmuseum
Jugendherbergsmuseum
Wandermuseum
Burg Altena
58762 Altena
☎ (02352) 200152
Open: Tues to Sunday 9.30am-5pm. All these museums are housed in the old castle above the town and cover local history, industry, youth hostelling and rambling. The old dormitories of the world's first youth hostel may be inspected. Admission charge to museums but castle courtyards and towers free. Very limited parkin at the castle: ample space in the valley close to the river. Café-restaurant.

Stadtgalerie im Hause Köster-Emden
Lennestrasse 93
58762 Altena
☎ (02352) 21270
Open: Tuesday to Saturday 10am-6pm, Sunday 10am-12.30pm.
The town art collection.

Arnsberg-Neheim-Hüsten
Sauerland-Museum
59821 Arnsberg
☎ (02931) 4098
Open: Tuesday-Saturday 9.30am-5pm, Sunday 9.30am-1pm. Closed on Monday and holidays.
Folk history of area. Finds from the Balve Cave. Conducted tours by prior arrangement. Admission free.

Litauen Museum
Burgstrasse 15a
59755 Arnsberg-Neheim
☎ (02932) 26858
Culture centre of Germans from Lithuania.
Open: Monday-Friday 9.30am-4pm; Saturday, Sunday and holidays by prior arrangement, Admission free.

Leuchtenmuseum
In Fabrik Thorn-EMI
Möhnestrasse 55
59759 Arnsberg-Hüsten
☎ (02932) 1499
Open: Monday to Thursday 10am-
12noon, 2-4pm. Friday 10am-12noon.
Museum of lighting equipment.
Admission free. Conducted tours by
prior arrangement

Deutsches Vogelbauermuseum
Cäcilienstrasse 11-15
59759 Arnsberg-Hüsten
☎ (02932) 4591
Open: Monday to Friday 9am-4pm.
Birdcages, paintings, literature, etc.
Admission free.

Attendorn
Attahöhle
Finnentroper Strasse
☎ (02722) 3041
Open: summer 9am-5pm, winter 10am-
4pm.

Kreisheimatmuseum
Alter Markt
57439 Attendorn
☎ (02722) 3711
Open: Tuesday to Friday 9am-1pm,
3-5pm, Saturday 9am-1pm, Sunday
11am-1pm.
Housed in the historic former *Rathaus*.
Local history and culture.

Waffenkammer
Burg Schnellenberg
57439 Attendorn
☎ (02722) 6940
Open: Tuesday-Thursday 12noon-5pm,
Friday to Sunday 10am-5pm.
Weaponry room in mighty thirteenth-
century castle. Hotel.

Balve
Balver Höhle
☎ (02375) 5380 or 4017
Open: April to October, Tuesday-
Friday & Sunday 10am-4pm.

Luisenhütte Wocklum
58802 Balve
☎ (02375) 3134
A mile north-east of Balve.

Open: May to October, Tuesday to
Saturday 10am-6pm, Sunday 11.30am-
6pm. During other months by prior
arrangement.
Significant museum of industrial
archaeology. Free Parking.

Balve-Volkringhausen
Reckenhöhle
☎ (02379) 209
Open: March to November, daily 9am-
4pm.

Bestwig-Ramsbeck
*Erzbergbaumuseum und Besucherer-
bergwerk*
Glück-Auf-Strasse 3
59909 Bestwig-Ramsbeck
☎ (02905) 250
Open: daily 9am-4pm (last admission);
closed December and Mondays mid-
October to mid-15 March. Parties book
in advance.
Mining history; underground tours on
old mining railway.
Free parking.

Ennepetal
Klüterthöhle
Höhlenstrasse 20
☎ (023331) 7865
Open: all year.
Recognised cure establishment for
asthma sufferers etc.

Hagen
Westfälisches Freilichtmuseum
Technischer Kulturdenkmale
Mäckingerbachtal
58091 Hagen
☎ (02331) 780744
South of city centre via Selbecker
Strasse.
Open: April to October, Tuesday to
Sunday 9am-6pm.
Huge open-air museum with many old
workshops and historic machines.

Museum Schloss Hohenlimburg
Im Schloss
58119 Hagen
☎ (02334) 2771
Five miles (8km) east of city.

Open: April to September, Tuesday to Sunday 10am-6pm, October and March, Tuesday to Friday 1-4pm, Saturday and Sunday 10am-4pm, November to February, Tuesday to Sunday 1-4pm.

More than twenty rooms of various exhibits in huge castle dating from 1230.

Karl Ernst Osthaus Museum
Hochstrasse 73
58095 Hagen
☎ (02331) 207576
Open: Tuesday-Saturday 11am-6pm, Thursday 11am-10pm, Sunday 11am-4pm.
Modern paintings.

Hattingen-Wengern Ost

Eisenbahnmuseum Bochum-Dahlhausen GmbH
Dr C-Otto-Strasse 191
44879 Bochum
☎ (0234) 492516
Trains usually run on first Sunday of each month April-October, with about five services in each direction. The museum at Bochum is open Wednesday and Friday 10am-5pm, Sunday and Holidays 10am-12.45pm. On Sunday and holidays February -November half-hourly shuttle service from Bochum-Dahlhausen station to museum.

Iserlohn

Städtisches Museum
Fritz-Kühn-Platz
58636 Iserlohn
☎ (02371) 2172247
Open: Tuesday to Friday 8am-12noon, 2-4pm and by prior arrangement.

Museum für Vorgeschichte und Höhlenkunde
Am Aufgang zur Dechenhöhle
58644 Iserlohn-Dechenhöhle
☎ (02371) 28890
Open: Monday to Friday 10am-12.30pm, Saturday and Sunday 10am-5pm. December to February only open at weekends.
Prehistory and caves.

Iserlohn-Letmathe

Dechenhöhle
☎ (02374) 71421
Open: April to October, 9am-5pm, November to March, 10am-4pm.
DB station Dechenhöhle. Restaurant.

Kassel-Naumburg

Hessencourrier (steam train)
Kaulenbergstrasse 5
34131 Kassel
☎ (0561) 35925 or 581550 or 21981
Service second Sunday each month June-October and on certain other days with a St Nikolaus special early December. Timetable (*Fahrplan*) for the year appears about February and obtainable from the address given. Reduced fares for children up to 12 years and families. Buffet car on all trains.

Kirchhundem

Stickmuseum
Rüsper Strasse 1
57399 Kirchhundem-Oberhundem
Open: Monday to Friday 9am-12 noon, 3-7pm, Saturday 9am-12 noon.
Embroidery.

Lüdenscheid

Stadtmuseum
Liebigstrasse 11
58511 Lüdenscheid
☎ (02351) 17445
Open: Tuesday to Saturday 9am-12.30pm, 3.30-6pm, Sunday 10.30am-1pm.
Includes the *Knopf* (Buttons) and *Feuerwehr* (Fire-Fighting) Museums. Admission free.

Museum Bremecker Hammer
58513 Lüdenscheid
☎ (02351) 42400
Open: May to mid-October, Tuesday-Friday 10am-5pm, Saturday & Sunday 10am-5.30pm.
Technical culture memorial and history of iron-making. Admission free.

Menden
Museum für Stadt- und Kulturgeschichte
Marktplatz 3
58706 Menden
☎ (02373) 164451
Open: Tuesday to Friday 9am-12noon,
3-5pm, Saturday 9am-12noon, Sunday
11am-12noon. Holidays closed.
Town and cultural history. Admission
free.

*Museum für Erdgeschichte und
    Naturkunde*
Marktplatz 4
58706 Menden
☎ (02373) 164452
Opening times as above.
Geography and natural history. Admission free.

Meschede
Heimatmuseum
Mittelstrasse 12
59872 Meschede-Eversberg
☎ (0291) 50674/51454
3 miles (5km) east of Meschede.
Open: Tuesday, Thursday and Saturday 3-6pm, Sunday 11am-12noon.
Closed Christmas-New Year.
Town history, rural working and
domestic implements, etc.

Plettenberg-Stahl-Hüinghausen
Märkische Museums-Eisenbahn eV
Postfach 1346
58840 Plettenberg
☎ (02391) 13035 (Herr Kodinger)
Metre-gauge museum railway. Workshop on premises of Firma Graeka,
Bredderstrasse, 58840 Plettenberg-
Eiringhausen (2 miles, 3km, from
centre) may be visited by prior arrangement. Activity confined mainly to
weekends. Trains usually run two
Sundays per month April-October, also
St Nikolaus excursions early
December.

Schmallenberg
Heimat- und Schieferbergbaumuseum
57392 Schmallenberg-Holthausen
☎ (02974) 6019 or 6825
Open: Wednesday and Saturday

2-5pm, Sunday 10am-12noon (also
during summer holiday period 3-5pm).
Local and slate-quarrying history.
Special exhibitions.

Soest
Burghofmuseum
Burghofstrasse
59494 Soest
☎ (02921) 103332
Open: Tuesday to Saturday 10am-
12noon, 3-5pm, Sunday 11am-1pm.
Art and culture.
Admission free.

Wilhelm-Morgner-Haus
Thomästrasse
59494 Soest
☎ (02921) 13524
Open: Monday to Saturday 10am-
12noon, 3-5pm, Sunday 10.30am-
12.30pm.
Art gallery. Admission free.

Osthofentormuseum
Osthofenstrasse
59494 Soest
☎ (02921) 103297
Open: April to September, Tuesday to
Friday 2-4pm, Saturday 11am-1pm,
Sunday 11am-1pm, 3-5pm; October to
March, Wednesday 2-4pm, Sunday
11am-1pm.
Art and culture housed in historic town
tower. Town history with models.

Warstein
Bilsteinhöhle
☎ (02902) 2731
On the road to Hirschberg.
Open: daily April to November, 9am-
5pm, December to March, weekdays
10am-12noon, 2-4pm, Sunday and
holidays 9am-4pm.
In addition to the caves, free adventure
playground and *Wildpark* with deer,
wild boars, etc. Restaurant. Free
parking.

Werl
Heimathaus 'Rykenberg'
Am Rykenberg
59457 Werl
☎ (02922) 800263

Open: Tuesday, Wednesday & Friday
2-4.30pm, Thursday 4-6.30pm, Saturday & Sunday 10.30am-12.30pm.
Folk Museum in thirteenth-century
building. Admission free.

Missionsmuseum
Meisterstrasse 15
59457 Werl
☎ (02922) 2635
Open: Tuesday-Friday 11am-1pm, 2-5pm, Sunday & Sunday 2-5pm.
Memorabilia of Franciscan missions
overseas.

Willingen
Wald- und Heimatmuseum
Alte Kirchstrasse 10
56479 Willingen
☎ (05632) 69625 or 6019
Open: May to October, Monday,
Tuesday, Thursday and Saturday
10am-12noon, 4-6pm.
Forestry and folk museum.

Schiefergrube Christine
Schwalefelder Strasse 28
56479 Willingen
☎ (05632) 6220
Tours of slate quarries Wednesday to
Saturday at 10 and 11am, 3 and 4pm,
Sunday at 10 and 11am.

Wuppertal-Kohlfurth-Cronenberg
Bergische Museums-Strassenbahn eV
Postfach 131936
42103 Wuppertal
☎ (0202) 470251 during opening hours.
A tramway museum with 1½ miles
(3km) of track. The Kohlfurth depot is
open all year Saturday 9am-5pm and
May-October Sunday 11am-5pm.
Groups at other times by prior
arrangement. Operations usually take
place two Sundays per month May-October. Entry free, but donation
invited.

Zoos and Wildlife Parks

Arnsberg-Vosswinkel
Wildwald Vosswinkel
59757 Arnsberg
☎ (02932) 25195 or 23004

On B7 12 miles (20km) north-west of
Arnsberg.
Open: daily until dusk.
Deer, foxes, wild boars, raccoons, etc.

Brilon
Brummerhagen
Three miles (4½km) north-west near
B516.
Open: daily.
Wild boars.

Madfeld
Nine miles east (14km) near B7.
Deer.

Ennepetal
Erholungspark Hülsenbeckertal
58256 Ennepetal
Open: daily.
Fallow deer, exotic birds, ornamental
fish.
Small animals enclosure.

Eslohe-Wenholthausen
Auf dem Eibel
Four miles (6km) north of Eslohe.
Open: daily.
Red deer, fallow deer, wild boars.

Finnentrop-Weuspert
Weuspert
Four miles (7km) north-east of
Finnentrop.
Open: daily.
Deer, fallow deer, wild boars.

Hagen
Wehringhauser Bachtal
Open: daily.
Deer.

Haspe
Three miles (5km) west of Hagen.
Open: daily.
Wild boars.

Fleyer Wald
North of Hagen.
Open: daily.
Wild boars, fallow deer.

Lennestadt-Kirchveischede
Heinrich Brill
Five miles (8km) west of Altenhundem
on B55.
Open: daily.
Deer.

Möhnesee-Völlinghausen
Am Wildpark
About 2 (4km) miles from Völling-
hausen at east end of the Möhnesee.
Open: daily.
Sika-deer, fallow deer, birds.

Warstein
Bei der Tropfsteinhöhle
Near the caves on road to Hirschberg.
Open: daily.

Deer, fallow deer, wild boars. Admission and parking free. Restaurant.

Willingen
Am Ettelsberg
56479 Willingen
☎ (05632) 6810 or 69198
2 miles (3km) south-west of Willingen.
Open: daily 9am-6pm.
Deer, fallow deer. Fairytale park.

The above list should not be regarded
as exhaustive. *Wildgehege* are not
necessarily always in exactly the same
location and a call at the local tourist
information office to check might save
a fruitless search.

Tourist Information Offices

Regional

Landesverkehrsverband
Westfalen
Südwall 6
44137 Dortmund
☎ (0231) 527506/7
(The main office for the
Federal State of
Westphalia).

Touristikzentrale
Sauerland
Postfach 1460
59929 Brilon
☎ (02961) 913229
(The main office for the
Sauerland in general and
for Hochsauerland, the
south-eastern segment,
in particular).

Kreisverkehrsverband
Südsauerland
Seminarstrasse 22
Postfach 1545
57462 Olpe
☎ (02761) 6822/6821
(For the south-western
corner around Olpe).

Märkischer Kreis, Amt für
Fremdenverkehr
Heedfelder Strasse 45
Postfach 2080
58509 Lüdenscheid
☎ (02351) 671873/671747
(For Märkisches
Sauerland, the north-
western corner excluding
Hagen and environs).

Local

Hagen
Mittelstrasse
Pavillon
58095 Hagen
☎ (02331) 13573

Kries Soest
Amt für Wirtschafts-
förderung
Hoher Weg 1-3
59494 Soest
☎ (02921) 302239
In addition to the principal offices listed, each
place has a *Verkehrsamt*
to which inquiries may
be addressed.

4 • The Saar Valley

The river Mosel, especially between Koblenz on the Rhine and Trier, is a fairly well-trodden tourist route and features in the itinerary of many 'package' holiday deals. Even the person who has not visited this famous valley of vineyards will probably be familiar with the names of many wine-producing areas such as Traben-Trarbach, Bernkastel and Piesport. The other two rivers of the Mosel-Saar-Ruwer wine-growing trio are comparatively little known and in this chapter we explore the larger of the two — the Saar.

This tributary of the Mosel comes over the border from France at Saargemünd and joins the Mosel some 56 miles (90km) to the north close to the Luxembourg border and just west of the ancient city of Trier. The traveller from Britain, whether by road or rail, will probably reach this area via Luxembourg since that is the most direct route. The motorist can choose a short sea crossing to Calais and drive east to join the continental motorway network near Dunkirk, proceeding then via Lille, Namur and Luxembourg. The night services on the longer crossings from Hull, Felixstowe or Harwich to Rotterdam or Zeebrugge allow ample time to reach any part of the Saar valley without another overnight stop.

The distance from Calais to Trier is around 290 miles (467km) and from the Dutch and Belgian ports a little less. Either way, the routes are predominantly motorway or fast dual carriageway. For the rail traveller a very direct route is that via Dover and Ostende, then through Brussels, Luxembourg and Trier. From there, trains run south to Saarbrücken calling at many of the places mentioned in this chapter. The railway enthusiast changing trains at Brussels Nord could spend an interesting half-hour in the excellent free railway museum in the station there.

The main international airports suitable for this area are Brussels or Frankfurt and possibly Cologne and Luxembourg from each of which the journey can readily be completed by train or hire car. The airport at Saarbrücken has connections from Frankfurt as well as from Düsseldorf, Munich and Berlin. The Saar valley is eminently

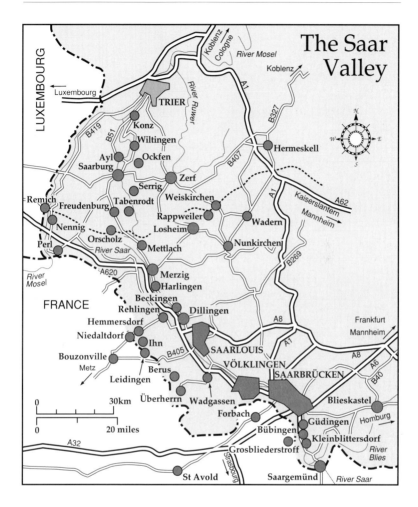

suitable for the visitor reliant upon public transport but there are, of course, advantages in having a personal motor vehicle.

At its north end, the Saar does not yet have the international water traffic of the Mosel but this will no doubt develop now that full canalisation has been completed. Southwards from the industrial area around Saarbrücken the river is extensively used, for just over the border at Saargemünd it gives access to the French canal system by means of which large freight vessels can reach places like Strasbourg or Paris.

There are many similarities between the Saar and the Mosel, particularly at the north end where extensive vineyards are much in evidence. Closer acquaintance reveals delightful towns and villages engaged in the wine industry, ruined castles, many traces of Roman occupation and countless hostelries serving good food and the fine wines of the region. The steep slopes either side of the river are the dominant feature of the landscape and as one travels south from Konz — the actual junction of the Saar and Mosel — the vineyards gradually give way to forested areas. The rambler and cyclist will find many well-marked touring routes, some of which lead to fine vantage points high above the river. At first the bordering hilltops rarely exceed 820ft (250m) but soon reach up to twice this height. Even at the south end where industrial activity often dominates the river banks it is only necessary to go a kilometre or two to escape the industrial fringe and be again in charming rural surroundings.

There is a lot of visitor accommodation in the area described in this chapter and the northern part is especially strong in self-catering facilities, both in bungalow villages and in individual private houses. It should be noted that while the north end of the valley is in the Federal State of Rheinland-Pfalz, from Mettlach southwards it is in Saarland. When writing to the principal state information offices, it is necessary to select the correct one. See the list of addresses later in the Further Information section. The self-catering houses and flats are comfortable, clean and well-equipped and offer very good value for money. Bed linen is nearly always provided but check when booking, also about any 'extras' although amounts for these are likely to be small. In private houses the hosts are usually delighted to welcome English speaking visitors. There are hundreds of small hotels, inns and pensions with modest prices but the bigger hotels in Saarlouis and Saarbrücken feature higher in the price-scale.

There are countless opportunities for walking in the countryside with waymarked footpaths everywhere and there are three important long distance paths. The European Long Distance Path from the Atlantic to the Bohemian Forest (Czech Republic) — waymark blue St Andrew's Cross — crosses the river Mosel from Luxembourg at Perl and reaches the Saar at the great Saarschleife, turns northward to roughly parallel the river which it crosses at Saarburg before resuming an easterly course.

The Grosser Saarrundweg — waymark black SR on white — is a circular route of some 37 miles (60km) with its approximate centre at Saarburg. The Saarland-Rundwanderweg is also a circular route. It is about 168 miles (270km) long starting and finishing at Saarbrücken and is confined to the State of Saarland. Optional extensions can add about 62 miles (100km). The waymark is a 10cm square sign with vertical red and white bars.

Maps for these major routes are readily available in book shops as are those for the more modest rambles. The shorter walks include various 'trails' and the visitor may see signs such as *'Naturlehrpfad'* (Nature Trail), *'Waldlehrpfad'* (Forest Nature Trail) and *'Weinlehrpfad'* (Vineyard Nature Trail). Keep fit paths will be found near principal towns and holiday centres with the signs *'Trimm Dich'* or *'Sportpfad'*; the paths are laid out with sixteen or twenty stations at which simple exercises are to be carried out using the equipment provided. There is no charge for using the facilities.

The first place actually in the Saar valley is **Konz** where there is an interesting open-air museum to be visited. A chapel from 1730, timbered houses and many rooms with domestic and agricultural exhibits may be seen. Cycles may be hired at the railway station in Konz. The Saartalstrasse (Saar valley road) and the railway closely follow the river as it winds southwards between the enclosing hills. The wine lover constantly comes upon villages with names familiar from wine bottle labels — Wawern, Wiltingen, Ayl and Ockfen for example. Most of the villages have a car park suitable for the start of a circular walk of a few kilometres through the vineyards and woods. For the more serious walker, a marked route (black G3 on white) starts at the south end of Konz off the road to Wiltingen and climbs rather steeply up into the vineyards. After about 3 miles (5km) through the vines the route enters a wood and just before the village of Oberemmel turns sharply westwards to drop down to the Saar at **Wiltingen**. Waymarks SR on this latter section refer to the Grosser Saarrundweg, as it makes its tour through the Saar valley recreation area. From Wiltingen, G3 climbs again into the vineyards but soon enters a wood from which it emerges 2 or 3 miles (3-5km) later into the extensive vineyards of **Ockfen**, reached in another 2 miles (3km) or so. From here, the route remains in the valley until it enters Saarburg, 14 miles (22km) from Konz. The very detailed map, *Erholungsgebiet Saartal* (Recreation Area Saar Valley) (1:25,000) is a useful asset and walkers will readily identify routes in keeping with their capabilities; G3 is typical of this northern part of the valley.

Saarburg is a charming little town overlooked by its castle ruin — an attractive viewpoint with a pleasant, but slightly expensive, restaurant nearby. The castle was built by Count Siegfried of Luxembourg in 964. He appreciated not only the picturesque charm of the landscape but the strategic importance of this rocky eminence and a town quickly grew up around the foot of the stronghold. After crossing the river, the direct route from the station enters the town by

*The Leukbach
waterfall, Saarburg*

means of a tunnel driven through a spur of the castle rock. On emerging from the tunnel, a short walk to the right (away from the town centre) leads to the lower station of the chair-lift up to the Ferienzentrum Warsberg (a holiday and leisure centre) and an extensive self-catering complex with many purpose-built bungalows. There is also a lot of self-catering accommodation in and around the town itself as well as a comprehensive range of hotels and guest houses, a youth hostel and a large well-appointed camp site. Leisure activities of every kind are provided for; walking on many kilometres of waymarked paths, cycling along recommended quiet routes (inquire at the tourist information office in the town centre about cycle hire and itineraries), canoeing on the Saar, riding and swimming. There is a fine heated outdoor pool and a spendid new indoor one. Considering the quality of the fare provided, prices will be found to be remarkably modest at several attractive restaurants in the town centre and the wine served may well have come from a vineyard only a few minutes away.

A remarkable sight in the town centre is the waterfall of the river Leukbach as it tumbles down past old water-mills to join the Saar in the valley. Over the centuries, flooding of the Saar has been a problem and in the *Altstadt*, beside the river, may be seen high water marks on several houses. Balconies used to be attached to the houses at first floor level so that the occupants could be rescued by boat in the event of a sudden rise in the water level. Although the balconies have been dismantled, their positions can still be seen; it is assumed that the river canalisation has removed danger of flooding in the future. The river improvement scheme has also been of advantage to the little motor-ships *Stadt Saarburg* and *Stadt Merzig* which operate cruises up and down the river, even as far as the Luxembourg border at Wasserbillig on the Mosel.

In the *Altstadt* the old Glockengiesserei (bell foundry) may be visited where bells of all sizes are for sale; an unusual idea for a souvenir, perhaps. Parking in the town centre is difficult; use the large free car park a few minutes walk away near the swimming pool. In Saarburg, as in all the other towns and villages nearby, a highlight of the year is the annual wine festival. Actual dates can be obtained from the local information offices.

An interesting excursion could be made eastwards from Saarburg, 24 miles (38km) along the B407 to Hermeskeil. After passing through Zerf, 7 miles (11km) from Saarburg, the road runs roughly parallel with the upper reaches of the Ruwer, the third of the famous wine-growing rivers. **Hermeskeil** is worth visiting anyway (there is a youth hostel here) but the object of the journey here is to visit two interesting museums. The first is the Dampflok-Museum at the station, where railway enthusiasts can see many of the last steam locomotives to have worked in this area, as well as many other railway technical rarities. From Hermeskeil one can travel on the museum railway line through the valley of the river Ruwer to the village of Ruwer itself on the Mosel, a distance of 31 miles (50km). The other museum, 2 miles (3km) away in **Abtei**, specialises in air transport. The *Flugausstellung* has a comprehensive display of civil and military aircraft, models, technical equipment and so on. There is a café in a full-size Concorde replica.

Three miles (5km) south of Saarburg the community of **Kastel-Staadt** west of the Saar is the goal for an excursion to a remarkable reminder of the Roman occupation of the area, the so-called *Klause*. Begun in the year 54, this was once an important complex centred on the palace of the Roman generals. Of particular interest is the use made of the rock to provide guardrooms and other apartments for the soldiers. Staadt is on the river bank and it is a fairly stiff climb of about half a mile (1km, waymark G7) to the *Klause* perched on the cliff 328ft (100m) above the river. Kastel is already at the upper level and it is a short walk from the car park to the *Klause*. The cemetery nearby, for Germans who fell in World War II, may also be of interest not least for its wonderful situation overlooking the Saar valley. The area is easily reached on foot from Saarburg by following waymarks G7 along the river or through forests and vineyards along a route marked by a blue St Andrew's cross on a white ground. The latter is along the old Roman road and is part of the European long-distance path from the Atlantic to the Bohemian Forest in Czechoslovakia.

There are few vineyards now on the shady west slopes of the valley, but across the river the attractive large village of **Serrig** has extensive plantations. Here, as elsewhere along these famous wine rivers, the growers often offer accommodation in their homes. Sometimes the accommodation is let on a self-catering basis but the guest may be treated to private *Weinproben* (wine tastings) with the family. Details of this and all other accommodation is available from the tourist information offices.

There is no lack of ruined hilltop castles but a visit should be paid to one of the more impressive ones which is prominent above **Freudenberg**, less than 4km south-west of Kastel. Continuing southwards from here, return to the river at one of its most spectacular and romantic places, the Saarschleife, a great hairpin bend in the river best seen from the west side near **Orscholz**. There is a free car park near the prime viewing location at **Cloef** and a forest and bird nature trail goes down towards the river through a little valley called the Steinbachtal. Adjacent to the car park is the Märchenpark Orscholz, a fairytale park with small animals.

Down on the river, the little town of **Mettlach** on the east bank has quite a number of sights of interest. Excavations around the former Benedictine abbey have revealed that there must have been a cruciform church here from about the year 700. Several later buildings occupied the site and an old tower from about 1000 has survived. It is not really a tower in the usual sense of the word but rather a chapel with a large dome, probably modelled on the Palatinate chapel in Aachen. Many of the important furnishings from this building, including a famous reliquary in the form of a triptych from about 1230, are now to be found in the Catholic parish church of St Luitwin. This church was only built around the turn of the century. It is an impressive and colourful building with rich mosaics. The decorations remind one of Italy and the terracotta Stations of the Cross, made and

The great loop in the river Saar near Orscholz

presented by the well known local ceramics firm of Villeroy and Boch, are copies of an Italian series.

The visual presentation 'Keravision' and the museum of Villeroy and Boch now occupy the former monastery buildings which have a baroque façade 367ft (112m) long. Admission to the presentation and museum is free and 1 to 1½ hours should be allowed for the visit. The Keramic-Symposium is a display of modern ceramic 'sculpture' which has been in the adjacent park since 1974. Note the fountain designed by K.F. Schinkel at the park entrance. Ceramics are also the principal theme of the museum in the nearby Schloss Ziegelberg.

A mile (2km) west of Mettlach the ruins of Burg Montclair occupy two cliff sites above the Saar with splendid views. There was a fortress here from about the year 1000 but the present ruin is that of a second rebuilding which took place in the period 1428-39. It finally fell into disrepair in the sixteenth century. Christian Kretschmar, who had been responsible for rebuilding the monastery in Mettlach in 1728, also built the Pagodenburg at St Gangolf 2 miles (3km) south-west of the town in 1745. It is an octagonal rotunda with five domes. Also worth seeing is the eighteenth-century former tithe house of the Mettlach abbey; the building with residential and service rooms is to be found at **Besseringen**, a mile (2km) south-east of Mettlach.

Four miles (7km) south of Mettlach along the B51 is Merzig and after this the road closely follows the east bank of the river for the

The town hall, Merzig

remaining 40 miles (65km) to Saargemünd. It is parallelled on the west bank by the A620 *Autobahn* which has come in from Luxembourg in the west. **Merzig** is a pleasant small town and, like Saarburg and Mettlach, makes a good base from which to explore the river and the surrounding countryside. From the second half of the fourteenth century until 1778, Merzig was the principal town in the Lorraine-Trier condominium of Merzig-Saargau. The people of Germany, France and Luxembourg have for centuries been used to moving freely about the area and today's frontiers have made little difference to this pattern so that there is a constant coming and going which the near common language of the border territory helps to encourage.

The former collegiate church of St Peter in Merzig was originally built in the twelfth century but modifications continued until well into the nineteenth century. The quite striking exterior is dominated by the massive west tower. Inside are very pointed arches similar to those often found in Lorraine. The lavish furnishings include a larger than life crucifix from about 1300 on the altar and various figures in the choir. Most of these are from the baroque period but some were added in the nineteenth century. The town hall was built between 1647 and 1650 as a hunting lodge for the elector of Trier. Later alterations affected the open-air staircase and the main doorway but it is a building worthy of inspection. The nearby Staadt-Marx'sche

Bürgerhaus, a citizen's fine house of about a hundred years later, was the work of Christian Kretschmar (1728-71), one of the two most significant baroque architects in this area and already mentioned for his work in the Mettlach area. The comfortable restaurant in the *Stadthalle* (Civic Hall) has a terrace overlooking an attractive park. Accommodation in Merzig is rather limited and mainly in small hotels and *pensions*. For the motorist, the *Verkehrsamt* has a free leaflet describing itineraries for three-day tours.

Before leaving the vicinity of Merzig, visit the unique *Wolfsfreigehege* just north of the town, the biggest wolf enclosure in Germany. There are really several enclosures, each housing a different kind of wolf, including the rare white arctic variety. As with most *Freigehege*, there is no charge for admission.

An excursion could be made to **Losheim** (8 miles, 12km, from Merzig) or **Nunkirchen** to travel a similar distance along an historic steam railway, the Saar-Hochwald-Dampfbahn. The rescue of this line from extinction came about in a strange way. In 1981 a small group of friends in Losheim got together to form a model railway club with the object of building a large HO scale layout. They were able to acquire a few items of redundant railway equipment which was put in store. Eventually they were given the old station building at Brotdorf to use as a club house and in 1982 they were allowed to take over the neighbouring redundant line for use as a museum railway. Operations became possible when like-minded enthusiasts from Luxembourg placed an old steam locomotive at the disposal of the Losheim club. In 1983 a locomotive was given by a local mining company. Since then, passenger services have operated each year on specified dates, usually on national holidays or in connection with local events.

A quite different interest requires a journey of a little over 12 miles (20km) in the opposite direction to the village of **Nennig** in the valley of the Mosel. In the year 1852, a farmer discovered the remains of a Roman villa which was eventually revealed as a splendid building 410ft (125m) long. The banqueting hall has a mosaic floor measuring 33 by 52ft (10 by 15m), the largest Roman mosaic yet discovered north of the Alps. At Nennig, a visit could also be made to Schloss Berg, a palace of which the oldest parts date from the twelfth century. Additional buildings were added in the fourteenth to sixteenth centuries and damage from World War II has since been made good.

About 5 miles (8km) north-east of Losheim, the health resort of **Weiskirchen** is the principal settlement in a group of idyllic villages — the others being Konfeld, Rappweiler, Thailen and Weierweiler —

in a very little known area in the so-called Schwarzwälder Hoch-
wald; no connection though with the better known Schwarzwald
further south. Weiskirchen is at an altitude of about 1,312ft (400m)
and the surrounding hills go up to 2,296ft (700m). The extensive
medical facilities here owe their existence largely to the healthy
woodland air and the generally mild climate which the area enjoys.
The ordinary holidaymaker though, will be more interested in the
possibilities of a base with access to some really charming scenery
but at the same time within easy reach of many places of interest.

Rappweiler has a 185 acre *Wildfreigehege* where the creatures to be
seen include boars, deer, bison and many varieties of birds. There is
a rustic restaurant here and during fine weather, meals may be taken
on the covered terrace with a view of the forest. The other resorts in
the group all have attractive camping and caravan sites and there is
a youth hostel in Weiskirchen. More conventional accommodation
will be found in the many hotels, pensions and private houses. There
is some self-catering accommodation in the area but farm quarters
are not easy to find; local information offices will furnish detailed
lists upon request. Needless to say, there are many well-marked
footpaths in the woods and Weiskirchen has indoor and outdoor
swimming pools and all the usual resort facilities — minigolf, outdoor chess, table tennis, band concerts and other entertainments.

However, this is essentially an area for open-air activities and
lovers of water sports find that the leisure centre at the *Stausee*
(reservoir) near Losheim offers boating, windsurfing, angling and
bathing amongst its facilities. There is a camp site here and some
Ferienhäuser (self-catering holiday homes) as well. The places mentioned are representative of a whole host of attractive little towns and
villages within quite a small area.

Back close to the river and about 2 miles (3km) south of Merzig the
little village of **Harlingen** boasts a chapel by Kretschmar. Another 3
miles (5km) or so and **Beckingen** is backed by a pleasant area of
woodland, on the fringe of which are several car parks giving access
to easy round walks of varying length. It will take the motorist but a
few minutes to reach **Dillingen** where the acknowledged industrial
activity is conveniently separated from the residential and business
area of the town, with its spacious *Fussgängerzone* (pedestrian precinct). In the district called Pachten close to the Saar, a number of
significant Roman buildings have been revealed. The remains of the
biggest Roman civil settlement in the Saarland, a cemetery and a
fortress, may be seen. Call at the *Kulturamt* (cultural office) in the
Rathaus, to obtain details of viewing arrangements. Dillingen is also

one of those places with a regular *Flohmarkt* (flea market) which takes place from March to September, usually on the third Saturday in each month.

There are a number of places of interest between the river and the French border. On the west bank, a short distance to the north there is a *Schloss* of 1624 in **Rehlingen**; the building probably stands on the site of the twelfth-century customs post of the dukes of Lorraine. A couple of kilometres to the south-east along a minor road through a *Naturschutzgebiet* (conservation area), is the ruined castle of Siersburg on a hilltop (1,010ft, 308m) with broad views over the valley and up and down the Saar; the original object of this stronghold was to keep watch on the river traffic. In this often disputed territory, the Siersburg was, for a long time, a bone of contention between the dukes of Lorraine and the bishops of Trier. The castle gave its name to the neighbouring village of **Siersburg** at the south end of which is **Itzbach**, home of a *Schloss* of 1740 which also owes its existence to the one-time Lothringian feudal lords. Like the *Schloss* in Rehlingen, this one is more like a superior farmhouse or manor house rather than the usual visualisation of a palace. A little more imposing is the recently renovated *Schloss* (1670) in **Grosshemmersdorf**. This village is about 2 miles (4km) west of Siersburg on the north bank of the little river Nied and gives a picture of a typical little old-Lothringian settlement. Once again the history of the *Schloss* reflects the influence of Lorraine with its ambitions and feudal traditions.

This is popular camping and caravanning country and there are many sites, especially around the Siersburg; there is another in **Hemmersdorf**, the part of this village south of the river Nied. A mile or two to the south-east, the village of **Niedaltdorf** is close to the present French border and is noteworthy for its stalactite caves (*Tropfsteinhöhle*) which may be visited. Just to the south in the village of **Ihn** there are Roman period excavations, and 4 miles (6km) to the east at **St Barbara** is a Roman copper mine which has survived virtually intact from its foundation by one Emilianus in the third century until the present day. The copper mined here was taken to the foundry in the Roman settlement in Dillingen already mentioned. Of more interest than the copper in recent times is the colouring agent azurite which it is said was used by the famous artist Albrecht Dürer in his painting. The mine may be visited by giving prior notice.

Wallerfangen, on the west bank of the Saar, from which it is separated by the A620, is now a suburb of the city of Saarlouis, it is actually a much older place. In 1850 a treasure trove of tools and

*The courthouse,
Saarlouis*

ornaments from the Bronze Age was discovered here and further exploration revealed that the area was settled also in Celtic and Roman times. Wallerfangen became the principal place in the domain of Franconian counts, but later appeared in the possession of Lothringian dukes and was probably elevated to the status of a 'free' town by Duke Friedrich III (1251-1303). Thereafter it was fortified by the construction of castles, walls and town gates and from the late Middle Ages became the headquarters of the officials dealing with the German speaking part of the duchy. The town suffered in the Thirty Years War when it was occupied by the French and the Swedes and was largely destroyed in 1635 during the counter attacks of the emperor's forces. The prehistoric finds of the Wallerfangen area may be seen in an exhibition in the *Rathaus* during normal business hours. The restaurant Epe (Bernard Epe is the name of the restaurant owner) has been awarded a coveted Michelin star and gourmets turn here with confidence for a memorable meal. Note, however, that this establishment is closed on Saturdays and for about 3 weeks between July and August. Many restaurants in this area specialise in French cuisine.

In 1680, Louis XIV, the Sun King, founded the modern city which was named after him and was acknowledged to be the political and strategic successor to Wallerfangen. **Saarlouis** remained a French stronghold until the fall of Napoleon in 1815 after which it came under Prussian rule until 1889. The original fortifications were the concept of the distinguished French military architect and engineer Sebastien Vauban of whom there are still many reminders. It is not surprising that in this town with its military tradition, two of its citizens became famous soldiers. Michael Ney, marshall of France, was called by Napoleon 'the bravest of the brave' and he is remembered in Saarlouis with a monument on the so-called Vauban island (in an old arm of the Saar) and by a tablet on his birthplace at Bierstrasse 11. General von Lettow-Vorbeck (born 1870) was the defender of German East Africa in World War I and had the honorary freedom of the city conferred upon him in 1956. His birthplace at 10 Silberherzstrasse has a memorial tablet and a street and a bridge have been named after him. Also on the Saar island is the interesting and striking little statue of the French soldier Lacroix; he somehow missed the retreat of his compatriots in 1815 — some say that he was asleep! — and remained at his post until the Prussians arrived. Saarlouis was very badly mauled in the course of the allied advance at the end of World War II, but is now a clean airy town around the *Grosser Markt*, the huge square which serves as a car park, except on market days. The visitor arriving by train must walk for about 20 minutes to reach the town. In so doing the heavy industry near the railway is left behind and after crossing the bridge over the canalised Saar, a route may be taken through the fine *Stadtpark* to the bank of the disused arm of the river. There is a woodland nature trail and the park also accommodates indoor and outdoor swimming pools and a fine camp site, noted for its international patronage. With war damage made good, the *Altstadt* is an area of some charm within the extensive pedestrian zone. The old military headquarters is now the main post office, facing the *Grosser Markt*, and there is a postal museum under the same roof. The town museum and library are found in former barracks in Alte Brauerei Strasse; the new *Rathaus* has Gobelins which were the gift to the town of Louis XIV. The *Glockenspiel* in the town hall tower plays at 8 and 11am, 6 and 9pm.

There is enough in Saarlouis to occupy the visitor for quite a long time but another excursion must be made to the west. Leaving via Metzer Strasse (B405), **Felsberg** is reached in approximately 2 miles (4km) and about half a mile beyond this village there is a car park in which a stop may be made in order to undertake the modest climb to the Teufelsburg castle ruins (1,161ft, 354m) for all-round views over the countryside. There has apparently been a fortress here since at least 1179 when it was in the possession of an obscure knightly line, the Herren von Felsberg. Another mile or two brings the visitor to **Düren** where a former *Schloss* (1760) is now a rather superior farming complex. In the Middle Ages most of the land around here belonged to the abbey at Lungfelden, near St Avold, which gradually bought

The chapel of St Oranna near Berus

out the property of the minor aristocracy. The Düren *Schloss* was built by one of the last of these, the French Franz von Bély.

Now close to the border, although there is nothing of particular interest there, it is worth going on to see the novel situation at **Leidingen** where the frontier runs right through Neutraler Strasse, so that the properties on one side are German and on the other French. Needless to say, border formalities are non-existent. Turn south-eastwards following the border as closely as possible to Berus. Just before reaching the village of **Berus** the ancient chapel of St Oranna should be visited. It is built in the early and late Gothic style and there are certainly parts dating from the thirteenth century, although much of the structure has been rebuilt much more recently. This has been a place of pilgrimage since the Middle Ages and the saint, or her memory, is credited with healing powers, especially in the realm of head and earache. The colourful windows were created as recently as 1950 by the Alsatian artist Tristan Ruhlmann, who illustrated ancient legends in this modern art form. The south side of the chapel has a large crucifixion group from the baroque period. The tomb of St Oranna is in the parish church in Berus which has other treasures also, including a high baroque altar and a Marienaltar (altar to the Virgin Mary) from about 1600.

On the outskirts of Berus is the startling and rather ugly Europäer-Denkmal, a monument dedicated to great post-war Europeans. It stands on historic ground and long disputed territory, with the reminders of successive battles all around and a population which, over the years, has had to allow itself to be called German, French, Lothringian, Prussian or Bavarian. Even the Russians have been here and Marlborough passed through with his armies, or would have done had not the then newly fortified Saarlouis halted his progress for a while. Here, where once in the confusion of war a whole village was destroyed, this new monument has been erected to commemorate the reconciliation and new friendship between the French and German peoples, bringing up to date as it were, the centuries old message of peace which has gone out over the Saar, Lorraine and the Mosel lands from nearby St Oranna. Remembered are those who overcame their experiences and prejudices to lay the foundation stones of the new post-war Europe, in particular Robert Schumann of France (first president of the European parliament), Konrad Adenauer (Federal German Chancellor from 1949 until 1963), de Gasperi from Italy and Josef Bech from Luxembourg. Do not leave Berus without a brief look round the substantial remains of some of the fortifications of the past.

Leave southwards through Überherrn and then turn east to follow a broad valley of many little water courses back to the Saar. In **Wadgassen** stop at the former Premonstratensian abbey whose history goes back to at least 902. It was in its heyday in the thirteenth and fourteenth centuries and until the end of the latter was the last resting place of the counts of Saarbrücken. It suffered badly in the Thirty Years' War, especially through the laying waste of its farms and the de-population of the countryside, but made a recovery in the eighteenth century when a lot of building was undertaken. At the beginning of the revolution, the abbey was occupied and plundered by French troops. The monks fled and the church eventually became a ruin while the remaining rooms of the abbey were given over to secular use in the construction of a crystal factory, now a gallery of the firm Villeroy and Boch.

The detours to places of interest in the countryside serve to conceal the fact that since Dillingen, the Saar has had a very industrialised aspect although it must be said that pleasant scenery is never very far away. From the river, or riverside paths, the scene is of an incongruous mixture of agriculture and heavy industry with steelworks predominating. Continuing upstream past Völklingen the hills can be seen behind the chimneys and cooling towers; within a mile or two there are numerous car parks giving access to walking and cycling routes, fine viewpoints, huts belonging to the various

The river Saar from the old bridge at Saarbrücken

rambling organisations, playing areas and even a *Wildpark*, an enclosure for deer or wild boars in Köllerbachtal.

But entry into the capital of the Federal State of the Saarland should be no longer delayed. The reader may find it strange that a city with a high population should feature in a book purporting to lead him or her off the beaten track. Yet few foreign visitors find their way to **Saarbrücken**, for in this corner of West Germany it is not on the direct route to any of the more well known tourist goals. Most people are hard pressed to think of a single fact about the city or even to pinpoint its precise location. As an important industrial centre it suffered grievous damage during World War II, in some parts the destruction being as much as 90 per cent, so it is hardly surprising that there is not a comprehensive picture today of its always stormy history. Nevertheless, much of interest has survived. Originally a Roman settlement stood at the intersection of the Lombardy road and the road from Metz to Mainz but by the end of the tenth century this junction had moved downstream as far as the trading post of St Johann. Saarbrücken was still separate at that time and both towns were granted charters in 1321. The Thirty Years' War and other conflicts inflicted damage on all the Saar towns and it was not until the end of the eighteenth century that they were again able to enjoy a period of peace and prosperity. In 1909, Saarbrücken and St Johann united and together with St Arnual and the industrial area of

Malstatt-Burbach, formed the basis of the modern city. In 1947 a university was founded and in 1957, after a short period as the capital of an autonomous region, Saarbrücken became the capital of the new German Federal State called Saarland.

Saarbrücken, nudging the French border, rightly regards itself as a cosmopolitan city and the influence of France is seen everywhere, not least in many of the restaurants. Indeed, the word *Salü*, which will be encountered frequently, has a French origin and can be used as a general greeting like the Bavarian *Grüss Gott*. Ther are river cruises varying in duration from 1½ to 2 hours, some of which go upstream to Saargemünd and into the French waterway system. The city is a member of a tri-partite partnership, the others being Nantes in France and Tbilisi in Georgia. The uncertainties about the role of Saarbrücken after the last war were finally resolved as a result of a referendum in 1955 and once France recognised the Saarland as part of the German Federal Republic, the way was clear to develop a peaceful and friendly relationship between the two countries. This new era is nowhere better symbolised than in the magnificent Deutsch-Französischer-Garten (Franco-German-Garden) which was opened in 1960 having been created as a joint effort between the two countries, the state of Saarland and the city of Saarbrücken.

The 123 acre (49 hectare) park has something for everybody. From the main north entrance, a miniature train takes the visitor round the large lake to be dropped off wherever the fancy takes him or her. From the south end of the lake there is a chair-lift for an effortless ride up to the eastern end of the park. There is boating on the lake which is also the location of the largest water organ in Europe. Young and old will enjoy the Land of the Lilliputians, models of famous buildings from all over the world built to a scale of 1:33 and set out in an area of some 5½ acres (2¼ hectares). Many people visit the garden just for the lovely array of flowers and trees which is to be found here. There are several eating places or one may picnic on the lawns at will.

Many historic buildings in the city have been carefully restored after the ravages of war. After the burning down of the Protestant Ludwigskirche in an air raid in 1944, there was much debate as to whether it should be rebuilt to the original plans of 1762-75 or in a modern style. The church, designed by the municipal architect F.J. Stengel, was considered to be the most important church in the Saar, and so it is fortunate that the final decision was to restore it to its original form and this is the building which faces the Ludwigsplatz. Stengel was also responsible for the Catholic parish church in St Johann (1754-58) and for the *Altes Rathaus* (1758-60) on Schlossplatz.

An earlier work of his was the *Schloss* (1738-48) which gives its name to the square. In 1793 it was looted and burned but was rebuilt to the architect's plans in 1810. Near the Schlossplatz and just over the Alte Brücke from the modern town, is the Protestant Schlosskirche and fifteenth-century town parish church, the funerary chapel of the princes of Nassau-Saarbrücken. Damage caused by fire in 1677 and by air raids during World War II was made good but most of the original furnishings were lost. The new windows should be noted.

Not to be missed is the Protestant parish church in **Bischmisheim** about 4 miles (6km) east of the centre. This is an octagonal, symmetrical rotunda designed in 1822. It is based on the palatinate chapel in Aachen with a tent-like pyramid roof and a lantern over the octagon. It is a typical Protestant preaching church with the altar, pulpit and organ in line one above the other.

From the Schlossplatz area, the Alte Brücke (1546-8), which was modified in the eighteenth century, leads over the Saar to the Staatstheater, built in 1937-8. The square which the theatre faces is now called Tbilisser Platz, acknowledging Saarbrücken's partnership with the Georgian city. Musicals and drama are staged by the resident company. The little Saarländisches Landestheater confines itself to 'straight' theatre. There are numerous museums and art galleries in the city and the tourist information office will gladly forward literature (largely in English) giving details of all places of interest. In addition to the international park already mentioned, the Saarbrücken zoo about 2 miles (4km) east of the city centre is a popular goal. It can readily be reached by bus and there is ample parking space. Be warned that it can be very busy indeed on Sundays and holidays when a thousand additional parking spaces are made available near the south entrance.

The holidaymaker may look askance at a big city as a base and there are certainly many smaller and more peaceful places within a short distance. But for the person dependent on public transport there are advantages in being at the focal point of rail and road services and as an international metropolis, Saarbrücken is able to offer a good range of hotel accommodation. There is ample provision for leisure activity with several indoor and outdoor swimming pools, many children's play areas, numerous tennis courts and so on.

The river Saar flows for some 5 miles (8km) through the Saarland capital and its inner suburbs and as the city is left to continue the journey southwards, the Saarland radio mast is seen on the Hallberg (840ft, 256m) where there is a good viewpoint and a rather romantic palace, the Schloss Hallberg. Most of the industrial activity is now left behind and in 4 or 5 miles (6 or 8km) **Güdingen** is reached, with its race course occupying an attractive site beside the river. For the next 6 miles (10km) the Saar itself forms the boundary between Germany and France. **Bübingen** almost adjoins Güdingen and is the last place within the administrative domain of Saarbrücken. There is little evidence of the national frontier and there is constant movement between the two countries. Between Kleinblittersdorf in Germany and Grossblittersdorf in France there is a footbridge built jointly by the two communities and known as the Bridge of Friendship. The French, however, call their town Grosbliederstroff; most of the towns and villages along here have French and German versions of their names creating a situation which can sometimes be confusing for the foreign visitor. A little further to the south the 430ft (131m) long railway bridge between Hanweiler and Saargemünd is another example of international co-operation. Along these last few kilometres of the Saar and to the west the coal mines and other necessary eyesores of the French industrial region across the river, with the continuous movements of buckets along overhead cableways may be seen. The German side of the river cannot lay claim to any outstanding scenic attractions either, but there are two surprises. The villages of Auersmacher and Sitterswald have both been gold medal winners in Germany's 'Beautiful Village' competition and are well worth visiting.

So far as Germany is concerned, this is the end — or rather the beginning — of the river Saar which, here at Saargemünd (Sarreguemines in French), comes up to the border from France where it has been called the Sarre. This too is where another long river, the Blies, adds its waters to the Saar and itself takes over the frontier watch for a while. It is surprising that it is the Blies and not the name-giving Saar which has the greater length in Saarland although the latter is, of course, the longer river in total.

Although the Saar journey is over, the visitor could be excused for cheating a little and following the Blies upstream to the rather charming baroque town of **Blieskastel**, a former royal seat and a present day spa, run according to the theories of the renowned Sebastian Kneipp. The historic buildings here include the *Schlosskirche* (1778-81) built for the imperial Countess Marianne von der Leyen. Also worth visiting are the Orangerie (1669), officers' and officials' houses on the Schlossberg (from 1765) and the *Rathaus* (1775). Adequate accommodation and leisure facilities, make this an ideal centre for the visitor wishing to explore the area yet not stay in Saarbrücken itself, which is only 14 miles (23km) away.

Further Information
— The Saar Valley —

Cycling and Rambling

Tourist information offices supply
brochures with suggested rambling
and cycling itineraries of 2 t0 9 nights
and details of 'packages' which include
maps, accommodation and sometimes
the transport of heavy luggage. Cycles
may be hired from the DB railway
station in Konz, Merrzig and Trier
where cyclists arriving by train pay
only half the normal hire charge.

Places to Visit

Hermeskeil
Dampflok-Museum
Am Bahnhof
Postfach 1166
54411 Hermeskeil
☎ (06503) 1204
Open: March to fourth Sunday in
Advent, weekends and holidays 10am-
6pm. Also July and August daily 10am-
4pm.
Nearly forty steam locomotives (festival at Whitsun) and other historic
railway equipment.

Hochwaldbahn-Ruwer-Hermeskeil
Hochwaldbahn eV
Postfach 2147
Trier
☎ (0651) 28718/300695
31 mile (50km) line operating Sunday
and holidays May to September with
historic diesel locomotive and railbus.
On one Sunday, usually in June, special
programme of steam-hauled trains.

Flugausstellung
54411 Hermeskeil-Abtei
☎ (06503) 7693
2 miles (3km) N of Hermeskeil on B327
Open: April to October daily 9am-6pm.
The history of air travel; military and
civil planes, models and equipment.
Café in Concorde. Free parking.

Konz
Volkskunde- und Freilichtmuseum
Roscheiderhof 1a
54329 Konz
Open: March to November, Monday to
Friday 9am-4.30pm, Saturday, Sunday
and holidays 10am-5pm.
Artisans' tools, agricultural exhibits.
Many furnished rooms, timbered
houses and chapel (1730). Groups
should make prior arrangements.

Losheim-Waldern-Nunkirchen
MECL Eisenbahnfreunde eV
Vierherrenwald 35
66679 Losheim
☎ (06872) 3592, (06887) 5497 or (06898)
87376 (all after 5pm)
Information also from:
Verkehrsverein Losheim
Postfach 1169
66679 Losheim
☎ (06872) 6169
Steam railway operating four or five
trains on Easter and Whit Mondays
and usually one Sunday per month
until November. St Nikolaus specials
early in December. Refreshments on all
trains. Cycles carried free. Steam
locomotive festival in August.

Merzig
Heimatmuseum
Fellenbergschlösschen
66663 Merzig
☎ (06861) 80290
Open: February-November, Sunday
and holidays 2-6pm.
Groups at other times by prior arrangement. Local history including Roman
finds. Admission free.

Mettlach
Mettlacher Keramik-Symposium
Abbey Park
Open: during daylight.
Admission and car parking free.
Close to town centre.

Burg Montclair
☎ (06864) 1774
Open: Saturday, Sunday, and holidays
8am-6pm. Other days by prior arrangement.
Impressive ruin overlooking the
Saarschleife.

Villeroy and Boch Keravision
In der alten Abtei
66693 Mettlach
☎ (06864) 81251
Open: Tuesday-Friday 10am-4pm,
Saturday 10am-1pm, Sunday 10am-6pm.
History and products of the famous
ceramics firm. Admission free. Free car
parking in adjacent abbey park.

Keramikmuseum
Schloss Ziegelberg
66693 Mettlach
☎ (06864) 81294
Open: Tuesday to Saturday 9am-12.30pm, 2-5.30pm, Sunday and
holidays 10.30-12.30pm, 2-6pm.
Exhibition of the products of Villeroy
and Boch, etc. Reduced admission for
students, children, etc.

Nennig
Roman Mosaic Floor
66706 Perl
☎ (06866) 279
Open: April to September, Tuesday to
Sunday 8.30-12noon, 1-6pm, October,
November and January to March,
Tuesday to Sunday 9-12noon, 1-4pm.
Finest Roman mosaic floor north of
Alps. Reduced charge for children,
students, clubs, etc. Groups should
telephone in advance. Free car park.

Niedaltdorf
Niedaltdorfer Tropfsteinhöhle
Neunkircher Strasse 10
66780 Rehlingen-Siersburg
☎ (06834) 444
Open: daily 10am-12noon, 2-6pm.
Prior telephone call appreciated.
Splendid underground spectacle with
caverns, passages and many stalactites
and stalagmites.

Saarbrücken
Abenteuermuseum
Im Alten Rathaus
Am Schloss
66119 Saarbrücken
☎ (0681) 51747
Open: Tuesday and Wednesday 9am-1pm, Thursday and Friday 3-7pm,
some Saturdays 10am-2pm.
Adventure experiences from Asia,
Africa, South America and New
Guinea. Facilities for groups, including
film show by arrangement.

Museum für Vor- und Frühgeschichte
Schlossplatz 16
66119 Saarbrücken
☎ (0681) 503486
Open: Tuesday to Friday 10am-4pm,
Saturday 10am-1pm, Sunday 10am-6pm.
Pre- and early history. Admission free.

Saarberg Geological Museum
Saarbergwerke AG
Hauptabteilung Ausbildung
Postfach 1030
Trierer Strasse 4
66111 Saarbrücken
☎ (0681) 4054098 or 4054330
Open: Monday to Friday 10am-5pm,
first Sunday in month 9am-1pm.
Closed holidays.
Geological history especially of the
Saarland, mineralogy. Admission free.

Saarland Museum
Bismarckstrasse 11-19
(near the Staatstheater)
66111 Saarbrücken
☎ (0681) 99640
Open: Tuesday-Sunday 10am-6pm.
Art gallery with paintings, sculpture,
porcelain, etc. Reduced admission for
children, students, etc.

Stadtgalerie, Kulturcafé
St Johanner Markt
66111 Saarbrücken
☎ (0681) 3001751
Open: Tuesday to Sunday 11am-7pm.
Admission free.

Free brochure of museums and galleries in Saarbrücken is available from the
Tourist Information Office.

*Botanischer Garten der Universität des
  Saarlandes*
Im Stadtwald
66123 Saarbrücken
☎ (0681) 3022864
Open: mid-April to mid-October,
Monday to Friday 8am-6pm (green-
houses Tuesday-Friday 10am-4pm),
Saturday, Sunday and holidays 1-5pm;
mid-October to mid-April Monday-
Friday 8am-4pm (greenhouses
Monday-Thursday 10am-4pm).

Deutsch-Französischer-Garten (DFG)
Metzer Strasse
66117 Saarbrücken
☎ (0681) 583595
Open: mid-April to mid-October 8am-6pm.
Splendid gardens and lake. Water-
organ, miniature train, chair-lift, etc in
summer. Admission free in winter.
Restaurants.

Saarlouis
Neues Rathaus
Grünebaumstrasse
66740 Saarlouis
☎ (06831) 443263 or 443228
Open: normal business hours.
Carillon plays from tower at 8 and
11am, 6 and 9pm.

Postmuseum
Grosser Markt
66740 Saarlouis
☎ (06831) 441216
On upper floor of main post office.
History of postal facilities and trans-
port in the area. Some exhibits may be
seen any time office open to public.
Main collection seen by arrangement.
Write in advance or call at administra-
tive office on south side of building.
Admission free.

Städtisches Museum
Alte Brauerei Strasse
66740 Saarlouis
☎ (06831) 443573
Open: Tuesday and Thursday 9am-
12noon, 3-6pm, Sunday 3-6pm.
Valuable treasures from the history of
Saarlouis and surrounding area.
Admission free.

Museum 'Haus-Ludwig'
Kaiser-Wilhelm-Strasse 2
(opposite the library)
66740 Saarlouise
☎ (06831 443574
Open: Wednesday-Saturday 11am-
5pm, Sunday 2-5pm. International
painting, sculpture and graphics of the
20th century. Changing exhibitions.

Wallerfangen
Römisches Bergwerk St Barbara
Schlossstrasse 98
66798 Wallerfangen
☎ (06831) 444488 (office of Landkreis)
Open: April-October with prior
notification to Landkreis office. Roman
copper mine in remarkable state of
preservation.

Zoos and Wildlife Parks

Ballweiler
Wildpark
South of village which is 4 miles (6km)
south-west of Blieskastel.

Differten
Wildgehege
South of road between Wadgassen and
Überherrn.

Karlsbrunn
Wildgehege
On the Steinberg. In southernmost tip
of Saarland, west of Forbach.

Ludweiler
Wildgehege
In the Scheidwald , 4 miles (6km)
south-west of Völklingen.

Merzig
Wolfsfreigehege
Two miles (3km) north of town.
Restaurant near entrance.

Nalbach
Wildschweingehege
2 miles (3km) north of Saarwellingen

Neunkirchen
Zoo
12 miles (20km) NE of Saarbrücken.

Orscholz (Cloef)
Märchenpark
☎ (06865) 434 or 505
Close to viewing area for Saarschleife.
Open: daily April to mid-October 9am-7pm, mid-October to March 2-5pm.
Fairytale park with small animals.
Reduced admission charge in winter.

Rappweiler
Wildfreigehege
A mile (2km) south-west of Weiskirchen
Open: daily 9am-8pm or dusk if earlier.
185 acres forest enclosure with deer, boars, bison and birds. Restaurant open all year. Free car park.

Saarbrücken
Zoologischer Garten
Graf-Stauffenbergstrasse
66121 Saarbrücken
☎ (0681) 812494
Open: in summer 8.30am-6pm, in winter 8.30am-dusk.
37 acres of park with animals of 250 species, Africa-house with nocturnal creatures, tropiquarium. Restaurants.

Wildgehege am Homburg
Two miles (3km) north of city centre on road to Dudweiler.

Saarwellingen
Wildfrei
hege Wolfrath On minor road L142 in direction of Lebach.

Schwalbach
Wildfreigehege und Tierpark
Grosswaldstrase
(opposite swimming pool)
3 miles (5km) south-east of Saarlouis.

Völklingen
Wildpark
In Köllerbachtal, 2 miles (3km) north of town centre.

There are also other forest enclosures (*Gehege*) for wild boars, deer, etc usually accessible at all times without charge. Contact local information offices for precise locations.

Tourist Information Offices

Rheinland-Pfalz
Fremdenverkehrsverband Rheinland-Pfalz
Postfach 1420
Löhrstrasse 103-105
56068 Koblenz
☎ (0261) 31079

Fremdenverkehrsgemeinschaft Obermosel-Saar eV
Granastrasse 24
54329 Konz
☎ (06501) 7790

Saarschleife Touristik
Postfach 10220
66693 Mettlach
☎ (06864) 8334

Verkehrsamt
Postfach 1365
54439 Saarburg
☎ (06581) 81215

Saarland
Fremdenverkehrsverband Saarland
Postfach 242
Dudweilerstrasse 53
66111 Saarbrücken
☎ (0681) 37088

Verkehrsverein Saarbrücken
Rathaus St Johann
Grossherzog Friedrich-Strasse 1
66111 Saarbrücken
☎ (0681) 96222/36901

Stadtverband Saarbrücken
Schlossplatz
66119 Saarbrücken
☎ (0681) 506247

Saarpfalz-Touristik, Landratsamt
Am Forum 1
Postfach 1550
66424 Homburg
☎ (06841) 1040

Kreisfremdenverkehrsverband
Schankstrasse 1
66663 Merzig
☎ (06861) 73874

Fremdenverkehrsstellung des Landkreises Saarlouis
Kaiser-Wilhelm-Strasse 6
66740 Saarlouis
☎ (06831) 444-488
or
Stadt Info
☎ (06831) 443-233

5 • The Palatinate Forest Nature Park

Most of the territory to be explored in this chapter lies within the boundaries of the Palatinate Forest (Pfälzer Wald) Nature Park along the east edge of which the German Wine Road (Deutsche Weinstrasse) runs from north to south. The nature park covers an area of 443,050 acres of which 71 per cent is wooded, making it the biggest uninterrupted forest in the Federal Republic. The forest, formerly the hunting land of emperors and kings, has over 4,375 miles (7,000km) of waymarked footpaths of which some 186 miles (300km) are cared for by the Pfälzerwald-Verein (PWV) with many shelters and parking places for ready access to the favourite viewpoints. Whereas the area is in general sparsely populated, the named road comprises a chain of closely spaced towns and villages, nearly every one being concerned, to a greater or lesser degree, with the production of wine. It is hardly surprising since this is part of Germany's biggest wine-growing area. This region enjoys warm and sunny summer months, and by the time the southern end of the Weinstrasse is reached it is one of the warmest parts of Germany.

By whatever means of transport, this area is easy to reach. Air travellers arriving at Frankfurt could reach Neustadt, fairly central on the Weinstrasse, by train in about 1½ hours. Rail travellers from Britain will find it quickest to travel via Cologne and Frankfurt. Motorists from Britain could well use the motorway network from Aachen. From there the route is at first eastwards in the direction of Cologne on *Autobahn* A4 and this is left near Kerpen after about 25 miles (40km) to join A61 going south-east. This is followed for 118 miles (190km) to Alzey, from where the B271 goes southwards, shortly to become the Weinstrasse. It could hardly be easier.

The 'Wine Road' is 50 miles (80km) long and starting at the north end the first village is **Monsheim**, 10 miles (16km) from Alzey and fairly typical of the places where the grape dominates life. There are no special attractions here, but watch out all along the route for

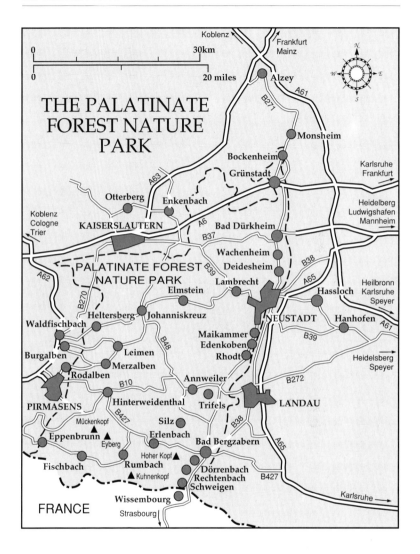

THE PALATINATE
FOREST NATURE
PARK

roadside stalls selling locally grown fruit and vegetables — a bonus
for the self-caterer, for prices are very reasonable. Needless to say,
wine is also readily available and occasionally *Weinproben* is invited.
In the small towns and villages not specially geared to the tourist
trade there is always a certain amount of modest accommodation
available and this may well appeal to the reader of this guide rather
than what is on offer in the more well known resorts. From
Bockenheim 2 miles (3km) further on (where there is a vineyard
nature trail), the Weinstrasse marks the eastern fringe of the desig-

nated nature park of the Pfälzer Wald and the traveller need not adhere strictly to the named road but can indulge at whim in attractive detours up to 25 miles (40km) to the west to enjoy the forest scenery or visit other places of interest.

Grünstadt, a little town 4 miles (6km) south of Bockenheim, is the former home of the counts of Leiningen and is today the economic and cultural centre of a vineyard district called Unterhaardt. Among the sights are the baroque Rathaus (1750-55), the charming baroque portal of the former royal court (1716) and the Gothic Martinskirche (1494-1520). The town has both a *Freibad* and a *Hallenbad* and on the hill above the pools the *Stadtpark* (town park), with a large free car park and tennis courts, provides fine views over the countryside and could be the starting place for local walks.

From Grünstadt, the motorist might well join the A6 for a speedy 15 miles (24km) westwards to the Enkenbach exit and turn north to **Enkenbach** where the former Premonstratensian monastery church of St Norbert is well worth a visit. It is now the Catholic parish church and is an essentially Romanesque building which was added to the then existing monastery complex in the thirteenth century. The porch is regarded as one of the most beautiful Romanesque constructions in Germany. In this little town the Protestant parish church has a fine organ and there are some interesting old houses in the Hauptstrasse. It would be worthwhile going a further 7 miles (12km) west to see the Cistercian monastery church (1181-1254) in **Otterberg**. There is a lovely rose window here and it is of interest to note that this building has been shared by Catholic and Protestant congregations since 1707. The stately *Rathaus* is also worthy of inspection. It was built by Walloon refugees in 1753 and is one of the most picturesque town halls in the Palatinate.

From here it is only a few kilometres into the city of **Kaiserslautern** where there are many sights of interest and a fine shopping area with a number of good restaurants. The 'Kaiser' in the name probably goes back to Emperor Frederick Barbarossa who built a fortified castle above the river Lauter in 1152; it was blown up by the French in 1703 during the War of the Spanish Succession. Churches include the former Premonstratensian church of St Martin and St Maria built for the monastery in early Gothic style 1250-90 and the former Minorite church (1300), now the Catholic parish church of St Martin. Nineteenth- and twentieth-century art is exhibited in the Pfalzgalerie at Museumplatz 1, and there is a local history collection in the Theodor-Zink-Museum at Steinstrasse 48. There are indoor and outdoor pools and there is a bathing beach on the tiny lake at

Gelterswoog, 4 miles (7km) to the south-west. Another heated outdoor pool is to be found in the little village of **Trippstadt** about 6 miles (10km) south of Kaiserslautern. The baroque palace (1766) here is now the home of the State Forestry School but it is for the rambling possibilities in this most beautiful part of the Pfälzer Wald that people come here. The Karlstal is a particularly picturesque valley and a favourite goal for walkers.

From the centre of Kaiserslautern the B37 is a pleasant road eastwards through the forest to reach **Bad Dürkheim**, back on the Weinstrasse, in 20 miles (33km). Dürkheim describes itself as the spa between the forest and the vineyards and was famous in Roman times for the same reasons as it is today, the forests, the wine and the thermal springs. It enjoys a mild climate and is a favourite centre for people wishing to undertake forest walks or to enjoy the good food and wine of the area. The *Kur*, the medical aspect of the spa, is not taken too seriously here but there is ample opportunity for bathing in either the *Thermalbad* (pool with water from the natural thermal springs), which maintains a temperature of 32°C (90°F) or in the leisure bathing complex called the Salinarium. Dürkheim also has the attraction of the only casino in the area covered in this chapter. The Dürkheimer Wurstmarkt (Sausage Market), despite its name, claims to be the biggest wine festival in the world and takes place on the second and third weekends in September.

The three-aisled former palace church of St Johannes is now the Protestant parish church. It dates largely from the fourteenth century but has a neo-Gothic tower added in 1865-6. The church is notable for its various tombs, including that of Count Ernich IX and his wife. The nearby Kästenberg has the remains of a Celtic ring, the so-called Heidenmauer (Heathen Wall), and on the east edge of this same hill there are rock drawings indicating the existence of a Roman quarry here. In the town, local history is recorded in the Heimatmuseum while the natural history of the area is dealt with comprehensively in the Pfalzmuseum für Naturkunde. The Kloster Limburg nearby is the remains of a former Benedictine monastery founded by Emperor Konrad II in about 1025 and now constitutes one of the most grandiose church ruins in Germany. Concerts and open-air theatrical productions take place here in summer. **Kallstadt**, to the north of Dürkheim, is a particularly attractive village straddling the Weinstrasse.

Wachenheim is only 2 miles (3km) south of Bad Dürkheim on the B271. The former *Schloss* is the headquarters of a wine firm specialising in *Sekt*, the German version of champagne. A peep into the well-preserved courtyard is worthwhile. Four miles (7km) to the south-west on the road to Lambrecht is the 395 acre Hochwildpark Kurpfalz, an area of great beauty in which many animals including deer, bears, boars and wolves live in natural surroundings. There are many pleasant paths through the woods with viewing platforms from which the animals in their large enclosures may be observed.

In another 3 miles (5km) along the 'Wine Road', the charming old town of **Deidesheim** is reached. This is a place which deserves more than a casual glance in passing. The over-riding influence here is the wine and much of the history and legend has to do with this desirable product of the area. For example, the inn Zur Kanne dates from the twelfth century and possesses a book in which Alexander von Humboldt made an entry on the subject. It still serves good wine and the Michelin guide has found the food worthy of mention too. In the *Marktplatz* (Market Square) the Catholic parish church is an important late Gothic building (1464-80), rebuilt in 1689. It is a basilica with a nave and two aisles and contains notable busts of the apostles and prophets from about 1480. The crucifix at the high altar is from about 1510. Also in the *Marktplatz* the historic *Rathaus* has a striking exterior staircase (1734) and the Museum für Weinkultur, tells the story of wine over the centuries with a varied collection of drinking vessels, literature and works of art on the subject. The Spitalkirche is a chapel of 1496 with adjoining sixteenth- to eighteenth-century hospital buildings; the chapel of St Michael, a late Gothic building of 1662, was restored in 1951 following war damage. The museum of modern ceramics at Stadtmauergasse 17 is also worth seeing.

Neustadt an der Weinstrasse (to distinguish it from many other towns with the same name) is by far the biggest place on this named route and is a centre of commerce and culture. One of the most important buildings in the Palatinate is the former Liebfrauen collegiate church here in Neustadt. It is mainly fourteenth century but the lower storeys of the south tower were inherited from an older building; under the baroque dome is the tower watchman's accommodation which was in use until a few years ago. Inside, the sculptural ornamentation includes monkeys and grotesque figures. The Casimirianum in Ludwigstrasse was founded in 1597 as a university for those members of the Reformed Church who had to leave the Lutheran Heidelberg University. It is a three-storey building with an attractive staircase tower and a fine Renaissance doorway. The *Rathaus* shares the market place with many houses which have fine courtyards. Numbers 4 and 11 Marktplatz, 4 Rathausgasse and 55 and 91 Hauptstrasse are all worth seeking out.

The *Heimat- und Weinmuseum* features local history as well as the

Deidesheim

history of wine. Two miles (4km) south of the town, above the suburb of Oberhambach is the eleventh-century castle called Kästenburg, the Hambach Schloss; its fame and interest derives from a student demonstration in 1832 in favour of the unification of Germany and the federation of Europe. The people of the Pfalz gave the castle to Crown Prince Maximilian of Bavaria as a gift and he had it rebuilt from 1846 in the style of a Venetian-Gothic palazzo. Major restoration work was carried out to celebrate, in 1982, the 150th anniversary of the events of 1832. Parts of the old building were incorporated in a new one which is now used for concerts and exhibitions, with fine views from the terrace café.

Those family groups who enjoy the modern style leisure park should take time for a visit to Holiday Park between Hassloch and Hanhofen about 7 miles (12km) east of Neustadt, where they will find entertainment and fun to keep them going all day. There are mechanical 'rides' of various descriptions, aquatic displays, a dolphinarium and much more. There is another *Weinmuseum* in the Holiday Park with a collection of wine artefacts and demonstrations of vineyard management. In this direction too, is the noble city of Speyer with its imposing cathedral and other places of interest. Although it is actually outside the scope of this chapter, it can be recommended as a possible excursion goal for it lies only some 12 miles (20km) from Neustadt.

Hambach Schloss

Railway enthusiasts will enjoy a visit to the railway museum near the Hauptbahnhof (main railway station) in Neustadt where they will see several notable historic steam locomotives and some thirty other vehicles. From time to time some of these are operated on the line which runs west from Neustadt to Elmstein, a distance of about 11 miles (18km). Between these places a stop could be made at **Lambrecht** to visit the Deutsches Schaustellermuseum (literally Showman's Museum) where a miniature representation of a *Kerwe* or *Kirmes* (old church fair) can be found.

The main road south from Neustadt is the B38 and although it continues for a while to mark the nature park boundary, the Weinstrasse now follows a less important road to the west to take in several wine producing communities such as Maikammer, St Martin, Edenkoben and Rhodt. There is access to numerous picturesque roads leading westwards into the hilly area known as the Haardt where the visitor will find the sources of many little rivers from which the waters eventually flow into the Rhine. There is a chair-lift, the Rietburgbahn, a mile west of **Edenkoben** which takes one quickly to the Rietburg castle ruin, at 1,804ft (550m) with another splendid viewpoint. There is a *Wildpark* at the top where the restaurant is open daily from Easter to October. In the Schloss Villa Ludwigshöhe near the foot of the Rietburgbahn, there is a collection of the works of the artist Max Slevogt and the rooms have wall and ceiling paintings and other works of art. This little palace was erected to celebrate the 90th birthday of Prinzregent Luitpold of Bavaria in 1911 — the Palatinate was formerly part of Bavaria. In Edenkoben there is a wine and nature trail to be followed and the exhibits in the Heimatmuseum are again strongly influenced by the wine industry. The area around **Maikammer** is particularly attractive in the spring when peach and almond trees blossom in the orchards.

The B38 continues into **Landau in der Pfalz** (to distinguish it from its namesake in Bavaria), a town which straddles the nature park boundary. Three-quarters of the medieval town was burned down in 1689 when Vauban, the architect who designed fortifications for Louis XIV was working here. However, a certain number of Vauban's works have survived, including the French and German gates. The Protestant parish church is the former collegiate church Unserer Lieben Frau which was built in the fourteenth century to serve an Augustinian canonry founded in 1276. It is a large, long building and the tower in 1458 had an octagonal belfry built on to the lower square storeys to create a somewhat unusual feature. In the course of restoration work in 1897-8, groin vaulting was added to the chancel and nave. The Catholic parish church of Heiliges Kreuz (Holy Cross) adjoins the Augustinian monastery. The church (1405-13) was damaged during World War II but was re-built to the original plans. Inside there is a font (1506) and the famous Landau Madonna, a wood carving from the seventeenth century, which has been in this church since 1893. The east section of the monastery buildings (1740-50) was destroyed in the war and has not been replaced. French influence can be seen in some seventeenth- and eighteenth-century houses and number 17 Martin-Luther-Strasse, 9 Kaufhausgasse and 1 Max-Josephs-Platz should be specially noted. 50 Marktstrasse (1827) was originally the garrison headquarters and is now the town hall. The *Heimatmuseum* in Villa Streccius has sections history and prehistory, folk art, military affairs and fortification systems. The oldest and biggest *Tiergarten* (zoo) in the Rheinland-Pfalz is home to more than 500 animals and birds.

The B10 leads westwards from Landau into the heart of the nature park. It soon crosses the Weinstrasse and in 9 miles (15km) reaches **Annweiler**. The outstanding attraction in this area is the imperial Burg of Trifels 4 miles (6km) to the east, so it is likely that, in the course of the journey from Landau, it has been seen. This fortress was

Sunflower crop near Landau

a stronghold of the reigning monarchs from as early as 1081. From 1124 until 1274 the imperial treasure was kept in the shallow oriel chapel on the east side of the castle and Norman treasure was also stored here in 1195. The castle served to protect the important highway from Metz to the Rhine and although it never fell to its enemies, it could not resist a natural disaster and much of it was destroyed by lightning in 1662. Its impregnable position resulted in it being used to hold distinguished prisoners, including the English king, Richard the Lionheart, who languished here in 1193-4. During the Thirty Years' War it was used as a refuge by the populace.

Since 1935 efforts have been made to restore parts of the building to its original condition and large sections have been completely rebuilt. The castle stands on a sandstone outcrop above the forest and can be seen from afar. From it there is a magnificent view in every direction and visitors should not fail to include this historic site in their itinerary. Exploration of the many rooms and towers will occupy the visitor for quite a while and there is a display of replicas of the Bavarian crown jewels — the originals are in Vienna. In Annweiler the displays in the *Heimatmuseum* understandably are influenced by the story of Trifels but there are also exhibits concerning the development of the tanning and textile industries.

Eleven miles (18km) beyond Annweiler turn southwards at

Hinterweidenthal onto the B427, a pretty road which reaches **Dahn** in 4 miles (7km). The Museum für Naturkunde, Handwerk und Waffentechnik combines displays illustrating the natural history of the area with creatures of the forests and rivers, tools used by the ancient trades and the weapons of the two world wars. The *Burgmuseum* has assembled finds from several of the castle ruins in the neighbourhood and there is a fine heated *Freibad*. A little way south of Dahn, leave the B427 and turn right towards Wieslautern to discover another of Germany's named roads, the Schuhstrasse. This leads to a string of interesting places, many of which are concerned with Germany's shoe manufacturing trade although an apparent paucity of retail outlets is rather surprising.

After passing through Wieslautern the road gradually assumes a westerly direction and a brief pause may be made in **Rumbach** to see the old frescoes in the Christuskirche. The route is now through the most hilly part of the nature park with summits like Kuhnenkopf 1,742ft (531m) on the left and Grosser Eyberg 1,683ft (513m), Grosser Mückenkopf 1,591ft (485m) and Hohelist 1,562ft (476m) on the right. The French frontier is but a few kilometres to the south. The attractive road continues through Fischbach to Eppenbrunn and the traveller will note the numerous possibilities for leaving his or her vehicle and rambling into the woods beside little streams or climbing up to one of the hilltops for rewarding views and perhaps a ruined castle. **Eppenbrunn** is an attractive little resort and makes an excellent base for an unsophisticated sojourn in this lovely countryside. In fairness the same might be said of almost every little place around here.

The Schuhstrasse leads on to **Lemberg** with its almost obligatory ruined castle and a forest nature trail and then into **Pirmasens** the shoe metropolis of Germany. This town on the fringe of the nature park is host each year to several international fairs concerned with the footwear trade and the leather industry. It is also a favourite venue for conferences of all kinds and there is an almost continuous programme of events of one kind and another. Unfortunately, there is little here of genuine historic interest since the town was almost completely destroyed during World War II. The late baroque *Rathaus* (1717-47) was one of the buildings which failed to survive but during 1959-63 it was rebuilt to the historic plans and is now a dignified building gracing the main square. It houses a museum of pre- and early history, the *Heimatmuseum*, the shoe museum and a gallery with the works of local artist Heinrich Bürkel (1802-69).

Pirmasens is well fitted to cater for its many fair and conference guests but it is not perhaps the ideal place for the general holidaymaker although the museum and gallery complex in the old town hall justifies a visit. The splendid and extensive pedestrian precinct has as a centrepiece a large artificial cascade which tumbles down the hillside opposite the restored *Rathaus*. At its head, the large rebuilt church stands behind a statue of its patron Pirminius who died in 753 and from whom the town takes its name. The rather charming *Schusterdenkmal* (Shoemaker's Statue) in the pedestrian precinct is a tribute to the trade from which the town derives its prosperity.

The Schuhstrasse now leads northwards into the countryside again, to **Rodalben** with its notable rock formations just 4 miles (6km) from the centre of Pirmasens and then east along a pretty road to **Merzalben** for the castle, Burg Grafenstein, and the Luitpoldturm which, when climbed, has panoramic views. After this the named road swings in a great anti-clockwise loop through Leimen and the valley of the little river Schwarzbach to its termination in **Waldfisch-bach-Burgalben** where Grafensteiner Schloss is worth a brief halt. The ruins of the castle Heidelsburg in the Schwarzbachtal and the place of pilgrimage, Maria Rosenberg, just to the south of Waldfischbach are favourite excursion goals.

The traveller must turn east to get back to the Weinstrasse but rather than retrace the way to Leimen it is suggested that a slightly more northerly route be taken via Heltersberg to Johanniskreuz, from where the B48 runs south-eastwards back to Annweiler and on to Bad Bergzabern. The whole of the route from Waldfischbach to Annweiler is picturesque and passes through an area with few sgnificant habitations. About 6 miles (10km) beyond Annweiler the Weinstrasse comes in from the north and the B48 is now the named road as well as being the boundary of the nature park. The ruins of Madenburg Castle nearby are quite extensive; it was one of the ring of hilltop castles which surrounded the Trifels.

In another 5 miles (8km) the spa of **Bad Bergzabern** is reached. This watering place is little known to English speaking tourists although quite popular with the French from Alsace for the border is only 5½ miles (9km) to the south. Bergzabern is an ideal centre for exploring this southern end of the Wine Road and the nature park, for it is the focal point of a useful road network and it is good also for excursions into France with the historic city of Strasbourg only some 43 miles (70km) away.

Bergzabern is in the sunniest tip of the Palatinate and the extensive vineyards come right to the outskirts of the town. Indeed, it is pleasant to wander through the quiet *Kurpark* with its thermal swimming pool, large boating lake and minigolf course and linger to listen

Gasthof zum Engel,
Bad Bergzabern

to a concert over a cup of coffee followed by a walk up through the vines to the cool woods beyond. On the southern fringe of the town there are fine modern indoor and unheated outdoor swimming pools although the former does not appear to open during the warm summer months. Much of the centre of this small town is a pedestrian zone and there is an extensive car parking area near the outwardly picturesque *Schloss*. This palace was the former seat of the dukes of Zweibrücken and the oldest of the four sections around the square courtyard dates from 1530. The others were added 1561-79 and the domes and baroque windows were added during a rebuilding in 1725-30. The three-storey Gasthof zum Engel (1556-79) was once the official residence of the dukes and is said to be the finest Renaissance building in the Palatinate. Its three gables are adorned with scrolls and obelisks and there is a lavishly decorated oriel at each corner and a fine courtyard gate. With its two staircase towers, it is the most beautiful of the several fine houses in the town. Not to be overlooked are the fourteenth-century Market Church, rebuilt in 1772 and restored in 1896, the Protestant Schlosskirche (1720-30) and the *Rathaus* (1705). The *Heimatmuseum* exhibits the history and crafts of the area. Cactus lovers should visit the remarkable exhibition of these plants at **Steinfeld**, 5 miles (8km) south-east of Bad Bergzabern.

About 7 miles (12km) west of the town along the B427, **Erlenbach**

is where the Burgmuseum der Raubritterburg Berwartstein recalls
the days when robber knights occupied many of the hilltop castles.
Emperor Frederick I presented Berwartstein to the Bishop of Speyer
in 1152 and although it has been largely in ruins since 1591, parts of
it are still occupied. It is one of many rock fortresses found in this area
and the upper castle has rooms and passageways hewn from the
living rock. Nearby to the south, another ruined *Burg* called Klein-
frankreich has a distinctive round tower dating from about 1480. For
those with children, a popular excursion from Bad Bergzabern is that
to the extensive Wild- und Wanderpark near Silz about 5 miles (8km)
to the north-west. Many varieties of animals roam freely over the
park which has a network of footpaths for modest rambles.

Climbing out of Bergzabern along the Weinstrasse — now the B38
— towards the French border, a minor road to the right leads to the
village of **Dörrenbach** less than a mile from the main road. Described
as 'das Dornröschen der Pfalz' (the Sleeping Beauty of the Palatinate)
this lovely old village is a real treasure. Since the road does not go
beyond the end of the valley in which it lies, there is no through traffic
so there is little to disturb the peace. Fine old timbered houses line the
narrow main street and include the *Rathaus*, a charming Renaissance
building with elaborate carved window frames dating from 1590.
There are several inns and restaurants serving excellent meals and
the local wines. The village church serves both the Catholic and
Protestant congregations. It is what is known as a *Wehrkirche*, that is
to say, it was fortified to protect it and its churchyard against vaga-
bonds, thieves and other marauders. Its stout walls and towers still
stand as evidence of those earlier less peaceful days. Many of the
newer houses on the fringe of the village offer guest accommodation
in private rooms or holiday flats. At the end of the village, tracks lead
directly and steeply into the forest where the lofty but unsightly
tower on the Stäffelsberg commands fine views back towards Bad
Bergzabern. A little further into the forest and one can discover the
remains of the Westwall, the defensive fortifications popularly
known as the Siegfried Line with which the Germans hoped to
discourage invasion from the west in World War II. These defences
were, in the end, no more successful than the French Maginot Line
had been some years earlier. The German 'wall' was blown up by the
Americans after the war, presumably to discourage later neo-Nazi
demonstrations but the French forts a short distance away over the
border were left intact to become something of a tourist attraction.
The forest has many marked paths and the walker could continue
another 6 miles (10km) or so north-westwards to another hilltop

Schloss Weikersheim, in the Tauber Valley
above: seen from the baroque garden; below: the Knights' Hall

Creglingen in the Tauber Valley

castle ruin, the Drachenfels, near Busenberg, or to the summit of the Böbenthaler Kopf (1,751ft, 534m), only about 4 miles (7km) from Dörrenbach but quite a climb.

Back on the main road, the way is lined by vineyards on the slopes of the Hoher Kopf (1,631ft, 497m) and the 'double' village of **Schweigen-Rechtenbach** is soon passed. Ahead, spanning the road, is the imposing Deutsches Weintor, a gateway marking the end of the Weinstrasse. Stop here to see the huge old wine press and to climb the gateway for a better view of the vineyards. A stall nearby provides a continuous opportunity for tasting and purchasing the local wines. There is a large restaurant here, as well as the inevitable souvenir shops. There is a vineyard nature trail to get one away from the crowds often encountered around the Deutsches Weintor. Just a few hundred metres on down the hill are the German and French border posts beyond which the French town of Wissembourg (Weissenburg in German) is well worth crossing over to visit.

For touring and sightseeing in the area covered by this chapter, the visitor could use the *'Aral' Tourenkarte Sheet 10, Hunsrück, Saarland/Pfalz (1:200,000)* obtainable from Aral filling stations in the area. Not only is it an adequately detailed map but on the reverse is a comprehensive summary of places of interest and much useful information. Incidentally, the same map covers the territory dealt with in the chapter on the Saar valley.

Finally, the fine city of **Karlsruhe** is less than 25 miles (40km) to the south-east of Bad Bergzabern and could well be the goal of an excursion should. A focal point of the city is the ducal *Schloss* which houses the Badisches Landesmuseum (Baden State Museum). The Kunsthalle is one of Europe's leading art galleries with a wide ranging collection, but particularly strong in the early German, baroque and Romantic periods.

Further Information
— The Palatine Forest Nature Park —

Cycling and Rambling

The rural roads are very suitable for cycle touring and suggested itineraries may be obtained from tourist information offices. Cycles may be hired from the DB railway stations at Annweiler, Deidesheim, Hassloch, Hinterweidenthal, Landau, Neustadt and Speyer. Cyclists arriving by train pay only half the normal hire charge.

Several resorts offer inclusive 'packages' of 3-15 nights for ramblers with one charge to cover bed and breakfast, maps, luggage transfer, visits to places of interest, swimming pools, etc. Information and bookings from information offices at Bad Bergzabern, Bad Dürkheim, Dahn and Kaiserslautern.

Details of these and many other holidays are in a booklet *Hobby-spezial* from
the state tourist office.

Places to Visit

Alzey
Museum Alzey
Antoniterstrasse 41
55232 Alzey
Open: Tuesday to Sunday 10am-
12noon, 2-5pm.
Geology, fossils, archaeology, rural
handcrafts, historic documents, etc.
Admission free.

Annweiler
Heimatmuseum
Quodgasse
76855 Annweiler
Open: daily mid-March to October
9am-12noon, 1.30-4pm. Local history
and exhibits relating to Trifels.

Burg Trifels
4 miles (6km) south-east of Annweiler.
Open: Wednesday-Sunday 9am-1pm,
2-6pm (5pm October to March). Closed
December.
Parking charge at nearest car park
(restaurant) with 20 minutes' climb to
castle. Several free car parks in forest
involving a longer walk.

Bad Dürkheim
Pfalzmuseum für Naturkunde
Hermann-Schäfer-Strasse 17
67098 Bad Dürkheim
Open: Tuesday to Sunday 10am-5pm
(8pm Wednesday).
Natural history, geology, mineralogy.

Heimatmuseum 'Haus Catoir'
Römerstrasse
67098 Bad Dürkheim
Open: Wednesday and Saturday
2-5pm, Sunday 9am-12noon, 2-5pm.
Local history, old dolls, vine culture,
paintings by local artists.

Dahn
*Museum für Naturkunde, Handwerk und
    Waffentechnik*
66994 Dahn

Open: Wednesday and Friday 1-6pm,
Saturday, Sunday and holidays
10am-6pm.
Local forest and water creatures, old
tools, weapons of the two world wars.

Deidesheim
Museum für Moderne Keramik
Stadtmauergasse 17
67146 Deidesheim
Open: Friday, Saturday and Sunday
10am-12noon, 2-5pm, Wednesday
6-8pm.
Closed in February and July. Ceramics
by leading artists world-wide.

Museum für Weinkultur
Historisches Rathaus
67146 Deidesheim
Open: Saturday 2-5pm, Sunday 10am-
12noon, Wednesday 6-8pm.
Wine growing, selling and drinking.

Edenkoben
Schloss Villa Ludwigshöhe
67480 Edenkoben
1 mile (2km) west of Edenkoben.
Open: Tuesday to Sunday 9am-1pm,
2-6pm (5pm October to March).
Wall and ceiling paintings, art gallery,
special exhibitions. Close to lower
station of Rietburg chair-lift. Ample
free parking.

Rietburgbahn
Chair-lift 1 mile (2km) west of Edenkoben to the ruins of Rietburg Castle at
1,800ft (550m). Journey time 8 minutes.
Operates Easter to November. *Wildpark*
and restaurant at upper station.

Erlenbach
*Burgmuseum der Raubritterburg
    Berwartstein*
76891 Erlenbach bei Bad Berzabern
Open: daily March to October 9.30am-
6pm.
Knights' armour, castle kitchen, torture
chamber, etc.

Hassloch
Weinmuseum
Im Holiday Park
67454 Hassloch

Open: daily April-September 9am-6pm.
Historic implements, bottles, glasses,
etc. Demonstrations.

Kaiserslautern

Pfalzgalerie des Bezirksverbandes Pfalz
Museumsplatz 1
67657 Kaiserslautern
Open: Tuesday to Sunday 10am-5pm,
also Tuesday 7-9pm.
Paintings, sculptures, glass, porcelain
figures etc from Middle Ages to present.

Theodor-Zink-Museum
Steinstrasse 48
67657 Kaiserslautern
Open: Tuesday to Friday 9am-5pm,
Saturday and Sunday 10am-6pm.
Town history and folk culture. Admission free.

Lambrecht

Deutsches Schaustellermuseum
Vereinstrasse 8
67466 Lambrecht
Open: Tuesday, Wednesday, Friday,
Sunday and holidays 10am-12noon,
1-6pm.
Miniature old church fair. Admission
free.

Landau

Heimatmuseum
Villa Streccius
Marienring 8
76829 Landau
Open: Tuesday to Friday 9am-12noon,
2-5pm, Sunday 10am-12noon.
Local history, pre- and early history,
culture and military exhibits. Admission free.

Neustadt

Heimatmuseum
Maximilianstrasse 25
67433 Neustadt an der Weinstrasse
Open: Monday to Friday 9am-12noon,
3-5pm.
Specially conducted tours arranged by
Fremdenverkehrsamt. Local history, old
inn signs, paintings, East Asian collection, etc. Admission free.

Hambach Schloss
2 miles (4km) south of Neustadt
through Oberhambach.
Open: daily March to November, 9am-5pm.
Cradle of German democracy. Rebuilt
1982 to celebrate 150th anniversary of
the Hambacher Fest. Charge for
exhibitions. Free parking. Terrace café.

Deutsche Gesellschaft für Eisenbahn-geschichte eV
Horst Kayser, Postfach 100318
Hindenburgstrasse 12
67433 Neustadt an der Weinstrasse
☎ (06321) 30390 or (06325) 8626
Steam-hauled trains with locomotives
and vehicles from the Neustadt Railway Museum operate between Neustadt and Elmstein, usually on Sunday
two or three times per month, May to
October also on some holidays. St
Nikolaus specials early in December.
Details in DB *Kursbuch*, table 669.

Eisenbahnmuseum
Schillerstrasse beim Hauptbahnhof
67434 Neustadt an der Weinstrasse
☎ (06321) 30390 or (06325) 8626
Open: Sunday and holidays10am-12.30pm, Saturday 9am-6pm.
Historic steam locomotives and railway
vehicles.

Pirmasens

Museum der Deutschen Schuhmetropole
Im alten Rathaus
Hauptstrasse 26
66953 Pirmasens
Locally made shoes from 1840-1967 and
world wide shoe collection.
Also at the same address:

Heimatmuseum
Local history, pre- and early history,
minerals, Bronze Age and Roman finds.

Bürkel-Galerie
Paintings of the Pirmasens artist H.
Bürkel (1802-69).
All the above open: Thursday 3-6pm,
Sunday 10am-1pm.
Group tours by prior arrangement.
Admission free.

Steinfeld
Kakteenland
Wengelspfad 1
76889 Steinfeld
☎ (06340) 1299
5 miles (8km) south-east of Bad
Bergzabern
Open: March-October Monday-Friday
8am-6pm, Saturday and Sunday 9am-
5pm; November-February Monday-
Friday 9am-5pm.
1,000 varieties of cactus in large greenhouses. Admission free. Shop.

Zoos and Wildlife Parks

Bad Bergzabern
Wild- und Wanderpark
76857 Silz
☎ (06346) 5588
Five miles (8km) north-west of Bad
Bergzabern at Silz.
Open: March to November from
8.30am, December-February 10am-dusk.
Extensive natural parkland. Deer,
goats, boars, etc roam freely. Many
footpaths. Café. Ample free parking.

Edenkoben
Rietburg Wildpark
Open: daily Easter to November.
Near upper station of Rietburgbahn
chair-lift a mile west of Edenkoben.
Restaurant with view of Weinstrasse.
Ample free parking near lower station.

Wachenheim
Hochwildpark Kurpfalz
67157 Wachenheim an der Weinstrasse
☎ (06325) 7805
Open: all year 10am-4pm.
Four miles (7km) south-west of Wachenheim. 395 acre park with native
animals in natural surroundings. Fish
ponds (angling possible), play area,
forest restaurant.

There are also many forest enclosures
(*Gehege*) for wild boars, deer, etc and
these are usually accessible at all times
without charge.
Contact local information offices for
precise locations.

Tourist Information Offices

Regional Offices

Koblenz
*Fremdenverkehrsverband
   Rheinland-Pfalz*
Postfach 1420
56068 Koblenz
☎ (0261) 331079
(Main office for the State)

Landau in der Pfalz
*Südliche Weinstrasse
   Zentrale für Tourismus*
An der Kreuzmühle 2
76829 Landau in der
Pfalz
☎ (06341) 380148
(Area office for the
Weinstrasse).

Local Offices

Bad Bergzabern
Kurverwaltung
Kurtalstrasse 25
76887 Bad Bergzabern
☎ (06343) 8811

Bad Dürkheim
Städtisches Verkehrsamt
67098 Bad Dürkheim
☎ (06322) 793-276

Dahn
Fremdenverkehrsbüro
Schulstrasse 29
66994 Dahn
☎ (06391) 5811

Kaiserslautern
*Verkehrs- und
   Imformationsamt*
Rathausplatz
67657 Kaiserslautern
☎ (0631) 852-231

**Neustadt an der
   Weinstrasse**
Rheinlandpfalz-Weinpfalz eV
Robert-Stolz-Strasse 18
67433 Neustadt an der
Weinstrasse
☎ (06321) 13093

Pirmasens
Büro für Touristik
Postfach 2265
66954 Pirmasens ˙
☎ (06331) 809126

6 • Franconia

The old duchy of Franconia, now administratively part of Bavaria, is to a large extent the valley of the Main. This river rises near the former East German border and flows west for some 300 miles (483km) to join the Rhine at Mainz. It is a valley of great beauty, lacking the castle-topped crags of the Rhine but with vine-clothed hillsides, pretty villages, and two of the finest towns in the whole of Germany. Yet for every hundred tourists who visit the Rhineland it is unlikely that five go up the Main. There are no regular boat services up its length but you can hire small cruisers for a week or so, and both road and railways run close beside it for long stretches.

The first big town, travelling upstream from Mainz is Frankfurt, but the traveller in search for off the beaten track attractions will not linger long here, though its airport would provide an excellent starting point. Almost a suburb of Frankfurt is **Offenbach**, with a unique leather museum, including a wonderful display of shadow puppets from Cambodia. A little further on is **Aschaffenburg**, with a fine Renaissance castle crowning the hill above the town and a painting by Grünewald in the abbey church. The river here makes a great loop round the Spessart, a forested range of hills that provides good walking country.

At this point one might well linger for a few days to explore the Spessart on foot. A good walk leads from the centre of the city along a route marked with red dots in the direction of Pfaffenberg. The path is at times narrow and difficult, but especially in the spring the flowers and the water-washed sandstone boulders will compensate for the labour of the climb. The Pfaffenberg is 1,417ft (432m) high, and easily recognised by the television masts on its summit. Descending from here, past a wayside shrine and through a beech wood, one can strike a marked footpath that leads to the Hohe Warte, a half timbered house on the site of an old hunting lodge that was used as a workshop for manufacturing matches in the nineteenth century. A footpath marked with a red circle leads from here to the edge of the wood, opening up a splendid panorama with a little

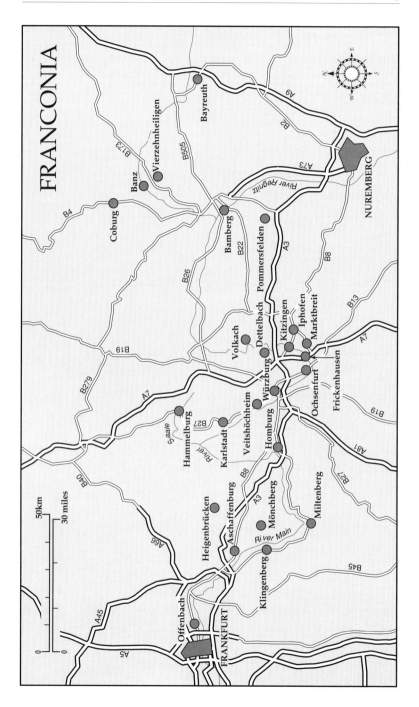

village lying in the meadows below. A meandering path, now marked with a red cross, leads under the hanging branches of hornbeams back to Aschaffenburg.

Penetrating a little further into the Spessart, you might move to the hill resort of **Heigenbrücken**, which is on the railway and easily accessible from the *Autobahn*. Footpaths lead from here in every direction. A particularly attractive area is through the Oberlohr- and Unterlohrgrund to Habichsthal. The Lohr, a tributary of the Main, is a stream that was loved and written about by Clemens Brentano, the writer of the nineteenth-century Romantic Movement, whose poems and stories are full of the atmosphere of German folklore.

In the bend of the Main, **Mönchberg** is another good centre, with one of the finest baroque churches in the area. There is a splendid walk through the woods whose stretches are designated with the rather fanciful names that Germans are fond of: Signalbuche (Beech Beacon), Schwarzer Keiler (Black Boar), Sandrain (Sandbank), Eichhörnchen (Little Squirrel), Märchenblick (Fairytale View) and Eichbaumweg (Oak Path). You can buy little books describing any number of splendid walks through the woods and hills, but if you rather resent following the routes marked out by the footpath signs you will have no difficulty in making your own variations.

Moving on, upstream from Aschaffenburg, another loop of the river brings us to **Würzburg**, that can fairly be described as one of the great cities of Europe. It can boast two superb buildings. The Residenz was built for the prince bishop between 1720-80 by a young artillery officer called Balthasar Neumann, selected, it would seem, largely for his skill in trigonometry, who turned out to be an architect of genius. The interior was decorated with glorious frescoes by Giovanni Battista Tiepolo. The great staircase leads to room after room in which the walls and ceilings are alive with mythological and historical figures whose limbs merge from two-dimensional paint to three-dimensional plaster and back again. It is simply the finest building of its kind anywhere in the world and stands today miraculously restored after the destruction of a terrible and totally unnecessary bombing attack in the last days of World War II.

The other great building of Würzburg is the Marienberg Castle crowning the hill on the other side of the river. This consists of seventeenth-century extensions to a medieval core and now houses a very fine museum, including a number of wood sculptures by the local artist, Tilman Riemenschneider. Riemenschneider, who died in 1531, bridges the Gothic and Renaissance styles with a mastery that has never been surpassed. It helps to form an appreciation of his

Marienberg Castle, Würzburg, with the bridge over the Main in the foreground

genius to go round the sculpture room in the museum deciding which pieces are by him and which by 'his workshop' before reading the labels. You are unlikely to go far wrong.

On the other side of a small lateral valley lies the Käpelle, a pilgrimage church designed by Neumann, approached up the hillside by a row of carved Stations of the Cross. On a hot day it can be a tiring climb, but it is worth the effort to inspect the delightful interior of this church, whose frescoes and stucco work represent the highest expression of rococo art. After this, if a further climb can be faced, push on higher still to the Frankenwarte, from which you can enjoy a superb view across the valley of the Main to the city of Würzburg. At the top you will discover that a bus could have taken you all the way from the city!

There is much more to see and admire in Würzburg, and many pleasant restaurants and *Weinstuben* to linger in. One visit that should not be missed is to the country palace of **Veitshöchheim**, a few miles down stream, which can be reached by boat. The garden is the attraction here, with baroque sculptures of milkmaids and shepherdesses tumbling all over the place and a delightful open-air theatre, with the wings and back-scene of the stage in well-clipped box hedges. The statues here are actually replicas; the originals are in the Marienberg Museum. This kind of garden architecture seems to go best with courtly eighteenth-century life and is perhaps not best appreciated on a Sunday afternoon in summer when the grounds are crowded with the twentieth-century citizens of the Federal Republic enjoying themselves. You may be more in tune with the atmosphere of the age, in which gardens like this were created, if you can pay your visit on a hazy morning in early summer or an afternoon in late autumn when the mist from the river lends a touch of magic and poetry to the alleys, vistas and gesturing figures who inhabit them. Balthasar Neumann, the designer of so many splendid buildings in Franconia seems, indeed, to have surrendered to the appeal of this atmosphere when he chose to propose marriage to his sweetheart in a swannery!

The hills around Würzburg are covered with the vines of the Stein and Leiste vineyards, which are Franconian wines. These are hardly known outside Germany, but for some drinkers they are the most enjoyable of all the German wines. In character, thanks to the shell-lime and Keuper soils on which the vines grow, they are full-bodied, pithy and vigorous. Over half of the wine produced is made from Silvaner grapes, which give a dry and somewhat earthy taste. To many connoisseurs this is preferable to the slightly sweet wines from Riesling grapes that are produced in other areas of Germany. But any one who prefers a slightly less dry Franconian wine (what the Germans call *halb-trocken*) can choose one made from Müller-Thurgau grapes, which constitute almost all the remaining volume of Franconian wine production. Both varieties are sold in bottles of a distinctive shape, called *Bocksbeutel*, which are reserved by German law to the wines of Franconia.

Almost all Franconian wines are white, but there is a small area south of Aschaffenburg, based on the beautiful medieval towns of

Miltenberg and Klingenberg, which produce very decent red wines from Spätburgunder grapes. Travelling upstream from Miltenberg on a wine drinking pilgrimage — what better pilgrimage to undertake in Franconia? — one comes to **Homburg** (another town of this name, near Frankfurt, gave its name to the hat), whose vineyards produce some of the greatest wines of Franconia, including some exceptional Rieslings. At the point where the Main turns south on another of its great loops the river Saale joins it from the north. This small tributary is flanked by good vineyards, especially at Hammelburg, lying below the old castle of Saaleck. Resuming the course of the Main, the visitor arrives at the attractive old town of **Karlstadt** with its medieval town walls, before reaching Würzburg.

A few miles beyond Würzburg is the large village of **Randersacker**, whose vineyards produce some of the finest wines of the district. In the past this was a favourite retreat for the prince bishops of Würzburg who owned and developed its vineyards. These were later inherited by the kings of Bavaria, and have now passed to the state domain, which owns large estates in the area and has done a great deal to preserve and improve the quality of Franconian wines. The *Weinprobier-Stuben* (wine-tasting inns) of Randersacker attract many citizens and students from Würzburg to taste the wines. There is nothing here now to remind the visitor of the 80-year quarrel with the neighbouring village of Eibelstadt over the right to a vineyard between them (which led to fixed battles with weapons), nor the sacking of the place during the Thirty Years War. On the hill above the town, where the *Autobahn* comes down towards the Main, there is a huge quarry from which the stone was dug that provided the building material not only for a large part of the castle at Würzburg but also for the Isar bridge in Munich, the town hall in Leipzig, and the Olympic Stadium in Berlin. An exploration of this labyrinth could provide an adventurous introduction to geology, especially for children.

Continue upstream, to the charming old village of **Frickenhausen**, with excellent vineyards on its southerly slopes. It lies between the old world towns of Ochsenfurt and Marktbreit. It is difficult to realise today, when visiting these well-preserved and prosperous communities with their fine churches, town halls, *Weinfeste*, and spring and autumn festivals that the Swedish troops passed through them, plundering as they went, in the Thirty Years' War, or that plague struck in the fifteenth and sixteenth centuries, leaving them deserted. A little further on, the walled and turreted town of **Sulzfeld** offers, as do many of these towns on the Main, a fine

Renaissance *Rathaus*, many old houses, a parish church enlarged in the seventeenth century, fishing, water sports, footpaths, wine-tasting, and a street *Weinfest* at the beginning of August.

After the Main has twisted once more to take a north-south course, one comes to **Kitzingen**, the largest town of this stretch of the river, the only place on the railway and a centre of the wine trade. A few arches of the old bridge stretch into the river, and the town can offer what claims to be the oldest *Weinkeller* (wine cellar) in Germany and a Fastnachtsmuseum (Carnival Museum) in the old Falter Tower. Moving upstream the visitor arrives at the walled village of Dettelbach, and then to **Volkach**, one of the oldest towns of Franconia and the site of some famous vineyards. This is now something of a show place, a resort noted for its fruit and vegetables as well as for its historic buildings, where a town councillor in Renaissance costume may welcome you on special occasions. The gem of the place is the pilgrimage chapel of Maria im Weingarten, set on a small hill outside the walls and surrounded by a luxurious wreath of vineyards. It contains a famous statue of the *Madonna im Rosenkranz* by Tilman Riemenschneider.

A little distance away from the river valley is the Steigerwald, a range of low wooded hills, whose lime and clay soil produces wine of a distinctive quality. The most attractive place here is the little town of **Iphofen**, with imposing walls, a splendid *Rathaus*, a fine Gothic church, and a *Zehntkeller* (tithe barn) housing one of the most popular hostelries in Franconia. An unexpected discovery here is the Knauf-Museum, an old mansion housing casts of famous monuments from the oldest civilisations in history that have been assembled from museums throughout the world.

Nearby is **Castell**, situated at the foot of a large baroque castle, with a *Schlossgarten*. The church here is particularly interesting as it is a rare example of the rococo style in a Protestant church. It might be thought that the florid rococo architecture was ill-suited for the sober manner of Lutheran worship, but in this church, built by the local lord in 1783, the spirit of the age has triumphed, substituting only the pulpit for the high altar as the main focus of attention. Generally in Germany the religious loyalties of the people depended upon those of the local lord, as recognised by the Peace of Augsburg in 1555. The older church buildings reflect this decision to this day. In many areas of mid-Germany, between the north and the south, adjoining villages may have either a Catholic or a Lutheran church.

After leaving the wine villages of the valley behind the visitor soon arrives at **Bamberg**, an historical town of great interest, almost

The thirteenth-century Bamberg Rider *in Bamberg Cathedral*

unvisited by British and American tourists and, for a merciful change, almost untouched by bombs. Among many buildings of great beauty is the outstanding old town hall. The Gothic structure, baroquised in the eighteenth century, stands like a ship on its own little island in the river. A little further up the hill is the cathedral, situated in what is claimed with justice to be the finest square in Germany. The cathedral contains some of the best examples of medieval sculpture in all Europe, among which the so-called *Bamberg Rider*, an ideal of knightly chivalry, is deservedly famous. Opposite is the Neue Residenz in full baroque style while further up the hill is St Michael's Church with fine Gothic, Romanesque and baroque features. There is a wonderful view of the old town from its terrace which makes the climb up well worth while. If one has seen and enjoyed Offenbach's opera, *The Tales of Hoffmann*, then one will be glad to know that this was E.T.A. Hoffmann's home town. His house is open to the public. If a visit to this attractive city coincides with a performance by the world-renowned Bamberg Symphony Orchestra it will be an added plus.

A few miles south of Bamberg is **Pommersfelden**; a baroque palace built for the Prince Bishop of Bamberg by Johann Dientzenhofer in 1711 with a grand staircase almost rivalling that at Würzburg. It also has a romantic grotto room, and amusing *trompe l'oeil* decorations. A similar distance to the north are two wonderful monastic churches. The earlier of these at **Banz** (1711), was designed by the same architect as at Pommersfelden, with walls, galleries and ceilings in sweeping curves, all under the control of a master plan.

On the other side of the valley, facing it and built in a spirit of unedifying competition that has not infrequently inspired architecture intended for the glory of God, is the even more remarkable church of **Vierzehnheiligen** (1744) and erected on a spot where a shepherd boy saw a vision of fourteen 'saintly helpers'. The architect here was Balthasar Neumann, the designer of the Residenz at Würzburg, but much of the decoration is somewhat later and in the full glory of rococo. The history of this building is a complicated story, but what it all builds up to is the erection of an extraordinary altar to the honour of these fourteen saints. This so-called Gnadenaltar (1762) seems more like the sort of fairy coach in which Cinderella might have gone to the ball than anything else and has been well described as one of the strangest and most brilliantly fantastic creations of late baroque. Whether this is a valid expression of religious art or not, it is certainly something to be seen, and this church still attracts thousands of devout pilgrims.

Only a few miles away, though not quite in the Main valley, is **Coburg**. This town has a special interest for British visitors as it was the home of Prince Albert, the husband and consort of Queen Victoria. This high-minded German prince, who was so deeply loved by his young wife, made a great contribution to the popular appreciation of art in England, with the titles of the Victoria and Albert Museum and the Albert Hall as reminders. Here we can see the surroundings that influenced him as he grew up: Schloss Ehrenburg, the princely palace in which classical, baroque, French Empire and Biedermeier styles all merge together within a nineteenth-century Gothic revival exterior; Veste, the old castle above the town, in which Martin Luther found a safe refuge in 1530 and in which his study can be seen; and the fine collection of prints and paintings housed there. Coburg may seem a sleepy provincial town today, but as so often there are treasures, pleasures and surprises to be discovered by the traveller who goes off the beaten track.

Finally, not far from the source of the Main, is **Bayreuth**. To most people Bayreuth means Wagner but long before Wagner was born it was the seat of a petty princeling who married a sister of Frederick the Great. She thus became the margravine who commissioned a number of splendid buildings in the town. The Markgräfliches Opernhaus (1745), in particular, was decorated by two of the Bibienas, the famous Italian theatre designers, and is even more magnificent than the Cuvilliés Theatre in Munich. Safety precautions limit the use of the building for theatrical performances, though it is sometimes used for concerts, but really it is enough just to stand and stare. This is probably the most glorious example of flamboyant theatre architecture in all Europe.

The Festspielhaus was built in 1872 solely for the production of Wagner's operas in a style intended to unite music, drama and design in a total art form — a *Gesamtkunst* — to be attended in an atmosphere of reverent absorbtion. It is still directed by his descendants for that purpose. During the summer festival, Wagnerites from all over the world flock here. For the rest of the year the theatre is closed, but at all seasons you can visit the house in which Wagner spent the last years of his tempestuous life and in whose garden he and Cosima lie buried.

Further Information
— Franconia —

Places to Visit

Bamberg
Cathedral
Open: summer 8am-6pm; winter 9am-12noon, 2-4pm.

E.T.A. Hoffmann House
Open: summer only May-October, Tuesday and Friday 5-6pm. Saturday and Sunday 10am-12noon.

Bayreuth
Festspielhaus
Open: April-September 10-11.30am.

Markgräfliches Opernhaus
Opernstrasse
Open: guided tours April-August 9-11.30am, 1.30-4.30pm; October-March 10-11.30am.

Coburg
Schloss Ehrenburg
Open: April-September10am-12noon,
1-5.30pm; October-March 10am-
12noon, 1-4.30pm.
☎ (09561) 7767

Iphofen
Knauf-Museum
Open: April to October, Tuesday to
Sunday 2-6pm. Tuesday and Thursday
10am-12noon.
☎ (09323) 31 4 87

Kitzingen
Deutsches Fasnachtmuseum
Open: April to November, Saturday
and Sunday, 2-5pm.
☎ (09321) 2 33 55

Würzburg
Residenz
Open: April to September, Tuesday to
Sunday, 9am-5pm. October to March,
Tuesday to Sunday, 10am-4pm.
☎ (0931) 5 27 43

Tourist Information Offices

Bamberg
Fremdenverkehrsamt
Hauptwachstrasse 16
96047 Bamberg
☎ (0951) 21040

Bayreuth
Fremdenverkehrsamt
Luitpoldplatz 9
95444 Bayreuth
☎ (0921) 88588

Coburg
Fremdenverkehrsamt
Herrngasse 4
96450 Coburg
☎ (09561) 7418-0

Würzburg
Fremdenverkehrsamt
Falkenhaus am Markt
97070 Würzburg
☎ (0931) 37398

Village Tourist Offices

97337 **Dettelbach**
☎ (09324) 808

97246 **Eibelstadt**
☎ (09303) 216

97252 **Frickenhausen**
☎ (09331) 2726

97762 **Hammelburg**
☎ (09732) 80249

97346 **Iphofen**
☎ (09323) 3095

97753 **Karlstadt**
☎ (09353) 8275

97318 **Kitzingen**
☎ (09321) 205

97340 **Marktbreit**
☎ (09332) 3418

97199 **Ochsenfurt**
☎ (09331) 5855

97236 **Randersacker**
☎ (0931) 708282

98617 **Sulzfeld**
☎ (09321) 5474

97209 **Veitshöchheim**
☎ (0931) 9009639

97332 **Volkach**
☎ (09381) 40112

Information about wine
seminars from:
Gebietsweinwerbung
Frankenwein-
Frankenland
Postfach 58 48
97070 Würzburg
☎ (0931) 12093

7 • The Tauber Valley

The little river Tauber enters the mighty river Main (pronounced 'mine') at Wertheim in Baden-Württemberg and this chapter traces its course for some 62 miles (100km) south-eastwards to the outskirts of the famous and well known medieval town of Rothenburg. The north bank of the Main is in Bavaria and parts of the route to be followed are within its boundary. By whatever means the Tauber is followed, the way is most pleasant but it is seen at its very best by those who go on foot or bicycle along the waymarked route called Liebliches Taubertal — Beautiful Tauber Valley.

Firstly, one must make the journey to Wertheim. The air traveller would best arrive at Frankfurt and could complete the journey by train in about 2 hours. This would also be the route for the rail traveller. Having arrived at Wertheim, there is a somewhat limited train service through the valley but places as far as Weikersheim and Niederstetten can be reached by this means. Unless it is intended to walk or cycle, however, the hire of a car is strongly recommended.

Motorists travelling from the west should follow *Autobahn* A3 (signs to Würzburg) from Frankfurt for about 43½ miles (70km) to the exit for Wertheim. Alternatively, leave at the Weibersbrunn exit 18 miles (29km) earlier and visit the picturesque *Wasserschloss* (moated palace) at **Mespelbrunn** about 4 miles (6km) to the south.Erected in the fifteenth century, this lovely little palace in its pretty wooded surroundings is just made for the photographer. The Knights' Hall, reached from the small courtyard, is the principal room on the ground floor. The Gobelinensaal contains a famous Gobelin tapestry from 1564 and the Chinese salon and other rooms with interesting furnishings are also open to view. From the direction of the *Autobahn* there is a strange lack of direction signs to the palace and one has to go almost to the end of the attractive but straggly village of Mespelbrunn before reaching the left turn to the car park.

Wertheim is now best reached along pleasant rural roads in about 18½ miles (30km). This is a little town and embraces fifteen outlying villages. There is a lot of accommodation in all categories, including

The market place at Bad Mergentheim, in the Tauber Valley

Aub town hall and baroque Virgin Mary pillar, in the Tauber Valley

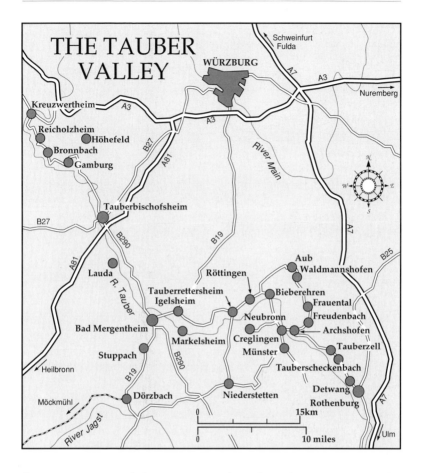

five camp sites, and there are a number of good restaurants. In the village of Bettingen, 6 miles (10km) to the east beside the Main, the peaceful but not inexpensive Schweizer Stuben earned a coveted Michelin star for its excellent cuisine. Before starting in earnest on the journey up the Tauber, time should be taken to explore this historic town. Needless to say, this is best done on foot, indeed, this is the only way for most of the centre is a pedestrian zone. However, there are several car parks nearby.

The first settlement here was in the seventh century on the other side of the river Main in the part now called Kreuzwertheim. With the building of the fortified castle in the twelfth century, the centre moved to the south of the river. In 1631, during the Thirty Years' War, the Swedes occupied the town and castle and as a result the latter was destroyed by the emperor's troops in 1634. It was never rebuilt but

Wertheim Castle

work has been carried out from time to time to prevent the ruins collapsing completely. The castle is seen at its most spectacular at night when it is floodlit. Several pleasant paths lead up from the town for rather splendid views over the river valleys.

The British visitor may well be astonished to come upon a red telephone box of the type so long familiar at home behind the market place. On it is a plaque recording that this was a gift of the people of Huntingdon and Godmanchester with which the community of Wertheim is twinned. The instrument within is of the standard German design, of course. The *Rathaus* has been created out of three former dwelling houses and has a staircase tower. Late Gothic fortified towers are vestiges of the old ring wall, and late Gothic is also the architectural style of the former Kilianskapelle (chapel of St Kilian), the basement of which served as an ossuary or charnal-house. The upper storey has ornate tracery and flying buttresses with finials and now houses the *Heimatmuseum*. It is just north of the late Gothic Protestant parish church which has a number of features of interest including the little choir of the Heilig-Geist-Kapelle (chapel of the Holy Ghost) and the seventeenth-century tomb of Count Ludwig II of Löwenstein-Wertheim and his wife, popularly known as the 'bedstead' because of its canopy.

In addition to the *Heimatmuseum* there is the interesting Glasmuseum in Mühlenstrasse with a collection of historic glass and recording the development of glass manufacture from the earliest times. Between the *Marktplatz* and the parish church the interesting Engelsbrunnen (Angel Fountain) of 1574 is so named because of the two angels at the top holding the Wertheim coat of arms. All around are artistic timbered houses, mostly from the sixteenth century. On Wednesday and Saturday the market place is colourful with the stalls of the fruit, vegetable and flower vendors. The visitor will find many more interesting corners as he or she wanders around and the photographer will be more than pleased if lighting conditions allow him or her to make the most of the medieval townscape. A small thirteenth-century church is to be found in the part of Wertheim called Eichel close to the Main.

Boating and angling are favourite pastimes here; cruises may be made up and down the Main in the summer months and private boats may be moored in the yacht-harbour just inside the mouth of the Tauber. Special package holidayss are on offer for anglers and their families, details available from the tourist information office. Cyclists and ramblers too, have special provision made for them; cycles may be hired at the railway station and elsewhere.

On leaving Wertheim, the densely wooded slopes of this north end of the Tauber valley are quickly in evidence on either side, the woods often giving way to the more open aspect of extensive or-chards or vineyards. This is a particularly attractive road in spring-time when the fruit trees are in blossom and again in the autumn when the leaves are about to fall. The village of **Reichholzheim**, four miles (6km) from Wertheim, has a vintners' co-operative and is one of several places in the area where *Weinproben* may be enjoyed and up to sixty persons can be accommodated. Note the colourful coats of arms on the vintners' building. There is a camp site near the river.

In another 2 miles (3km) **Bronnbach** with its former Cistercian abbey church of St Maria is reached. This is now the Catholic parish church and is one of the most interesting early Cistercian churches in Germany with traces of Provençal and Burgundian influence. Al-though building began in 1157, the church was not consecrated until 1222; the baroque interior dates from the seventeenth and eighteenth centuries. Externally, the long cruciform three-aisled basilica has a ridge turret above the crossing as the only decoration. The lavish baroque altars with twisted columns are of artistic merit. Apart from peering through the wrought-iron grille, one must summon the custodian (bell-push nearby) to inspect the interior of the church. The abbey buildings are worth seeing too. The cloisters date from about 1230, the chapterhouse is twelfth century and has late Romanesque rib vaulting on four columns. The Josephsaal dates from 1727.

The picturesque road continues along the east bank of the river past the village of Hohefeld and in about 5 miles (8km) reaches **Gamburg** where there is an old stone bridge which enables one to cross to the twelfth-century castle on the west side. There is an old mill here as well and one may also see examples of *Bildstöcke* — posts at the wayside bearing a likeness of the Virgin or a saint. The next stop is Tauberbischofsheim, 17 miles (27km) from Wertheim, although there are several attractive villages along the way.

Tauberbischofsheim is not a big place and nearly everything of interest is in the compact old town with its extensive pedestrian zone within a ring road, adjacent to which are several spacious free car parks. It is not worth the hassle of trying to park in the narrow streets.

The history of Tauberbischofsheim goes back to the year 735 when the first German nunnery was founded here by St Lioba, a relative of St Bonifatius. Both of these saints have churches dedicated to them here, the Liobakirche at the end of the Marktplatz being that formerly associated with the *Kloster*. It was considerably enlarged in the baroque style in 1735. The church of St Bonifatius is east of the town beyond the river Tauber and is a modern building. The Catholic parish church of St Martin is an impressive structure dominating the town centre. It was built between 1910 and 1914 and is considered to be one of the best examples of neo-Gothic architecture. The 226ft (69m) high tower and many of the valuable relics within are, however, from the previous church on the site. The bells are of various ages, the oldest having been cast about 1380 and the newest — the Liobaglocke — in 1953. The high altar was created in traditional style during the years 1915-32 by one Professor Thomas Buscher, one of five brothers, who were all sculptors. The pulpit from around 1700 came from the old church as did several side altars. The late Gothic Marienaltar is the pride of St Martin's and came from the School of Riemenschneider, if not from the great man himself. The Kreuzaltar nearby, for centuries housed two of the finest works of the artist Matthias Grünewald, *Christ on the Cross* and *Christ Carrying the Cross*. In 1882 these paintings were sold to the Kassel Gallery for 2,000 gold Marks but 6 years later at the behest of the church authorities were bought back for 7,000. In 1900 they were sold again, this time to the Baden Art Gallery for 40,000 Marks. Today they are to be seen in the Hall of Art in Karlsruhe, their place in Tauberbischofsheim having been occupied by acceptable copies of the originals.

At the north end of the *Marktplatz* the *Rathaus* (1865) is another building in neo-Gothic style. The former *Schloss* of the electors of

*A modern fountain in
Tauberbischofsheim*

Mainz now houses the Tauberfränkisches Landschaftsmuseum, a treasure-chest of exhibits for those with an interest in the history of landscape, domestic life, dress and culture. The *Schloss* was originally built around 1250 but most of the present building is from the fifteenth and sixteenth centuries. Nearby are the remains of the one surviving watchtower from the thirteenth-century town fortifications. Originally there were twenty-one of them but the rest of these and the walls were finally demolished in 1812. The first weekend in July sees the medieval town centre, with its numerous picturesque timbered houses, hosting the annual Altstadtfest, a general merry-making, dancing in the streets sort of festival facilitated by the spacious traffic-free areas. The second or third weekend in October is the time for the Martini-Messe (Festival of St Martin) in which some religious activity is combined with the annual Winzerfest (Vintage Festival), for since 1935 Tauberbischofsheim has again been a centre of the wine industry after some years of neglect.

In and around Tauberbischofsheim there is ample accommodation and leisure activities. This is one of the overnight stops on a 3-

Tauberbischofsheim

day cycle ramble between Wertheim and Rothenburg. Although the cycle route closely follows the river Tauber it is almost entirely along little-used rural roads, agricultural roads, etc, most of which although surfaced are barred to normal motor traffic. The cycle way is marked by a sign depicting a bicycle above the words *Liebliches Taubertal*, a tourist route which is equally available to walkers.

The motorist must now join *Bundesstrasse* B290 which is designated the Romantische Strasse. This 'Romantic Road' is one of Germany's many named routes and runs from Würzburg in the north to the Alps close to the Austrian border 199 miles (320km) away to the south. After 10½ miles (17km) is **Bad Mergentheim**, a very pleasant spa with many activities and sights of interest. Unlike some spas, Mergentheim is a place for the general holidaymaker just as much as for the person coming for health reasons. The leisure centre Solymar caters especially for water activities; there is a *Wellenbad* (pool with artificial waves), a mineral spring pool and a heated open-air pool. Those not wishing to participate can watch from the bar or restau-

A pause on the Liebliches Taubertal *cycle route*

rant. In the town centre, the massive Deutschordensschloss (a castle of the Teutonic Order) houses the museum of the order but is not otherwise of outstanding interest except for its now Protestant church with its gigantic ceiling frescoes. The Catholic *Münster* of St John was built in 1250-70 by the knights of St John of Jerusalem and taken over by the Teutonic Order in 1554.

The fine *Rathaus* stands in the centre of the *Marktplatz* which is surrounded by many well-preserved ancient buildings. The 'historic' post-box on the *Rathaus* wall — there is another between here and the *Schloss* — is not, apparently, a genuine antique. According to the German Post Office authorities, these boxes have been manufactured to resemble the Württemberg town letter boxes of 1877 but are not an exact copy. Just off the *Marktplatz* is the Auto-Mobil-Museum with an interesting collection which includes several old racing cars, saloons, motor-cycles and many pictures and souvenirs of famous international racing drivers. In addition to irregular concerts, theatrical productions and so on, Bad Mergentheim has a calendar of regular events which includes the departure of the Teutonic Order Company and the historic Rifle Corps (both in April) and the re-entry of the latter in October, a veteran car rally (May), the festival 'Around the Town Hall' (June), Catholic and Protestant church festival (June to July), citizens' and folk festivals (July and August) and a Christmas market in December. In nearby Markelsheim the wine festival is

*The former railway
station at Dörzbach*

the first weekend after Whitsun and Herbsthausen has its *Bockbier* (strong Bavarian beer) festival the first weekend after Ascension.

About 4 miles (6km) south of Bad Mergentheim on the B19 in the parish church (1607) of the village of **Stuppach** is the so-called *Stuppach Madonna* by Matthias Grünewald, painted 1517-19 and one of the most important works of old German painting. Also to the south of Bad Mergentheim but on the B290, is the excellent *Wildpark* with many animals in natural surroundings together with a comprehensive animal museum. Falcons and other birds of prey are allowed to fly freely twice daily between 1 May and the latter half of September, but if these demonstrations are missed, there is a continuous television presentation in the museum. Also twice daily one may see the feeding of the zoo's baby bears and thereafter of the wolves which emerge from the dim recesses of their large wooded enclosure to devour enormous quantities of meat. The wolves here constitute the largest pack in Europe. Both the *Madonna* and the *Wildpark* are well signed from the town centre.

Weikersheim

The Romantische Strasse and the visitor's route now turn generally eastwards to follow the Tauber, leaving Mergentheim on the B19 (direction Würzburg) but shortly turning off right (sign-posted Rothenburg) past Igersheim and Markelsheim vineyard nature trail along a broad valley with extensive vineyards right down to the roadside. About 6 miles (10km) further on the health resort of **Weikersheim** is reached and must be considered an essential stop for the visitor. This is the last place in the lower end of the Taubertal directly accessible by train. The outstanding sight here is the Renaissance *Schloss* with its brilliant interior. The most important room is the Rittersaal which reflects the hunting passion of Count Wolfgang von Hohenlohe for whom it was built. Many other furnished rooms are to be seen, but this can only be done on a conducted tour which is included in the admission price. The commentary is in German but an English language guide book is available.

The *Schlosspark* was laid out from 1709 onwards and is one of the finest baroque gardens in Germany. There are colourful flower beds, a pond, an orangery and many grotesque and amusing statues. From June to September concerts or operas are given in the *Schloss* or its courtyard by the Musical Youth of Germany. The nearby Haus der Musik (Music School) was opened in 1981. There is a pleasant town centre with many historic buildings and each year on Christmas Eve there is traditional carol singing in the illuminated *Marktplatz* in front of the town church. On New Year's Day a concert is followed by a festive supper; on the second Sunday in May (Mothers' Day) there is spring music in the *Marktplatz*. The first Sunday in September is dedicated to the Weikersheimer Kärwe, a traditional folk festival with an historic procession. In the *Marktplatz* the Tauberländer Dorfmuseum has a large collection devoted to village culture in the area. There is accommodation of all types in Weikersheim. Prices are generally moderate and especially good value is obtainable in the many private houses which have a few rooms set aside for guests. There is an indoor pool in the town and a heated outdoor one in very attractive surroundings in the village of Neubronn a few kilometres away. Also just outside the town above the village of **Laudenbach** is the Bergkirche, a pilgrimage church dating from 1412. This charming building impressed the poet Eduard Mörike so much that he dedicated a poem to it.

Leaving Weikersheim Bavaria is soon reached. **Tauberrettersheim** lies on the far bank of the Tauber and to reach it one must cross the bridge of 1733 built by Balthasar Neumann (1687-1753), the distinguished engineer and architect from Würzburg. On the bridge there is a statue of St Johann Nepomuk, the patron saint of bridges, who is often encountered in this area. Tauberrettersheim has its wine festival early in May and this is followed by Wine Week in **Röttingen**, a little town a few kilometres further along the road. For about 4 weeks in July and August the town is again a hive of activity for there is a theatre festival here which attracts its audience from a wide area. The baroque *Rathaus* presides over the small *Marktplatz* presenting a fairly unspoiled medieval scene and there is a small historical exhibition in the *Rathaus* lobby. The old town wall has seven towers and the new bridge over the Tauber is once again under the eye of Nepomuk. There is an archaeological trail and a rather surprising one with the theme of sundials which are found in considerable numbers around here.

Only a few minutes are needed to reach **Bieberehren** and the last of the vineyards. Turn off the main road here and cross the river to the foot of the Kreuzberg, a modest hill surmounted by a chapel to which the approach from the roadside — 274 steps — is flanked by the Stations of the Cross in a series of very detailed reliefs. From the chapel there is an extensive view eastwards over the valley. Back on the Romantische Strasse the visitor soon passes through the village of **Klingen** and upon crossing the Tauber re-enters Baden-Württemberg to arrive in a few more minutes in **Creglingen**, an attractive town lying mostly aside from the main road with ample free parking.

The carved wooden altar in the Herrgottskirche, Creglingen

This is a central location in the upper Taubertal and makes a fine base for exploring the area . This is one of the places where the *Verkehrsamt* is happy to arrange accommodation for visitors.

The principal attraction in the town is the Herrgottskirche

(Church of the Lord God) which contains what is regarded as Tilman Riemenschneider's finest wood carving, the altar of the Virgin Mary. Riemenschneider (1460-1531) was a modest citizen of Würzburg who worked hard at his trade, producing altarpieces, sepulchres, reliefs and statues for churches and dignitaries. While running his business he also helped to run the city serving variously as councillor, judge, tax-collector, head of local defence and finally *Bürgermeister* (mayor), the highest civic post. In 1525 his peace and prosperity were shattered when the Peasants' Revolt against the ruling princes erupted across Germany. Riemenschneider stood firm with other councillors in refusing to send troops to quell the uprising but the revolt failed and he was imprisoned. Eventually released, he died 6 years later at the age of 71. Many of his works are now collected in a gallery in the Mainfränkisches Museum in Würzburg. No other artist has been able to portray with such feeling and accuracy the features of man: the title 'Master Carver of the Middle Ages' is certainly well-deserved.

The triptych in Creglingen was probably created in the period 1505-10 and was designed specifically for this little church. The wooden part surmounts the stone altar to give a total height of 36ft (11m) and it is about 13ft (4m) wide. The work depicts the Assumption of the Blessed Virgin and the various scenes are carved in the most intricate detail. The light limewood is unpainted giving a specially soft and warm effect and contrasting well with the reddish hue of the pinewood frame. The church itself dates from 1389; it became a place of pilgrimage and by 1500 sufficient funds were available to have the interior adorned with various art treasures including the altar already mentioned. In 1530 the church became a Protestant one and the Riemenschneider masterpiece was closed up and only re-opened in 1832. Across the road from the church is the unique Fingerhutmuseum, a collection of thimbles from all over the world and from Roman times until this day.

Creglingen's pleasant little heated *Freibad* is in the village of **Freudenbach** about 4 miles (6km) east and open-air bathing is also possible in the artificial lake near the camp site at Münster 2 miles (4km) to the south. Those staying in this area should not fail to obtain from the tourist office the *Urlaubspass* (visitor's pass) for which there is a nominal charge and which allows reduced entrance fees for museums, swimming pools, cycle hire, minigolf, tennis and so on in the towns of Creglingen, Weikersheim, Röttingen and Niederstetten, a resort about 6 miles (10km) south of Weikersheim. The *Schloss* in **Niederstetten** is the home of a hunting museum and of the

Archshofen

Albert-Sammt-Zeppelin-Museum which has many exhibits, photographs, etc concerning the history of the Zeppelins. It is named after Albert Sammt, the last German airship captain, who died in 1982.

The popularity of cycling in the Taubertal has already been mentioned and Creglingen is a good centre for this with cycle hire facilities in the town and a leaflet of useful suggestions from the tourist office. Many hosts can provide cycles for their guests at no extra charge. Obviously a car is an asset in this area but travellers by public transport can reach Creglingen by bus from the railheads at Weikersheim or Ochsenfurt. The river Tauber is popular with anglers — the trout and other fish seem almost to be jostling for space in the shallow water.

Modest excursions from the town include the Fire Brigades Museum (housed in a former Renaissance *Wasserschloss*) at **Waldmannshofen** about 6 miles (10km) to the north and 2 miles (3km) beyond there is the little Bavarian town of **Aub** where the parish church has a crucifixion group by Riemenschneider. The 1482 *Rathaus* there overlooks the pleasant little square which has a notable baroque pillar bearing a gilded figure of the Virgin Mary. Outside the nearby village of **Burgerroth** is a chapel dedicated to St Kunigunde dating from about 1200 and in the churchyard is a lime tree reputed to be 1,000 years old. Unfortunately the chapel, which is in an isolated position, has suffered from vandalism and if one desires to see the interior the key must be obtained in the village. About 3 miles (5km) north-east of Creglingen in the village of **Frauental** one can find the former *Klosterkirche* founded by the Cistercian order in 1232. The church, which now serves as the Protestant church for the area, is well worth seeing. Just outside Frauental at the farm called Fuchshof, is an interesting collection of old farming implements, fittings and furnishings which may be seen by prior arrangement. The tourist information office in Creglingen will assist if necessary.

There are endless rambling possibilities and numerous car parks in the countryside with marked circular walks. The 1:25,000 map *Oberes Taubertal* enables routes to be selecte,d but the following easy ramble of about 7 miles (11km) may be regarded as typical.

Go southwards from Creglingen along the west side of the little stream called Herrgottsbach (waymarked by a blue rectangle) and after half a mile (1km), turn sharp left past the Kohlesmühle (Thimble Museum) to reach the main road near the Herrgottskirche. Turning right, continue to follow this for 500yd (457m). Turn right to re-cross the stream and resume the southerly direction along the west bank for a mile until **Münster** is reached. The meals at the Gasthaus Zur Traube near the church can be recommended. Following the way-marks, cross the stream and carry on to the far end of the village. Continue along the road close to the stream for about 500yd (457m) if it is desired to visit the camp site and bathing facilities mentioned. Otherwise turn sharp left to an almost due north direction and climb fairly steeply out of the valley on a minor road for about half a mile (1km). Turn sharp right reversing direction and continue to climb. Gradually this very minor road curves left to assume a roughly easterly direction towards **Archshofen**. Soon one is on the ridge between the valley in which Münster lies and the Taubertal. The road is called Archshofer Weg but there is no need to identify it. Once on the ridge the water tower in the village of **Schön** on the far side of the Taubertal will be visible and can be used as a point for which to aim. There are no waymarks between Münster and Archshofen which is a distance of about $2\frac{1}{2}$ miles (4km), but by whatever road or track, one will eventually join a more important road to drop down steeply into Archshofen. About 250yd (229m) past the first houses note the signs where the *Liebliches Taubertal* cycle route crosses the road, turn left and follow this back to Creglingen about 2 miles (3km) away.

Again leaving Creglingen, travel either along the Romantische Strasse, a picturesque and fairly quiet road or, if cycling or walking, along the designated route on the south side of the river. After about $2\frac{1}{2}$ miles (4km), just past the village of **Archshofen** a turning off the

The 1,000-year-old church of St Peter and St Paul in Detwang

main road leads steeply up the valley side to a splendid viewpoint, the *Panoramablick*. A round walk is marked from the nearby parking space. The road leads on through Schön to the village of Freudenbach for the swimming pool mentioned previously. The riverside road continues through the villages of **Tauberzell** and **Tauberschecken-bach**. In the latter a bridge over the now quite small river enables a visit to be made to the Flax Museum in **Burgstall** about half a mile (1km) to the west. Prior arrangements are necessary — see Further Information at the end of this chapter.

Shortly before the road climbs out of the valley to the historic town of Rothenburg, a stop should be made in the village of **Det-wang**. The little church of St Peter and St Paul was founded here in 968. It belonged to the Neumünster monastery in Würzburg until 1258 when it was taken over by the Teutonic Order and when the order was dissolved in 1544, it became the Lutheran parish church. Romanesque elements in the architecture date from 1200-50 and Gothic ones from the fourteenth century. Baroque elements were added later; the gallery with its balustrade decorated with garlands of flowers in about 1650, the painted font in 1720 and the inlaid and gilded pulpit in 1723. There are many treasures in the church but the outstanding work is Tilman Riemenschneider's altarpiece of the Holy Cross. It was originally made for St Michael's Chapel in Rothenburg in 1508 and was moved to Detwang in 1653. It is one of the great master's finest works and time is needed to absorb every detail of the carving. The lifelike faces and hands of the figures depicted are quite remarkable.

A description of **Rothenburg** would not be appropriate in the present volume for it is one of the most popular places on the tourist trail. This is by no means an undeserved honour for it is a really lovely town and if the reader is not already familiar with it, then a visit should certainly be paid, preferably in an evening when the hundreds of coach-borne visitors will have departed, or at a quiet time in spring or autumn when there is peace to enjoy the old place.

Further Information
— The Tauber Valley —

Cycling and Cycle Hire

From April to October cycles may be hired at the DB stations at Bad Mergentheim, Lauda, Rothenburg, Weikersheim and Wertheim. Cyclists arriving by train pay only half the normal hire charges. Cycles may also be hired in Tauberbischofsheim and Creglingen (addresses from local tourist information offices). A selection of cycling holiday suggestions is available from Tauberbischofsheim tourist office.

Places to Visit

Bad Mergentheim
Deutschordensmuseum
Schloss
97980 Bad Mergentheim
☎ (07931) 57209
Open: Saturday, Sunday and holidays all year, also March-October Tuesday-Friday, 10am-12noon, 2.30-5.30pm. Closed 24 December to 5 January. Rooms furnished in baroque, rococo and classical styles housed in the palace of the Teutonic Order.

Wildpark
97980 Bad Mergentheim
☎ (07931) 41344
Situated on B290 south of town. Open: daily from around Easter until about end of October depending on weather.
Extensive zoo with many animals in natural surroundings. Free-flying birds of prey, baby bears, large wolf pack, animal museum. Restaurant. Children's amusements. Free parking.

Bronnbach
St Maria
☎ (09341) 820
Open: Easter-October with daily 9.30am-12noon, 2-5pm. At other times tours by prior arrangement.
Former Cistercian abbey church. Baroque interior from seventeenth to eighteenth centuries. Fine choir-stalls. Gothic-Romanesque cloisters.

Creglingen
Herrgottskirche
Half a mile (1km) from town centre. Open: April-October daily 8am-6pm,

November-March, Tuesday-Sunday
10am-12noon, 1-4pm. (20 December to
end of February afternoons only, closed
24, 25, 31 December.) Admission
charge.
Noted for its fine works of art, especially St Mary's Altar by Riemenschneider.

Flachsbrechhüttenmuseum
Burgstall
97993 Creglingen
☎ (09865) 643
Situated mid-way between Creglingen
and Rothenburg.
Open: throughout the year. Guided
tours by prior arrangement with Herr
Beck at above number or contact
Creglingen tourist office.
The story of flax-growing and prepara-
tion.

Bäuerliches Museum
Fuchshof
97993 Creglingen-Frauental
☎ (07933) 572
4 miles (6km) north-east of Creglingen.
Open: throughout the year. Guided
tours by prior arrangement with Herr
Fuchs. Old farming implements and
furnishings, etc.

Feuerwehrmuseum
Waldmannshofen
97993 Creglingen
☎ (07931) 45959
Six miles (10km) north of Creglingen.
Open: daily Easter to October 10am-
12noon, 2-4pm and at other times by
prior arrangement.
Comprehensive display of fire-fighting
equipment, etc housed in former
Renaissance moated palace.

Fingerhutmuseum
97993 Creglingen
☎ (07933) 370
Opposite the Herrgottskirche.
Open: April to October daily 9am-6pm
and November to March daily 10am-
12noon 1-4pm.
Thimbles from all over the world
dating from Roman times to present
day.

Detwang
St Peter and St Paul
☎ (09861) 3113
Open: daily April-October 8.30am-
12noon, 1.30-5pm (6pm June to mid-
September). November-March 10am-
12noon, 2-4pm. Closed on Monday in
winter. Admission charge.
Many fine works of art, in particular
the altarpiece of the Holy Cross by
Riemenschneider.

Langenburg
Schloss Mit Deutschem Museum
74595 Langenburg
☎ (07905) 264
16 miles (25km) south of Bad
Mergentheim, 13 miles (20km) south-
west of Niederstetten.
Open: Easter to mid-October daily
8.30am-12noon, 1.30-6pm.
Automuseum only: November-Easter,
Sunday and holidays 1.30-5pm.
Large castle complex with interior
showing development of furnishings,
etc from Renaissance to nineteenth
century. Motor museum with collection
of seventy vehicles including historic
racing cars.

Lauda
Heimatmuseum
97922 Lauda-Königshofen
☎ (09343) 4517
Situated in Lauda between Tauberbischofsheim and Bad Mergentheim.
Open: April to October, Sunday and
holidays 3-5pm and at other times by
prior arrangement.
Guild and workrooms, agriculture and
wine-growing in the Tauber valley.
Housed in the birthplace of the re-
former of Franconian agriculture, Dr
P.A. Ulrich.

Niederstetten
*Jagdmuseum and Albert-Sammt-Zeppelin-
   Museum*
Schloss
97996 Niederstetten
☎ (07932) 205

Open: April-October, Saturday and
Sunday 10am-12noon, 2-5.30pm.
Parties of ten or more at other times by
prior arrangement.
General hunting museum with trophies
from home and abroad and the history
of the Zeppelins with many objects of
interest, photographs, etc.

Röttingen
Rathaus
97285 Röttingen
☎ (09338) 200 or 8181
In town hall facing the market place.
Open: during business hours.
Collection of old furniture, Franconian
costumes, guild treasures and flags,
weapons, etc. Sundial exhibition.

Stuppach
Parish Church
☎ (07931) 2605
Four miles (6km) south of Bad Mergen-
theim on B19.
Famed for its *Madonna* by Matthias
Grünewald painted 1517-19.
Open: daily April-October 8.30am-
5.30pm, November 9.30am-4pm,
December-February 11am-4pm, March
10.30am-4.30pm. Admission charge
includes explanatory talk in German.

Tauberbischofsheim
Landschaftsmuseum
Im Kurmainzischen Schloss
97941 Tauberbischofsheim
☎ (09341) 2036 or 3377
Open: Easter to October, Tuesday-
Saturday 2.30-4.30pm, Sunday and
holidays 10am-12noon, 2.30-4.30pm.
Varied collection of sacred art, furniture of Renaissance, baroque, etc
periods, rural costumes, household
implements, tools, etc.

Weikersheim
Tauberländer Dorfmuseum
97990 Weikersheim
☎ (07934) 8320
Open: April to mid-November Tuesday-Sunday 10am-12noon, 2-5pm.

Special arrangements can be made for
parties of ten or more. Biggest collection of Franconian village culture in the
Tauber area.

Schloss Weikersheim
97990 Weikersheim
☎ (07934) 8364
Open: guided tours daily April-October
9am-6pm, November-March 10am-
12noon, 1.30-4.30pm.
Mighty Renaissance palace from
around 1600; splendid baroque garden.
Entry to grounds only also possible.

Wertheim
Burg
Ruins of twelfth-century castle com-
plex. No admission charge.

*Historisches Museum für Stadt und
Grafschaft*
Mühlenstrasse 26
97877 Wertheim
☎ (09342) 301155/6
Open: Tuesday to Friday 10am-12noon,
2-4pm, Saturday and Sunday and
holidays 2-4pm.
History of the counts of Wertheim, the
fishing guilds, folk customs (costumes
and ceramics), sacred art, furniture, etc.

Wertheimer Glasmuseum
Mühlenstrasse 24
97877 Wertheim
☎ (09342) 6866
Open: April-October Tuesday-Sunday
10am-12noon, 2-4pm. Entry free.
Special Christmas exhibition between
first Sunday in Advent and 7 January.
Glass technology from ancient Egypt to
the present day.

Tierfreigehege
On the Karlsberg.
Deer, wild boars, etc in pleasant park
surroundings above the town. Baroque
country seat (1725-42) of Count Carl
Ludwig.
Forestry museum open April to mid-
November Sunday 2-5pm.

Tourist Information Offices

Bad Mergentheim
Städtisches Kultur- und
Verkehrsamt
97980 Bad Mergentheim
☎ (07931) 57135

Creglingen
Städtisches Verkehrsamt
97993 Creglingen
☎ (07933) 631 and 70-111.
Outside office hours
(09335) 300.

Niederstetten
Stadtverwaltung
97996 Niederstetten
☎ (07932) 534

Rothenburg
Kultur- und Verkehrsamt
91541 Rothenburg ob der
 Tauber
☎ (09861) 40492

Röttingen
Verkehrsamt
97285 Röttingen
☎ (09338) 200 or 8181

Tauberbischofsheim
Gebietsgemeinschaft
 'Liebliches Taubertal'
Postfach 1254
97941
Tauberbischofsheim
☎ (09341) 82-0

Weikersheim
Kultur- und Verkehrsamt
97990 Weikersheim
☎ (07934) 10255

Wertheim
Fremdenverkehrsgesellschaft
 'Romantisches Wertheim
 mbH'
Postfach 1242
97877 Wertheim
☎ (09342) 1066

8 • The Bayerischer Wald

The Bayerischer Wald, an area of outstanding natural beauty, lies at the most south-easterly corner of the Federal Republic of Germany and still retains an aura of old world courtesy and dignity. Tourism, with all its bustle and commercialism, is only just beginning to appear and for that reason alone the area must appeal to those who still prefer a get-away-from-it-all type of holiday.

It has two natural boundaries; to the south is the river Danube as it flows eastwards from Regensburg to Passau, while on its eastern flank lies the border with the Czech Republic. The land lying between these two boundaries is part of the old Bohemian Forest that covered so much of Bohemia up to the last century. Bohemia was famous for its manufacture of glass and this tradition is still found in the Bayerischer Wald with Zwiesel as the main distribution centre.

Industry is only found along the Danube valley and is not an intrusion on the countryside. The economy is otherwise supported by agriculture, forestry and the newly found tourism. Each village and town is fiercely independent with a pride in its local history, as evidenced by festivals, museums and folk evenings. Most resorts are small but visitors will find accommodation with modern comforts, while food is of an excellent quality and well prepared.

The 'House of the Guest' is an institution unique to Germany and offers assistance and information to visitors. Some provide reading rooms containing the German national newspapers as well as local ones. In resorts such as Garmisch-Partenkirchen, Bad Reichenhall and Berchtesgaden, foreign newspapers may be available as well. A television room is also fairly common. Unfortunately not all resorts offer this facility but each year more are added.

The air here is reputedly some of the cleanest and finest in Europe, mainly due no doubt to the lack of pollution. Nearly all the brochures offer their town as one with a *Luftkur* (air cure) even if they have no medicinal waters to use as a bath or drinking therapy. Health in Germany is not taken for granted and each year many take a cure of some sort for two or three weeks, some of which is paid for by

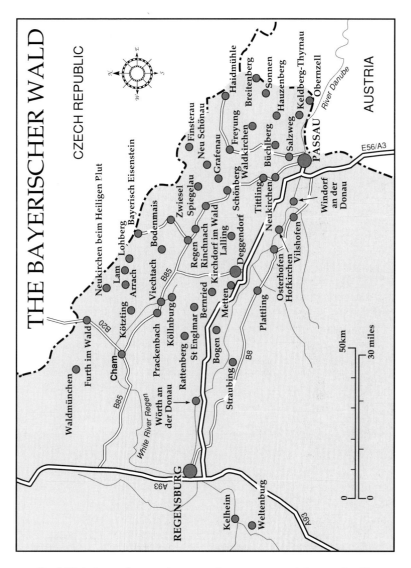

medical. This large demand means that to attract visitors who like to combine therapy with a holiday, resorts advertise the health benefits they can offer, ranging from the non-polluted air to the sophisticated treatments of sulphurous springs and vapours to mud baths, mineral waters and whirlpools.

Why then is the Bayerischer Wald not so well known as it might be? The answer is probably twofold. The first is transport, as it does not have an international airport but has to rely on Nuremberg and

Munich with onward travel by either train or coach. The Deutsche Bundesbahn (German Railways) run a fairly comprehensive network over much of the area but it is true that sometimes journeys have to be finished by either bus or taxi, although quite a few hotels will organise this for the visitor. Having arrived, getting around presents no problem as every village has organised excursions as well as regular local bus services. For the private motorist there is the *Autobahn* which runs right through to Passau, and will join up with the Austrian *Autobahn* direct to Vienna.

The second factor may be because the people did not realise that there was scope for exploring further afield, a fairly valid reason until a few years ago whenthe Czech Republic lifted its restrictions, and it is now possible to undertake day excursions to Prague. Anyone wishing to make this particular excursion should contact the local tourist office and ask for particulars well in advance as one requirement is that a form be filled in at least a week before the proposed date of travel together with a valid photograph. Other excursion destinations, to name but a few, range from Regensburg and Passau to Nuremberg, Munich and Salzburg.

Sporting facilities throughout the Bayerischer Wald are excellent with the emphasis definitely on water sports, tennis and riding. Walking however is the number one attraction whether it be from one village to the next, through woods or across open fields, to ascending the Grosser Arber the highest mountain hereabouts at 4,780ft (1,457m), or exploring the National Park covering 300sq miles (788sq km), with its wildlife reserve and forests.

The National Park issues a brochure called *Der Goldene Steig*, once the historic salt trade routes but now a network of marked walks, which shows the four main routes ranging from 7 to 19 miles (11 to 31km) in length. The two longest trails lead right to the frontier where they connect with routes on the other side but unless one is a practised long distance walker it is advisable not to try to continue.

The Prachatitzer Weg runs from Röhrnbach via Waldkirchen, Schiefweg, Böhmzwiesel, Fürholz, Grainet, Bischofsreuth and on to the border, a distance of 17 miles (27km).

The Bergreichensteiner Weg runs from Freyung via Kreuzberg, Mauth to Finsterau and the frontier, a distance of 19 miles (31km).

The Winterberger Steig runs from Hinterschmiding via Herzogsreut to Philippsreuth a distance of 14 miles (23km).

The Gulden Strass runs from Grafenau via St Oswald, Waldhäuser to Lusen, a mere 7 miles (11km).

For long distance walking either boots or stout walking shoes are advisable although all the above mentioned routes are by way of minor roads or good paths with wayside halts providing benches and tables while on the longer routes there are huts for shelter. The rolling countryside is adorned with small villages and ancient castles, some of which are only ruins but often the setting for historical plays or pageants which abound here. The most famous and colourful of all is probably the Drachenstich (Dragon Sticking Festival) at Furth im Wald.

The churches in the rural parts of the Bavarian Forest are on the whole small and without the rich paintings and stucco work found elsewhere in Bavaria. In the seventeenth and eighteenth centuries when most of this work was carried out the area was sparsely populated and most definitely off the beaten track to the more famous artists. However this in no way detracts from the many delightful interiors by local artists. For example it is impossible but to admire the wonderfully carved 'Fisher of Men' pulpit at Weissenregen on the outskirts of Kötzting.

Although the area is small it has two of the finest and loveliest cities in the whole of Germany in Regensburg and Passau. Both owe much of their delightful architecture to the Italian influence through trading with the Venetian merchants in the Middle Ages. The cathedral at Regensburg is undoubtedly a Gothic masterpiece and the organ in the cathedral at Passau the largest in the world.

The Danube Valley

Regensburg and Passau

The historic town of **Regensburg** is the gateway to the Bavarian Forest and is therefore a natural starting point, especially as it is also the capital of East Bavaria.

This gracious city, whose history goes back as far as the Stone Age, offers its visitors one of the warmest welcomes to be found anywhere in the whole of Germany. In Celtic times (500BC) it was called *Radasbona* , then came the Romans who built a fortified camp and renamed it *Castra Regina*. The settlement had four gates and above one was placed a 26ft (8m) stone slab in 179 to commemorate the fortification. This historical monument is now on view in the town museum and part of the massive walls erected during the Roman occupation can still be seen at the Porta Praetoria.

Regensburg attained its greatest fame during the Middle Ages, which is why the *Altstadt* (Old Town) is so important for it is here that the real heart and soul still flourishes, as it did centuries ago amid the gracious buildings erected during this period.

The cathedral of St Peter is one of the few Gothic cathedrals to be found in Germany and by any standards is a masterpiece. Even from the motorway that bypasses the city it still dominates the surrounding countryside. It was built in 1275 on the site of a previous building of which the Eselsturm (Donkey's Tower) still remains, but its twin towers and west façade were added during the fifteenth century. The baroque high altar, Gothic side altars and superb stained glass windows are just some of the fine features of the beautiful interior.

The Alter Kornmarkt stands on what was the inner fortification in 200 and is the setting for the Ducal Court, the Roman Tower and St Ulrich's Church. The Ducal Court, in Carolingian times known as the Herzogshof, was one of the most important palaces in southern Germany under Charlemagne. The timbered ceiling of the Romanesque Great Hall is adorned with coats of arms.

The Roman Tower still contains some of the original masonry in the 12ft (4m) thick walls which form the base. Its original function was that of a keep; later it became the treasury and could only be reached by an enclosed bridge linking it to the palace. St Ulrich's Church dates from the early thirteenth century and has recently been restored and now house the diocesan museum.

The Alte Kapelle is the oldest church in the city as its foundations date back to the Carolingian period but its fame dates from 1000 when it was restored to full glory. Additions and alterations were made in the thirteenth and fifteenth centuries. The detached bell tower was constructed with Roman blocks of stone. The interior is rococo with the high altar and golden triumphal arch flanked by statues of Henry II and his wife Kunigunde as patrons of the church. In the tiny Chapel of Grace there is an icon of the Virgin Mary reputedly given to Henry II by the pope in 1014 and is set in an exquisite frame made of silver gilt and embellished with precious stones. The painting unfortunately is now known to be of the thirteenth century and because it was painted in a Byzantine style, the legend maybe destroyed, but the beauty remains.

The Niedermünster Church was once a convent but in 1806 became the cathedral's parish church and while renovations to the cathedral were in progress the Domspatzen (Cathedral Sparrows) were heard. They are the Regensburg equivalent to the Vienna Boys Choir and have the same excellence of quality.

The *Altes Rathaus* in the Kohlenmarkt was built between the fourteenth and sixteenth centuries. The main entrance is reached by a flight of well worn stone steps. The door itself is a massive wooden one black with age and embedded in the masonry, by its side, are the

St Peter's Cathedral and Steinerne Brücke (Stone Bridge)
across the river Danube, Regensburg

old iron rods which were the official measures used to settle disputes. The Reichssaal (Imperial Hall) has a beautiful timbered ceiling supported only by a massive central beam that is held in place by the roof framework. The ceiling is studded with 22-carat gold studs, and in the centre of the main beam is the city coat of arms. The walls are hung with Flemish tapestries from the late fifteenth or early sixteenth centuries. The Reichsaal became the home of the Imperial Diet from 1663 until the dissolution of the Holy Roman Empire in 1806.

At the far end of this long chamber and raised on a dais is the Imperial Throne, flanked by two benches covered in a red cloth on which the electors sat while the side walls have benches covered in a green cloth for the princes temporal and spiritual. The benches across the floor of the chamber were for the representatives of the Free Imperial Cities and other visiting dignitaries. Other interesting rooms to be seen are the Electors' Chamber with its single handed clock dating from 1624 and massive furniture. The Antechamber is delightful with its Renaissance panelling but in some respects the adjoining room with its deep blue ceiling and silver stars denoting secrecy is more romantic.

The dungeons house the medieval torture chambers with many of the original gruesome instruments which are on show to the visitor. Two of the well preserved rooms are the Inquisition Room and the Folterkammer Chamber where the furniture includes such items as the 'Spanish Donkey' and 'The Maiden's Chair'. Spine chilling is almost an understatement but children seem to revel in it.

One item down here not connected with torture is the old salt scales. It is very crude to look at having only two pans either side of a moving pointer, but if one piece of paper was placed on one of the pans the pointer would register.

Another feature of the old town are the patrician houses built by wealthy merchants during the thirteenth and fourteenth centuries. Some were built as towers while others were erected around court-yards but both show the influence of Venetian trading partners. Many of these noble houses have fallen into disrepair but it is the policy of the city council to renovate them for use, for example, as student residences for the university.

The Runtingerhaus was originally built in the year 1200 by the Runtinger family who were as rich and famous as the Fuggers of Augsburg. The first dwelling was built in tower form but, with increasing wealth, the family pulled down the tower and rebuilt it on a lavish scale to include a large banqueting hall. After restoration in the 1970s it has now become the home of the City Archives whose collection contains the 'Runtinger Book' a ledger which shows the family's trading from 1383-1407.

The oldest stone bridge in Germany and certainly the first to span the Danube is the Steinerne Brücke, a medieval engineering feat of the first magnitude taking only 11 years to build (1135-46). The original bridge was constructed with sixteen arches and three towers but time has seen the removal of several of the arches and two of the towers. On the parapet halfway across is the famous statue of the Bruckmandl (Little Bridge Man). The stories surrounding its origins are many but one amusing theory is that the engineer in charge of the construction made a pact with the Devil in order to complete the bridge as quickly as possible. The payment was to be that the first eight legs to cross the bridge would be handed to the Devil. The engineer honoured this bargain but instead of sending four humans across he sent a dog and two chickens.

On the waterfront at the city end of the bridge is the Historische Wurstküche (Old Sausage Kitchen) whose history is as old as that of the bridge. It was built to provide food and drink for the workmen employed on the bridge construction. Eight hundred and fifty years later it is still fulfilling the same function but the clientele is some-what different; the working man has now disappeared and tourists as well as some of the local inhabitants have taken his place. The fare provided is excellent: home made potato soup, pork sausages and *Sauerkraut* (pickled cabbage) washed down by beer brewed by the local prince. Ruling over the hot kitchen stove is the cook who provided meals every day, apart from Christmas Day when the premises are closed.

There are many interesting places to visit, mostly in the the old town. Guided walking tours are the best way of getting to know this city and are arranged by the local tourist office which is situated on the ground floor of the *Altes Rathaus*. The following are just a few of the important places that should not be missed.

Keplerstrasse is named after the famous astronomer Johannes Kepler who lived at No 2. Number 5 is now known as Kepler House for it was here that he died in 1630 and is now a museum showing his work on the Copernican theory of the solar system together with instruments and drawings that helped him in his work.

The Bischofshof (Bishop's Palace) whose foundations are the old Roman walls, was built round a central courtyard with one of the most delightful and original fountains in a land that produces so many. Called the 'Goose Sermon Fountain' the central figure is a fox dressed up as a cleric preaching to some geese. The back of the cassock is slightly open to reveal the face of the fox leering at the innocent geese. The water from the fountain spills into a trough whose sides show historical episodes connected with the palace. In summer the courtyard is an outdoor restaurant for a first class hotel.

Haidplatz is a large elegant square dominated by the Haus zum Goldenen Kreuz (House of the Golden Cross), five storeys high and surmounted by battlements and a tower. Its function from the six-teenth to the nineteenth centuries was that of an hotel where the famous and wealthy used to stay while in Regensburg. It was also the setting of a true romance when Emperor Charles V fell in love with a commoner, Barbara Blomberg, whose father was a city alderman. This alliance produced a son who later became famous in his own right as Don Juan of Austria, the victor of the naval Battle of Lepanto against the Turks in 1571 and later governor of the Netherlands. The building is no longer an hotel although a café still remains together with a violin workshop, an art gallery and a set of small boutiques, known as the Golden Cross Arcade.

The Thon-Dittmar Palace is also on Haidplatz and it originally consisted of two fourteenth-century patrician houses which were amalgamated in the early nineteenth century. Built round a central courtyard with balconies on two floors it has now become a natural open-air theatre during the summer. Shakespearian plays find much favour and figure prominantly in the season's programme. The German-American Institute is also to be found within its portals.

Schloss Thurn and Taxis is the home of the family who bear this name and who in the past were known as the postmasters of Europe through founding the first post and mail coaches back in the sixteenth century. The castle was originally St Emmeram's Monastery but after secularisation in 1808 it was taken over by the Prince of Thurn and Taxis who proceeded to turn the south wing into a turreted palace. When the family are not in residence, and they do have other homes throughout Germany, the palace is open to the public and includes the state apartments, Throne Room, Ballroom, Chamber of Mirrors and the Green and Yellow Drawing Rooms.

The Marstallmuseum housed in the indoor riding school contains a fascinating display of horse transport, from ceremonial coaches and carriages, phaetons which were used around the extensive parkland, to sleighs and sledges. Upstairs in the gallery are equestrian paintings and ornate harnesses used over the years.

Last but by no means least is the City Museum in Dachauplatz in what was a former monastery of the thirteenth century. It has over a hundred rooms on three floors which indicates the magnitude of wealth that is and was in Regensburg. The ground floor contains relics from prehistoric and Roman times and includes the foundation stone of 179 as well as a model showing boats bringing the stone up river, being unloaded and carried away to where the fortifications are being built. On the first floor are exhibits illustrating the historical development of the city while the second floor concerns art history from medieval to present day in the form of paintings, sculpture, tapestries and craft work which naturally includes glass and furniture. A series of rooms also shows the varying styles of different centuries. The third and top floor draws attention to the cultural pursuits that have been enjoyed in east Bavaria.

Regensburg is blessed by having not only the mighty Danube flowing past its walls but also because the Regen joins its larger brother. The Rhine-Main-Danube canal will bring new prosperity by opening up the navigable waterways right through the heart of central Europe. This new project can be visited by motor boat and is proving a popular pastime. It is a journey of approximately 17 miles (27km) upstream to Kelheim and is spectacular. The excursion by river takes about 2 hours but includes passing the Befreiungshalle (Hall of Freedom), a rotunda-shaped building in Greco-Roman style designed by Leo von Klenze and built in 1842 to commemorate the War of Liberation against Napoleon. Adorning this eighteen-sided

*A wayside shrine in
the Bayerischer Wald*

edifice are eighteen buttresses, each topped by a female statue holding a plaque with the name of a German tribe inscribed upon it. The
number '18' has been deliberately incorporated as a reminder that on
18 October 1813 that the Battle of Leipzig was fought and Napoleon
defeated. The interior is reminiscent of a Greek marble temple with
Valkyrian figures illuminated only by the small amount of daylight
which finds its way through the cupola high above.

Kelheim is a small town at the confluence of the Altmühl and the
Danube and is extremely picturesque with its old town gate. It has a
long and noble history for the dukes of Bavaria resided here from
around 1200. The main attraction though is undoubtedly the Benedictine monastery of Weltenburg dating back to 612 and even then
built on the site of a former Roman settlement. To reach **Weltenburg**
the Danube flows through a rocky gorge known as the Donaudurch-
bruch. Here the rugged limestone cliffs rear up to a height of 400ft,
(122m) and at the end where the river bends, stands the monastery
with its splendid baroque church built by the Asam brothers in the
early eighteenth century. Inside is St George's Altar with its larger

than life sculpture of St George attacking the dragon.

For the energetic it is extremely rewarding to take the well marked footpath from Befreiungshalle to Weltenburg as it follows the ridge close to the river (approximately an hour). The return can be made by boat in order not to miss the gorge from the river.

Downstream from Regensburg is **Donaustauf** and yet another famous landmark — Walhalla, a classical white marble temple perched high on a wooded hillside with commanding views over the winding river to the flat and fertile plains beyond. It was built on the orders of King Ludwig I of Bavaria by Leo von Klenze in 12 years and he took the Parthenon in Greece as his inspiration.

The temple (one can call it nothing else) can be reached by road or more romantically by river steamer even though it entails climbing the 366 steps leading up to the main entrance flanked by a double row of Doric columns. Inside the floor is a colourful marble mosaic. Set back against the outer walls are plinths holding marble busts of famous men and women, most of whom are German as one would expect, but there are quite a few exceptions. Outside the view is superb along the river valley. It stretches from Regensburg in the west and southwards over the vast plain known as the 'Grain Store of Bavaria', a reference to the maize that flourishes here. Another good viewing point nearby is from the ruined Romanesque castle that was once the seat of the bishops of Regensburg.

From here onwards the river winds its way past the low fertile plains to the south while on the northern shore the foothills of the Bavarian Forest begin to rise. Apart from the motorway that also runs to the north of the river there are tiny farming communities, sometimes with castles or monasteries, not all of which are inhabited for some have fallen into ruins. Minor roads lead up into the foothills and so into the hinterland of the forest itself. One such road is at Wörth an der Donau, a small community which boasts a fortified castle adorned by eight turrets. Courses in painting and sketching are among the facilities to be found here.

From Wörth the minor road leads to the small village of **Falken-stein** recommended for its views over the surrounding countryside. The village is unpretentious with its small main street, a couple of *Gasthöfe* and a few shops but the climb up through the woods to the summit for the panoramic views of vast tracts of forest interspersed with tiny communities is a reward for the long toil involved. The castle up here on the heights is, during the summer, the setting for a drama festival mainly during June and July. Falkenstein is also called the 'Pearl of the Bavarian Forest'.

Rejoining the Danube valley one can follow the river as it flows on to **Straubing** on its southern bank. Twentieth-century Straubing is a flourishing market town but it has a long and varied history. Once a Celtic and Roman settlement the old town grew up around the church of St Peter in about 1180. But the old town did not form the nucleus for expansion, and it remained outside the fortified new town which was developed in 1218. St Peter's was built in Roman-esque style although the towers were added as late as 1886. The interior has a particularly fine crucifix from 1200, but it is the burial vaults of 1486 with their Dance of Death frescoes (1763) that have become famous. In the churchyard is the chapel and tomb of Agnes Bernauer whose fame is due to the fact that she was the daughter of an Augsburg barber and because of her outstanding beauty caught the eye of the heir to the dukedom of Bavaria. Albrecht married her in 1432 against the wishes of his father who in turn sought to discredit his unwanted daughter-in-law by successfully accusing her of witchcraft and sorcery. The penalty was death by drowning in the Danube. Friedrich Hebbel wrote a tragedy recalling her life and death and it is now performed every 4 years in the Ducal Palace.

The so-called new town with its fortifications became the capital of an independent duchy in 1353 but lost this status in 1425 when it was incorporated into the duchy of Bavaria.

The main square in the centre of the town is the Theresienplatz notable for its fourteenth-century 200ft (61m) city tower surmounted by five pinnacles. Opposite is the Gothic town hall of 1382. Also occupying a central position in the square is the Tiburtius Fountain of 1685 and the tall graceful Trinity Column erected in 1709 to commemorate the town's liberation after a siege by Austrian troops.

There are some fine old medieval houses with high gables to be found in Ludwigsplatz and Fraunhoferstrasse. The parish church of St Jakob is fifteenth century, and its most notable feature is the high altar with valuable figures, and painted panels of 1590 from an altar in Nuremberg. The side chapel of the Maria Hilf contains some early fifteenth-century paintings. The altar and paintings in the Maria Tod Chapel are by the Asam brothers. Other churches of note are the Carmelite church, begun in 1371 but not finished until the fifteenth century, and the extremely ornate even sumptuous Ursuline church of 1738 which is again the work of the Asam brothers.

The Schloss or Ducal Palace by the bridge across the Danube was built in 1356 by Duke Albrecht I. The chapel was added during the fourteenth and fifteenth centuries and the courtyard is the venue of the Agnes Bernauer Festival.

Straubing is also a noted agricultural centre for cattle and grain, both of which have long flourished on the well irrigated land surrounding the town. Each year, during the month of August, the Gauboden Volksfest (Fertile Land Festival) takes place with its processions, singing, dancing, barbecues and vast quantities of ale to refresh the revellers. The Gauboden Museum houses a prehistoric collection together with the Römischer Schatzfund (Roman Treasure Trove) with its wonderful array of gold masks, bronze figures and armour which were only excavated in 1950. A point of interest is that a model of the medieval town of Straubing was made in 1658 by Jakob Sandtner and is now considered so important that it is in the Bavarian National Museum in Munich.

Eight miles (13km) north-east of Straubing is **Bogen,** an old established small town with a museum and a reading room for visitors to use. The Marienkirche on the Bogenberg dates from the thirteenth century and is the setting for the annual Whitsun Festival. Close by is Oberalteich a former Benedictine monastery church of 1630 with a splendid rococo interior containing a hanging staircase that leads up to the galleries.

Before reaching Deggendorf it is worth visiting **Metten** and the Benedictine monastery of St Michael whose origins date back to the eighth century when it was founded by the Emperor Charlemagne. The present church with its fine carvings and lavish baroque interior dates from only 1720. The superb entrance porch has a frescoed ceiling which is rather unusual. Above the high altar is a particularly fine painting of St Michael destroying Lucifer by C. D. Asam but even more interesting is the wonderful monastery library; a veritable work of art and Aladdin's Cave all rolled into one. The ceiling frescoes all relate to the books that can be found in the very ornate bookcases that line the walls. The equally elaborate decor of the vaulting and cornices are of marble and held up by Atlas like figures mounted on plinths. The banqueting hall continues in this ornate style with rococo stucco work while the ceiling is as fresh and vibrant as when it was painted 250 years ago. In the inner courtyard there is a fountain which is dedicated to the founder Charlemagne.

Deggendorf, a pleasant town with a delightful promenade, is at the confluence of the three rivers, namely the Regen, Isar and Danube. Trees give shade and it is from here that the river excursions call to load and unload passengers. This prime site has enabled Deggendorf to be an important town since 750, and the only one of any size on the north bank of the Danube. Naturally it is a busy commercial centre these days and the main thoroughfare, especially

Deggendorf

on weekdays when it is lined by stalls selling everything from fresh produce to clothing. Like all modern towns, Deggendorf has traffic problems and the stalls, although colourful, do not aid the flow of traffic. The Luitpoldplatz at the centre of the town has a sixteenth-century *Rathaus* incorporating the St Martin Chapel of 1296, and two charming fountains of the same era. There is a local museum containing many fine paintings, weapons, clocks, local crafts and prehistory.

The church of the Maria Himmelfahrt (Assumption) was Romanesque but destroyed by fire in 1240. The succeeding years have seen reconstruction in varying styles but something to admire on the wall of the Wasserkapelle is a relief over the door which dates from the mid-thirteenth century. At present the church is closed for interior restoration. The other noteworthy church in the town is that of the Holy Sepulchre with a Gothic nave and basilica of 1360.

Deggendorf is also the scene of several festivals which include the annual Music Week in August covering a wide range and taste in this field. July sees what is called the Deggendorfer Kaffeehaustage which recreates the old coffee house traditions. The *Volksfest* (Folk Festival) is held annually in late-July/early-August with processions, games, music, drinking and jollifications.

Across the river lies **Plattling**, a pleasant old town on the Isar and

also on the fast railway line from Passau to Munich and Nuremberg.
This provides a first class service for visitors without their own
transport. The Isar provides an excellent venue for oars-men and
during the summer rowing regattas are held there.

The Danube now flows in a more southerly direction away from
the foothills and here the Benedictine monastery of St Mauritius can
be seen. It was at its most powerful in the Middle Ages and the
foundations which are fourteenth century are all that remained after
a disastrous fire. The current building is early eighteenth century.

The river now forms a loop and on the southern bank is **Osterhofen** with the monastery church of St Margaretha in the *Alter Markt*.
The original medieval building fell into decay but in 1727 the best
artists of that period, namely J. M. Fischer and the Asam brothers,
undertook its restoration. Taking 13 years to complete, it is now
regarded as the most elaborate baroque church in Bavaria; some may
feel that it is too elaborate but that is a matter of personal choice. Let
us just say that the sheer beauty is almost overpowering!

Once again the river forms a long loop before straightening out
where the village of **Hofkirchen** on the north bank is to be found.
This peaceful rural community has an ancient but picturesque ruined castle, the Hilgartsberg, perched high above a narrower stretch
of the valley. It has had a chequered history with ownership changing hands many times but has been used since the last century as a
setting for festivals as well as a viewing platform. Hofkirchen may be
small but there is a heated open-air swimming pool and other sporting attractions, river cruises and easy access to the *Autobahn* or
alternatively train services from Vilshofen on the southern bank.
Vilshofen has grown up between the river Vils and Wolfach just as
they enter the Danube and its history goes back 1,200 years, as
witnessed by the Renaissance Tower, the baroque parish church and
the twin towers of the Benedictine Abbey of Schweiklberg. There is
a splendid new leisure centre complex with swimming pool and
medicinal salt baths. Many sporting activities are held here as well as
lessons at the flying and gliding school.

Windorf is a little old market town on the north bank of the
Danube slightly downstream from Vilshofen. Offshore it is the largest river island between Ulm and Vienna with its nature reserve
attracting many species of birds who find this a haven especially
during the nesting season. Along the banks there are over 40 miles
(64km) of marked country walks and because of its location and
proximity to Passau, Windorf has now become a summer resort with
two 'holiday villages'. **Ebersberg**, the larger of the two, is set on

The river Danube with a view of the Veste Oberhaus, Passau

rising ground and affords splendid views over the city of Passau. Each chalet contains two or four furnished apartments and within the complex is a restaurant, swimming pool, sauna, table tennis and children's playground. **Buchelberg** is both smaller and quieter, surrounded by gentle wooded hills and facilities for riding, tennis and bowling are near at hand.

Aicha vorm Wald, lying just north of the river before it reaches

Passau, is a small village surrounded by green pastures. Its origins date back to the tenth century and details together with its subsequent history can be found in the local museum housed in the moated Schloss Aicha. The village lies on the banks of the Gross Ohe river as it flows through a narrow but pretty valley, providing an ideal location for anyone wishing to find peaceful surroundings linked to an activity holiday. Accommodation is of the simple traditional variety, but it is advisable to have a car for staying here.

Passau is said by some connoisseurs, including Alexander von Humboldt, to be one of the seven most beautifully situated cities in the world. Its setting is certainly delightful with the old city being built on a spit of land that narrows to a point as the rivers Danube and Inn come together. The waters mingle to become a mosaic of blue and brown and the modest Ilz is the third river to join the tide here.

The old waterfront is lined at the narrowest point with old buildings of varying heights and colours. On the north bank of the Danube, wood covered slopes sweep up to the Veste Oberhaus, a mighty fortress dominating the skyline. It began life in the early thirteenth century in quite a small way, but succeeding generations of prince bishops added to the complex turning it into the vast domain that it is today. It has now become the home of the town museum, art gallery, Bohemian Forest Museum and Fire Brigade Museum. There is also a restaurant and observation tower here.

The old city is dominated by St Stephen's Cathedral which took 113 years to build (1407-1520). The architecture is mixed; Romanesque, Gothic and baroque are all found here. It is however the organ that attracts the vast crowds that flock each day for the concert given at noon. The seats in high summer are all taken half an hour before the concert commences and then there is only standing room left in order to listen to the wonderful instrument. With 17,000 pipes and 208 stops it is the largest church organ in the world.

Flanking the cathedral is the shady Residenzplatz on which stands the New Residence Palace of the prince bishops with a beautiful staircase leading to the state rooms which are all in an ornate rococo design. The Residence may be the largest and grandest but the other stately houses here once belonged to wealthy merchants.

There are many interesting places to visit in Passau such as the Rathaus Ratskeller (1298), the Old Residence of the prince bishops (now the Law Courts) and the Jesuit church of St Michael. Niedernburg is a former benedictine convent of the eighth century with the Maria Parz Chapel containing the tomb of the abbess Gisela, sister of the Emperor Henry II and widow of St Stephen, King of Hungary.

Hotel Wilder Mann, Passau

Passau does not live in the past. It is a modern city with first rate theatre and concert programmes and is the host city to the European Weeks Festival each year. All sports, either for watching or participating, are given first rate facilities.

The Glass Museum, Passau

The town is one of the major departure points for the short cruises to Regensburg while longer ones can go as far as the Black Sea. This would seem to be a city of perpetual movement. Large and small craft load and unload passengers from all corners of the world while every language imaginable assails the ear. All this however just seems to lend enchantment to the cosmopolitan city.

Down by the waterfront stands the Hotel Wilder Mann. Apart from being a first class hotel it is unusual that it also incorporates a unique collection of glassware which has now been established as the Passauer Glass Museum. It is also home to the suite of rooms once occupied by the Empress Elisabeth of Austria and still furnished as it was during her stay. More than 10,000 pieces of glassware are on show here, Biedermayer to Art Nouveau are displayed in over 150 show cases. All the principal glass manufacturers are represented

here with either full collections or several pieces covering the last 200 years and grouped together period by period in separate rooms. Every colour and shade of glass imaginable can be seen. Some of it is engraved, some is hand painted, some is small, and some large, but all have a story to tell. The museum is open daily and the visitor is permitted to wander at leisure. The hotel also has a rooftop café and a lift to whisk visitors up to the top floor. One of the cakes on offer here is called Sissi's Delight and it is extremely rich.

Six miles (10km) downstream from Passau is **Kellberg-Thyrnau**, noted for its clean pure air. Surrounded by meadows and gently rising hills it is an excellent centre for exploring this corner of Germany together with the adjoining countryside of Austria and the Czech Republic. The riding school here has acquired a first class reputation. Other activities include swimming, tennis and bowling and as an alternative there are well marked nature trails to delight walkers and naturalists. Concerts, folk evenings and a lending library all help to create a full programme and there is also a bus connection to Passau.

The last town in this section of the Danube valley is **Obernzell**, a market town and once the summer residence of the prince bishops of Passau who had a castle here. It is now part of the Bavarian National Museum, includes pottery for which Obernzell was once famous and is strategically placed on the banks of the Danube as the river begins to enter a gorge. There is a ferry to convey passengers to the opposite shore and a boarding point for travellers by river steamer to Austrian territory. The town itself is well laid out with an imposing market square and an eighteenth-century church with twin towers. An additional sporting facility here is the 11 mile (18km) stretch of water for skiing enthusiasts. Cycling is another popular attraction here thanks to the 30 mile (48km) long track which runs alongside the river. The local tourist office organises a weekly programme of events guaranteed to keep visitors well occupied with sporting and cultural activities. A local speciality here is the fruit wine, more associated with the Black Forest area but very welcome as an alternative to wine and beer on warm days.

Bavarian Forest

The South

From Passau the B12 road runs along the valley of the river Ilz till it reaches **Salzweg**; a small rural community that offers its visitors a warm welcome, but especially to those who are interested in flora and fauna. A river information trail with a total length of over 45 miles (72km) has been set up here in the Ilz valley enabling those interested in such things to see for themselves the unique species of flora and fauna found here. Swimming is in a dammed up section of the river while other sports on offer are tennis and shooting. A bus service from Salzweg to Passau, only 4 miles (6km) away, allows the attractions found there to be enjoyed quite conveniently.

Following the B12 northwards one reaches the fair sized village of **Hutthurm**, lying in a sunny part of this wild but romantic valley. Holidays here are simple and relaxing, spent in small private pensions and private houses where the cost can be quite inexpensive depending on the length of stay. Sports include tennis and a bowling alley, while there is swimming in the neighbouring village of Büchlberg less than a couple of miles away. However the village does offer its guests a reading room and arranges local folk evenings. There is a distinct advantage in having one's own transport here as it enables one to cover the delightful surrounding countryside without having to rely on the local bus service. The nearest railway station is 10 miles (16km) away at Passau.

East of Hutthurm is the slightly smaller **Büchlberg** on what used to be the old salt trade route known as the Golden Path, for in the Middle Ages salt was as precious as gold is today. Close to the winding river Erlau, Büchlberg is fast gaining a reputation as an ideal centre for leisure activities with its keep fit trails, riding, tennis, fishing and swimming in the heated outdoor pool. Relaxation is catered for with excursions by old stage coach and in the evenings there is music and dancing as well as special folk performances. The newly found prosperity is reflected by the medium sized hotels that have recently been built. Like Hutthurm the close proximity to Passau makes this an attractive destination.

Hauzenberg is ideal for a relaxing holiday amidst the unspoilt forested countryside which surrounds it, and is still only 13 miles (21km) from Passau to which it is connected by a regular bus service. It is very much a family resort with children warmly welcomed, both in the self-catering apartments as well as the many farms that offer accommodation and allow the children to 'help' in feeding the farm animals. Children's adventure play areas have been set up to help keep them fully occupied.

Other facilities here are a reading room, cinema, open-air chess and stage coach trips. Every year, normally in May, Hauzenberg runs cultural weeks. The school hall becomes a theatre and the new church, with its excellent acoustics, is transformed into a concert hall with seating for 800 people.

On the sporting front, both indoor and outdoor tennis, swimming and smallbore shooting are available. There is also a well organised rambling association which awards special commemorative badges to those who cover enough mileage. There is an animal museum which attracts many who come here, but without doubt the biggest attraction is the Kropfmühl Graphite Mine which is the last working mine to be found in Germany. A visit enables one to descend to the fourth floor where the mining is now carried out. Also on show is the machinery used to extract this mineral both now and in the past. Woodcarving is a local interest and courses in this subject are held.

Heading north-east from Hauzenberg and passing the small Freudensee the road reaches **Sonnen** which, true to its name, is a dear little village on a sunny plateau. As the border with the Czech Republic draws closer, one really begins to realise that nothing could be more off the beaten track and away from tourist routes. Here the local people really enjoy meeting visitors from other parts of Europe and further afield. Absent are the hotels and larger pensions and in their place stand the small traditional inns that have seen many a year, together with houses let out as apartments and a few private houses and farms. After a day spent in the open air discovering the pleasures of nature, the evening is a welcome time for relaxing over a glass of beer, watching television or making merry at a barbecue. There is a local bus service to Passau but a car is really essential.

Breitenberg is tucked into a corner where the three countries of Germany, Austria and the Czech Republic meet. It is also one of the finest and loveliest of rambling areas with the Dreisessel mountain rising to a height of 4,333ft (1,321m). Although this is real border territory the paths and trails are well marked and, providing one does not attempt to stray from them, there is no real likelihood of crossing any borders unwittingly. Additionally there are red and white marked posts driven into the ground at intervals which all add up to security for the uninitiated. Breitenberg itself is an agricultural area of which one of the crops was flax. The farmers' wives and village women used to weave it into linen and there is a museum here devoted to this cottage industry, with the old implements used in the long process needed before the material could be woven.

An open-air swimming pool with an extensive sun bathing area as well as an adventure playground all adds to the fun to be found here. Breitenberg certainly extends a home from home welcome.

Waldkirchen is roughly mid-way between Passau and the National Park on a sunny incline overlooking the pleasant rolling countryside. It is an ancient town that grew due to its position on the Goldener Steig (Golden Path) which was the old trade route between Passau and Moldau in the Czech Republic. It has developed into a thriving modern town and at one end of the main town square stands the parish church known locally as the cathedral of the Bavarian Forest because of its size and 200ft (61m) slender tower. This not only dominates Waldkirchen but acts as a landmark to those approaching it. Well laid out parks and gardens together with a wildlife park help to give the town an air of prosperity, enhanced by the addition of a 'House of the Guest' with its library and reading and television rooms. Other amenities include a museum and an art gallery.

Sporting activities are extremely well catered for with a golf course and school together with an excellent tennis centre and instruction for those wishing to perfect their game. Riding over the surrounding countryside is also another popular sport with the additional facility of an indoor school.

Waldkirchen

An interesting point regarding Waldkirchen is that the number of beds on offer in private houses and farms is equal to the number on offer in the hotels. The town is served by both a bus and train service although it is probably preferable to use the inter-city trains to Passau as the local line is slow and infrequent.

North of Waldkirchen and on the B12 road is **Freyung**, close to the National Park. On the outskirts of the town is the purpose built holiday complex, Ferienpark Geyersberg, with its modern, well equipped apartments, restaurant, two swimming pools, fitness centre, volleyball, minigolf and table tennis. Slightly smaller is the Kur- und Sporthotel Bavaria offering apartments as well as normal hotel rooms. In and around Freyung there is approximately 2,000 apartments and holiday homes with plenty of shops to cater for visitors.

Freyung has two swimming pools; the indoor one also has a sauna and solarium while the outdoor one is heated to a set temperature. As befits an old forest town there are three local museums to be found here; the one at Schloss Wolfstein deals with art over a wide range of subjects. The second is in the Schraml-Haus, the oldest building in Freyung and built mostly of wood in the year 1700. The living quarters on the first floor are reached by steep wooden steps with only a single handrail for guidance. Inside is an interesting collection of old costumes, handwork and glassware. In the *Rathaus* is a collection of old book printing as well as glass from Winterberg in the Böhmerwald which, many years ago, was one of the famed centres in these ancient crafts. The countryside surrounding the town is ideal for walking with over 75 miles (121km) of marked paths.

Haidmühle situated between the Dreisessel mountain and the National Park is surrounded by wooded slopes, many of which have marked nature trails as opposed to just paths for walking. Here the simple outdoor life can be exchanged for the modern amenity of the indoor swimming pool with the addition of a sauna and solarium. Other facilities found here include a reading room and a museum on the forest as well as the legends that surround it. During the summer visitors almost outnumber the locals mainly through the two apartment hotels and holiday homes that have sprung up here. There is both a bus and a train service to serve this border community.

The next five villages all border on to the National Park itself and it is therefore appropriate that the reader is acquainted with both its history and function before proceeding further. The Bavarian Forest is the most easterly section of the Federal Republic and part of the old Bohemian Forest that extended into the Czech Republic. The forest is estimated to be at least 10,000 years old and was the home for wildlife and the final refuge for animals, as their natural habitat was taken from them for urban development.

The Bavarian government, conscious of this natural heritage disappearing for ever, decided to establish a National Park within the forest. Secondly a nature reserve area was set up so that plants and shrubs could be studied. The forest itself was to be protected but marked paths and routes, giving information on the various trees and birds, would be available to the public in order that they might come to see, understand and appreciate their surroundings.

Not all the walks are in the wooded zone; some are over alpine pasture, upland moorland as well as rocky terrain that is found in this region. Overall there are thirty-six marked routes, each one being provided with places to rest or shelter and drinking troughs containing delicious ice cold water, as it has been taken off the mountainside. The park itself covers an area of 50sq miles (130sq km). A large car and bus park is here for which a small fee is payable but it does cover a full day's parking so is relatively inexpensive. Across the road in the modern building is the Information Centre, built on Scandinavian lines where postcards, maps and books on the park and forest may be purchased. There is also a cinema which shows an interesting film about the forest and is helpful in deciding just what to see first. This building also houses the toilets, although there are several more scattered over the park itself. The self-service restaurant is in a building between the Information Centre and the car park and has a terrace furnished with wooden tables and benches for those preferring to eat outside.

There are two areas adjacent to these buildings to demonstrate, in their natural surroundings, the animals who live or once lived in this wild part of Europe. One area which is small, recreates compactly the various conditions under which plants in the National Park live. Thus the plants of the marshes and streams can be seen only yards from plants living on the dry rocks of hilltops. A complete tour of the second section would take about 2-2½ hours depending on the speed of walking and how long is spent looking at the animals that are housed here, including lynx, bears, wolves, bison and wildboar as well as many birds. The way is at times steep and convenient benches are placed at strategic intervals for the weary.

Within the National Park are two villages, **Alt Schönau** and **Waldhäuser**. The latter consists of a few houses and farms together with the odd *Gasthof* as the steep road nears its journey's end at Martinsklause; from here one can take the summer route by foot which is rough going (boots are a must) or by the winter path which, for most part, is gravelled up to the rocky outcrop of the Lusen at 4,128ft (1,258m) where a mountain inn will revive the footsore and weary with both food and drink.

Alt Schönau is much lower, set amid open fields where several *pensions* may be found and are a delight for those hoping for a quiet location. The highest point in the National Park is the Grosser Rachel at 4,722ft (1,439m) with the Rachelsee lake just below the summit. On

Traditional farmhouse at the open-air museum, Finsterau

fine clear days there is a tremendous view which makes the climb well rewarded. This is the setting for the villages of Finsterau, Neu Schönau, St Oswald, Riedlhütte, Spiegelau and Frauenau.

Finsterau straggles along a narrow winding road that climbs continually up past the Mauther Forest to the border. It is an agricultural community with a large camping site and is also the setting for a new museum that is still in its early stages of being constructed; the Freilichtmuseum Bayerischer Wald in Finsterau is its long and complicated name. Opened for the first time in 1980 it is re-erecting historical Bavarian Forest farmhouses and furnishing them with traditional old furniture and cooking utensils.

Neu Schönau is the sister village to Alt Schönau and has grown up on the rolling farmland just outside the National Park. It is compact and has its own church, village store, butcher and local tourist office which arranges excursions, natural history tours and gives advice on the local arts and crafts that can be seen in the area. Fishing is also allowed (with permits). There is a new self-catering accommodation complex here as well as hotels and private houses.

The twin villages of **St Oswald** and **Riedlhütte** are linked together for administration purposes, but they are in fact two quite separate communities, lying in sunny open countryside with views across to the Grosser Rachel and Lusen. Apart from being in a prime position for visitors wishing to go to the National Park there is an

Farmhouse bedroom, Finsterau

added attraction in Riedlhütte. At one of the area's many glass works visitors can see the molten glass being blown into various shapes, as well as cutting and decorating.

Short courses in the old crafts of woodcarving and basket weaving are on offer as is also breadmaking, using the old outdoor ovens for the baking process. The importance attached to retaining these old crafts can be seen in the newly constructed Forest Museum which was opened in 1982 by no lesser person than Bavaria's own minister, Franz Josef Strauss who died in November 1988. Swimming in the lake as well and tennis and riding can be enjoyed here. Short excursions by horse-drawn wagons is another popular pastime.

Next to Riedlhütte is **Spiegelau** with its own railway station on the line to Zwiesel. Situated at the foot of the Grosser Rachel it is both sheltered and sunny which affords an ideal base for exploring the surrounding areas. Guided tours of the local glass and pottery works are possible. There are also study tours on geology and animal husbandry, but for this undertaking a good working knowledge of German is needed. A large wooded park which incorporates an adventure playground for children is proving extremely popular. Swimming can be in either the modern indoor pool or on warm summer days in a heated outdoor pool. Fishing permits may be obtained for use on the Stausee. Evening entertainment comes in the form of folk evenings with local songs and dances or just listening to the haunting strains of a zither. A large and excellent camping site is to be found here in Spiegelau.

Frauenau is a small town over 650 years old. A Benedictine monk, so history recalls, came from the Danube valley and built himself a refuge at the foot of the Kleiner Rachel. He then set out to fell some of the densely packed trees to make a clearing in order to build a pilgrimage shrine. Today Frauenau possesses an eighteenth-century rococo church but the humble origins have not been forgotten.

During the Middle Ages glass workers came and settled here; their trade depended on wood with which to fire their kilns and there was an abundance here. So in 1420 the first glass works was established. Although in the twentieth century Zwiesel is regarded as the main glass works centre, Frauenau is the recognised centre for the decorative coloured glassware. Visits to the factories and glass museum to see both the old and new processes is not only interesting but well rewarding and one can buy the wares at factory prices in the showrooms. There are courses held here for painting on glass; further details are available from the local tourist office.

Also to be seen in Frauenau are some rather attractive old houses which photographers seem to find irresistible. Walking, either on the marked trails or by guided moorland, is extremely pleasant. The sporting activities of swimming, tennis, riding and even cycling can fill the days and by night there are folk entertainments, band concerts, zither music and wine tasting.

Rinchnach is a small village, adjacent to the Ostmarkstrasse in the heart of the Bavarian Forest, whose history goes back to 1011 when a monk called Gunter came to settle and live the life of a hermit; he was later canonised and the last week in June sees a festival to commemorate St Gunter. In alternate years there is an historic pageant as well, depicting the life of the saint and the founding of the village. The baroque monastery church is also worth visiting. Although small in size Rinchnach caters well for its visitors with theatrical productions as well as folk and zither evenings. Fishing in the Rinchnacher Ohe is popular with guests and local folk alike. There is a train service to Regen with an onward bus connection.

Kirchdorf im Wald is a pretty little place lying just off the Ostmarkstrasse. Admittedly it offers only simple accommodation and camping but because of its central locality offers an ideal opportunity to explore the countryside.

Lalling is a small resort north of Deggendorf which nestles at the foot of the Kleiner Rachelberg, in the area known as the Lallinger Winkel. Due to its sunny south-facing position there are many or-

Stuppach parish church, in the Tauber Valley

Maria Gern, Ramsau, in the Bavarian Alps

chards to be found here and in the late spring or early summer, when the fruit trees are in full blossom, this fruit bowl of the Bavarian Forest is a truly wonderful sight. The women here make spice bouquets which are then sent to Passau and Regensburg for sale. Courses are held for painting on glass and well marked paths and nature trails here cover more than 60 miles including the Tote Au, an area of high moorland. Hang-gliding takes place on the Buchlstein and swimming, apart from in the hotels, at Hengersberg or Deggendorf.

At the end of May or beginning of June there is the Mostfest (*Most* is fruit juice, wine and cider) when quantities of these beverages are downed; there is also a pottery market. The third weekend in August sees a folk and craft festival, when the local country crafts are displayed. Local costume is also worn and there is spirited country music to dance to.

Schönberg has grown up on a plateau perched above the Ostmarkstrasse with views across to the Kadernberg. Although close to Grafenau, Schönberg's amenities make it very independent with a swimming pool, riding school, guided walking tours and even a flying club which puts on displays from time to time.

Grafenau itself is a small compact little town with several outlying districts. The major part of the town lies in a hollow with encircling pine-clad hills so making it sheltered from the winds while in winter they claim to have the best snow. Once up and out of the town the countryside is undulating with scattered farms and small communities of just a few houses.

Grafenau is proud of its heritage for in 1376 it received a charter from the Emperor Karl IV to become a town. The reason for this honour was mainly because Grafenau was the last place in Bavaria on the salt route from Passau and Vilshofen which ran over the border ridge of the great forested mountains into Bohemia. As this trade brought prosperity to the territory over which the emperor ruled he naturally liked to reward up and coming communities. Regretfully there are no original records for the Grafenauer Strasse although it is on record that the monastery of Niedernburg at Passau in 1010 received the taxes levied on the salt trade using the Goldener Steig which led from Passau-Ilzstadt through the princely bishopric country (this was the territory of the old district of Wegscheid and Wolfstein) to Prachatitz. Another known fact is that around the middle of the fourteenth century the Guldensteig (one of four main trails) became the new trade route through the dense forests surrounding the Lusen mountain and in the year 1366, on the order of the emperor, the route was to be open for all to use.

The importance of salt in the Middle Ages cannot be over empha-
sised since it was used in the preservation of food through the winter
months. The salt in this particular case was brought from Hallein and
Reichenhall by barges down the rivers Salzach and Inn to be stored
in Passau and Vilshofen. Later it was put into barrels and loaded onto
horses which were driven by salt seamers. These pack trains would
carry other merchandise as well. The return journey would be made
with furs, hops and malt from Bohemia.

Today, Grafenau is a bustling market town with a tree-lined main
square and a main shopping area except for two large supermarkets
on the outskirts of town.

The town museum deals not only with the town's history but has
a specialised section on snuff. The Bauernmöbel Museum is in the
attractively laid out *Kurpark* and houses old farmhouse furniture and
equipment. Also in the *Kurpark* are the fountains that throw spectacular jets of water into the air and the open-air swimming pool with
four different sections, surrounded by an extensive sun bathing lawn
with protective bushes. The indoor pool is in the local high school
and only in use late afternoon and early evenings during term time.

A local festival held here in Grafenau takes place on the first
Saturday in August and is the Salzsaumerfest (Salt Drivers' Festival),
when period costume is donned and the old salt drivers once again
lead their horses into the town.

Overlooking the town are several large first class hotels including
one of the Steigenberger group; small private pensions as well as
private houses are scattered over a wide area. Self-catering apartments are also well to the fore with a purpose built holiday village of
Vogelthenne at **Haus im Wald** 6 miles (10km) out of the main town.
This holiday village draws its supplies of fresh milk, bread and eggs
from the neighbouring farms but bulkier produce has to be brought
from Grafenau.

Tittling is an old market town in the area around the Ostmarkstrasse known as the Dreiburgenland (The Three Castles Land, ie
Saldenburg, Fürstenstein and Englburg). It is also the home of the
excellent Dreiburgenland Riding School with its indoor riding hall as
well as special routes over the countryside which pupils have the use
of. The House of the Guest has a reading room for public use. There
is an indoor swimming pool but on fine summer days many find
their way to the Dreiburgensee which is located on the east side of the
Ostmarkstrasse. The name of Tittling is synonomous with the
Museumsdorf which has now grown up beside the Dreiburgensee.

Museumsdorf is a unique village which came about almost by chance when the Höltl family, who have lived in this area since the seventeenth century, built a hotel beside the Dreiburgensee. This hotel provides not only full board to its guests but lays on a full weekly programme of sporting events, excursions and evening entertainment. Guests without their own transport are met at Passau and brought to the hotel.

In 1972, just after the hotel had opened, Georg Höltl acquired the Rothau Mill which was falling into disrepair. The mill itself dates back to 1430 and took 2 years to restore. It opened as a museum in 1974 under the blessing of the Bavarian prime minister. The interior was furnished so that visitors might see how a miller and his family lived and worked in years gone by. Other local history was also incorporated under this roof. However this was not to be the end of the story, for over the succeeding years other old buildings have been added and now there are fifty complete farms together with outbuildings as well as chapels, sawmills, a blacksmith and one of Germany's oldest schools. In 1985 Neil Armstrong the astronaut came to visit this re-creation of old east Bavaria.

Apart from the enormous amount of history that unfolds before the eye Museumdorf is a delightful place to wander around. To try and describe all the buildings to be seen here would almost be a book in itself, but the following are a cross section to be found.

The *Gasthaus* Mühlhiasl was built as a farmhouse in 1760 but extended over the years with its upper floor surrounded by a stout wooden balcony. After being fully restored it was opened in 1980 as an inn to offer hospitality to the thirsty and hungry visitors.

The *Sägewerk* (sawmill) next door to the Rothau Mill had its old wooden saw replaced by one dating from 1876. Apart from the working area there is a small living room where a small stove provided the only means of cooking a meal. All mills depended on a supply of water to turn the wheels and the *Hammerschmiede* (blacksmith) was no exception. So next to the sawmill is the single storey dwelling built above the wooden wheel where the smith and his family lived. On the ground level with stone walls was the workshop for shoeing horses and making farm implements, as well as smaller utensils like picks and shovels.

The *Dorfkapelle* (village church) is a small wooden building, with a simple bell tower consisting of four wooden beams supporting a tiled campanile adorned with a cross. The bell dates from 1725 and was brought from the pilgrimage church in Büchlberg.

There are several of the free standing *Backofen* (baking ovens) on view. Before the eighteenth century farmhouse ovens were all in the

Traditional farmhouses and duck pond, Museumsdorf

kitchens but they proved to be fire hazards with so much timber about that the idea was conceived of building brick ovens outside the main building. On baking days huge fires were lit, the fuel used being logs hewn from the forest. The bread made in the kitchen would then be placed on long handled spatulas and pushed into the centre of the oven. When baking had been completed the warm ovens would be used for drying fruit and even flax.

The village school on view here was built in the mid-seventeenth century and served several purposes. Built on two floors, the lower one consisted of the largest room and was used as the main living room for the village clerk and his family as well as being used as the local council chamber for meetings; at the back of this floor was an oven and a toilet. The first floor was reached by a steep flight of wooden stairs; the largest front room was used as a classroom and the village clerk then became the schoolmaster. Three other smaller rooms were probably used as bedrooms. Incorporated in the ground floor but only accessible from the outside was the jail and so the clerk schoolmaster then became the jailor as well; one can only wonder what his salary was for all the tasks that he was called upon to undertake. This building was in fact used as a dwelling until 1976. No village would be complete without its duckpond and this one is no exception. It is inhabited by a whole family of both ducks and geese who, from time to time, march in single file to some other pasture.

Only buildings that cannot be kept in good repair by the owners on the original sites are brought to the Museumsdorf and all buildings before they are taken down have detailed plans made to ensure accurate reconstruction. Currently around thirty workmen are employed by the Museumsdorf, repairing, renovating and rebuilding this village of the Bavarian Forest which is open to the public daily.

Eging am See in the southern most part of the Bavarian Forest is on the shores of a pretty tree-fringed lake. It was once just a small very ordinary village in pretty rural surroundings but is now becoming popular as a centre for various medical treatments centred on water therapy; from artificially induced wave movements to vapour baths. In fact it has almost attained spa status and indeed the newly laid out park is designated as such. The lakeside really is enchanting with one section turned into a large bathing beach with rowing boats and pedaloes for hire with which to explore other parts of this man-made lake. Green lawns sweep up to the newly built sport and leisure complex with the excellent swimming pool, restaurant and terrace. Over 25 miles (40km) of marked walks and forest information trails together with tennis, riding and minigolf, offer those seeking an activity holiday plenty of scope.

Neukirchen is another small village close to the Ostmarkstrasse in the Dreiburgenland with a mixed countryside of meadows, woods, lakes and rivers all near at hand. One certain factor is that you will be hospitably welcomed here for in 1986 Neukirchen received a commendation in the competition on hospitable Bavaria; quite a feat for a village. There are plenty of outdoor activities here with woodland and river trails, keep fit courses, riding, tennis and fishing, all of which may be necessary to those taking advantage of the bread that has been baked in the old style ovens—the warm bread not only smells delicious but tastes it as well. Neukirchen is a quiet oasis to the more hectic life of Passau 11 miles (18km) away.

The North

Regen stands on the Black Regen river which flows on eventually to Regensburg. On warm sunny evenings the riverside walks under leafy trees give the relaxation that the area is known for. They are also just as pleasant in the evenings when illuminated by electric light.

The large town square is overlooked by shops and cafés, as well as the parish church of St Michael, while on the fourth side is the House of the Guest with its reading and television rooms and information office all under the same roof. A decorative touch to the square is the flower beds and the old fountain.

Courses on glass painting and pottery are held here, and details can be obtained from the local tourist office. There are also many sporting facilities with two swimming pools, an excellent riding school with its own jumping arena and well defined country rides up to 7 miles (11km) long. In addition there is tennis and football. Fishing is definitely a major sport here and rules are laid down and strictly adhered to regarding the quantity and size of fish that may be caught in any one day. Apart from fishing the river is used for rowing and canoeing and even shooting the rapids is a possibility for those with a strong nerve.

The last weekend in July sees the Pichelsteiner Festival celebrated. It is without doubt the longest extended weekend in the Bavarian Forest as it lasts for 5 days. The origins of this festival are certainly strange as it is derived from a stew called the 'Pichelsteiner' which is made from meat, vegetables and seasoning. The result is an excellent and very filling meal which even the Iron Chancellor Otto von Bismarck was delighted with. Apart from eating and drinking during the day, there are water sports and musical processions with those taking part wearing an historic *Tracht* (traditional or historic costume). At night gondola trips illuminated by Venetian lighting all contrive to make this a genuine Bavarian carnival.

To the south of the town is the ruined castle of Weissenstein where, or so it is alleged, a certain Count Hund buried his wife alive in retaliation for having drowned their baby in the river. Here also is the Frassenden Haus Museum where the Baltic poet Siegfried von Vagesack and his Swedish wife, also a poet, lived and worked, producing more than eighty literary works. The ground floor is in fact devoted to their work and the rooms are furnished with their belongings. The first floor houses a collection of snuff boxes, 1,300 examples in all, and is claimed to be the largest private collection in Europe. It is the work of a former Bürgermeister, Alois Reitbauer, over a period of more than 46 years.

The second floor has varying themes from the world of literature, art and folklore, but note that the exhibitions change from time to time. The third floor is set aside for special exhibitions by well known artists of which there may be two or three during the summer.

The attics up under the roof show the linen industry that once flourished widely in these parts. Both implements and illustrations show the process, from the growing of flax to the final woven linen.

The name Weissenstein means 'White Stone' and the entrance hall shows the geology of the quartz with its strange formation that creates this phenomenon known as Pfahl. The Pfahl is in fact a quartz ridge which stretches from Freihung in the north to Freyung in the south and is estimated to be around 150 to 300 million years old. It can only be seen above ground at certain locations, namely Thierlstein near Cham, Viechtach and Weissenstein where it appears as a white rock. Outside the museum a massive dragon has been sculptured from this rock and then beautifully coloured in blues, greens and red with its jaws wide open showing its wicked fangs as if ready to swallow unsuspecting visitors.

Following the river Regen upstream one comes to **Zwiesel** which is acknowledged as the centre of the glass industry as well as that of the loveliest part of the Bavarian Forest. The town itself consists of a steep main street which, until the new bypass was opened this year, was heavily congested. It is still very busy but at least the queues are not quite so long for anyone wishing to drive through the town.

There is a small well laid out garden at the lower end of the town with benches and a pool whose fountain attracts birds who use it as a shower in summer. This peaceful haven also has a small free car park adjacent to it, with no limit making this a very useful starting point for exploring the town and various glass works. Most of these works have their own showrooms which the public may browse round and purchases are beautifully packed to ensure no breakages on the journey home however far that may be. The main street also has some showrooms for works that are not as central. At the top end on the north side in a quiet courtyard is the Waldmuseum. The ground floor mounts a comprehensive introduction to the forest in the way of trees and insects that they often harbour to their detriment as well as the uses that the felled trees are put to. One may also see a representation of a forester's house in bygone days. Animal life in the forest is also there together with the fungi that grow within its boundaries and information on how to distinguish between those that are edible and those that are poisonous, even fatal. The upper floor shows the glass that has been produced in this area over the years. The parish church is noted for its statue of *The Whipped Christ*.

Zwiesel can offer over 3,000 beds to visitors ranging from hotels to private houses and in addition there is a youth hostel and a camping site that is open all year round. Recreational facilities here

A master glass-blower at Theresienthal, Zwiesel

are also good with two outdoor pools, one of which is heated, as well as the indoor swimming pool. There are also guided walking tours as well as an information trail to the Grosser Falkenstein. Seven miles (11km) to the north of Zwiesel at **Scheuereck** is a nature reserve where you can see wild animals being fed without prior booking.

Zwiesel and the glass industry are synonymous and glassware bought here is far cheaper than in the shops or departmental stores in other parts of the country. Each manufacturer has a distinctive design and most are known for cut glass wares (eg Royal Bavarian Crystal). A good example which illustrates this art more fully is 'Theresienthal'. The factory and showrooms are outside the main town of Zwiesel on the road to Bayerisch Eisenstein and the firm is one of the oldest and most famous in Germany. It produces the finest quality glass, 80 per cent of which is for the home market, the other 20 per cent being divided between Europe, America and Japan. It was founded in 1421 by the Rabenstein family and remained in their hands until 1636. From then on it passed through several family ownerships but since 1982 has been a public company.

The current production of Theresienthal glass has been developed from the old traditions. Indeed the company policy is to retain the old hand crafted methods and to this end the old wooden moulds are still used to give the final shape required. The molten glass is taken by a learner (glass industry term for an apprentice) from the gas fired furnaces to the glass-blower who blows through a long pipe to form the basic shape of the glass. This is then transferred to the wooden mould where the final shaping is undertaken before being passed to the master glassmaker who applies the decorative additions before checking the precision of the finished product. Each piece of glass bears the unmistakeable stamp of Theresienthal in its superb colouring, shape and decoration. The mass production market is not for this firm; quality before quantity is their motto. It is no wonder the royal houses of Europe placed their orders here.

By modern standards the factory is quite small. Each morning the glass-blowers work from 8.30am-1.30pm and in summer the heat from the furnaces becomes almost unbearable — hence the amount of liquid that is consumed while working. After the glass-blowers have finished the men who mix and smelt the glass take over in order that the next day's shift may have enough molten glass to work with. When the glass has been fired and cooled some of it is passed on for hand engraving or painting. Factories, which can be visited, are well stocked with a wide range of table glassware, vases and decorative pieces which may be bought as single items or in larger quantities. There are at least ten glass works in the area which welcome visitors.

The road from here to the frontier village of **Bayerisch Eisenstein** climbs up through an ever narrowing valley whose slopes are covered with dark green conifers. To the east is the 4,258ft (1,298m) high Grosser Falkenstein mountain while to the west is the highest peak within the forest, the Grosser Arber at 4,778ft (1,456m). This small resort is for the active. In winter it is a skiing area while in the summer the paths ring to the sound of boots and *Wanderstock* (stout walking sticks), for it is here that the true alpine hiking and climbing comes into its own. At the far end of the main street is the border and customs post with a large car park. Once past the barrier the road continues to run on through the wooded heights for roughly another couple of kilometres before reaching the Czech Republic border post.

There is a winding narrow road which turns off westwards at the actual border or a slightly better road 4 miles (6km) back towards Zwiesel that leads directly to the Grosser Arber. Even before reaching the chairlift that carries one up this mountain, cars and coaches are parked along the roadside and in the parking bays. To avoid long queues at the chairlift it is advisable to arrive early — the lift commences at 8am! Having reached the top of the lift additional warm clothing can be a good idea as one is exposed to any wind that may be blowing. It is possible to continue on foot past a chapel to reach two rocky outcrops. The one above the chapel is the point where the visitor has extensive views over the Schwarzer Reger and on across the Czech Rebublic frontier to the almost hidden village of Zelezná Ruda. From the other rocky spur with its cross, one has the whole panorama of the Bayerischer Wald and the Lamerwinkel, albeit on fine days only. At least half a day is recommended to make this particular trip worthwhile. At the foot of the Grosser Arber is the enchanting and magical Grosser Arbersee lake with its surrounding pine trees reflected in its still waters; a very popular spot for family picnics and leisurely boating.

The road from here to Neukirchen beim Heiligen Blut covers some of the loveliest unspoilt and wooded landscape to be found anywhere in Europe with a rare elusive beauty that once found is hard to forget. The highest village in the forest is **Lohberg**, surrounded by woodland with a game enclosure for the deer and other wild animals. Marked walks radiate out from the village as well as a keep fit trail with its series of exercise stops along the shores of the Kleiner Arbersee. The open-air swimming pool, tennis courts and the fishing are gaining popularity with those in search of active holidays. A 'House of the Guest' with a reading and television room is an added attraction.

As the road commences its descent panoramic views over the Lamerwinkel unfold. The grandeur of the Grosser Osser towers over the gentler hills and the open sunny valley where the attractive but small resorts of Lam, Haibühl and Arrach form a triangle. **Lam** has a splendid new recreation centre which includes an indoor swimming pool and a gymnasium. There is a local folk museum with emphasis on the minerals found in these parts and a reading room in the House of the Guest. As well as the folk music and dancing there is a very good folk theatre which puts on plays dealing with some of the legends which the Bayerischer Wald is steeped in. Quieter forms of entertainment are zither music and for the railway enthusiasts on certain summer weekends there is the Regen Valley Railway steam locomotive *Mizzi* which operates, with nineteenth-century rolling stock, for excursions either between Kötzting and Lam or from Viechtach to and from Blaibach and Gotteszell.

Arrach, the third village of this trio, is linked for administration purposes to the tiny community of **Haibühl**. Whether one approaches this cluster of villages from either the north or the south they do represent some of the most attractive villages to be found here in the forest. Only a short distance separates Arrach from the wood covered slopes with their well signposted routes for walking. There is a riding stable with its own indoor school and jumping

The Dragon Festival, Furth im Wald

arena. Evening entertainments include folk evenings and film shows about the past and present Bavarian Forest.

Neukirchen beim Heiligen Blut is part of a developing holiday area. It is surrounded by densely wooded slopes and has the longest chairlift in the forest which ascends the 3,482ft (1,061m) high Schwarzriegel which is part of the Hoher Bogen ridge. At the top there is a restaurant and a newly constructed summer toboggan run. Neukirchen is a 500-year-old village due, in no small way, to the fact that pilgrims were drawn here to pay homage to a miracle that is alleged to have occurred back in the Middle Ages. The village itself is neat with some rather nice old houses and a well tended park. Sporting facilities on offer here are tennis, riding and hang-gliding.

Furth im Wald is an old border town and famous for its Drachenstich (Dragon Sticking Festival) which takes place from the second Sunday in August for a week and is the oldest folk festival in Germany. Nowadays this is no ordinary country pageant but a first class production that costs over a million Deutsch Marks. The festival and play are performed in the main street which is closed during this period; seating for 2,225 people is erected along the route. The seats at the front are the most expensive but as it is tiered all have a good view of the proceedings. Its fame has spread worldwide, mainly due to television coverage as well as having been filmed by Walt Disney.

The real origin of this particular festival is obscure although it

The town hall, Furth im Wald

probably had something to do with the Magyars who used to sweep down from the Hungarian plains and terrorise this region. In fact until a 100 years ago this pageant was always performed at the religious festival of Corpus Christi. With a 500-year-long history the play has changed slightly as successive authors have rewritten the script. The current production is the work of Josef Martin Bauer in 1952 and shows the fate of a frontier people during the worst moments in the Hussite Wars of the fifteenth century. The heart of the

Fountain, Furth im Wald

story is simple; a young and lovely maiden falls into the clutches of a wicked dragon and is rescued by a gallant knight. The play itself is performed on a raised stage, with a procession through the streets consisting of 1,100 participants in medieval costume. Some are dressed as mounted knights in full armour, for which 200 horses are needed, not forgetting the flag bearers, musicians and dignitaries.

The Dimpl family have long been associated with the pageant and many a son has played the noble knight who wins the lady. In 1967 Volkmar Dimpl and Rosemarie Percher were the *Ritterpaar* (leading lady and gentleman) and a few years later actually married.

Once the procession is underway the dragon must be attacked by the mounted knights with spears until the final death blow. Only then is the maiden free to be claimed. In a way the real hero is that of the dragon who, in these modern times, is a fabulous creation. The current monster was designed by the Pyrkos family and built by the engineering firm of Fischer in Mühlausen, close to the city of Nuremberg. The sensation caused when the finished article was mounted on a long trailer and towed by lorry for around a hundred miles over well used roads probably had to be seen to be believed.

The monster, for that is what it really is in more ways than one, measures 58ft (18m) long, 13ft (4m) wide, 10ft (3m) high and has a comprehensive hydraulic system enabling its wings to flap. It is also fully mechanised and has two drivers ensconced inside. Painted red and green with flashing eyes, the huge jaws open and shut to show the wicked teeth while the nostrils emit billowing smoke. It is strange but for all this the spectacle is not a frightening experience. Children adore the dragon and when he is killed there are tears of real sorrow to be mopped up. During the rest of the year the dragon may be visited in his lair in the *Schlossplatz* for a minimal fee.

Furth im Wald, even without the festival, is a delightful place with a charming *Rathaus* whose main entrance portrays St George slaying the dragon. A carillon of bells plays at 11am at the entrance to the *Schlossplatz* where the Landestormuseum can be found. It is housed in the former hospital and town tower and has a special collection of figures of saints as well as paintings of them. The museum has recreated a furnished room that would have graced a town house at the turn of the century and has a glass division which shows something of the glass and other local industries. It also outlines the history and geology of the town and surrounding countryside including that of Bischofteinitz in the Sudetenland over the border in the Czech Republic. Overall it is a most interesting and comprehensive account of how people lived and worked throughout the ages.

The Voithenberghammer is an extension of the main museum although a little way out of town there is an old blacksmith's dwelling house and workshop in the Kalten Pastritz valley. Built in 1823 it has now been renovated to its former glory and displays the tools and implements used by the smithy.

At **Steinbruch** on the other side of the town, is the Waldmuseum with its animals, plants, flowers, insects and fungi that are, or were, found in the woods and streams in this part of the world. Amongst the larger stuffed animals on view are the brown bear, lynx, European bison and the capercaillie, a local and long extinct bird. Outside there is an enclosure for red deer and various species of wild goat that children find enthralling. Walks, fishponds, a children's play area and a restaurant make this a favourite haunt for a day out.

In addition Furth also offers its guests a wide choice in the way of accommodation. Sporting facilities are not forgotten with an indoor and outdoor swimming pool, tennis, riding, and golf, making this a really worthwhile place to stay for either a long or short period.

Waldmünchen

Just north of Furth is the 1,000-year-old town of **Waldmünchen** noted for its splendid network of marked walks. It is a great favourite of those who prefer walking holidays alone or with a guide. It also has an annual pageant, known as Trenck the Pandour Pageant, performed during July and August. This has nothing to do with the world of dragons as it originated during the eighteenth century. A certain Baron Trenck and his mounted troops pillaged the town of Cham. The inhabitants of Waldmünchen were afraid of what would happen to them and so they gathered together a large sum of money and offered it to the baron in order that he would leave them in peace; this he agreed to do. The pageant is now celebrated by the enactment in full costume of the baron and his troops arriving and being paid off. The standard of riding, coupled with the colourful costumes as well as the merrymaking that ensues, makes this a joyful occasion.

The small town square has a *Rathaus* with a gilded statue outside. This forms the focal point around which the compact town has arisen. A modern riding school with its own grounds takes groups of riders out to discover the surrounding countryside. Sailing and windsurfing as well as boating take place on the Perlsee (Pearl lake). Tennis and pistol shooting are also available while swimming can be enjoyed either in the lake or the indoor and outdoor pools. For an after-dinner stroll there is a newly laid out town park.

Cham is an old market town dating back to the tenth century and owes its existence to being at the crossroads of the Ostmarkstrasse running north and south and the Regensburg or Nuremberg road to the Czech Republic which runs west to east, and so was a focal point in the days of the Emperor Charlemagne. It is also the boundary between the Bavarian Forest and the northern territory known as the Oberpfälzerwald. The town centre can boast two main squares; the *Marktplatz* which was the scene of much bartering (especially in the Middle Ages) and the *Stadtplatz* with the fifteenth-century *Rathaus* which has had alterations including a neo-Gothic extension in 1875.

The parish church of St Jakob has some nice old features, but notably the towers that date back to the thirteenth century, while the interior has some fine stucco work and paintings from the mid-eighteenth century. The museum devotes itself to the history of the town and countryside as well as a section on some of the ancient folklore. Every year at the end of July Cham plays host to the largest and most traditional folklore festival in the forest.

Cham was the birthplace of Count Nikolaus Luckner in 1722 who later became a marshal of France and commander of the army in the north in 1792. It is to him that the *Marseillaise* is dedicated. Before questions are raised as to how a German should have the French national anthem dedicated to him it must be remembered that armies employed foreign nationals in high ranking posts in that era. The composer Claude Joseph Rouget de Lisle was a captain in the engineers stationed at Strasbourg when ordered to join Luckner's army. The Mayor of Strasbourg regretted that the soldiers had no patriotic song to march to, so de Lisle wrote the words and music of what was later to become the *Marseillaise* and thus achieved fame. Marshal Luckner was not so fortunate as he was executed in 1794.

Kötzting is a medium sized town situated on the Black and White Regen rivers. The hills rising in the background are the Kaitersberg, whose highest point is the Mittagsstein at 3,660ft (1,115m); a favourite of the high altitude walkers whether with a local guide or not. A 'House of the Guest' has recently been built in Kötzting and the town

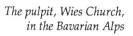

The pulpit, Wies Church, in the Bavarian Alps

The old chapel at Museumdorf, in the Bayerischer Wald

Attractive cottages on the Fischland-Darß-Zingst peninsula of the Baltic Coast
The beach and pier at Ahlbeck, Usedom, on the Baltic Coast

is also keen on keeping up the old traditions through folk evenings and film shows. The local festival here is the Kötzting Ride and dates back to 1412. The legend tells how the parish priest had to ride through the night to administer the last rites to a dying farmer in neighbouring Steinbühl. He was accompanied by some of the young men of the town who acted as a bodyguard should the priest run into a band of robbers or cut-throats that roamed the countryside at night. Today the whole of the Whitsun weekend is taken to mark the occasion. The festival play *Pfingstrittehr* is performed on the Saturday, Sunday and Monday, but the culmination of this festival is on Whit Monday when a procession of more than 600 people on horseback ride from Kötzting to the Zeller valley. This is then followed by a service held in the tiny Nicholas Church at Steinbühl. On their return to Kötzting the 'Whit Bridegroom' receives the wreath of virtue in the market square.

Other places of interest worth visiting are the *Rathaus*, the *Alte Schloss*, the parish church and the church of St Veit. Approximately a couple of miles out of town, on the road to Viechtach in the tiny hamlet of **Ried**, is the 1,000-year-old lime tree Wolframslinde.

Arnbruck is a quaint little village set in the Zeller valley at the foot of the Kaitersberg and not far from Kötzting. With a fairly reasonable bus service to the larger resort all the facilities at Kötzting may be enjoyed by anyone staying in Arnbruck. Again there are well signposted walks in the surrounding woods with the addition of a game enclosure and there is a 'House of the Guest' with a library and reading room which is also used for film shows. The small parish church has a high altar and two side altars, each flanked by statues with triumphal arches. These are adorned by large oil paintings which act as a focal point. Craft work here is glass cutting and painting on wood. Swimming is in both an outdoor and an indoor pool and on the edge of the village there is the gliding and flying club where visitors are welcome and flights available. For such a small community Arnbruck is quite a lively centre.

Bodenmais is quite different from any other resort in the Bavarian Forest as it is fast becoming a first class health resort and has grown enormously over the last 20 years. Lying in an open sunny position, sheltered from the easterly winds by the majestic Grosser Arber, it certainly can be justly proud of its climate. The village itself is quite ordinary but with the reasonably new *Kurhaus*, surrounded by a well laid out and tended park where concerts are held, Bodenmais has risen from near obscurity to becoming a prosperous spa town.

Inside the *Kurhaus* is a whole range of medicinal baths and massage rooms and also a reading and television room. After spending the day concentrating on health and fitness the entertainment scene covers just about everything from folk-dancing and singing to plays, concerts, film shows and festivals of one sort or another. If these do not appeal to the visitor then an evening can be spent in a wine tavern listening to zither music.

Every sport imaginable is on offer here and for swimmers there is the choice of a heated open-air pool or a superb indoor one. Thirteen hotels here have their own pools as well as sauna and solaria.

There are several large glass showrooms doing a brisk trade although prices are not as low as in the smaller villages.

Bodenmais has a very interesting museum with minerals, fossils and precious stones that have been collected from all over the world. Some local geological exhibits and silver and bronze articles from the eighteenth and nineteenth centuries when Bodenmais was a mining centre can be seen. It is also possible to visit the 500-year-old Erzbergwerk to see where and how the silver was mined.

Viechtach is a small bustling town on the Black Regen river and often called the Green Heart of the Bavarian Forest through its mild climate and especially in the spring and autumn when there is a lack of fog. The countryside which surrounds the town is open farmland with gentle wooded hills. Here and there are ancient ruined castles, once the home of some feudal baron. Such a castle is at Neunussberg, a suburb of Viechtach, which belonged to the Nussberg family and was built over a period of 10 years between 1340-50 with the chapel being added 3 years later. A festival is held here annually during July but the castle may be visited at other times by obtaining permission from the farm that adjoins it.

In the centre of Viechtach is the seventeenth-century *Rathaus* and the rococo parish church of St Augustinus built in the mid-eighteenth century. The interior has some beautifully carved choir stalls, while the painted ceiling is the work of Otto Gebhardt. Next door is St Ann's Chapel in Gothic style with a baroque altar. The oldest building in the town is that of the Hospital Church of the Holy Ghost which was founded in 1350 by Conrad of Nussberg. It is now the home of the Crystal Museum with over 1,200 exhibits of world-wide minerals and crystals making it one of the finest collections in Germany. In fact, if one takes the museum at Bodenmais into consideration, then this area is definitely the home of the largest collection.

Many activities are on offer here; tennis, riding, rowing and of course fishing both in the Black Regen river or the Höllenstein lake can be pursued. For the swimmers there is a heated outdoor swim-

Totenbrett boards on the side of the road

ming pool surrounded by extensive sun bathing lawns affording views of the Great Pfahl, where it has risen above ground. Concerts are held both indoors or in the park. Folk evenings, film shows with slides and lectures all make Viechtach an excellent centre. Accommodation here is in either hotels, pensions, farms or camping at the Pirka and Schnitzmühle sites. The Knaus-Luxury camping site is open all year round and has its own indoor swimming pool and sauna. Viechtach has both bus and train services.

Prackenbach is only 2 miles (3km) from Viechtach and is a small rural community. It provides an inexpensive base to anyone seeking a quiet and simple holiday but wanting more facilities within easy reach. For fishing in the Blaibacher See or the Höllenstein reservoir, enquire locally regarding permits.

The following resorts are all situated on the western side of the Ostmarkstrasse beginning with **Rattenberg** which is perched on a small ridge overlooking the rolling countryside that appears almost as a patchwork quilt with its fields, farms and small woods rising and falling as far as the eye can see. This scattered farming community comes together on a Sunday morning for church services and then goes on to the local inns where, over *steins* of beer, the latest news is discussed with vim and point.

The district of Neurandsberg, a little way from the main village, has a ruined castle and is also one of the remaining places where the old Totenbrett boards can be seen at the side of the road. These boards are an old east Bavarian custom which derived from the deceased being placed on a funeral board and taken to the churchyard for burial. Afterwards the board was decorated and inscribed with the loved one's details before being placed near wayside shrines or on walls of houses and so acting as a memorial.

Haibach is another small hamlet and together with Elisabethzell offers peace and tranquility in open countryside which both walkers and naturalists enjoy. There isan open-air pool and hang-gliding.

St Englmar is known for its winter sports but is an ideal choice in summer as well, with wooded slopes that lead up to the Proller (3,406ft, 1,038m), the Predigstühl (3,328ft, 1,014m) and the Hirschenstein (3,559ft, 1,085m) by well marked and timed routes. There is an annual festival held on Whit Monday incorporating the old religious and folk play *Englmari Suchens* (Englmar Search) which recalls how the holy hermit Englmar was murdered around 1100 and the body later found in the forest without having decomposed. The festival commences at 9am in the Kirchplatz with an opening fanfare by the town band followed by a mass and the blessing of the animals.

St Englmar has first class riding facilities with an indoor swimming pool as well as medicinal baths, massage and sauna. There are indoor and outdoor riding arenas as well as tennis courts. For entertainment there are plays and folk evenings in the local folk theatre and concerts or zither music at one of the hotels.

Köllnburg is set on a broad ridge away from the sound of traffic but in a particularly delightful part of the Bavarian Forest with its panoramic views over the surrounding countryside. The village is clean and neat with a baroque church and a twelfth-century castle that once belonged to the Nussberg family before its partial destruction in 1468. Like Viechtach this is also a fog free climate. Sporting facilities within the village are tennis and bowling but with a quick and easy access to Viechtach the extensive facilities there can be used with little inconvenience.

Bernried is a small resort in a sheltered sunny position at the commencement of the foothills of the Bavarian Forest, just above the Danube valley and only 7 miles (11km) from Deggendorf. The Bernriederbach is a clear mountain stream that rises close to the summit of the Hirschenstein and flows past the wooded slopes and the village of Bernried before joining the Schwarzach which then flows into the Danube. The trees that surround Bernried are mostly silver birch and make a pleasant contrast to the darker conifers. In spring and early summer the meadows are carpeted with flowers adding to the already colourful scene. Although very much a walking area, Bernried has an open-air swimming pool as well as riding and tennis.

Halfway between Bernried and Deggendorf in the Perlbach valley is Schloss Egg, a real fairytale castle, built in the twelfth century high above the surrounding forest and now open to the public from April to November to view the chapel and the main hall. The castle is guarded by ramparts while in the courtyard is the Hungerthurm (Hunger Tower). This is a tall square windowless building except for the narrow lancet windows that throw a minimal amount of light on the stairs leading to the top of the tower with its pyramid shaped roof and the four small turrets that decorate each corner. An ideal setting for Rapunzel to let down her long golden tresses.

The castle now forms part of an hotel. In fact the former stables and coach house have been turned into first-class restaurants in historic surroundings; meals here are not cheap but a splendid way to wind up an excellent holiday

Further Information
— The Bayerischer Wald —

Places to Visit

Bodenmais
Museum Bodenmais
Bahnhofstrasse
Open: daily 10am-4pm except November and December. Times of guided tours vary. Car park .

Breitenberg
Weberei Museum
Open: daily during main summer months but only on three afternoons a week in early and late season.

Finsterau
Freilichtmuseum Bayerischer Wald
Open: daily May-September; afternoons only January-April and October.

Zwiesel
Theresiental Glass Factory
Open: 9.30am-1pm for factory visits. Showrooms open: 9am-4pm Monday-Friday.

Tourist Information Offices

Regional

Fremdenverkehrsverband Ostbayern
Landshuter Strasse 13
93047 Regensburg
☎ (0941) 57186
Regional office for East Bavaria

Local
These are all *Verkehrsampt* unless stated otherwise

Aicha vorm Wald
Gemeinde Aicha vorm Wald
Am Kirchplatz 1
94529 Aicha vorm Wald
☎ (08544) 7511

Arnbruck
93471 Arnbruck
☎ (09945) 414

Bayerisch Eisenstein
Hauptstrasse 16
94252 Bayerisch Eisenstein
☎ (09925) 327

Bernried
94505 Bernried
☎ (0995) 217/451

Bischofsmais
Rathaus
Hauptstrasse 34
94253 Bischofsmais
☎ (09920) 1380

Bodenmais
Bahnhofstrasse 56
94253 Bodenmais
☎ (09924) 77835/77836

Bogen
Stadtverwaltung
Stadtplatz 56
94327 Bogen
☎ (09422) 505-52

Breitenberg
Gemeindeverwaltung
94139 Breitenberg
☎ (08584) 411

Büchlberg
Hauptstrasse 5
94124 Büchlberg
☎ (08505) 1222

Cham
Propsteistrasse 46
93413 Cham
☎ (09971) 4933

Deggendorf
Oberer Stadtplatz 34
94469 Deggendorf
☎ (0991) 296-169/296-170

Eging am See
Rathaus
94535 Eging am See
☎ (08544) 8052

Falkenstein
Marktplatz 1
93167 Falkenstein
☎ (09462) 244

Frauenau
Rathausplatz 34
94258 Frauenau
☎ (0992) 6710

Freyung
Rathaus
Rathausplatz 2
94078 Freyung
☎ (08851) 588-50

Furth im Wald
Fremdenverkehrsamt
Schlossplatz 1
93437 Furth im Wald
☎ (09973) 3813

Grafenau
Rathaus
Rathausgasse 1
94481 Grafenau
☎ (08552) 42743

Haibach
Fremdenverkehrsamt
94353 Haibach
☎ (09963) 1030

Haidmühle
Gemeindeverwaltung
94145 Haidmühle
☎ (08556) 567/1064

Hauzenberg
Rathaus
Schulstrasse 2
94051 Hauzenberg
☎ (08586) 30-30/30-31

Hofkirchen
Gemeindeverwaltung
8359 Hofkirchen
☎ (08545) 213

Hutthurm
Gemeindeverwaltung
94116 Hutthurm
☎ (08505) 833 and 834

Kellberg-Thyrnau
St Blasius Strasse 10
94136 Thyrnau
☎ (08501) 320 and 282

Kirchdorf im Wald
Gemeindeverwaltung
Marienbergstrasse 3
94261 Kirchdorf im Wald
☎ (09928) 355/416

Kollnburg
94262 Köllnburg
☎ (09942) 5091

Kötzting
Rathaus
Herrenstrasse 10
93444 Kötzting
☎ (09941) 602150

Lalling
Lallinger Winkl
94551 Lalling
☎ (09904) 374

Lam
Marktplatz 1
93462 Lam
☎ (09943) 1081

Lohberg
Rathaus
Rathausweg 1
93470 Lohberg
☎ (09943) 3460

Neu Schönau
Alt Schönau
94556 Neuschönau
☎ (08558) 850/858/667

Neukirchen vorm Wald
Pfrundestrasse 1
94154 Neukirchen vorm
Wald
☎ (08504) 1763

Obernzell
Rathaus
94130 Obernzell
☎ (08591) 1877

Osterhofen
94486 Osterhofen
☎ (09932) 403-0

Passau
Fremdenverkehrsverein
Neuburgerstrasse 7
94032 Passau
☎ (0851) 33421

Plattling
Stadtverwaltung
94447 Plattling
☎ (09931) 708-0/2241

Rattenberg
94371 Rattenberg
☎ (09963) 703

Regen
Haus des Gastes
Stadtplatz 4
94209 Regen
☎ (09921) 2929

Regensburg
Tourist Information
Altes Rathaus
93047 Regensburg
☎ (0941) 507-4411
/507-4410

St Englmar
Rathaus
94379 St Englmar
☎ (09965) 221

St Oswald-Riedlhütte
94568 St Oswald
☎ St Oswald (08552) 4666
or Riedlhütte (08553)
6083

Salzweg
Fremdenverkehrsverein
Goldener Steig Salzweg
Passauer Strasse 18
94121 Salzweg
☎ (0851) 41372

Schönberg
Rathaus
94513 Schönberg
☎ (08554) 821

Sonnen
Gemeindeamt
94164 Sonnen
☎ (08584) 808

Tittling
Im Grafenschlossle
Marktplatz 10
94104 Tittling
☎ (08504) 401-14

Viechtach
Stadtplatz 1
94234 Viechtach
☎ (09942) 1661

Vilshofen
Fremdenverkehrsbüro
Stadtplatz 29
94474 Vilshofen
☎ (08541) 208-0

Waldmünchen
Fremdenverkehrsamt
Marktplatz
93449 Waldmünchen
☎ (09972) 261

Windorf
Marktplatz 24
94575 Windorf
☎ (08541) 8500

Wörth an der Donau
Verkehrsverein
93086 Wörth an der
Donau
☎ (09482) 472

Zwiesel
Stadtplatz 27
Rathaus
94227 Zwiesel
☎ (09922) 9623

9 • The Bavarian Alps (Oberbayern)

The state of Bavaria is the largest in Germany and is therefore divided into various regions. The Bavarian Alps are found in the extreme south of Upper Bavaria (Oberbayern) and form a natural boundary with Austria. It is an area of striking contrasts, where the lakes and flat plains in the north give way to the mountainous region in the south and where the Deutsche Alpenstrasse runs from Lindau in the west to Berchtesgaden in the east. Although the peaks here are more dramatic than those found in the Bayerischer Wald, they are still somewhat lower than the French and Swiss Alps.

This is the land of alpine villages whose balconied chalets are garlanded in summer with a colourful floral profusion. Music is never far away for every town, village or hamlet boasts a brass band. Zither music in the inns helps foaming tankards to be downed to slake thirsty throats and outside the air rings to the melody of cow bells as cream coloured cattle graze in the lush village meadows or high alpine *Almen*. Churches, usually rococo or baroque in style, have interiors beautified by ornate carving and delicately hued frescoes. From the late seventeenth to the mid-eighteenth century Bavaria was fortunate to have the Asam family living in their territory. It is in no small way that the ecclesiastical art treasures found here is due to them. Hans Georg Asam was born in 1649 and started the family tradition but it was his two sons, Cosmas Damian born in 1686 at Benediktbeuern and Egid Quirin born in 1692 at Tegernsee, that became so famous. The two sons did much of their work together and so became known as the Asam brothers.

In winter, when the snow comes, many of the mountain villages turn into winter wonderlands and the inhabitants put away their agricultural implements and become ski instructors, while the sports shops change their summer wares to those more suited to skiing. For those interested in trying a winter sports holiday off the beaten track, an application to any of the local tourist offices will bring information regarding facilities in their area.

The region is well served with means of transport. The main

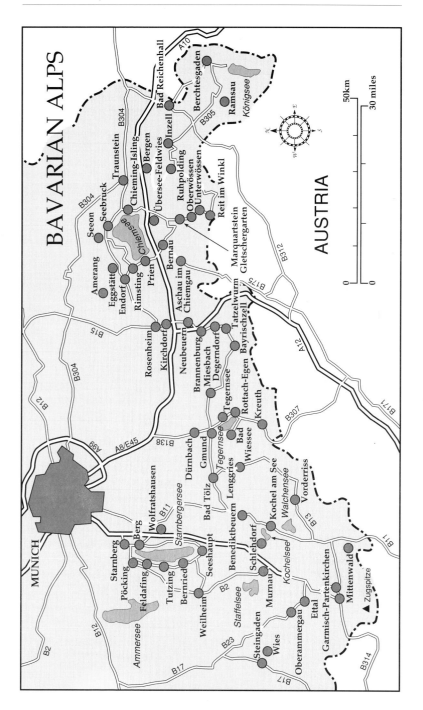

airport is at Munich Riem which is capable of taking the biggest transatlantic jet aircraft. Hire of cars from firms like Avis and Hertz is a mere formality at the airport or the main railway station (*Hauptbahnhof*). Fast inter-city trains from all parts of Germany will convey the traveller by day or night services in comfort. Travellers coming from those channel ports which do not have a through service change at Cologne, but there are seat reservations for the entire journey; thanks to the computerised system the required carriage in the next train is opposite the one just vacated. The budget conscious traveller can make the journey by coach and be whisked at high but comfortable speeds along what must be one of the finest motorway systems outside of America.

For the motorist there are good and frequent filling stations, restaurants (waiter and self-service) as well as parking bays with toilet facilities on all motorways. A free motorway service booklet can be obtained from German National Tourist Offices or at *Autobahn* filling stations; it provides valuable help in calculating distance and services available on route. Most towns and villages have their own local tourist office that helps visitors to find accommodation as well as giving out local information on transport and places of interest; some are incorporated with the House of the Guest.

The climate during the summer months ranges from warm to very hot but in the more mountainous regions thunderstorms can break out quickly especially during July and August. Walkers are therefore well advised carry protective clothing as well as insect repellent. Snakes are rarely a hazard.

Accommodation varies from farmhouses to first class hotels but all offer well kept rooms. A simple room will contain a bed, chairs, wardrobe, bedside table with reading light and a washbasin with hot and cold running water. At the other end of the scale the rooms have balconies, bathrooms or shower and a WC, some may have televisions and refrigerators for drinks.

Self-catering standards, whether in apartments or whole houses, are first class with fully fitted kitchens containing ovens and refrigerators; some have washing machines and dryers. Bed linen is usually supplied but sometimes not towels (always check at the time of booking just what will be on offer). The cost of heating may or may not be included and the final cleaning charge is usually extra.

Meals, whether in hotels or restaurants, are of excellent quality and quantity, not highly seasoned and therefore usually very acceptable to the majority of palates. *Konditorei* (confectioners) have mouth watering displays of luscious cakes attracting either personal shoppers or those wishing to sit down and avail themselves of coffee as well. Regrettably this does prove rather an expensive pleasure.

Bavaria is where comfort, leisure, kindness and geniality are combined and known as *Gemütlichkeit*. Although it is a holiday area popular with the Germans it is well worth exploring. Even the better-known places, especially those associated with King Ludwig, will reward the visitor, despite being busy during the peak periods. Try to avoid school holiday times to avoid the crowds, advice which applies to much of Continental Europe, not just Bavaria.

The Deutsche Alpenstrasse

Back in the 1930s an alpine road was constructed to enable visitors to enjoy the splendours and hospitality to be found in this rural corner of Germany. The route to be covered commences at Steingaden, south-west of Munich where Oberbayern and the Allgäu meet, and ends where the Alpenstrasse finishes at Berchtesgaden.

Steingaden is an unpretentious village with a lovely old Romanesque church of St John; built in the twelfth century it has twin towers with saddle roofs which are unusual in this region. During the Peasants Rising of 1525, 15,000 peasants attacked the church and set fire to the outer buildings; the damaged areas were subsequently rebuilt but again suffered in 1646 at the hands of the Swedish army during the Thirty Years' War. This is very much a rural community and the inhabitants are mainly farmers or employees of the factories which turn the milk from the famous Allgäu cattle into cheese.

Coupled with Steingaden is **Wies** whose fame lies in its church which was built between 1746-56 on the orders of the abbot of Steingaden. This glorious rococo church is set in alpine meadows, shielded by dark pine forests and was the work of two famous brothers, Dominikus and Johann Baptist Zimmermann. Viewed from the outside this yellow and white church gives no indication of the wealth or beauty that lies within. The interior walls are painted white as is the stucco work, but this merely serves to enhance the rich glowing colours of the painted ceiling which represents the Day of Judgement. The side altars form a marked contrast with a rich red marble (in truth it is merely layers of red stucco, polished to a high degree) and the main altar has been treated in the same way. In the central alcove pay particular attention to the rough wooden statue of Christ, for this statue attracts pilgrims from all corners of the world; a legend says that real tears were seen running down its cheeks.

On the way to Oberammergau the road crosses a 250ft (76m) gorge, spanned now by the Echelsbacher Bridge built in 1929. Prior

The famous rococo church at Wies

to that, motorists had to cross the river Ammer by raft pulled by oxen. There is a commemorative monument on the left bank.

The road runs south through the Ammergebirge to reach **Oberammergau**, home of the famous passion play which is performed every 10 years; the next performance is in 2000 but in the intervening years this village is well worth a visit. Situated at the foot of the Kofel it is a good centre from which to explore the surrounding areas which include the Zugspitze and the Karwendel mountains.

The village itself, although not strictly off the beaten track, when not overcrowded with tourists coming for the play, is delightful. The houses are gaily painted and two great favourites are those painted with scenes from *Red Riding Hood* and *Hansel and Gretel*. The parish church was built in the early part of the eighteenth century and the interior has some first class frescoes.

The Echelsbacher Bridge

Oberammergau is famous for its woodcarving and houses an international school to instruct pupils in this most delicate of crafts. There is an arts and crafts museum in the Dorfstrasse exhibiting all manner of local craft work. One of the finest pieces is that of a crib made almost 200 years ago.

With the mountains rising all around this is definitely walking territory — either on the well defined paths or real mountaineering if preferred — for which guides are available. Each year, on 24 August, there is an organised walk (*Gebirgswandertag*) in King Ludwig's footsteps. As dusk falls bonfires are lit and the mountain peaks catch the reflected glow turning a rich rosy red.

A few kilometres further on is **Ettal** in the Ammergauer range; a mere hamlet but dominated by a magnificent Benedictine monastery. It was founded in 1330 by the Emperor Ludwig after a traumatic journey from Rome where he had been crowned by the Pope. His homeward route had taken him to the northern Italian cities where he had tried unsuccessfully to obtain taxes from the wealthy merchants. A battle ensued and Ludwig was soundly defeated and had to flee for his life. Weary and dejected he knelt and prayed for help, whereupon a monk appeared and offered him money and a statue of the Virgin Mary. In recompense the monk required him to found a monastery in his homeland of Bavaria. To this Ludwig agreed and when his horse eventually collapsed in a lonely valley he took it as

The painted façade of the Hansel and Gretel Haus, Oberammergau

a sign that this was where the monastery should be built.

The façade is decorated with figures representing the twelve apostles and its magnificent green dome is about 200ft (70m) high. The eighteenth-century interior is a combination of baroque and rococo and is comparatively modern. The paintings adorning the dome are the work of Jakob Zeiller. The cloisters that surround the church are now a school and the pupils are taught by the monks when they are not distilling a potent liqueur made from twenty-six different alpine herbs and known as Ettal Klosterlikör. With the steady stream of visitors that the church attracts there is a ready market for this beverage. Across the road from the monastery is a general shop, a couple of inns and one or two houses.

After leaving Ettal the road claws its way upwards by a series of hairpin bends before descending to the Loisach valley and **Garmisch-Partenkirchen**, the famous expensive winter sports resort, a leisure centre for the American forces in Europe and also a base for some of the highest walking and hiking expeditions in Germany. It is possible to take advantage of the delights that Garmisch-Partenkirchen has to offer outside the main centre for a fraction of the cost and enjoy some of the superb natural facilities as well.

Grainau is a small village only 4 miles (6km) away and close to the Eibsee, a small delightful lake at the foot of the Zugspitze. For those who like gorges the walk to Partnachklamm, 2 miles (3km) from

Garmisch, should not be missed. The river Partnach forces its way through a wild gorge while a path runs alongside the turbulent water which can at times dampen one with a fine spray; sometimes the path is cut out through the rock face and in other places becomes a platform built out over the river. The Riessersee, even closer to town, is another small lake with views across to the Waxenstein and behind that the towering Zugspitze itself.

A more strenuous walk is to the Höllentalklamm just below the Waxenstein where a path follows a rocky gorge. The Zugspitze is the highest mountain in Germany and the summit can be reached by more than one route. There is a rack and pinion railway via the Riessersee, Grainau, Eibsee and Riffelriss and then by a tunnel to the Schneefernhaus. The final ascent to the summit and viewing platform is by a cable car. On clear days there are fantastic views across range after range of mountains into Austria, Italy and Switzerland.

The second route is by cable car from the Eibsee and is a must for those who enjoy an unfolding panorama. The third route is by cable car from the Austrian side of the mountain followed by a walk through the mountain with windows cut out of the rock face to enable visitors to look out onto the Schneeferner — a natural bowl that is used for skiing most of the year. Having passed through to the German side one can take the cable car to the summit.

A small detour from the Alpenstrasse which is well worthwhile is to **Mittenwald**, the last town in Germany before crossing the border into Austria. This medieval town might well have stepped straight out of *Grimms Fairy Tales*, set in the vividly green valley of the river Isar and protected by the towering massif of the Karwendel Gebirge to the east and the Wetterstein massif to the south. Added to this are five charming lakes around the town; the Schmalensee, Luttensee, Wildensee, Lautersee and Ferchensee which attract visitors who are happy to picnic on the shores and partake in the aquatic delights offered by these sheltered lakes.

The town has some beautiful old houses decorated with colourful frescoes which are mainly to be found in the Unter and Obermarkt. Here also is the church of St Peter and St Paul built in the mid-eighteenth century. In front of the church is a statue of a man seated on a stool carving a violin; this is Mittenwald's most famous son — Matthias Klotz (1653-1743).

Matthias Klotz was sent as a young boy to Cremona in Italy to learn the art of violin making under a master craftsman Nicolo Amati, where they also worked with Stradivarius (a native of Cremona). After 20 years of absence, gaining experience in various

The Riessersee with the Zugspitze in the distance

locations, Klotz returned to his native Mittenwald. At the rear of the altar in St Nikolaus Church in Mittenwald he carved the following inscription 'MK 1684 violin maker for twenty years'.

Klotz found all the wood suitable for violin making in and around Mittenwald and soon became successful in selling his instruments, especially to monasteries and princely residences. He recruited talented members of his own family and then, to expand his trade, extended this to other families. To start with they sold the violins themselves which meant travelling a good deal, but eventually they sold their instruments to merchants enabling the craftsmen to spend more time on the manufacturing.

In 1858 a state violin-making school was founded at Mittenwald; today the school is in the Partenkirchenerstrasse and has an annual competition for the twelve places available. Applications are received from throughout the world and out of the hundreds only forty are short listed and then the final twelve lucky ones are chosen.

Alpine meadows near Mittenwald

The pattern of training has changed very little since the Middle Ages. The successful applicant becomes an apprentice for 3½ years. The second stage as a journeyman lasts a further 3 years under a master craftsman before the final examination is taken to become a master. The time to make a violin is about 160 hours so it is not surprising that these instruments are expensive to buy.

There are abundant facilities in the district but above all this is an area for the walking enthusiast with routes ranging from a 10 minute stroll to an all day 8-hour hike. The local tourist office can give further information on the choices available and on special guided tours.

This next section leaves the Alpenstrasse to take in some of the lakes that lie in the Voralpenland. From Garmisch-Partenkirchen one follows the road that runs along the Loisach valley until one reaches the busy market town of **Murnau** which was on the old medieval trade route between Germany and Italy. There is the fine old parish church of St Nikolaus as well as the charming Mariahilfe-kirche here and was the home of Wassily Kandinsky, a painter of the early abstract Blue Rider School. Murnau is also noted for its water sports facilities on the Staffelsee and Riegsee. The Staffelsee is the larger lake and has sharply indented shores forming reed-fringed bays. The lake itself is dotted with small wooded islets and sailors make full use of these obstacles in races. There are two excellent bathing beaches close to Murnau and accommodation in the district

Weilheim

to suit all tastes and prices, including a large camping site.

Weilheim is a small but busy market town between Murnau and the Starnbergersee, dating from Roman times. During the Middle Ages the town was encircled by a city wall built, so it is said, by prisoners from the local jail. Much of the old fortification has disappeared but the remaining parts give an indication of the size of the town during that period. Weilheim, in the Middle Ages, was used to store that most precious of commodities, salt.

The small village of **Polling**, now a suburb of Weilheim, was the major community back in the eighth century, as it housed a Benedictine abbey whose abbot ruled over the surrounding countryside. It is well worth stopping to see the abbey church and the ancient houses that still remain in its shadows. From Weilheim the road goes on to Starnberg, the main resort on the Starnbergersee, but before reaching it there is one place of particular interest and that is **Pöcking**.

It is a small unpretentious town and the home of the now famous chain of Post Hotels found throughout German speaking countries. In the days when everything had to travel by road, including the mail, coaches pulled by teams of horses and carrying a few passengers as well, needed a few stopping places where horses could be changed and passengers provided with a meal and overnight accommodation. Local inns were used and eventually the regular ones became known as Post Hotels; the first of them is at Pöcking.

The Starnbergersee covers an area of approximately 22sq miles (8sq km) and is a mere 18 miles (29km) from Munich, the capital of Bavaria. It is naturally a great attraction to the city dwellers who, during the summer months, come by car or train for a day on or near the lake. The wealthy have villas in the small resorts that lie around its shores. From Starnberg there is an *Autobahn* link into the city centre as well as a fast electric train service as far as Tutzing on the western shore. The lake itself is plied by large ships very similar to those used on the Rhine for daytime cruises. Why not take a complete tour of the lake or use it as a ferry to one of the lakeside resorts?

During the sixteenth and seventeenth centuries the Starnberger-see was the venue for many great water carnivals while the guests watched from luxurious gondolas. Even now there are wooden gondolas that take passengers on short excursions.

The resort of **Starnberg** lies at the northern end of the lake and is overlooked by a sixteenth-century castle, once the home of the prince bishops but now alas a mere tax office. In the centre of the town the tall blue and white maypole, like those found in most communities in Bavaria, is decorated with figures representing the various trades carried out in and around the town. Perched on the top is a starling which is the town symbol; Starnberg means Starling Hill.

The parish church of St Josef dates from 1765 and is built in the rococo style. The main altar is flanked by white marble figures and gives a pleasant lightness to the interior. In the Possenhoferstrasse is a local history museum showing the various activities in this area down through the ages. As befits the largest resort there is a fine yacht harbour and during the summer months regattas take place most weekends and holidays.

The eastern shores of the lake are less populated than the western side but **Berg**, a short distance from Starnberg, is where Ludwig II, famed for his fantastic castles of Neuschwanstein, Linderhof and Herrenchiemsee, met his untimely end. After being declared insane and deposed from the throne, Ludwig was sent to Schloss Berg under the supervision of a doctor. Two days later he and the doctor took a small rowing boat out onto the lake. When they failed to return a search party was sent out and found the boat overturned in shallow water and the bodies of the two men who had drowned. The actual spot is marked by an iron cross rising from the lake and on the shore is the tiny Votivkapelle. Each year, on the 13 June, a service is held here in memory of this tragic king who nevertheless left behind a rich heritage that succeeding generations flock to see.

Berg is essentially for those wishing to spend their days out on the lake and evening entertainment is sought either in Starnberg or Munich. Except for the small hamlets of Leoni (named after the Italian baritone Giuseppe Leoni), Aufkirchen and Ammerland, most of the shore is inhabited by wildlife. This quieter shore has attracted some famous names who value the peace it affords and have made their homes here — Christian Morgenstern the poet and currently the well known German baritone Dietrich Fischer Dieskau.

On the western shore after leaving Starnberg is **Possenhofen** and the *Schloss* that looks out over the lake. This was the childhood home of the Empress Elisabeth (Sissi), wife of Franz Josef of Austria. Sissi and her sisters loved this castle and would ride through the woods and countryside; after this carefree existence it is little wonder that Sissi found the life at the Austrian court in Vienna stifling and rebelled against the restriction it imposed. The castle is not open to the public but a pleasant walk across the public park enables the inquisitive to see the exterior.

The neighbouring village of **Feldafing** is a busy little resort which offers splendid water sports facilities as well as one of the most delightfully laid out golf courses in Germany. Its view is of the lake and, in the distance, the rising alps. Feldafing boasts only one large hotel, the Golf Hotel Kaiserin Elisabeth, which is renowned for its old world charm and hospitality as dispensed in the halcyon days when the Empress Elisabeth returned to the scene of her childhood and stayed in this hotel for several weeks during the summer. In the course of her stay she would cross to the small offshore Rosen Insel (Rose Island) to meet her cousin Ludwig II for whom she had a great affection. Doubtless these two unhappy people exchanged confidences and sought comfort in each other's company.

The hotel is the starting point for excursions in the old yellow and black post coaches drawn by four horses, and is where courses are held for driving four in hand.

The hill rising at the back of the town is the Kalvarienberg (Hill of Calvary) with its Stations of the Cross, and is also a good vantage point for surveying the surrounding countryside.

The town also boasts a well laid out park thanks to Maximilian II (father of Ludwig II) who had intended to build a castle as well; in the event he only managed the Roman villa, in the style found at *Pompeii* on the Rosen Insel, before his early demise.

The Rosen Insel can only be reached by boat; at weekends one can cross by a pole propelled gondola, but during the week visitors either have to hire a boat or swim. On the island one can visit the villa or just stroll along the paths that have been laid out amongst the thousands of rose bushes; the perfume-scented air on a still warm afternoon is wonderful. Richard Strauss, the composer, used to come here frequently, perhaps to gather inspiration for his next work.

Lothar Günther Buchheim, noted painter, author, photographer, publisher and collector, lives in Feldafing. His work *The Boat* was the story of a U-boat crew during World War II, and has subsequently been televised and received with acclaim.

The next lakeside resort is **Tutzing** where the emphasis is again on the watersports facilities with sailing and windsurfing predominating. Just outside the town at Deixlfurt is another golf course and at weekends and holidays is extremely popular. In theory it is possible for visitors to use local courses, but in practice it may prove more difficult because golf courses are not as numerous as in Britain or America and therefore they become well patronised. Prior contact with a club or course is advisable to save disappointment. Golf is still regarded in Germany as a sport for the few rather than the majority. Tutzing also offers shooting as an alternative sport and the local club organises tournaments and welcomes entries from visitors.

Another local sport (perhaps craft might be a better term) is that of fish sticking. Instead of rod and line a long pole, sharpened to a fine point at one end, is used. This method does not yield a large catch but it does provide an insight into the lengths the fisherman in bygone days used to go to. Anglers employing more conventional methods are rewarded with pike, renke, rainbow trout, carp, eels and tench.

Every 5 years Tutzing holds an historical play which depicts a fisherman's wedding. As one might imagine it is a highly amusing affair with one of the funniest parts centring round the bridegroom and the party he holds the night before the wedding.

The castle, Schloss Tutzing, dates from the early part of the seventeenth century but was completely rebuilt at the beginning of the nineteenth century and now houses an evangelical college.

Bernried, with its lovely old timbered houses, is the last resort on the western shore and in 1983 was awarded a gold medal and title of *Schönstes Dorf* (Most Beautiful Village). Peace and tranquility prevail here and is an ideal place for anyone in need of relaxation. A former Augustinian monastery founded in the twelfth century is close to the lakeshore and after restoration is now used for educational purposes by the Benedictine Order.

Over 70 years ago an American, Wilhelmina Bush-Woods, came to Bernried and was so enchanted with the place that she built a castle, Schloss Hohenried, on the northern slopes overlooking the village. She also founded a trust which supports the nature reserve here. In 1950, to ensure the future environment and welfare of the local people, she arranged for her Bernried estate (195 acres) was to be given to the community in perpetuity for all people but with special reference to mothers and children, nature and animal lovers for their relaxation and enjoyment as well as to stimulate and inspire artists and students. In 1952 she died at the age of 62 and is buried in the now private grounds of the Schloss Hohenried Clinic.

The final lakeside resort is situated at the southern end of the lake and is **Seeshaupt**, a mere hamlet where accommodation and pastimes are simple. Apart from the sailing and windsurfing school the only other sport is tennis. Visitors who come here are mainly ornithologists and are attracted by the numerous birds which find a haven for nesting within the tall reeds which grow in profusion.

Wolfratshausen is an old eleventh-century market town to the north of Seeshaupt in the valley of the Isar. The Munich to Garmisch-Partenkirchen *Autobahn* almost clips the western side of the town but does provide for quick and easy motoring. In the Marktstrasse there are some very fine old houses to be seen, dating back several hundred years. The ancestral home of the counts of Diessen-Andechs was built in the eleventh century to withstand marauders but not unfortunately, a thunderstorm that occurred in 1734. The parish church of St Andreas with its dominating 210ft (64m) high tower was built in 1484 but partially destroyed in 1619 by fire. The real gem here though is the early baroque church of 1286 in Nantwein which is dedicated to St Nantovinus, a pilgrim who after being falsely accused of treachery was burnt at the stake.

At the confluence of the Loisach and Isar rivers is the Pupplinger Au, the largest nature reserve area in Europe. An added attraction for visitors are the raft trips that ply between Wolfratshausen and Munich. These large rafts, made of logs and propelled by a long oar, have wooden benches for the passengers to sit on. The 2-hour journey is a merry one as beer is dispensed straight from the barrel and there is often music to which the passengers are invited to join in and sing.

Leaving the Starnbergersee area, head south-east through the tiny village of Penzberg to **Benediktbeuern**. This village is at the foot of the Benediktenwand that rises to a height of 5,853ft (1,784m). The village offers simple accommodation, a few shops and is the home of a magnificent Benedictine abbey which was founded in 730. It is the oldest monastery in Upper Bavaria and the present building dates from the latter half of the seventeenth century. It is baroque in style with frescoes painted by Hans Georg Asam whose son Cosmas Damian was born here. Scenes from the life of Christ are depicted in

The monastery at Benediktbeuern

rich glowing colours in the painted frescoes that adorn the ceiling and walls of the basilica and are the work of Hans Georg Asam. The pillars and arches are literally smothered in white plaster stucco and very reminiscent of Grinling Gibbons work in wood. Above the high altar is a clock, probably the only one in such a prominent position inside a church. One of the abbots considered that sermons should

The rich baroque interior of Benediktbeuern

not exceed 45 minutes and so had the clock installed to ensure that the preacher did not overrun the allotted time.

The separate chapel of St Anastasia is situated at the northern end of the abbey and was built in 1751. It is the work of Johann Michael

Fischer, who later went on to build Ottobeuren in the Allgäu in the same style, and now recognised as a masterpiece of baroque architecture. Concerts are held in the precincts of the abbey during the summer and guided tours are available daily, one in the morning and afternoon, to other parts of the abbey including the old refectory now used as a library; note the frescoed ceilings by J.B. Zimmermann. The Alter Festsaal on the second floor is now used for concerts and is an extremely elegant room with six full length windows that light up the ornate ceiling with its glorious paintings of 1674 by Kaspar Feichtmayr. The Kurfürstensaal, again the work of J.B. Zimmermann and his son Josef in 1731, is now used as a house chapel and has modern seats and kneeling rests. Hanging from the ceiling are four sparkling glass chandeliers.

Originally the occupants of this abbey were of the Benedictine Order but since 1930 it has been inhabited by the Salesian Order who have established a theological college in the cloisters of the church.

The Frauenhofer Museum in Frauenhoferstrasse is the old workshop of the scientist Josef von Frauenhofer (1787-1826). It is hard to believe in this modern age that the almost crude apparatus here helped to improve the specialised field of optics.

The Alpenstrasse now runs on to the pretty lakeside resort of **Kochel am See** that nestles at the foot of the rising alps with painted houses adding to its charm; the Hotel Zur Post (1356) and the Alpenhotel Schmied von Kochel are two buildings that prove this point.

One cannot fail to notice that the name of Schmied von Kochel is uppermost in this village. The main square bears the name as well as the bronze statue of this mighty man, a giant in more ways than one, who in 1705 died fighting in Munich and became the hero of the Peasants Uprising. The parish church of St Michael is typical of the area with white walls and a steep black roof with an onion dome on the tower. Franz Marc, the famous painter, was killed in France in 1916 and now lies buried in the churchyard here.

Its situation on the shores of the lake makes Kochel a popular place for holidaymakers and town dwellers at weekends who take part in all sorts of aquatic sports which includes a splendid outdoor swimming pool. Wildlife abounds in the marshy territory at the northern end of the lake and especially at nesting times. This is also a good starting point for walking and hiking with a choice of taking the low or high routes. There is plenty of accommodation for visitors whether in hotels, private houses, farms or camping sites.

Schledorf is a farming community that is adjacent to Kochel but dominated by yet another Benedictine abbey. The first church to be

built was in the fifth century by the Kochelsee, but in 742 the holy
Tertulin persuaded Otto von Freising to found and endow a Benedictine abbey here in Schledorf; alas in 907 it was destroyed by the
Hungarians. Rebuilt again in 1140 as an Augustinian monastery it
was replaced in 1718 with another new building but this time with
an inner courtyard and then greatly extended in 1812 to become the
imposing edifice that stands today. From 1892-1904 it was a Dominican convent but changed hands to become a missionary monastery.
The abbey church of St Tertulin, with its double staircase leading up
to the main entrance, is incorporated in the main buildings; the views
afforded from here over the Kochelsee to the Herzogstand are magnificent. The interior of the church with its plain classical features
and simple geometrical patterned decoration of the late eighteenth
century is in marked contrast to that of Benediktbeuren. The high
altar has a massive painting of the *Shepherds Paying Homage*.

At the southern end of the Kochelsee is the hydro electric power
station which draws its supplies from the neighbouring and much
larger Walchensee. From Kochel the road runs alongside the lake
before climbing and twisting up through the woods to reach the
vividly deep blue Walchensee ringed by dark green woods against
the rising majesty of mountain ranges to the south, the Karwendel-
gebirge in the foreground and the Stubai Alps on the horizon. The
Walchensee is not overpopulated, but one or two small hotels and
camping sites can be found at Urfeld and Walchensee.

From the village of **Walchensee** there is a chair-lift taking visitors
to the Herzogstand, the ascent affording visitors glorious panoramic
views over the surrounding countryside. From the top of the chair-
lift a 30-40 minute walk along a well defined path leads to the summit
itself. On clear days the mountain ranges that can be identified
include the Karwendel, Stubai, Wetterstein, Zugspitze, Grossglock-
ner and the Gross Venediger.

From Walchensee it is possible to follow the road to Wallgau and
the Isarfall. Use the small side road to visit this cascade of water,
which has been formed by diverting part of the river Isar before
taking the toll road which follows the main stream of the Isar as it
passes through the mountains to **Vorderriss**. Here, the visitor will
find a cluster of chalets a *Gasthof* and the long Sylvenstein lake with
its dam at one end constructed in 1959 to regulate the river and
control any flood of water. The excess water is now used by an
underground power station. At Vorderriss the small toll road continues alongside the river Rissbach before crossing the border into
Austria and the tiny mountain retreat of Eng.

From Vorderriss the national road runs along the southern shore of the Sylvenstein before crossing back in mid-lake via the magnificent high stone bridge where once again the road divides. One branch continues to the end of the lake and the Walchental to the frontier, from where the Achen Pass leads to the Achensee and eventually to the Inn valley. The other branch is the B13 which continues to follow the Isar as it flows northwards to reach the small town of **Lenggries** in the area known as the Isar Winkel, lying between the Tegernsee and Walchensee.

The town itself is mainly situated on the eastern bank of the river and in the centre, with the 182ft (55m) high tower topped by a copper dome, stands the parish church of St Jakob built in 1772. First and foremost Lenggries caters for activity holidays, with excellent facilities for sailing, windsurfing, canoeing, hang-gliding and tennis.

For the walker this is an area of natural unspoilt beauty and in early summer the surrounding countryside is a picture with a profusion of wild flowers which includes some protected species such as the ladys slipper orchid, the turks-cap lily, alpen roses and gentian.

Opposite the town on the west bank the cable car whisks visitors up to the Brauneck where there are even more splendid vistas. In winter this open sunny plateau becomes a skiers paradise with its connecting network of lifts producing runs of various gradings. In summer the ski runs become trails for hikers who find much enjoyment in the sharp mountain air. The highest point is the Benediktenwand and can be reached from Brauneck with about 4 hours good walking. There are mountain *Gasthöfe* up here, some providing full meals and overnight accommodation as well as mountain huts selling drinks only. For the wildlife enthusiast, watch out for the ibex that can, on occasions, be seen perched on their rocky vantage points.

Overlooking the town is Schloss Hohenberg, originally an eleventh-century fortress belonging to the lords of Thann but destroyed in 1707 during the War of the Spanish Succession. It was rebuilt in 1712-18 as a stately home with a chapel added in 1722 with a fine rococo altar. In 1953 the castle became the property of the Ursulines and is now a boarding school.

From Lenggries the road and river continues down the valley to **Bad Tölz**, whose history goes back as far as the fifth century when the Romans formed a settlement on the river bank. Today the river Isar divides the old town from the new spa that has developed on the west bank. It is here in the modern town with its wide tree lined streets and well kept parks and gardens that clinics and hotels offering cures for various ailments are to be found, together with the

*The town hall,
Bad Tölz*

municipally run Cure Centre. Here, as in most parts of Bavaria, guests pay a *Kur Tax*. In return they receive a visitor's card enabling them to use certain local facilities such as swimming pools at reduced charges. It may be noted that the waters on offer here for drinking are iodine based and slightly more palatable than the sulphur ones!

The old town with its steeply sloping Marktstrasse is the main shopping area where the small shops and cafés have gaily painted façades lending a piquant charm of its own, while at the top end of the street is the beautiful *Rathaus* with its delicately painted façade. In the centre of the street, opposite the *Rathaus* entrance is a statue of a warrior holding a lance, in memory of Kasper Winzerer, a knight and leader of a local mercenary band 450 years ago.

Bad Tölz offers visitors many attractions one of which is a delightful Marionette Theatre with a seating capacity for 161 persons. There is a most comprehensive local museum in Marktstrasse exhibiting arts and crafts, a geological collection and items of special local interest. A wander through the old side streets lined with venerable aged houses topped by steeply gabled roofs, painted façades and gay window boxes is a step back into history; worthy of note are the Marienstift, Höflingerhaus, Sporerhaus and the former *Rathaus*. Now that the new bypass is open it is possible for pedestrians to wander and view these delights less dangerously than before.

The parish church of the Maria Himmelfahrt dates from 1262 and is well worth a visit. The ecclesiastical gem however has to be the church and tiny chapel on the Kalvarienberg. The Kalvarien-bergkirche dates from 1718 while the chapel is slightly later at 1743 and dedicated to St Leonard, a pious hermit who spent his life in the welfare of prisoners and horses. The chain that can be seen girding the chapel is a reminder of his prison work. Each year on the 6 November there is the Leonhardt Ride when farm carts and wagons, drawn by horses and attired in elaborate harnesses, form a stately procession up the hill bordered by the Stations of the Cross to the church and chapel where a special service is held.

A remarkable feature for this town is the number of specialists and other medical practitioners. Apart from this aspect of what is after all a spa town, Bad Tölz is a delightful place to stay; the riverside walks, tennis, fishing and even golf all add to the enjoyment of visitors of whom many are young and active.

One of Bavaria's most beautiful lakes is the Tegernsee, east of Bad Tölz, surrounded on three sides by mountains whose tree-lined shores afford shade during the summer but in the autumn turn to a burning gold and with the mountain tops already white with snow make this a veritable paradise. The main resorts on the lake are Bad Wiessee, Rottach-Egern, Tegernsee and Gmund. **Bad Wiessee** on the western shores is now known for its spa facilities discovered only this century. Here the iodiferous and sulphurous sodium chloride springs are to be found which the clinics, sanatoriums and hotels offer to their clients who come to find relief for heart and circulation problems as well as rheumatics. There is a splendid partly open-air concert pavilion close to the lakeshore where orchestras as well as brass bands entertain. Lakeside gardens enable the afternoon stroller to combine light activity with perhaps a game of outdoor chess. For this particular pastime the chess board is at ground level and meas-ures 12ft by 12ft (4m by 4m). The chessmen although 2ft high are quite light to pick up and move around the board.

The lakeside café's in the afternoon are well patronised as visitors partake of coffee and cake while enjoying the activities that are taking place on the lake from sailing regattas to the disembarkation of passengers on the lake steamers, or just listening to the back-

A quiet game of outdoor chess, Bad Wiessee

ground music from the afternoon concert. There is a theatre for more formal concerts as well as plays. Bad Wiessee is not just for the elderly who come to relieve their aches and pains for the young are catered for with sailing and windsurfing; for inclement weather there is a first class swimming pool. Other sports include tennis and a nine hole golf course of which the whole of the Tegernsee is justly proud.

A whole range of walks either along the lakeshore or into the surrounding hillside makes this a most attractive resort. For those wishing to walk further afield a local bus will take you to the departure points or there are ample car parks at all the strategic places which usually have large maps showing the area and suggested routes and times. Most of the walks that commence at Bad Wiessee take between 2-3 hours but it is quite simple to undertake only a part of a route. For idyllic views the walk to Bauer in der Au (Farmer in the Meadow), is a must. The building is an inn where one can sit outside to quench the thirst while gazing at the green clad slopes surrounding the meadow on three sides. Cattle are up here grazing on their summer pastures and as they move the bells that hang round their necks jangle, filling the air with a melodious tune. After leaving the inn the ground drops away steeply and the whole panorama of the lake and hills rising on all sides unfolds.

To the south, where the road commences its climb towards the Achen Pass, are the villages of Kreuth, Wildbad Kreuth (a tiny spa) and Glashütte. These three tiny villages are strung out along the final stretch of road before the border. The further one goes the wilder and more remote the territory becomes as the mountains close in. **Kreuth** is the largest of these resorts and, in fact to begin with, is almost an extension of Rottach-Egern. It does however have its own delightful small *Rathaus* and a *Bürgermeister* and looks after its own affairs while offering a quieter alternative to the bustling lakeside resorts with some first class accommodation as well as the simple variety. Kreuth is an ideal base for those who are predominantly interested in walking in the day and by evening are content to sit and discuss the following days route over a glass of beer or wine. There is however an indoor tennis hall and squash courts for those still with energy to spend and indeed it takes only a few minutes to reach the other lake resorts for further evening entertainment.

Perched high above the south-west corner of the lake is Schloss Ringberg. It is open to the public as it is part of the Max Planck Institute, a renowned scientific research establishment whose head-quarters are in Munich.

Rottach-Egern standing at the southern end of the lake is perhaps the most elegant and sophisticated town to be found in this valley. The lakeside is bordered with first class hotels including the five-star Hotel Bachmair with its own night club that attracts international cabaret artists. Leading off the lakeside are small quiet roads and it is here that the small privately run pensions are to be found. All offer excellent accommodation but instead of having a lake view there is an equally attractive panorama across meadows to the mountains. The offer here is usually on a bed and breakfast basis but in the town itself or just outside there are plenty of restaurants so that it presents no real problem. Indeed one of the most popular restaurants with both visitors and locals alike is out at Berg. A pleasant stroll along-side the tiny Rottach stream takes about 20 minutes or even along the road past meadows and cattle. Until early evening there is even a local bus service. This rural inn, the Angermaier, offers accommoda-tion as well as lunches and dinners while during the afternoon a splendid array of home made cakes are on offer together with coffee and other drinks. Apart from one other restaurant in this neighbour-hood the gastronomic delights are to be found in or around the centre of Rottach-Egern. Self-catering is widely featured here and is re-flected in the fact that the town can boast three large supermarkets as well as smaller shops. Apart from food the shops are geared to the

Lake promenade, Rottach-Egern

fashion market and *hautcouture* is displayed in the windows of the boutiques; footwear, from climbing boots to the latest fashion shoes from Italy, are also tantalisingly exhibited.

The 'House of the Guest' is situated in the *Rathaus* on the main street next door to the Post Office. Accommodation, information, reading and television rooms are all housed here under one roof. Across the street is the office for the local tour operator whose windows display various excursions on offer ranging from a half day to extended day-long trips to Venice or Vienna.

There is a fine outdoor pool adjacent to the lake with wide sun bathing lawns and a restaurant; for cooler days there is a solarium. Part of this complex is the concert hall, used for plays and exhibitions.

The bandstand set in an open garden offers concerts at least two evenings a week and again on Sunday mornings. This is also a popular spot for feeding the swans and ducks that inhabit the lake, and seems to encourage anglers during the evening. By standing on the landing stage for the lakeside steamers, one can see fish of various sizes swimming just beneath the surface of the clear water.

The author Ludwig Thoma lived in Rottach-Egern and is buried in the *Alter Friedhof* (Old Cemetery) and is also the opera singer Leo Slezak. The parish church of St Laurentius dates from the fifteenth century with a pleasing interior. The nave was originally late Gothic but in 1671 was altered into baroque style. Although there are no paintings by internationally famous artists the work that decorates this church is pleasing to the eye. The Miesbacher School evidently believed in being slightly more restrained than Hans Georg Asam who was working in the area during this period.

Rottach-Egern was originally two villages and was primarily a farming and fishing community. In 1320 a road was constructed over the Achen Pass which opened up a trade route from Bavaria into the Tyrol and ultimately Italy, thus bringing prosperity to the area which over the years has continued.

Apart from the boating, swimming, surfing and fishing there are some splendid tennis courts on which is held an annual tournament with first class prizes. In this walkers' paradise escorted day hikes are arranged by the local tourist office twice a week, usually on Tuesdays and Fridays, weather permitting. The routes vary in length but range from around 4-8 hours.

For those who prefer to combine walking with a modicum of transport a pleasant stroll either along the road or up through the woods to Sutten and the Moni Alm is ideal. At Sutten there is a long chair-lift up to the Stumpfling Alm and its *Gasthof*. From here one can either take a second lift down into the next valley and the Spitzingsee or take one of the many mountain paths that eventually lead home. Moni Alm is a peaceful sunny valley with rough meadowland gay with flowers and where the dark green forests give way to more rocky pinnacles; the slience is broken from time to time by the call of one of the birds at the Greifvogelpark Adlerhorst. The birds on view here range from the great condor, vultures and eagles down to small owls under the care of a naturalist. Here, at close range, one can view these birds of prey that inhabit this region. Each bird is contained by a long chain attached to a foot enabling them to move around their tree-lined enclosure at will. They are also taken out hunting in order that they may retain their natural way of life. Close by is a small lake whose placid waters are broken only by small families of ducks that swim out of the reeds when strangers appear in the hope of food.

At the rear of the town is the 5,599ft (1,707m) Wallberg mountain which can be ascended by a twisting mountain road where James Bond survived a desperate chase, or by the cable car. At the foot of the cable car is the Alpenwildpark which is a reserve for the wild animals (mostly deer) while close to the top of the lift is the Wallberg Hotel with its large terrace used in winter by skiers to relax in the sun. In summer its function is the same but the boots and skis are replaced by somewhat lighter attire. A short but steep track leads to the Wallberg summit with its tiny mountain chapel. There is a network

A picturesque corner of Tegernsee

of walks up here but it is advisable to have a map of the area because some parts are for climbers who have had some training or practice under difficult conditions.

The resort of **Tegernsee** on the eastern shores of the lake is, apart from Gmund, the resort with the smallest population. However that is of no consequence in the major role it has played throughout the ages. Dominating the town is Schloss Tegernsee as it is known today but in fact its origins go back to the eighth century when a Benedictine monastery was founded and became, in the succeeding years, an important cultural focal point as can be seen in the *Heimatmuseum* housed in the castle. The present building dates from the seventeenth century with the frescoes and stucco work by H.G. Asam. In 1803 it was secularised and became a royal residence for Maximilian Joseph I, so receiving the title *Schloss*.

The twin towers that grace the castle are reputed to be the oldest in Bavaria. The church contains three aisles although many of the side altars have disappeared. The side chapels are embossed with ornate rococo decorations while the Rekreationsaal's stucco work is by J. B. Zimmermann. Apart from the church and rooms used for the museum this magnificent building is now the home of a local brewery which also provides good food at reasonable prices to go with the beer in its own *Stüberl* (a room where one can both eat or drink).

The large wooden boat houses on the edge of town house the lake steamers that provide not only round cruises but also a ferry service to the other lakeside resorts from dawn till dusk.

There is a privately owned train service known as the Tegernseebahn which links up with the more modern Deutsche Bundesbahn at Schaftlach to take passengers on to Munich. Most Sundays during the summer special steam trips are arranged by the railways and the carriages are pulled by one of the lovely old steam engines that are now becoming such a thrill to young and old alike.

Tegernsee has a thriving yacht club and regular weekend sailing regattas. Windsurfing and rowing are also prominent. The town authorities have been busily renewing the *Kurpark* and the bandstand as well as the indoor swimming pool. The House of the Guest, situated on the main street in sight of the lake, houses the local tourist office, a library, reading room, television room and a music room.

The small streets that lead off the main road are an artist's dream and further on they give way to marked paths that wander the hillside, sometimes finding farms or *Gasthöfe* whose terraces look out over the lake before winding their way down into the next valley.

During September there is an annual festival when the streets take on a carnival air. Brass bands gather to play for folk dancing and all the local customs and traditions are brought to the fore. The local theatre puts on plays and poetry readings and concerts are held in the Baroque *Saal* of the *Schloss*.

Gmund, at the northern end of the lake though the smallest resort, does have its own railway station as well as a seventeenth-century parish church, St Ägidius, with work by H. G. Asam. Today Gmund is probably better known for the traffic congestion at weekends and on sunny days. The T-junction has traffic lights but it still causes long delays at peak times. Unfortunately there is no real alternative route for those heading towards Holzkirchen and the motorway.

Once away from the traffic problems of Gmund the road reaches **Dürnbach**. It is only a couple of shops and inns but important to British and American visitors, for the Commonwealth War Graves Commission sign at either side of the traffic lights indicates the Dürnbach War Cemetery on the road to Miesbach. It is mainly for RAF personnel that died in World War II but there are others buried here that have, for one reason or another, been brought to make their final resting place in this quiet and peaceful corner of Bavaria. The cemetery is surrounded on three sides by trees; the fourth side is open and commands views across the fields to the distant mountains. The grounds are beautifully kept by gardeners who are all recruited locally, take tremendous pride in their work and are more than willing to talk to visitors. It is regrettable that the visitors' book shows a lack of British tourists; as well as the Austrians and Germans, it does appear to be known to some North Americans and therefore it would be regarded that even the specialised tour operators have overlooked or forgotten that this cemetery exists.

The Alpenstrasse now continues eastwards and bypasses the old market town of **Miesbach**, but for those interested in making a short detour into town some history may be in order. The original town was destroyed in 1312 and was rebuilt only to be destroyed by fire in 1783. The old town now offers a peaceful setting with its houses and ancient Café Beer (1623) in the *Marktplatz*. Apart from being a busy commercial centre it has a museum covering the town's history together with farming and art exhibits from the seventeenth century. The parish church of the Maria Himmelfahrt was originally a pilgrimage church but rebuilt after the town fire of 1783.

Rejoining the Alpenstrasse leads to **Schliersee** at the north end of the delightful lake of the same name. Set amid vivid green meadows and dark green forests it also incorporates the districts of Neuhaus-Fischhausen and the charming mountain village of Spitzingsee.

This area has a long history going back to 779 when the monastery of Slyrse was founded but burnt down 200 years later by the Huns. In 1170 Bishop Otto I of Freising built another monastery where the present parish church now stands. This monastery survived even the troubles of the Reformation and the Thirty Years' War. In the eighteenth and nineteenth centuries the peaceful charm of the area attracted painters and poets as well as the actor Konrad Dreher and his gifted pupil Franz Xaver Terofal who together created the world famous Schliersee Folk Theatre. Customs and costumes (*Tracht*) have remained unchanged in this area up to the present day. As in Bad Tölz there is a Leonhardt ride on the 6 November each year to the saints chapel in Fischhausen.

The *Rathaus*, which is well worth a visit, dates from the fifteenth century when its function was that of the law courts and offices. The parish church, originally built around 1350, was rebuilt in 1712 in a baroque style. The interior is light and airy, the woodwork being of walnut which, with the ornate gilding, gives an impression of eternal sunlight. The ceiling frescoes are again the work of J. B. Zimmermann and were done when the church was rebuilt. Three early pieces are the painting by Jan Pollack in 1494 of the Virgin, the statue of St Sixtus

A wayside chapel at Schliersee

(1520) who was the patron of the church and the Throne of Grace dating from 1480. Schliersee is noted for its folk evenings and plays showing the history of the area as far back as the fourteenth century. Accommodation can either be in hotels, pensions, private houses, farms or the large camping site on the shores of the lake itself.

A tour of the lake by the small steamer takes about 45 minutes but is extremely pleasant. The further shore of the lake is for the most part uninhabited, although the railway line to Bayerischzell passes by. The lakeside gardens are attractively laid out and also provide a congenial setting for open-air concerts. Aquatic sports naturally flourish here and some of the hotel gardens slope down to the lakeside where they have their own moorings and bathing platforms which are sometimes used for fishing as well. Swimming, apart from in the lake, may be undertaken in either the indoor or outdoor pools.

After leaving Schliersee the road leaves the lake and runs on through increasing mountain grandeur. Another short detour is to the Spitzingsee, a tiny lake surrounded by mountains which can be reached by a good but steep and winding road, up over the 5,473ft

(1,668m) Brecherspitze. Around the lake a small resort is emerging with good facilities so that in a relatively short time this quiet mountain retreat will attract many more visitors. The return journey to the valley below is quite spectacular. Descending from a height of this magnitude the views alone are well worth the effort but not really recommended for those who do not have a head for heights.

Bayrischzell, a quaint and picturesque mountain resort well patronised in both winter and summer, has grown up over the years at the foot of the Wendelstein, a mighty giant of just over 6,000ft (1,829m). Ascents can be made by either cable car or the oldest rack and pinion railway in Germany. Near the terminus is the Wendelsteinkirchl which was designed at the end of the last century by Max Kleiber. He carried the cross that adorns the roof from the foot of the mountain on his own back. This small chapel is the scene of weddings for those who prefer something different and can afford the price. The summit is marked by the tiny stone chapel of St Wendelin built in 1718. From this vantage point are some of the finest panoramic views. To the north lie the low, flat open plains around the Chiemsee giving way to the Berchtesgaden Alps, Loferer, Leoganger Steinberge, the grey limestone massif of the Kaisergebirge and finally the Tauern Heights with their glittering glaciers.

From Bayrischzell the way lies amidst the mountains; the Tatzelwurm waterfall is a sight to behold in early summer when the melting snow high above increases the velocity and volume of the flow of water. It can only be reached on foot but it is not really hard or difficult walking. From Tatzelwurm to **Degerndorf** a toll road descends fairly steeply and runs through the mountains by means of a tunnel. When emerging at the other end one finds that the scenery has undertaken a dramatic change; the high encircling mountains disappear and instead the green fertile plains irrigated by the river Inn are in view, stretching away in the distance as far as the Chiemsee. Degerndorf's most noticeable features are the sturdy chalets whose wooden balconies from late spring to early autumn are a riot of colour with their flower filled boxes spilling over. Further on the villages of Brannenburg and Kirchdorf follow the same pattern being quiet and attractive as well as offering reasonably priced accommodation to those who wish to explore this part of Germany.

Chiemsee and Berchtesgadenerland

The Chiemsee is part of the Chiemgau region which is the flat and mainly agricultural land lying south-east of Munich. The centre is dominated by the Chiemsee, the largest of all the Bavarian lakes. This area being close to Munich attracts not only visitors from all parts of Germany and Europe but the city dwellers who pack into their cars in the early morning to enjoy a day in rural surroundings combining fresh air and aquatic facilities from yachting to surfboarding.

Small pretty villages are the norm here and accommodation for those wishing to stay overnight or longer is to be found in small family run pensions and hotels. It is a great camping area and camp sites are both numerous and well equipped. Because of its proximity to both Salzburg and Munich, should the weather be inclement the attractions offered by these two major cities can be easily reached.

Although much of the region is flat it is the beginning of the alpine territory which becomes Berchtesgadenerland, and in fact places like Aschau, Marquartstein, Inzell, Reit im Winkl and Ruhpolding are true mountain resorts offering both winter and summer sports.

Berchtesgadenerland is the mountainous region from Bad Reichenhall to the Austrian border with Berchtesgaden as its focal point. It is first and foremost a centre for alpine activities, from walking to mountaineering, riding to kayaking or the more gentle although not always less strenuous sports of golf and tennis.

Here, on fine summer days, the sky is a really deep blue against which the giant peaks of the encircling mountains rise majestically, also etched against the sky the dark shadow of a circling eagle looking for its prey. Lower down the mountainside is the dark green forest, quiet and tranquil except for the occasional call of a bird or the sound of rushing water forcing its way over rock strewn channels.

It is also an area strong in keeping the old traditions alive, from the ceremonial return of the cattle from the high alpine pastures to their winter quarters in early to mid-autumn depending on the weather. The Buttnmandle is celebrated at Christmas time when Santa Claus and his wife escort the Buttnmandl as devils covered in straw and wearing grotesque animal masks make a hideous noise shaking chains and cow bells while Whitsun is the time to see the Miners Annual Day with its 400 year old ceremony consisting of a parade with bands and festive uniforms and an open-air concert.

Rosenheim is not technically part of the Bavarian Alps but as it lies just off the main Munich-Salzburg *Autobahn*, as well as close to the Chiemsee and Chiemgau region that do form part of the Bavarian Alps, it has been included. The town itself dates back to Roman times when two major roads (routes is perhaps more accurate), namely the one from the Brenner Pass to Regensburg and Salzburg to Augsburg, formed a cross roads. Later a medieval town grew up around Burg Rosenheim which currently is a thriving industrial centre and railway junction. The old and new towns are separated by the Mittertor Gate, now home to the town museum. The *Heimatmuseum* shows the cultural history of the town as well as shipping on the river Inn and prehistoric and Roman collections. The Inn Museum on the Innstrasse houses a collection of boat building and shipping on the river Inn. There are displays of models of the old boats as well as the flora and fauna found around the river banks.

The old town is of the most interest with the old shopping arcades which can be found as well as graceful aged buildings like the *Altes Rathaus*, Ellmaierhaus (1568) and the Nepomukbrunnen fountain. The parish church of St Nikolaus was originally built in the fifteenth century but only the tower and some cross beams remain from the original building for the church was rebuilt in neo-Gothic style in the late nineteenth century. The church of the Holy Ghost was built by a wealthy merchant, Hans Stier, in 1449 and connected to a domestic dwelling; its *Volto Santo* mural dating from 1499. The hospital church of St Josef (1618), the Capucine monastery of St Sebastian founded in 1635 but rebuilt in 1889, and the Loreto Chapel of 1635 are some of the ecclesiastical buildings of the town.

Two villages well worth a visit lie on the west side of the *Autobahn*. **Neubeuern** must rank as one of the loveliest gems to be found even in this land of enchanting villages. It is hardly surprising therefore that in 1981 it was awarded the title of 'Loveliest Village in Upper Bavaria' and is now in great demand with film and television companies who are in the market for picturesque locations. This small community owes its existence to the river Inn on whose shores it has grown up — the reason being that in olden times one method of transportation was by river. The boats that used the Inn needed places to moor and their crews had to take provisions on board, so communities like Neubeuern were established. The main square with its old houses is a photographer's dream, decorated with sepia tinted murals and crimson geraniums spilling over the window boxes. It would seem that time has stood still. Perched on its rocky outcrop stands the castle which is now a hotel and a chapel dating from 1751. The parish church is even earlier, being built in 1672.

The neighbouring village, a mere kilometre away, is that of **Altbeuern** whose church dates from 1494 although the high altar is of a much later date, namely the seventeenth century.

The other picturesque village is **Aschau im Chiemgau**, through which the river Prien flows and, along with the following resorts, is in the area known as the Chiemgau. Overlooking Aschau is the Burg Hohenaschau, a fortified castle set on a rocky cliff and the perfect

Painted houses in Neubeuern

setting for any fairytale. The outer walls date from the twelfth century, while some additions were made during the sixteenth and seventeenth centuries. The chapel was built in 1637 with a rococo style interior, although the high altar is of early Italian baroque, purported to have come from Verona and is a recent addition. The two side altars are again the work of J. B. Zimmermann.

Inside the main building the ballroom with its gallery of ancestors, containing twelve gigantic statues on pedestals and the ornate stucco work of the ceiling and walls, have to be seen to be believed. The parish church of St Maria dates from the fifteenth and eighteenth centuries and has a baroque chancel and rococo side altars. Jacob Laub's *Madonna*, with a protection cloak should also be seen. The Hotel Zur Post next to the church is a relic of the seventeenth century and many of the houses in this village are extremely old. Accommodation here ranges from hotels and pensions to farms and camping. Sporting facilities are also extremely good with hang-gliding, minigolf, riding and swimming in both an outdoor and indoor pool. Entertainment is not forgotten with a library and reading room, folk theatre with folk evenings and concerts.

Close to the castle is a cable car which ascends the 5,330ft (1,625m) Kampenwand from whose summit the glories of the Chiemgau unfold. There is a café and terrace to welcome those returning from one of the many walks that radiate from here and for those wishing to venture no further.

Bernau, separated from the Chiemsee only by the *Autobahn*, is small but in quiet rural surroundings and prides itself on being *Gemütlich* — a word that has different meanings to different people. It is true however, that Bernau extends a warm welcome to its visitors and trusts that they will enjoy themselves. With the Chiemsee in the foreground, mountains in the background and green pastures all around, it certainly makes an idyllic holiday setting. Naturally all the facilities of the Chiemsee are open to anyone staying in Bernau and it does have its own windsurfing school. Swimming is either in the lake or in the new indoor pool. The new tennis and squash complex has its own sauna and a small restaurant, while those more attracted by the mountains can take the cable car from Aschau to the Kampenwand. Accommodation here is extremely good but it is a popular resort at weekends and the vacancies are quickly filled.

Chiemsee is the largest lake in Bavaria covering 32sq miles (83sq km) and it naturally attracts a large number of visitors. Not all of them are holidaymakers who camp or stay around its shores for some are city dwellers who enjoy a day out on the unusually placid waters. Another reason for its popularity is easy access, with the Salzburg-Munich *Autobahn* running along its southern shores. By far the most popular sports here are aquatic but it also attracts the anglers as this lake is as rich in fish as any in the country with renke, bream, pike, eel and trout. Naturalists also abound in the areas where the reeds grow in profusion for it is possible to see up to 250 types of bird as well as a multitude of different plants around Bernau. This incredibly beautiful lake, sometimes called the Bavarian Sea, could hardly have a better setting — an immense sheet of blue water with partly wooded surroundings, reed-fringed banks and a backcloth of mountains to the south and east.

Prien in the south-west corner is the major resort but the others, although small, are equally attractive in their differing ways. The town of **Prien** is situated about half a mile from the actual shores of the lake but its baroque and rococo buildings provide an attractive ambience. The *Heimatmuseum* is housed in a delightful old farmhouse dating back to 1837. Inside the rooms are given over to different periods and traditions. There is a farmhouse living room together with a kitchen and bedroom. Other rooms are furnished in the

Prien

Biedermeier or baroque style while another displays local costumes. There is also a dug out canoe which was used for fishing on the Chiemsee and handwork that includes painting on glass. Outside is a charming garden which makes a visit here almost a necessity. The art gallery in the *Altes Rathaus* has some delightful pictures, the work of many a local artist, especially over the last 200 years. The parish church of 1735, which is larger than one would imagine, is adorned

The Chiemsee ferry at Prien Stock

with frescoes and stucco work by the celebrated J. B. Zimmermann. The intricately worked wrought iron handrail that leads up to the pulpit is a fine example of local craft.

There is a nineteenth-century steam locomotive known as the

Fraueninsel

Fiery Elias that runs from the main railway station to the lake shores, and judging from the numbers who avail themselves of it this mode of transport is extremely popular with both young and old alike. Situated on the lakeside is the heated outdoor pool surrounded by green lawns but by mid-day they are covered with sun bathers. The town's harbour (Prien Stock) is close by and it is from here that the ferries ply, not only to the other resorts but also to two islands. The **Fraueninsel** or Ladies Island derives its name from the Benedictine convent founded on it in the eighth century by Duke Tassilo III who was later disposed of by the Emperor Charlemagne.

It is ironic that Charlemagne's granddaughter Irmengard later became abbess here. The present building is Romanesque and dates from the eleventh century while its interior is baroque with a beautifully painted ceiling and high altar with a carved Madonna all dating from the seventeenth century. Its bell tower is distinctive with its octagonal shape and was built beside the church to be a place of refuge. The dome was added in 1626, almost 600 years later. The *Torkapelle* (Gate Chapel) of St Michael and St Nikolaus probably dates from Carolingian times and parts of the wall paintings from the eleventh century. The picture of Christ on the east wall is thirteenth century. The convent is now a boarding school.

The village, that has grown up over the years around the convent, offers sanctuary to the many artists who come here to paint the

King Ludwig II's palace at Herrenchiemsee

surrounding landscape as well as the fishermen who try their luck and skill. Courses in both painting and pottery are on offer here.

The larger and more famous island is **Herrenchiemsee** where Ludwig II built his largest and last palace. The entire island was bought by the king in 1873 as a setting for his replica of Versailles, but it was this final extravagance that brought the king's downfall. Although not as spectacular as Neuschwanstein it is larger and the furnishings so lavish that both he and the state were bankrupted.

The craftsmanship is superb; the Meissen porcelain chandelier is quite exquisite in its delicacy and detail. The palace is surrounded by formal gardens copied from Versailles and offer the visitor a chance to wander and reflect on this strange young man and his dreams of everlasting beauty. During the summer the ballroom, or to give it its correct name the 'Hall of Mirrors', is the venue for candle-lit concerts.

The island's history goes back to the eighth century when a Benedictine abbey was founded in conjunction with the Fraueninsel convent but regrettably destroyed by the Magyars. It was re-established again in 1730 and prospered until secularisation in the early nineteenth century. Part of what was the Bishop's Palace is now used as a hotel and restaurant.

On the north-west shores of the Chiemsee are the lakeside villages of Rimsting, Breitbrunn, Gstadt and Gollenshausen. Nearby **Eggstätt** on the small Hartsee offers visitors the choice of swimming, sailing, windsurfing, boating and fishing. **Rimsting** and Eggstätt also have indoor pools even though the Chiemsee is the warmest of all Bavarian lakes on account of its size. All these resorts share in offering other activities especially to those seeking an active type of holiday, well catered for with tennis and riding including short courses of instruction in these pursuits.

Endorf is not on the lake and is known more for its iodine thermal springs and the benefits these can offer. In addition there are concerts and plays as well as a good range of sporting facilities.

North of Endorf is **Amerang** a quiet village surrounded by gentle wood-covered slopes. The parish church of St Rupert was originally Gothic in design but was altered into baroque in 1720. Perched on a hill above the village of Amerang is a delightful old *Schloss* with a picturesque wedge-shaped Renaissance courtyard three storeys high with Tuscan columns. The balconies are bedecked with flowers and trailing creepers which relieve the stark white walls. The acoustics are so good that during the summer regular concerts and plays are performed here with seating for 255 people.

Entry to the *Schloss* is by guided tour only at rough hourly intervals but should the visitor have to wait he or she is invited to visit the fish pool teeming with carp, golden trout as well as several other varieties of fish. On reaching the pool there is a machine dispensing food with which the visitor may entice the fish to fight over tasty morsels. At the same time chickens scurry underfoot to catch pieces that are dropped; a notice helpfully informs one that the chickens like the granules intended for the fish.

Across the stone bridge over the moat is the outer stone flagged hall where entrance tickets are purchased as well as postcards, home baked bread, smoked fish and new-laid eggs. One cannot fail to be amused that during the summer visitors not only pay to feed fish and fowl but are then encouraged to buy the produce as well!

The guides, young students some of whom are members of the von Grailsheim family who own the *Schloss*, are well informed and welcome questions. From the courtyard the tour enters the main building where one can see the Rittersaal with its restored frescoes and hunting trophies and the music room with a delicately painted ceiling from which hangs a chandelier in shot glass with hues of blue, pink and green. The games room with its Biedermeier furniture and billiard table is housed here, along with the sitting room with intricate inlaid furniture. On the first floor is the Gothic St George's Chapel which was established in 1245 and extended in 1512. Under the recently cleaned walls Gothic paintings have been found. The painting at the rear of the altar dates from 1762 while on a side altar stands the small wooden sixteenth-century figure of Anna, the Virgin Mary's mother.

On the top floor is a small museum housing a collection of fishing and household utensils used in days gone by. There is also a cabinet with military uniforms and caps.

East of Amerang and north of Seebruck is **Seeon** known for the former monastery founded in the tenth century by the Count Palatinate Aribo whose monument in the form of a tomb is in the St Barbara Chapel of the monastery church of St Lambert. Aribo's feet are shown resting on his faithful hound. The church has had a Romanesque basilica added and converted to a Gothic style in the fifteenth century. The flat roof was changed to net vaulting whose unusual green and gold designs contrast with the white columns supporting them, thereby focusing attention on the representation of the Ascension and other themes.

The original famous *Madonna of Seeon* sculpture, also of the fifteenth century, is now in the Bayerisches Nationalmuseum in Munich, but a copy is on the high altar. Other interesting parts are the chapterhouse, refectory and chapel of St Nikolaus built in the eighteenth century.

Seeing the whole complex as one approaches, it is quite understandable why this small island was chosen for the site of what was to become such a massive building. The setting really is superb as the red roofs and white walls contrast with the green grass and the leafy trees surrounded by the deep blue of the lake water. Then, rising above everything else, the twin octagonal towers from the eleventh century which received their onion domes in 1561 are in view.

This prosperous monastery was able to encourage art and science so that among its visitors were Haydn and Mozart. Nevertheless with secularisation at the beginning of the nineteenth century, this work was destroyed and the buildings are now in private hands. In the monastery courtyard a 6 week season of plays is held in July and August. Shakespeare's *Twelfth Night* was one of the choices in 1987.

Of special interest to motor enthusiasts is the Oldtimer Museum with some twenty-two veteran cars and motorcycles. It is open on Wednesday and Sunday afternoons at the Hotel Schanzenberg.

Seebruck was originally a flourishing Roman military camp called *Bedaium* on the Salzburg to Augsburg road. This is substantiated by the treasures that have been unearthed over the years and which are now in the museum.

Today Seebruck is a holiday resort at the northern end of the

Chiemsee where the river Alz leaves the lake. The church of St Thomas belongs to the Fraueninsel convent and was built in 1474. In the entrance are two antique fragments.

During the summer this resort is a busy water sports centre with its sailing and windsurfing school together with a fine yacht marina and bathing beaches. For entertainment there are concerts and folk evenings. The local museum Römerhaus Bedaium exhibits Celtic and Roman items discovered locally.

The road out of Seebruck towards Chieming soon reaches **Ising**, well known for its pilgrimage church of Maria Himmelfahrt. It was probably built in the late fourteenth century but there is conjecture that a villa was erected here in Roman times. Although the church was altered in the eighteenth century there are interesting carvings and paintings, some of which recall disasters on the Chiemsee.

The last resort on this eastern shore is **Chieming** with 4 miles (6km) of beach, and a charming lakeside promenade. A well equipped 'House of the Guest' has an indoor swimming pool. Other sports include riding, shooting and an eighteen-hole golf course.

Traunstein is an old market town approximately 5 miles (8km) from the eastern shore of the Chiemsee and only a short distance from the Munich-Salzburg *Autobahn*. With a history dating back to the thirteenth century this town has seen many changes. During its early days it suffered from the plague and was plundered by foreign troops and often partially destroyed by fires, the last of which was in 1851. Today it is known as a flourishing health resort thanks to its salt and mud bath therapy. Even with its chequered history there are some fine old houses together with the fourteenth-century Brothaus-turm (Breadhouse Tower) and the sixteenth-century Lindlbrunnen (a small lime-tree fountain) which have managed to survive.

The town museum houses household effects as well as various implements and costumes that have been in use through the ages along with religious and secular art. There is a section devoted to the salt trade with which the town was and still is associated.

The parish church of St Oswald, originally built in the fourteenth century, was rebuilt in the late seventeenth century. The Salinen-kapelle dedicated to St Rupert in der Au was built in 1630 in early baroque style with frescoes also dating from this time.

As befits a town of this standing, there are many facilities to be found here with concerts, folk plays and good sporting attractions. On Easter Monday the Georgiritt (George Ride) takes place with a mounted procession of over 400 and includes a sword dance.

Bergen is a small village on the south side of the *Autobahn*. It is not, at first sight, any more remarkable than some of the other places that surround it, but if one was to visit the church one would not only see its slender delicate spire but also a lump of rock! According to legend it is the rock that Tannhäuser had to carry on his back as a penance. For those not acquainted with Tannhäuser the story tells how he had sinned by having an affair with Venus the Goddess of Love on the Venusberg. Tiring of her he wished to return to his mortal love but in order to do so had to receive absolution from the pope himself who in turn imposed this burden. Tannhäuser carried this heavy rock back across the Alps but on reaching Bergen dropped it and to this day it still remains there. The opera written by Richard Wagner was taken from this legend.

Just outside the village is the cable car that will take visitors up to the Hochfelln at 5,440ft (1,646m) in a two stage journey which can be terminated at the middle station if desired. The summit itself can be reached by a rough path and the weary can regain their breath by taking a look inside the wooden chapel, or watch the hang-gliders launching themselves into space. This is one of the many places in the Chiemgau where one can enjoy the superb views of both mountains and extensive plains.

Übersee-Feldwies is an attractive quiet village in rural surroundings with flower decked chalets lining the roads. The village is justly proud of its local theatre where plays, quite a few of them comical, are produced. The local brass band gives concerts as well as accompanying the folk songs and dances at the folk evenings. Sporting facilities include tennis and riding as well as a full aquatic programme on the Chiemsee. Accommodation ranging from hotels to self-catering and camping can be found here.

Once again the visitor rejoins the Deutsche Alpenstrasse as it parts company with the *Autobahn* at **Grabenstätt**, known for its Roman museum, as the former now heads directly towards the Alps as it follows the merry little Tiroler Ache stream. At first the way is flat until **Marquartstein** is reached; a lively village whose way of life is steeped in the old traditions which include its own folk theatre. On Sundays and feast days (of which there are plenty) the local costume is proudly worn. The women are attired in full black skirts with velvet bands. The matrons wear black tops with long sleeves edged with white lace, white kerchiefs tucked into their necklines, pinafores of blue or mauve silk and small black boater style hats trimmed with gold tassels perched on their heads. The unmarried girls are clothed in a black velvet bodice over crisp white blouses. Their pinafores are white with gaily coloured embroidery and they wear white knitted stockings and black shoes with silver buckles. Their bodices jangle with silver medallions that are looped from side to side by silver chains. All the women wear fresh red flowers (usually carnations) and sprigs of rosemary tucked into their necklines.

The men are just as gaily attired in their *Lederhosen* with massive chased leather belts around their middles as well as gaily embroidered braces and knee length socks. But as often happens in rural areas, the part from ankle to mid-calf is missing; in other words there is only the foot and top piece. The reason for this is not really clear. Two favoured explanations are that it economised on wool when these areas were poor and the other one is that when walking through long wet grass the wool got wet and uncomfortable. White shirts are worn under either brown and green or grey and green jackets. Their hats are of green velour adorned with long white feathers. Activities here are of the simple outdoor variety with the emphasis on walking although there are plenty of organised excursions with the local tour operator or by one's own transport.

Leaving Marquartstein behind, the scenery once again becomes more and more alpine as the road climbs steadily to the villages of Unterwössen and Oberwössen which have grown up along the road that runs through them. **Unterwössen** (the larger of the two) has an indoor swimming pool and is the home of the German Gliding School. Halfway between the two villages lies the Wössnersee — a pretty little lake at the foot of the Rechenberg. Sheltered from the wind it offers an ideal place for swimming, a large children's play area and rowing boats for hire. This is only open during the summer months as the lake is fed from streams coming straight off the mountain side and therefore the water is fairly cold. At **Oberwössen** there is an enclosure for feeding the wild deer that make their homes in the surrounding woods. In winter these shy wild creatures need this regular source of food if they are to survive but even in summer, when food is more plentiful, they will probably come once a day.

The road swings in a wide arc past the Walmberg before reaching the open and sunny plateau and the attractive, peaceful village of **Reit im Winkl,** perhaps best known as a winter sports paradise. Here the mountains rise on every side in majestic splendour and the dark green forests sweep down into the valley. From the first moment one is never in any doubt that this is a true alpine resort. At an altitude of 2,500ft (762m) the air has taken on the crisp fresh tang that comes straight off the mountains. Pass the daylight hours in exploring the surrounding countryside on foot, over meadows bright with wild flowers, through the woods or take a chair-lift to the high pastures where some of the cattle are grazing. On the rocky outcrops you may find the deep blue gentian and the deep pink alpine roses — edelweiss is found only on the highest peaks and is a protected flower and must not be picked; the penalties for doing so are quite severe.

Facilities here include first class indoor and open-air swimming pools. There are several small lakes set amid meadowland and are popular venues for families who bring inflatable dinghies and picnics. Other pursuits include riding, tennis, rock-climbing, minigolf and a new nine-hole golf course. To launch the new project the first spit of turf was removed by Rosi Mittermaier-Neureuther who, before her marriage, was the famous ski racer. In the municipal park there are band concerts sometimes combined with *Schuhplattler* dancing and the local theatre where plays are performed; some amusing, some historical. They are of course given in German but it is not too difficult to follow them even if one cannot understand every word that is said. The Kuhstall is a great favourite in the evenings and is where one may be entertained with a large repertoire of yodelling. As Reit is on the Austrian border many find it useful as a base to combine an Austro-German holiday.

From Reit im Winkl to Ruhpolding the road passes four lakes and a nature reserve. The lakes are the Weitsee, the Mittersee, the Lodensee and finally the Förchensee. All are attractive alpine lakes either completely or partially surrounded by areas suitable for use as bathing and windsurfing beaches. They also attract families from the nearby towns on both sides of the border who arrive in their cars and park them along the roadside or just off the highway amongst the bushes. They bring with them dinghies, surf boards, canoes, sunbeds and hampers to ensure a pleasurable day away from busy town life.

The town of **Ruhpolding** lies just off the main Alpenstrasse, although the road that runs through the town does connect up with the *Autobahn* and provides a short cut avoiding the slower but more scenic route. With this almost direct access Ruhpolding attracts visitors not only from Germany but Austria as well. This beautiful alpine town set in the Chiemgau Alps is perhaps the last place that one would expect to find English and American newspapers but in fact both the *Daily Telegraph* and the *New York Herald* are on sale here albeit 24 hours late. Usually the only daily papers available in these parts are German ones and those who must have a paper from home have to go to Munich, Salzburg, Berchtesgaden or Bad Reichenhall.

The setting may be rural but the town is an elegant and popular one. The houses combine town elegance with touches associated with those found in the more remote areas and are set in well tended

Ruhpolding

gardens. Built in the first half of the eighteenth century, the parish church of St George has the reputation of being one of the finest in Upper Bavaria. The interior has exquisitely carved and decorated choir stalls and pulpit. To the right of the main altar is an early thirteenth-century wooden sculpture of the *Madonna and Child.*

The large *Kurpark* is an oasis of lawns, flowerbeds, paths and trees with a lily pond and an open-air bandstand, while the tourist office is to be found here. The town has many fountains derived from tree trunks and adorned with carvings; some are drinking troughs. The wayside shrines always seem to have fresh flowers placed in them.

The facilities here are first class and include two outdoor swimming pools with high diving boards. Tiled surrounds give way to smooth lawns surrounded by colourful and well tended flower beds, adjacent to which is the immaculate indoor pool.

Ruhpolding caters specially for its young visitors. There are adventure play areas and indoor activities like painting and modelling here, with pony-riding, a miniature train on which one may ride, and a miniature town. Most of these attractions are to be found at the Märchenpark on the outskirts of the town on the banks of the Urschlauer Ache. Across the river is the Märchenwald (Enchanted Forest) with its well sign-posted woodland walks. The local mountain is the Rauschberg, whose heights can be reached by cable car from where an even wider choice of mountain walks is available.

Ruhpolding also possesses two excellent indoor riding schools and tennis halls. There are two museums: the one in the Schloss-Strasse is housed in an old hunting lodge dating from the sixteenth century and depicts the town's history and growth through the ages. The second one is in the Friesingerstrasse and houses the art gallery as well as old painted furniture and glassware. One is constantly aware how much anything 'folk' means to this alpine resort.

After Ruhpolding the Alpenstrasse climbs and weaves its way past the Froschsee where it is joined by the B306 road and where the resort of **Inzell** is found. Like Reit im Winkl it is both a winter and summer resort and the new ice stadium built just outside the village is open all the year and provides a stark contrast to a day spent out in the warm sunshine. The village itself lies in an open sunny valley at the start of the Bavarian Alps. Plenty of amenities are on offer here with a modern bathing complex consisting of a full sized swimming pool and a separate diving pool with both springboard and high-board. There is another pool for children only. This complex has also been built just outside of the main village and is surrounded with lawns and flower beds. Also here are sauna and solarium facilities.

The village is small and compact, and close by the parish church of St Michael is the 'House of the Guest', incorporating the local tourist office as well as a library and reading room for visitors. Although small, Inzell is a lively resort and attracts visitors from near and far. Many of these are on excursions to sample the delights of the various mountain villages before going on to Berchtesgaden or Salzburg. Inzell is an ideal centre for touring and the local tour operator offers excursions to the Salzkammergut as well Vienna and Venice.

Rejoin the main Alpenstrasse and almost immediately one comes to the Gletschergarten (Glacier Garden). Parking is available on both sides of the road enabling visitors to proceed on foot to view this phenomenon. Steps have been cut into the hillside for those wishing to climb to the higher part. It takes about 15 minutes for the round trip but quite frankly the best part can be reached in about 2 minutes. This is a rare opportunity to see the result of massive geological upheavals of 15-20,000 years ago, bringing rocks through the surface from far underground. They now look very smooth and grey from the movement of glaciers and are very different to the surrounding jagged rocks. A pipeline for water was built over these hills in 1617 and remained in use till 1958 but has now been sadly replaced by a more modern method.

The Chiemgau area now gives way to what is known as the Berchtesgadenerland and to reach Bad Reichenhall take the small turning via the Thumsee: a delightful lake and much loved by the local inhabitants. The marshy area has now been turned into a protected reserve for rare water plants. Perched high above is the church of St Pancras of Karlstein.

Bad Reichenhall is an elegant spa town in this modern age but has in fact been famous since Celtic times due to its vast salt deposits. Its history can be followed in the museum showing how the town drew its wealth from the salt mines as well as the life and customs that flourished here. Bad Reichenhall has provided well laid out parks with colourful flower beds; a botanical garden will attract those who lean towards horticulture. Many of the visitors that throng the streets here have come to take the waters and baths that they feel may relieve many of their ailments. Visits to the old salt workings are available during the summer both in the mornings and afternoons, decreasing to twice a week in the winter. Check locally for the times of these visits.

Bad Reichenhall has a cathedral, St Jeno, originally built at the beginning of the thirteenth century and is the largest Romanesque church in Upper Bavaria. The main entrance is decorated with alternating red and grey marble. The interior was severely damaged in a fire at the beginning of the sixteenth century and had to be replaced using the newer techniques available at that time.

The old cloisters of the adjacent monastery are open to the public on Sunday mornings and are noted for the relief embellishments found on the columns. The parish church of St Nikolaus dates from 1181 but, perhaps unfortunately, was extended in the latter part of the last century which has made the transept rather dark and gloomy for the windows have been set high up in the vaulted roof.

Two roads leave Bad Reichenhall for Berchtesgaden, the B20 and the B21. The former follows the railway while the latter after passing the Saalachsee, a long and rather narrow lake, rejoins the Alpenstrasse to climb up to the Schwarzbachwacht Pass where the scenery is dramatic. The road runs through the densely wooded valley of the river Schwarzbach behind which, on the western side, rises the stark peaks of the Reiter Alpe. On the eastern side are green alpine pastures scattered with farms, a few chalets and browsing cattle. This is the beginning of Ramsau but before actually reaching it take the turning to the right for the Hintersee. This picturesque lake has, as a background, the jagged cruel peaks of the Reiter Alpe while to the south is the mighty Hochkalter. The lake itself is surrounded by meadows and woods which in the autumn turn to a glowing gold. It is known as the Zauberwald (Enchanted Forest) and provides delightful walks along shady river banks in clear mountain air broken only by the cries of a bird, the mellow sound of bells as cattle wander in search of fresh pasture and the sound of rushing water as it flings itself headlong over the rocky terrain.

Ramsau is adored by painters and climbers alike. The small cream church with its tiny cemetery sits above the mountain torrent, crossed only by a rustic wooden bridge and surrounded by old knarled trees. This small remote sixteenth-century church attracts so much attention because Josef Mohr was once the priest here and when he was a young curate at Oberndorf he wrote the carol *Silent Night, Holy Night*. Many come to see for themselves the real picture that appears on so many jigsaw puzzles.

Artists, both professional and amateur, find the scenery enthralling and never seem to tire of trying to recapture on canvas the changing light on the Watzmann. The Hochkalter is famed for its blue ice glacier and the streets of Ramsau, in the early hours, ring to the clatter of heavy boots and the clinking of ice picks as mountaineers start out on their long and hard climbs. For those left behind the House of the Guest offers a reading room, library and television room. A quieter and relaxing outdoor pastime is fishing or boating. There is accommodation to suit all tastes and pockets here from hotels to farmhouses.

Finally **Berchtesgaden**. Although not off the beaten track and one of the most expensive towns in Bavaria outside Munich it should be visited if in the area. It attracts not only Germans but is a rest centre for the American army stationed in and around Europe. Apart from those who actually stay in the town, many more arrive by train, coach and car to spend the day and see the sights, of which there are many. The Kehlstein attracts enormous crowds with its spectacular journey by bus before the final ascent by lift through the mountain itself to the summit and the Kehlstein Haus. It is now a café although probably better known by its other name of Eagle's Nest. Many people thought, and indeed some may still do so, that this was the home of Adolf Hitler but that is not true. His home at Berchtesgaden was the Berghof at Obersalzburg where Neville Chamberlain came in September 1938. The buildings were mainly destroyed in an air raid in April 1945. It was later completely demolished and traces of habitation were removed.

The historical part of the town is the *Schlossplatz*; a dignified square around which are the old buildings with an arcaded gallery of the sixteenth century. The Residenz was once a monastery and was later owned by the ruling family of Bavaria, the Wittelsbachs.

The last resident of this family was in fact Crown Prince Rupert who during World War I was the commander in chief of the Bavarian troops and died in 1955. During his lifetime he collected fine furniture, oriental art and fifteenth- and sixteenth-century German woodcarvings. These treasures are now on view to the public in the castle museum housed in some particularly fine Renaissance style rooms as well as the fifteenth-century canons' dormitory.

To one end of the square is the church of St Peter and St Johannes. Originally built in 1122 it was superseded by a new building during the thirteenth century and combines both Romanesque and Gothic architecture. The choir stalls, beautifully and intricately carved and the quaint niches, shaped like swallows nests used for prayers, should not be missed. Massive red marble tombs are the final resting places of some of the priors.

A really outstanding visit is to the salt mines on the Bergwerkstrasse. Trips take approximately an hour but due to its popularity it is almost essential to pre-book and so ascertain when a tour can be taken. At peak periods it may be a couple of hours away and this time can then be fully utilised. Before the tour commences warm protective clothing in the form of trousers, jacket, felt hat and a leather 'seat' (used on the long slide which descends to the lower parts of the mine where it is very cold) should be worn.

Anyone who suffers from claustrophobia is advised not to embark on this adventure. Having donned the warm but unglamorous outfits, the journey commences on a small train which conveys the visitors along galleries to where a single rail descends 1,640ft (500m) into the bowels of the earth; hence the need for the leather seat which is strapped around the waist so that, when invited to sit on the rail, the leather can act as a cushion. Groups of about ten visitors, each with arms around the person in front, swoop down the shute before emerging into a real fairytale world, where the walls shimmer and sparkle with salt crystals of varying hue (not all salt is white). An illuminated underground lake is crossed by means of a raft, and small islets with wee caverns lit by tiny bulbs all cast their magic spell. There is also a film describing the history and importance of salt over the years before one regretfully leaves this underground paradise to emerge into the everyday world again.

Last but certainly not least one can visit the loveliest and also slightly mysterious lake in Bavaria, the Königsee. It is accessible only by an electrically powered boat that glides silently through the dark still waters so reminiscent of a Norwegian fjord. The round trip takes around 2 hours but can be shortened by only going as far as St

Bartholomä. The area surrounding the lake is a nature and wildlife reserve and it is for this reason that noise is discouraged although on most boat trips a horn is blown to evoke celestial echoes (at least that is possibly what it is intended to do). The tiny chapel of St Bartholomä, whose shape resembles that of a three leafed clover, was built in the eighteenth century and together with an inn and one or two chalets are a world apart from the twentieth century. Two famous names that have spent some time out here are Sigmund Freud and Max Reger. In the autumn this mosaic of greens turns into a fiery furnace of flames and gold. The lake steamer goes as far as Salet but it is possible to reach the Obersee on foot in about 10 minutes to view the Rotbach waterfall which cascades down from the Teufelshorner (Devils Horns). This is wild and remote country where the real alpine walkers and climbers commence their battle against nature. A more off the beaten track spot would be hard to find and it is therefore fitting that this remain the final destination.

Further Information
— The Bavarian Alps—

Places to Visit

Amerang
Schloss Amerang
Open: June-September, Easter & Whitsuntide. Guided tours only, approximately one per hour.
☎ (0807) 5230

Aschau
Schloss Hohenaschau
Open: May-September Tuesday & Friday 9.30-11.30am. Guided tours only.
☎ (08052) 932

Bad Aibling
Heimatmuseum
Wilhelm-Leibl Platz 2

Bad Reichenhall
Altes Salinenwerk
Salinenstrasse
Open: April-October 10-11.30am, 2-4pm. In winter Tuesday and Thursday only. Guided tours only.

Heimatmuseum
Getreidegasse 4

Bad Tölz
Heimatmuseum
Marktstrasse 48

Benediktbeuren
Frauenhofermuseum
Frauenhofer Strasse 2
Open: daily 9am-6pm.

Berchtesgaden
Schlossmuseum
Schlossplatz 2
Open: October-April Monday-Friday 10am-1pm, 2-5pm; May-September Sunday-Friday 10am-1pm, 2-5pm.

Heimatmuseum
Schroffenbergallee 6

Salzbergwerk and Museum
Bergwerkstrasse 83
Open: May to mid-October daily 8am-5pm; mid-October to April Monday-Friday 1-4pm.

Chiemsee
Herzog Tassilo Museum
Frauenchiemsee
☎ (08054) 672

Schloss Herrenchiemsee
Open: daily, April-September 9am-5pm, October-March 10am-4pm.
Guided tours, some in English.

Dürnbach
British War Cemetery
Mainly RAF personnel.

Garmisch-Partenkirchen
Werdenfelsmuseum
Ludwigstrasse 47
Open: Tuesday-Sunday.

Richard Strauss Villa
Zoppritzstrasse 42

Kochel am See
Freilichtmuseum Glentleiten
1 mile north of Schledorf.
Open: April to October Tuesday-Sunday 9am-6pm. November Saturday & Sunday 10am-5pm.

Walchenseekraftwerk
Hydro-electric works.
Further information from *Verkehrsamt*.

Franz Marc Museum
Herzogstandweg 43
Open: Tuesday-Sunday 2-6pm.

Königsee
Heraldry Museum
Jennerbahnstrasse 30

Lenggries
Tiermuseum
Bergweg 12
☎ (08042) 2510

Mittenwald
Geigenbau and Heimatmuseum
(Museum of Violin-Making and
    Regional Life)
Ballenhausgasse
Open: daily May-October Monday-Friday 10-11.45am, 2-4.45pm.

Murnau
Münter-Haus
Kottmüllerallee 6
Open: Wednesday, Saturday & Sunday 4-6pm.

Prien
Heimatmuseum
Friedhofweg 1

Art-gallerie im Alten Rathaus
☎ (08051) 3031

Rosenheim
Heimatmuseum
Ludwigsplatz 26
Open: Tuesday-Friday 9am-12noon, 2-5pm; Saturday 9am-12noon; Sunday 10am-12noon. Closed public holidays.

Inn Museum
Innstrasse
Open: Friday 9am-12noon, Saturday & Sunday 10am-4pm.

Rottach-Egern
Greifvogelpark-Adlerhorst
Moni Alm
Open: daily in fine weather 9am-5pm.

Ruhpolding
Heimatmuseum-Jagdschloss
Schloss Strasse 2

Bäuerlich-Sakrales Museum
Roman Friesingergasse 1

Schliersee
Heimatmuseum
☎ (08026) 8162

Seebruck
Römerhaus-Bedaium
Open: Tuesday-Saturday 10am-12noon, 3-5pm; Sunday 3-5pm.

Seeon
Oldtimermuseum
Hotel Schanzenberg
Open: Wednesday & Sunday afternoon.
☎ (08624) 2031

Starnberg
Heimatmuseum
Possenhofener Strasse 9

Tegernsee
Heimatmuseum
Schloss Tegernsee
Open: daily.

Olaf Gulbransson Museum
Im Kurpark
☎ (08022) 8180

Deutsche Bundesbahn (Steam Trips)
For details of dates apply to
Bayerischer Localbahn Verein
PO Box 116
83684 Tegernsee

Traunstein
Stiftung Heimathaus Traunstein
Stadtplatz 2-3
☎ 0861 65258
Open: with guided tour only May-June
& September to mid-October weekly
2pm & 3.30pm, Sundays & public
holidays 10am.
July-August Thursday 9am-12noon, 2-
5pm without guided tour, Sundays &
public holidays 10am.

Unterwössen
Radio und Plattenmuseum
☎ (08641) 8772

Tourist Information Offices

Bavarian Tourist Office
Fremdenverkehrsverband
München-Oberbayern
Sonnen Strasse 10
80331 Munich
☎ (089) 597347

Regional

Bad Reichenhall
Kur und Verkehrsverein
Hauptbahnhof
Nebenbau
83435 Bad Reichenhall
☎ (08651) 1467

Bad Tölz
*Fremdenverkehrsgemein-
    schaft Isar-Loisachtal/
    Tölzer Land Gaste-
    information*
Landratsamt
Bad Tölz
Postfach 1360
83646 Bad Tölz
☎ (08041) 5051

Berchtesgaden
*Kurdirektion Berchtes-
    gadenerland*
Postfach 2240
83471 Berchtesgaden

☎ (08652) 5011
Information on Berchtes-
gaden, Bischofswiesen,
Marktschellenberg,
Ramsau, Schonau and
Königsee.

Garmisch-Partenkirchen
*Fremdenverkehr Werden-
    felser Land*
Kurverwaltung
Postfach 1562
82467 Garmisch-Parten-
    kirchen
☎ (08821) 53093

Prien am Chiemsee
Verkehrsverband Chiemsee
Alte Rathaus Strasse 11
83209 Prien am
Chiemsee
☎ (08051) 2280/6905-0

Rosenheim
*Fremdenverkehrsverband
    Wendelstein*
Landratsamt Rosenheim
Wittelsbacherstrasse 53
83022 Rosenheim
☎ (08031) 392379 or
392324

Schliersee
Kuramt Schliersee
Postfach 146
83727 Schliersee
☎ (08026) 4069
Information on Bayrisch-
zell, Fischbachau
Schliersee.

Schongau
Fremdenverkehrsverband
Pfaffenwinkl
Postfach 40
86956 Schongau
☎ (08861) 7773/211117/
7216

Starnberg
*Fremdenverkehrsverband
    Starnberger Fünf Seen
    Land*
Postfach 1607
8130 Starnberg
☎ (08151) 15911/13274

Tegernsee
*Fremdenverkehrsgemein-
    schaft Tegernseer Tal*
Haus des Gastes
83684 Tegernsee
☎ (08022) 3985/180140

Traunstein
Verkehrsverband Chiemgau
Ludwig Thoma Strasse 2
83278 Traunstein
☎ (0861) 58223/65273

Local
These are all *Verkehrsampt*
unless stated otherwise

Amerang
83123 Amerang
☎ (08075) 230

Aschau im Chiemgau
Kurverwaltung
Kampenwandstrasse 37
83229 Aschau im
   Chiemgau
☎ (08052) 392

Bad Reichenhall
Wittelsbacherstrasse 15
83435 Bad Reichenhall
☎ (08651) 3003

Bad Tölz
Stadt Kurverwaltung
Ludwig Thoma Strasse 22
83646 Bad Tölz
☎ (08041) 70071

Bad Wiessee
Kuramt
Adrian Stoop Strasse 20
83707 Bad Wiessee
☎ (08022) 82051

Bayrischzell
Kuramt
Kirchplatz 7
83735 Bayrischzell
☎ (08023) 648

Bernried
See Starnberg

Berchtesgaden
Kurdirektion
Königsseer Strasse 2
83471 Berchtesgaden
☎ (08652) 5011

Bernau am Chiemsee
Aschauer Strasse
83233 Bernau am
   Chiemsee
☎ (08051) 7218

Chieming-Ising
83339 Chieming
☎ (08664) 245

Ettal
See Oberammergau

Garmisch-Partenkirchen
Bahnhof Strasse 34
82467 Garmisch-Parten-
   kirchen
☎ (08821) 1800

Gmund
Reise und Verkehrsburo
Bahnhof
83703 Gmund
☎ (08022) 7391

Grainau
Waxensteiner Strasse 35
82491 Grainau
☎ (08821) 81281

Inzell
Verkehrsverein
Rathausplatz 35
83334 Inzell
☎ (08665) 862

Kochel am See
Kalmbach Strasse 11
82431 Kochel am See
☎ (08851) 338

Kreuth
Kuramt
Rathaus
83708 Kreuth
☎ (08029) 1044

Lenggries
Rathausplatz 1
83661 Lenggries
☎ (08042) 2977

Marquartstein
Bahnhofstrasse 3
83250 Marquartstein
☎ (08641) 8236

Mittenwald
Dammkar Strasse 3
82481 Mittenwald
☎ (08823) 1051

Murnau
Kohlgruber Strasse 1
82418 Murnau
☎ (08841) 2074

Neubeuern
Markt
83115 Neubeuern
☎ (08035) 2959
(Part-time office)

Oberammergau
Verkehrsbüro
Eugen-Papst-Strasse 9a
82487 Oberammergau
☎ (08822) 4921

**Pöcking and
   Possenhofen**
See Starnberg

Prien am Chiemsee
Rathaus Strasse 11
83209 Prien am
   Chiemsee
☎ (08051) 69050/690555

Ramsau
See Berchtesgaden

Reit im Winkl
Rathaus
83242 Reit im Winkl
☎ (08640) 8207

Rottach-Egern
Kuramt
Rathaus
Hauptstrasse 60
83700 Rottach-Egern
☎ (08022) 26740

Rosenheim
Kulturamt
83022 Rosenheim
☎ (08031) 37080

Ruhpolding
Kurverwaltung
Hauptstrasse 60
83324 Ruhpolding
☎ (08663) 1268

Schliersee
Kurverwaltung
Am Bahnhof 13a
83727 Schliersee
☎ (08026) 4069

Seebruck
83358 Seebruck
☎ (08667) 7133

Seeon
83370 Seeon
☎ (08624) 2155

Starnberg
Verkehrsverein
Kirchplatz 3
82319 Starnberg
☎ (08151) 13274

Tegernsee
Kuramt
Hauptstrasse
83684 Tegernsee
☎ (08022) 180140

Tutzing
Kirchenstrasse 9
82327 Tutzing
☎ (08158) 2031

Übersee-Feldwies
Feldieserstrasse 27
83236 Übersee
☎ (08642) 295

Unterwössen
Oberwössen
Rathaus
83246 Unterwössen
☎ (08641) 8205

10 • The Upper Danube

The Danube river rises in the eastern slopes of the Black Forest and flows for some 1,770 miles (2,849km) to the Black Sea. There are those who claim that in the whole of its famous course there is not a more beautiful stretch than the 35 miles (56km) near its source between Tuttlingen and Sigmaringen when the infant stream makes its winding way through the Swabian Alb. The river here is narrow — not more than 10yd wide — and shallow, because it has lost a great deal of water through a curious geological phenomenon shortly before it reaches Tuttlingen, known as the Donau Versickerung. What happens here is that up to 4,000 gallons (20,000 litres) of water escape every second from the river bed through cracks in the limestone, to surface 10 miles (16km) away in the south, from where it finds its way into the upper waters of the Rhine.

After leaving Tuttlingen the river sweeps in huge curves in a narrow valley between beetling limestone cliffs to which thick woods precariously cling; lush meadows line the stream and ruined castles crown the crags. In the spring the bright green of the foliage contrasts starkly with the white rocks, and in September and October the warm colouring of the trees creates a romantic river landscape that sets the cameras clicking and causes every painter's hand to itch. If you are an artist, bring an easel and paints.

Yet this idyllic area is totally unknown to tourists, and not greatly visited even by Germans. It is true off the beaten track country. No main road passes through it, and in some stretches of the river there is no road at all. A branch railway does run down the valley but much of the view is lost in tunnels. It can only be explored on foot. There are no large hotels, and indeed not all that many small pensions and inns and yet it is not difficult to reach. The *Autobahn* from Stuttgart to the Bodensee (Lake Constance) passes near Tuttlingen. A railway links Stuttgart with Sigmaringen, and the railway between Freiburg and Ulm provides easy access to the small towns and villages on this stretch of the river.

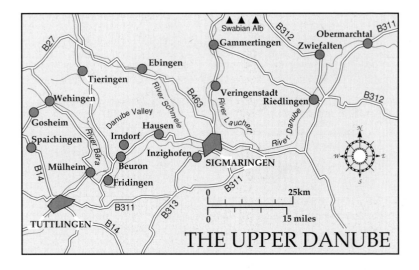

THE UPPER DANUBE

Sigmaringen

In practice there are just three places offering a choice of accommodation where you can stay. These are Sigmaringen, Tuttlingen, and Beuron half way between them. Of these, Sigmaringen is well worth visiting for itself. A huge castle on the rock above the river dominates the town, and it is surprising to find this small provincial town is graced with noble buildings and parks, worthy of a capital city. The bewilderment of visitors will be increased when they find, placed here and there about the town, statues of the Princes of Hohenzollern — a name that is always associated with Prussia.

To understand how this came about it is necessary, and interesting, to be aware of the complicated history of the German states, principalities, kingdoms, empire, and republics — a subject that few of us learn anything about at school! The family of Hohenzollern originated in Swabia, not far from Sigmaringen, in the eleventh century. In the thirteenth century it split into two main lines: the Swabian Line, which remained based in this area and the Franconian Line, which gained great power in the German states, ruling over the area of Nuremberg; from the fifteenth century becoming electors of Brandenburg, and from the eighteenth century kings of Prussia. After the reign of Frederick the Great, Prussia became recognised as one of the chief European powers.

Meanwhile the Swabian branch continued to play a more modest but still distinguished role as aristocratic rulers in this region, remaining faithful to the Catholic faith in distinction to the Prussian

*A statue of Prince Leopold of Hohenzollern
standing in front of Prussian government buildings, Sigmaringen*

branch that was a leading adherent of the Protestant cause in the Reformation. In 1535 a member of the Swabian Line was created a count of Hohenzollern by the Holy Roman Emperor and obtained possession of the castle and estates of Sigmaringen. In the seventeenth century the line was elevated to the rank of Princes of Hohenzollern. Although Prince Karl, in the nineteenth century, was an enlightened ruler, his reign was disturbed by the social unrest that followed the French Revolution, and he abdicated in favour of his son, Prince Karl Anton. In 1849 Karl Anton took the decisive step of relinquishing his power in favour of the related royal house of Prussia — an action seen as a contribution towards the unification of Germany. From that date the principality of Hohenzollern became absorbed in the distant kingdom of Prussia. Sigmaringen and the surrounding territory remained part of Prussia for just over a hundred years: under the Prussian kingdom from 1849-71; under the German Empire, ruled by Hohenzollerns from Berlin, from 1871-1918; and under the Weimar Republic and the Nazi Third Reich from 1919-45. It was finally absorbed into the *Land* of Baden-Württemberg under the post-war constitution of the Federal Republic in 1952. The fine administrative buildings erected by the Prussian authorities bear witness to this chapter in its history, and a frontier post bearing

The castle of the Hohenzollern family dominates the town of Sigmaringen

the words 'Preussen Hohenzollernsche Lande' can still be seen in the town today. The town was, indeed, in its day a provincial capital of some importance, in which Prussian administrative efficiency was partnered with Swabian south German culture.

The history of the castle of Sigmaringen is equally complicated and equally fascinating. The oldest part of the building, the square tower in its centre, dates back to the twelfth century. The present shape of the structure was established by the Counts of Werdenberg in the fifteenth century. After the Swabian Hollenzollerns acquired possession of the castle it received further additions in about 1600, but 30 years later it was sacked by Swedish troops during the Thirty Years War and required considerable reconstruction. A number of embellishments in Gothic revival style were carried out in the nineteenth century, including its most obvious landmark, the octagonal and pointed helm to the central square tower. But then part of the castle was gutted by fire in 1893 and restored early in the present century. What can be seen today therefore, is a product of many different periods and its furnishings represent the domestic style of a wealthy aristocratic family in the early 1900s. It is not a homogeneous piece of architecture, nor indeed a great work of architecture of any period, but a great building that has grown with the centuries to achieve a unity of a very special kind.

The castle is open to the public (except in December and January) and presents not only a history of architectural styles but also a history of the princely family that has lived in it for so long. Prince

Karl Anton, the last Swabian Hohenzollern to rule his principality, had many connections with the royal families of Europe: a daughter married the King of Portugal; his son and successor married a Portuguese princess; his second son became king of the recently established state of Rumania; another daughter married the Count of Flanders, and became the great-grandmother of the present King of Belgium. Crown Prince Leopold was offered the throne of Spain, and although he declined the honour this provoked the Franco-Prussian War. These royal associations are all illustrated by splendid portraits on the walls of the apartments today. As a pendant to these illustrious figures from a vanished age, the last rulers of any kind to dwell in the castle of Sigmaringen were the members of the Vichy government of occupied France, who were moved here by the retreating Germans in the last months of World War II, and who must have gazed with mounting disquiet from the windows of their opulent apartments as they waited for the American army to transfer them to a different kind of captivity.

Two features of the interior call for special mention. The armoury contains weapons of every kind from the fourteenth to the twentieth centuries, and constitutes the largest private collection in Europe. The museum, built in Gothic revival style in 1867, houses a very distinguished collection of the work of Swabian painters and sculpters of the fifteenth and sixteenth centuries; in its own field this collection is unmatched anywhere.

The interest of Sigmaringen is by no means limited to its castle. It is a pleasant small town, with the nearby Wildpark Joseflust which houses many wild animals of the region in their natural habitat. It would make an admirable centre for excursions into the surrounding countryside, but before any further exploration it would be as well to describe the other places in the Upper Danube valley that might provide a base for such expeditions.

Beuron

Beuron lies in an idyllic situation in the Danube valley where a bend of the river has left sufficient flat ground for a settlement to grow up. A legend maintains that when an eleventh-century count was out hunting in this area a beautiful stag that he was pursuing laid down and indicated to him the spot where he should found a monastery. The stag certainly showed excellent taste! The monastery prospered in the hands of the Augustinian Canons, the adjoining land was acquired bit by bit or donated, and the abbey church was rebuilt in the fashionable baroque style in the eighteenth century. But then disaster struck. Although southern Germany, in general, remained Catholic during the Reformation, the influence of the French Revolution and the general secularisation of society at the end of the eighteenth century, combined with the conquests of Napoleon over the greater part of Europe, led to the acceptance in all these European countries that vast land-owning monasteries should be suppressed. Today it is hard to understand why the monks were not left to say their prayers in peace while the bulk of their property was confiscated, with or even without compensation. Perhaps this solution never appealed to the various abbots involved. Anyhow Beuron, like many others, was suppressed in 1802.

Germany today is full of great monastic buildings that were secularised in this period but now serve other purposes: Fürstenfeldbruck, near Munich, is a police college and Zwiefalten, which is described later, is a psychiatric hospital. But Beuron is a monastery again, and this is how it came about.

Early in the nineteenth century a group of idealistic German painters, who came to be called the Nazarenes, rejected the conventional art style of the period and sought to recreate an early Christian school of painting. They set up a studio and a quasi-religious brotherhood in Rome, and from this inspiration a number of Germans had joined the Benedictine monastery of St Paul's Outside the Walls in Rome. In 1862, just 60 years after the suppression, two young German monks from St Paul's moved into the ruins of Beuron. The widow of Prince Karl Hohenzollern, who now owned the site, gave them the property to enable them to refound the monastery. Barely had the work of restoration begun when the monastery found itself caught up in the quarrel between Prussia (in whose territory it now stood, as explained earlier) and the Catholic Church. This was Bismarck's *Kulturkampf*, under which all Catholic religious institutions were closed down. But after 12 years the situation improved and the monks could return. The monastery prospered, more monks joined the community and under its inspiration there grew up a new school of Christian art, which would be less sentimental and more truly religious than what had passed for religious art previously.

The artistic style of what came to be known as the Beuron School of Art is not very fashionable today, and one must regret that the original altarpiece by Josef Feuchtmayer, by all accounts a masterpiece of baroque sculpture, was destroyed in the process of redecorating the church. Perhaps it seemed too worldy for these idealistic reformers. But where one can see Beuron art in its own setting, as in the new Lady Chapel of the church or in the Saint Maurus Chapel a few miles down the river, one cannot withhold one's admiration, especially when one sees the crowds of genuine pilgrims who come to pray there.

Beuron not only founded a new school of art but revived the ancient art of Gregorian plainsong, which had fallen into neglect. Today the offices of High Mass and Compline are sung daily, in Latin, by the monks in the choir. For anyone who has any feeling for this form of worship, in which prayer is transmuted into a high form of art, this is an experience that should not be missed.

As every monk will tell you, the main purpose of their life is to pray. But they also have to work, and Beuron supports itself (and the hotel where visitors probably stay) by an efficiently and ecologically run farm. It contains monk craftsmen in almost every form of activity; it runs a printing press and a publishing house and houses an institute for the study of biblical palimpsets that has an international reputation. If you are male you can ask to stay in the guest house, where you can share, as far as you wish, something of the monastic atmosphere. Women must stay in a hotel or *pension* in the village!

While Beuron will make a particular appeal to those who appreciate the religious atmosphere of the abbey, it is an excellent centre for any one who wants to explore the Danube valley. Wonderful walks stretch in every direction from outside your door.

The Danube Valley

The third place in the district that can offer a fair choice of hotels and inns is **Tuttlingen**. This is a larger town than Sigmaringen, and more industrial in character, with firms that specialise in the manufacture of medical instruments. It is well situated at the point where the romantic Danube valley closes in, and would provide an excellent base for exploration, especially if accomodation in Sigmaringen or Beuron is fully occupied.

As to the exploration of the Danube valley it is difficult to give advice, as it is wonderful wherever you go. Try to walk beside the river, and climb to the top of the cliffs on either side to take in the views. You should try to reach some of the castles on the peaks, though these are mostly either in ruins or in private hands. Among the most attractive are Burg Wildenstein, which is now a youth hostel, Schloss Bronnen, which is used by the Stuttgart School of Art, and Schloss Werenwag, where the Minnesinger Hugo von Werenwag sang in the thirteenth century, and there are several others. An

The Danube between Tuttlingen and Sigmaringen

effort should be made to visit some of the caves that the action of water has worn out of the limestone. This whole area is honey-combed with caves, of which about 1,200 are registered. Some are little more than small depressions in the rock but others stretch for hundreds of yards; a dozen or so have been fitted with electric lights as show caves. Of these the most convenient to visit is the Kolbinger Höhle near Mülheim which stretches for 65yd into the rock and contains fine stalactites; it is only open to the public at weekends. There are several other caves near Mülheim, some of which should be entered only with caution. The Ziegelhöhle near Fridingen is similar to the Kolbinger Höhle but it is not illuminated; you are warned not to enter it without three good torches, of which you may expect to use up two. The Falkensteinhöhle, near the ruined castle of that name, is much smaller in size but bears signs of having been inhabited in the middle Stone Age; some 9,000 tools and ornaments

The Upper Danube near Möhringen, where the river drains away through cracks in the limestone bed

have been excavated from it. The views from the cliffs are superb.

The whole area is covered with well-marked footpaths, but it is advisable to get a good map; these marks occasionally disappear in the most inconvenient places. There are, of course, inns in many of the small villages, with some offering a room for the night, and walkers of any age in search of simple and inexpensive accommodation may use the Wanderheim Rauber Stein at Irndorf. A facility which could be of great help to walkers laden with heavy rucksacks is a service which will send your luggage by car from the place where you spent the night to the place you intend to walk to; this scheme — 'Wanderung ohne Gepäck' — is organised by the *Verkehrsverein* at Reutlingen, Tuttlingen, and Sigmaringen, from whom details may be requested.

The Swabian Alb

The interest of this area is not limited to the valley of the Danube. The Swabian Alb, through which the river has cut its way, is well worth exploring. Do not be confused by the word Alb. These are not Alps but a range of limestone hills, about 35 miles (56km) wide, inter-sected by picturesque valleys which are partly clothed by fine beech forests. It runs in a north-east direction from near Tuttlingen for over a hundred miles. In general the ridge facing north-west provides the finest scenery; behind this stretches a wide plateau. It is only the south-western area of the Alb that falls within the scope of this chapter. It is now registered as the Naturpark Obere Donau, guaran-teeing a measure of protection from undesirable development.

An attractive expedition may be made up the river Bära, which runs into the Danube near Fridingen. After about 7 miles (11km) the river divides, and the right hand fork leads, after a further 7 miles, to **Tieringen** at the foot of the Lochenstein, said once to have been a pagan place of sacrifice, from which there is a fine view. This may be as far as you want to walk in one day. The next day can be spent comfortably reaching Wehingen or Gosheim, on the way climbing Lemberg, which at 3,330ft (1,015m) is the highest peak in the Swabian Alb. To round off this expedition a return can be made to the Danube via the Klippeneck, a popular site for launching gliders, and the Dreifaltigkeitsberg, which offers a splendid view from the tower of the pilgrimage church at the top. On a fine day the Swiss Alps from Jungfrau to Karwendel can be seen. This plateau at the top of the mountain was regarded as a sanctuary in the past. If enough walking and climbing has been done for the day a train or bus could be caught to Tuttlingen from Spaichingen, which does not offer much interest today but was the centre of an active manufacture of articles for pedlars in the past.

Another expedition into the Swabian Alb could be to take the train from Sigmaringen up the wild valley of the Schmiere. Just after Ebingen the line crosses the watershed between the Danube and the Rhine. A few miles after Balingen you come to Hechingen, the station for the imposing Hohenzollern Castle. This was the original seat of the Hohenzollern family. The first castle on this magnificent site seems to have been erected in the eleventh century; it was destroyed in the fifteenth century after a siege in which only thirty-two knights survived out of a garrison of 500. The second castle stood from the fifteenth to the eighteenth century. In 1819 the Hohenzollern King of Prussia, William IV, obtained possession of the ruin of the former

The nineteenth-century Hohenzollern Castle, on a site that has housed the family's castles since the eleventh century

castle and set in hand plans for a new castle. What is seen today was completed in 1867, an impressive example of nineteenth-century German Romanticism. It was intended to be a monument to the Hohenzollern line of German emperors. Today the Hohenzollern emperors have vanished, but the tombs of Frederick William I and of Frederick II, 'the Great', in the Protestant chapel are from time to time bedecked with flowers from visitors who wish to honour their contribution to the great but tragic history of this gifted nation.

A third excursion into the Swabian Alb is by the branch railway from Sigmaringen that follows the river Lauchert. Note that the station for this line is not the main Sigmaringen station but adjoins it. The line goes through pleasant landscape as far as Gammertingen, you may however wish to leave the train, after a 35 minute ride, at **Veringenstadt**, an old village round which the river curves. There are two easily accessible caves here, not very deep but of interest as they seem certain to have been used as temporary dwellings by Stone Age hunters of mammoths. The local archaeologist who excavated the finds here buried them so securely for safety during World War II and died without telling anyone where they were, so that they now wait to be discovered all over again! The ruins of a castle and chapel with sixteenth-century frescoes grace the hill above the village and in a house, by one of the bridges, there lives a keen collector and dealer in minerals, who has decorated the outside of his house with strange metallic surrealistic sculptures and who — if an intelligent interest is shown — may demonstrate his collection. The metallic structures are frames for the mounting of translucent minerals that glow like stained glass when a light is placed behind them.

There is one further expedition that should be pursued. Leaving Sigmaringen down the Danube, the hills recede and the country is flat. The river widens and after 16 miles (26km) we come to the charming medieval town of **Riedlingen**. Pleasant though this is with a fine Gothic church, a fifteenth-century town hall, and a somewhat more touristy hotel than is usual in these parts, the real object of the visit is two churches in the neighbourhood that are of great importance in the development of rococo architecture.

The earlier in date of these is at **Obermarchtal**, a little further downstream from Riedlingen. This is an early example of what is called the Vorarlberg School of Architecture. Towards the end of the seventeenth century there grew up a group of artists and architects in the Vorarlberg, which is a province of Austria at the east end of Lake Constance. Under their influence churches came to be constructed in what is called the 'wall-pillar' style. Builders had, of course, long known that the thin high walls of a long building needed some extra support. In the Middle Ages this was supplied by external buttresses. The contribution of the Vorarlberg School was to place the buttresses inside the building, thus creating what appear to be wall-pillars. These pillars often flank side chapels, and are linked by galleries above; sometimes they are pierced to provide a side aisle; sometimes their structural function is so disguised that they appear to be purely ornamental. You can find this style of building all over southern Germany and Switzerland. Just as constructional problems in Gothic architecture were solved by buttresses and vaulting, so the solution of constructional problems in a later age again produced architectural forms of great beauty.

Obermarchtal was built in 1686 by an architect from the Vorarlberg called Michael Thumb. After noting the wall-pillar construction, observe that there are no frescoes. The walls and ceiling are white, which is relieved by very fine stucco decoration. The altar and chapels are in dark brown, which provides a pleasing contrast. There are some good statues, but the general effect is somewhat heavy. The new spirit of baroque was still struggling to find perfect expression.

At **Zwiefalten**, a few miles away, the art of baroque has taken wings in a flight of purest rococo. This is one of the finest of the many fine rococo churches in Germany. It was designed in 1741 by Johann Michael Fischer, one of the greatest of the architects of this period. The situation in a wooded valley at the foot of the Alb is beautiful; the exterior is imposing; the interior is a dream of white and gold, with walls flanked by stucco pillars. It is hard to believe that they are not real marble. The ceilings are painted in frescoes that seem to whirl the visitor up into the company of the saints in heaven. The statues, in contrast, are in pure white: Ezechial, on one side of the transept crossing, gazes in prophetic ecstasy at his vision of the valley of dry bones grouped round the pulpit opposite. The eye is led on, past the older pilgrimage statue of Mary in its nimbus of golden rays, through the ironwork grille, to the choir whose dark wooden stalls seem alive with movement, to reach the climax of the church in the high altar set between clusters of pink and white columns.

It would be best to visit this church on a Sunday. This is the only day on which it is open to all to walk round it as wished. On weekdays in summer there are guided tours every hour, but that is no way for a visitor to slowly absorb the atmosphere of such a building. In the winter there are not even guided tours. One can always enter the large vestibule at the west end and gaze at the rest of the interior through an ironwork grille, but this is a poor substitute for a careful and perhaps prayerful visit. One must appreciate the problems for the authorities who have the charge of a church like this. It was built for the use of a large community of monks, and was closed down in the suppression of 1803. It is now simply the parish church of the small village that surrounds it. The German state has done magnificent work and at enormous expense in restoration, which was completed only in 1984, but the state is not responsible for the day-to-day care of the building. Obviously proper care must be taken to guard the superb artistic treasures that it houses; the provision of this care may well be beyond the resources of a small village. But the consequence for a visitor, who perhaps has travelled thousands of miles to see one of the greatest buildings of its kind in Europe and who arrives on a winter weekday, is not one of which Germany or Zwiefalten can be proud. So, till this situation is improved, visit on a Sunday!

When you are at Zwiefalten there is one other visit you may like to make. The Wimsener Höhle, a mile or so from the village, is one of the most dramatic of all caves in the Swabian Alb, and the only one that has to be visited by boat. A river rises here, giving a depth of 9ft (3m) of crystal-clear water. Boats take you into the cave for about 100yd. It goes much further, and has been explored in conditions of great difficulty and some danger for nearly half a mile; no one knows quite how far it reaches.

This visit to Riedlingen and the churches nearby is the only excursion that has been described for which a car would be useful. In general, visitors to the nature park of the Upper Danube who have come by car are advised to leave their cars in the hotel car park, to abstain from blocking the narrow roads with their vehicles, and to make use of the excellent public transport that is available both by train and bus. If you haven't got a car, it is easy to travel to Riedlingen by train; there are buses from there to Zwiefalten and (occasionally) to Obermarchtal, but these are timed rather to the requirements of school children than to the convenience of independent travellers with a taste for rococo architecture. It is possible to walk from Riedlingen to Zwiefalten in 3 hours by pleasant footpaths, and return by bus; or to take a taxi at either place, or hire a bicycle at Sigmaringen railway station.

While you are here you will be very conscious of the fact that you are staying in Swabia. It is a long time since this has been an administrative or political area of its own, but the Swabians are, like all Germans, very conscious of their own regional identity. They have the reputation of being hard working, thrifty and inclined to introspection, and have produced many poets. It is not uncommon to find a memorial on a house in some little village recording that such and such a poet lived there — a name perhaps quite unknown elsewhere but fondly cherished in his homeland. If the visitors' German is good enough they will recognise the Swabian accent, and even the Swabian dialect. A common diminutive suffix is *-le*: a small rucksack becomes *Rucksäckle*, a small inn, *Wirtschäftle* and a little house might even be *ein kloins Häusle*. However elementary your German, you will certainly notice, and hopefully eat dishes on the Speisekarte that you will not meet elsewhere: *Maultaschen* is *Spätzle* (dumpling) filled with meat and spinach and bound with egg; a *Gaisburger Marsch* is a stew with *Spätzle*, potato, sausage, fried onions and meat gravy. There is no local wine, but the Württemberg vineyards are not far off and provide good wine that is not often listed in other areas.

As has been indicated, the Swabian Alb is of special interest to geologists. It is, indeed, the largest limestone range in central Europe. As well as the numerous caves and evidence of past volcanic activity, the rocks are rich in fossils. It also offers good opportunities to rock climbers; in particular the stretch of river between Beuron and Inzighofen is known as a climber's playground. Skilled climbers may reach the nests of eagles and peregrine falcons (but not to take their eggs), and find one of their few surviving breeding grounds, but visitors should beware of loose rocks. Climbers and cavers who are attracted to this area would do well to make contact with similar German societies through their own clubs for advice before venturing alone.

Riding holidays are popular here and the gently rolling plateau of the south-eastern Alb provides good riding country. Several farms offer horses for hire. The river also offers scope for fishing and boating and canoes may be hired. There are camping sites at Sigmaringen and Hausen, and open-air swimming pools at all the chief places in the area. Flying gliders is popular and there are several good spots for launching them. In the winter you can ski all over the hills, and there are many ski lifts; the plateau is particularly suitable for cross-county skiing (Langlauf Skiwanderung).

Further Information
— The Upper Danube —

Places to Visit

Beuron
Kolbinger Höhle
Near Mulheim
Open: only March-November at
weekends.

Sigmaringen
Schloss Sigmaringen
Open: February to November, daily
from 8.30am-12noon and 1-5pm.
Tour of castle takes about 45 minutes.

Tourist Information Offices

Sigmaringen
Verkehrsamt
Postfach 249
72488 Sigmaringen
☎ (07541) 106 233

Tuttlingen
Verkehrsamt
78532 Tuttlingen
☎ (07462) 6217/6243/340

Information about other
specialist activities may
be requested from the
following organisations:

*Fremdenverkehrsgemeinschaft
'Bergland junge Donau'*
78532 Tuttlingen

*Gebietsgemeinschaft
'Schwäbsche Alb'*
72072 Tübingen
An der Neckarbrücke

*Geschäftsstelle Naturpark
Obere Donau*
88631 Beuron

Schwaber International
70173 Stuttgart
Charlottenplatz 6

*Verband Deutscher
Höhlen- und
Karstforscher*
72622 Nürtingen
Jusistrasse 4/2

11 • Eastern Germany — An Introduction

To visit eastern Germany is to witness a land in metamorphosis. A land breaking free from the economic and social constraints of an authoritarian society like a butterfly from its cocoon. The dilapidated centres of many historic towns are being restored to their former grandeur. Pot-holed roads are giving way to smooth asphalt highways. For better or worse the East has become one giant building site; scaffolding has become the outward, if mundane symbol, of the advent of western prosperity after years of socialist stagnation.

No time could be better for visiting eastern Germany than now. No time more fascinating. After all, how often is it in a lifetime that one has a chance to witness a whole society in the process of radical change? How often can one witness the results of a peaceful revolution? Everywhere it is possible to see the contrast of old with new. The concrete housing blocks, utilitarian to the point that they seem to embody the monotony of daily life, stand next to freshly painted half-timbered buildings, which a few years before were nearly in ruins. In some places the name of Karl Marx still clings tenuously to a street sign nobody has had time to remove. The lack of money, or interest, has meant that much from the past has survived in eastern Germany, even if it is only in the slightly moth-eaten condition that one might expect of a badly tended museum.

The People and their Situation

With the fall of the Berlin Wall people who had lived all their lives under an authoritarian communist system were confronted, virtually overnight, not only with all the positive benefits but also with all the negative aspects of a democratic system. There was no time for gradual adaptation, no time to come to terms with concepts like 'private enterprise' or even something as mundane as 'personal insurance'. People who had, for forty years, been taught *not* to think for themselves, that the accumulation of property and competition (except in sport) were sins, now had to learn that precisely the

254

opposite was expected of them. They were left hanging in a kind of limbo, unwilling to go back but uncertain as to how to go forward.

What has hit the East Germans hardest since the fall of the Wall is unemployment. Unemployment was unknown in East Germany as the State followed a policy of full employment, even if that meant massive government subsidies for unprofitable industries or giving two men the work that could be done by one. The loss of a job has been particularly traumatic for those people in their thirties or forties. Instead of the hoped for prosperity a growing number of East Germans have to get by with a cheque from social welfare. The bitterness and disappointment felt by such people, who believed that the West was a kind of 'promised land', is not hard to imagine.

The problems of reunification are as great as the benefits it may eventually bring. The financial burden, even for a country of Germany's economic stature, is immense. It is therefore hardly surprising that reactionary elements in German society have tried to capitalise on this (temporary) mood of discontent and uncertainty for their own ends. The 'anti-foreigner' attitude that has taken its ugliest form in the shape of right-wing violence against refugees is not an attitude shared by the majority of Germans. Travellers will find that most people in eastern Germany in fact welcome the opportunity of talking to foreign tourists. They are eager to hear about lands which they were once prevented from visiting. Many also have a need to explain what they have been through, to make the 'outside world' (above all West Germans!) understand what it was like to live in a society where the secret police were able to penetrate every aspect of their private and public lives. Because of this it is often easier for travellers to make contact with people in Germany's eastern states than in western states like Bavaria, where tourists have long since ceased to be a novelty.

Travelling by Car

With a few exceptions the 'B' roads (*Bundesstrassen* or trunk roads) and highways in eastern Germany are in reasonable condition but it is still advisable to avoid exceeding 100kph except where the road has obviously been repaired. The secondary roads — usually marked in yellow on maps — can be rather poor and those minor roads which are not distinguished by a colour of any kind are best left alone, unless you own a four-wheel drive vehicle! Though the minor roads in the north tend to be better than in the south the authors encountered a few in the Uckermark that hardly deserved the title of track let alone road.

In contrast to western Germany the road signs in the east can be very confusing. Some towns and villages are not signposted at all or in an illogical fashion; the sign is visible from one direction but not the other. Quite often the signs are placed a kilometre or so before a road crossing but not at the crossing itself! A good road map is therefore indispensable if motorists do not want to get lost.

Some recommended maps are: *Euro-Atlas Deutschland/Europa* published by RV Verlag 1:300,000; *ADAC-Karte Altmark und Havelland* 1:150,000; *Touristenkarte Uckermark/Untere Oder*, Tourist-Verlag 1:150,000; *Freizeitkarte Allianz No.64, Dresden/Oberlausitz/Sächsische Schweiz*, Mairs Geographischer Verlag 1:100,000; *RV No.11131, Ostseeküste (Baltic Coast), Rügen, Usedom, Mecklenburger Seenplatte*, 1:200,000; *ADAC-Karte XXII Harz, Magdeburger Börde, Hoher Fläming* 1:150,000 (all available in Germany).

Within towns it should be borne in mind that many streets that were named after socialist heroes will change. For instance Karl-Marx-Platz might become Marktplatz and Ernst-Thälmann-Strasse might become Hauptstrasse again. Please bear this in mind when reading the descriptions of towns in this section. Locals will invariably know which street you mean if the name has changed since this book was written.

Until recently it was difficult to find a petrol station that sold unleaded (*Bleifrei*) fuel but now it can be difficult to find a station that sells normal leaded petrol. This is particularly the case in some of the more off the beaten track places. Larger petrol stations usually have both types of fuel but because the network of stations is not as dense as in the west it pays to fill up as soon as the opportunity arises.

Traffic signs and regulations are generally the same as in the west. One important difference is the green arrow for traffic turning to the right at traffic lights. This means that motorists can turn right even if the traffic light shows red. There has been talk about getting rid of the green arrow but the possibility has also been considered of introducing it all over Germany. At the moment it only applies to the east and motorists should, in any case, exercise care at intersections where the green arrow is used.

Accommodation

The accommodation situation in eastern Germany is improving with every year but in those places that are off the beaten track visitors will find that the standards are not always up to those in the west of Germany. The cheapest, and sometimes also the best accommodation, is that offered by the small privately run 'bed and breakfasts'

(*Privatzimmer*). The tourist offices should have up-to-date and comprehensive lists (some will even help to arrange accommodation) but many people also advertise their rooms with signs in front of their houses like '*Gästezimmer*' or '*Zimmer frei*', which means room to let. Not all *Privatzimmer* offer breakfast and one should inquire whether or not it is '*mit Frühstück*' (with breakfast). At the cheapest places it is not uncommon to find that there are no showers and that the toilet is either in the courtyard or has to be shared with your hosts. However there is always a sink to wash in.

The prices and standards in hotels and boarding-houses (*Pension*) vary greatly but a *Pension* or *Gasthaus* is generally cheaper than a hotel and they often offer better value for money; they usually have a more homely atmosphere than larger hotels. Such hotels are more likely to offer western standards and visitors are more likely to be able to find somebody who speaks good English at reception.

Camping grounds are fairly widespread in eastern Germany and they are usually much cheaper than in the west. Although many have been modernised some camping grounds are still without adequate sanitary facilities such as hot showers and flushing toilets. Most are open from 1 May until 30 September, though some are open throughout the year.

Youth Hostels (*Jugendherberge*) in eastern Germany are listed in the *German Jugendherbergsverzeichnis* which is available from bookshops or from the Deutsches Jugendherbergswerk, Bismarckstrasse 8, 32756 Detmold, ☎ (05231)74010, as well as in the *International Youth Hostels Guide to Budget Accommodation* vol 1, which lists basic information on all hostels in Europe. Groups are strongly advised to reserve places in advance and individual travellers should reserve a bed at least a day ahead.

Please note that although hotels (and restaurants) are listed at the end of this book according to their price categories, these categories are by no means fixed in eastern Germany. As soon as the owner can afford to renovate his *Pension* or *Gasthaus* it might easily catapult from the cheap to the medium or even expensive category. Always ask the price beforehand. For stays of three or more days it is usually possible to ask for reduced rates.

Language

English is not as widely spoken in eastern Germany as in western Germany. Travellers should make sure that they have a phrase book and it would pay to learn a few polite greetings and so forth before setting off.

Telephoning

Telephoning can sometimes be a bit of an ordeal in the east because the antiquated telephone system has not yet been completely modernised. The dialling codes given in the Further Information sections are all valid for calls from the west of Germany to the east but not always for calls within the eastern states. Because of all the changes taking place it could be that some of the phone numbers listed in the text are no longer valid. If a local telephone book is handy then check first.

Not every house or hotel in eastern Germany had or has a telephone. The German Bundespost is doing its best to rectify this problem as quickly as possible, but in some rural areas the only way to place a call is from a public phone booth. They are not everywhere either but when they do exist they are often modern card-operated phones. If you cannot find a phone booth then look for the nearest post office (*Postamt*). Telephone cards (*Telefonkarten*) can be bought at the post offices. Although it is usually possible to find a coin-operated phone next to a card phone the queues tend to be shorter outside the card phone booths.

12 • The Baltic Coast

Between the Hanseatic splendour of Wismar and the provincial charm of Ueckermünde lies a fascinating coastal landscape composed of long sandy beaches, wind-swept coastal pine forests, and shore hugging islands that have been frayed by the constant gnawing of wind and waves. Into this scenery the hand of man has set immense Gothic churches, tiny thatched cottages, stately villas and aristocratic spas. Each bit of coast seems to have a special character of its own with the only unifying factor being, perhaps, the cool salt breeze of the Baltic Sea (known to the Germans as the Ostsee).

Starting point for this exploration of the Baltic coast is **Wismar**. The town is quickly reached from Hamburg and Lübeck on the A1/B105. From Berlin the motorway goes as far as Schwerin, from where it is only a drive of some 32km (20 miles) along the B106. There are rail connections from both Hamburg and Berlin. It is also possible to take the hydrofoil from Travemünde (near Lübeck).

Wismar's heyday was during the fourteenth and fifteenth centuries when it took part in the flourishing sea-trade of the Hanseatic League. In those days beer must have been an especially lucrative export as around 1480 there were no less than 180 private breweries here — at present there are none! This period of prosperity was put to an end by the Thirty Years' War after which the town belonged to Sweden until 1803. It was not until the middle of the nineteenth century that the economic situation really improved and in the twentieth century Wismar's harbour was expanded to make it the second largest port in the former German Democratic Republic.

A good place to start a tour of town is in the *Marktplatz*, one of the largest and prettiest in eastern Germany. It is lined on one side by some very picturesque gabled houses among which is the Alter Schwede (1380), the town's oldest burgher house. Also here is the classical *Rathaus* (1817-19) and Renaissance *Wasserkunst* (1579-1602). In medieval Germany the term *Wasserkunst* referred to bucket eleva-

The Alter Schwede in Wismar's market place has been used as a restaurant since 1878

tors and pump-rooms. Wismar's *Wasserkunst* functioned as a central reservoir from where the town was supplied with drinking water until 1897.

A number of interesting buildings are loosely grouped to the west of the *Marktplatz* and they include the gabled houses along Lübsche Strasse, the Heiligen-Geist-Kirche, the Fürstenhof (Princes' Court, 1535-55) and the mighty tower of the Marienkirche. This tower is all that is left of the church which was destroyed by bombing in 1945. Near the tower is the beautifully restored fifteenth-century Archidiakonat (Pastor's House).

To the north of the *Marktplatz* is the Schabbelhaus (1569-71) which houses the town museum (*Stadtgeschichtliches Museum*). The house was built in Dutch Renaissance style and once belonged to the wealthy owner of a local brewery. Not far from here, and next to the old town canal that was built in the Middle Ages as part of a system linking the Baltic Sea to Lake Schwerin, is the monumental structure of the brick Nikolaikirche (1380-1403). Built to inspire awe the vast central nave towers 37m (121ft) over the heads of the congregation making it the highest in eastern Germany. Only the Münster in Ulm and the cathedral in Cologne are larger. Not far from this church is the *Alter Hafen* (Old Harbour) from where boats depart for the island of Poel. Standing here is the Wassertor, a gate remaining from the medieval town wall.

In the vicinity of Wismar are a number of places worthy of closer investigation. A few kilometres to the north is the beach resort of **Wendorf**. An interesting walk taking about 20 minutes goes from the beach to the fishing village of **Hoben**, where there are a number of houses in traditional Mecklenburg style. Another beach resort is **Boltenhagen** located some 25km (15½ miles) to the west. Around 15km (9 miles) to the east of Wismar the small town of **Neukloster** is located next to a lake of the same name. In the church belonging to the Cistercian nunnery (Zisterzienserinnen-Kloster Sonnenkamp) here are stained glass windows dating from the thirteenth century. They belong to the oldest and most significant in all of northern Germany. A bit further south is another lake known as Wariner See. Bathing is possible in both lakes.

Continuing east from Wismar it is possible to take either the B105 or to follow minor roads which run much closer to the coast. Naturally, those visitors who wish to find out-of-the-way places should choose the latter alternative. Though secondary roads can be a bit rough in this part of Germany the unspoiled towns and countryside they often go through make the few extra jolts worth it.

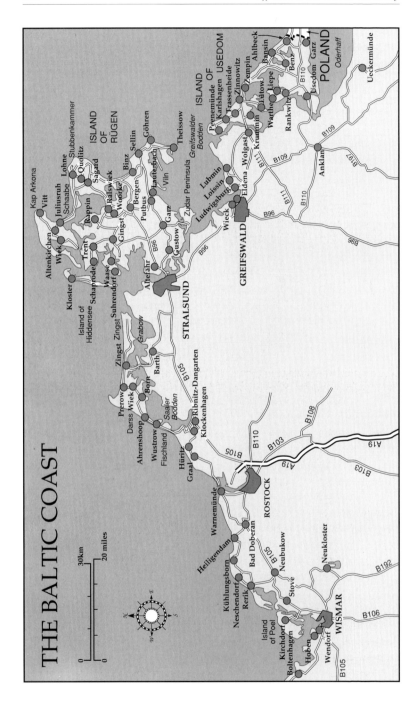

THE BALTIC COAST

This old windmill near Stove is one of the few left along the Baltic coast

The island of **Poel** can be reached by boat from Wismar (1 hour) or by road via the village of Groß-Strömkendorf. A road embankment links the island to the mainland. The main settlement here is **Kirchdorf** with an *Inselmuseum* (Island Museum) and *Dorfkirche* (village church) from the fifteenth century. Apart from the popular beaches at Timmendorf and 'Am Schwarzen Busch' there is not much else to the island which is flat as a board and covered mainly by farmland. This lack of anything spectacular has not prevented the island being described as one of the nicest holiday areas on the Mecklenburg coast, though mainly for those who like beaches.

Back on the mainland Neubukow can be reached via Blowatz and Boiensdorf along a slightly elevated road which offers some nice views over the coastal scenery. On the way it is worth stopping at the tiny settlement of **Stove** where one of the few windmills left along the Baltic coast can be visited. It was erected in 1889 and remained operational until 1977.

Neubukow is the birthplace of the archaeologist Heinrich Schliemann (1822-90), the discoverer of Troy. A memorial dedicated to

Schliemann is located in the town library (*Bibliothek*). There is also a working windmill here that can be visited.

North of Neubukow is the Ostseebad (beach resort) **Rerik**. Apart from some 4km (2½ miles) of beach there is a very impressive early Gothic church with baroque interior that is well worth a visit. In nearby **Meschendorf** are some dolmen (megalithic graves) as well as a nudist (FKK) beach. Situated as it is next to the Salzhaff (a sheltered bay) Rerik makes a good base for those keen on sailing. International yacht regattas are held in the bay.

Only a short distance further east of Rerik is Ostseebad **Kühlungsborn**. It is the biggest beach resort on the Baltic coast and has a wide range of accommodation as well as some very good restaurants. The resort's indoor salt-water swimming pool (*Meerwasserschwimmhalle*) ensures that guests can go for a dip in all weathers. South of town is a beautiful area of forested hills known as Die Kühlung. It is possible to walk from town (start at Bahnhof Kühlungsborn-Mitte) to the Diedrichshäger Berg (130m, 426ft), which is not only the highest elevation in Die Kühlung but also along the entire Baltic coast. The trail goes past a windmill, now used as a restaurant, that was built in 1872.

Anybody who stays any length of time in Kühlungsborn is bound to come across '*Molli*'. This is the affectionate name given to a steam train that has puffed its way along the narrow-gauge railway between Kühlungsborn and Bad Doberan since 1886. With a top speed of 40km/h (25mph) there is plenty of time to enjoy the scenery along the way. In summer *Molli* covers her 15km (9 miles) journey up to fifteen times a day and stops close to a number of beaches.

Next stop on the coast is Ostseebad **Heiligendamm**. Founded in 1793 by Grand Duke Friedrich Franz I it is the oldest German seaside resort. The idea of starting a resort came to the grand duke when some eminent doctors were able to convince him of the curative properties of sea water. In those days such a resort or spa was usually close to an aristocratic residence and only open to the very highest circles but in the mid-nineteenth century the development spread to farming and fishing villages. The clientele now belonged to the upper middle-class and offered locals a welcome opportunity to improve their meagre incomes. Not until the start of the twentieth century did the taint of snobbism disappear from 'a day at the beach' and the first family resorts were opened (no singles allowed). The dignified buildings along Heiligendamm's beach, all resplendent in white against the cool blue of the sea, were built in classical style and are reminders of the resort's exclusive beginnings.

*Classical architecture
at the seaside resort
of Heiligendamm
gives it a noble
character*

Heiligendamm also has a FKK beach. The abbreviation stands for *Freikörperkultur*, literally 'free body culture' or nudism. Nudism began in Germany in 1906 with the founding of the Deutsche Luftbadegesellschaft in Berlin. At a time when prudery dominated German seaside resorts (beaches were separated according to men and women, no binoculars or cameras were allowed) the idea was revolutionary. Berlin was however a progressive, open-minded city and the idea was in any case more puritan than it might at first seem. No doubt as a reaction to the confining, stressful conditions of a major city the people who joined this 'movement' sought a lifestyle that was more in keeping with the rhythms of nature. The emphasis in the various nudist clubs was on sport and comradeship; alcohol, tobacco, gambling and vulgarity were frowned upon. Although there are of course FKK beaches in Germany's western states nudism seems to have been even more widespread in the former German Democratic Republic. Everywhere along the Baltic coast it is possible to find FKK beaches, as well as around the numerous lakes of Mecklenburg-Vorpommern.

Bad Doberan lies a few kilometres inland and is reached along a road flanked on one side by beech forest. The town as a whole is quite pretty, especially in the area of the 'Kamp', a park surrounded by buildings in classical style with two Chinese pavilions from the nineteenth century providing some exotic contrast. The main attraction is, however, the *Münster* (1294-1368). This brick Gothic church is richly furnished and ranks as one of the finest in the entire coastal region. In 1807 Bad Doberan gained distinction with the opening of Europe's first horse-racing circuit.

The city of **Rostock** is quickly reached from Bad Doberan and though not described in detail here (to concentrate on less well-known attractions) it is certainly worth a look for those with the time. Among Rostock's many sights are the Gothic Marienkirche, the thirteenth century *Rathaus* and several very interesting museums including a *Schiffahrtsmuseum* (Shipping Museum) and *Schiffbau-museum* (Shipbuilding Museum), which is located on board a ship permanently at anchor in the suburb of Schmarl.

Warnemünde can be reached by taking the road north from Bad Doberan via Ostseebad Nienhagen. This seaside resort is now a suburb of Rostock and is a favourite excursion for city-dwellers as it is only some 13km (8 miles) from the city centre. A pleasant stroll is to go along that part of the harbour known as 'Alter Strom' to the *Leuchtturm* (lighthouse, 1898). The ascent of the 135 steps to the look-out platform at the top is rewarded by grand views over the harbour. Next to the lighthouse is a restaurant known as the Teepott. Also of interest is the *Heimatmuseum* (Local Museum) which is housed in a typical fisherman's house from the eighteenth century. Sight-seeing trips around the harbour start from the Alter Strom.

In order to avoid driving through Rostock a car-ferry can be taken from Warnemünde across the River Warnow. The road continues through the attractive landscape of the Rostocker Heide to Ribnitz-Damgarten. On the way **Graal-Müritz** lures visitors with its 6km (4 miles) of sandy beach and a rhododendron park, whereas **Klocken-hagen** possesses a *Freilichtmuseum* (Open-Air Museum) with thatch-roofed farm cottages and a windmill. In **Ribnitz-Damgarten** visitor's should not miss having a look at the superb collection of amber in the Bernsteinmuseum (Amber Museum). With a little luck amber can still be found washed up on the beaches of the Baltic coast. Also of note is the *Klosterkirche* (monastery church) and Rostocker Tor, a medieval town gate.

The harbour at Prerow is linked to the coastal inlet of Bodstedter Bodden by the Prerower Strom

North of Ribnitz-Damgarten is the Fischland-Darß-Zingst peninsula. Much of the peninsula falls within the boundaries of the Nationalpark Vorpommersche Boddenlandschaft which stretches across to the island of Hiddensee. The peninsula was formed when the channels between the mainland and between what used to be the separate islands of Fischland, Darß and Zingst silted up. Fischland and Darß were already connected and joined to the mainland by the fifteenth century. Zingst was connected in 1872 after a storm washed up sediments and closed the channel separating the island from Darß. The scenery is a pleasant mixture of deciduous woods and broad, flat meadows. Bird-watchers will be interested to know that the peninsula is one of the few places of refuge for the rare osprey (Fischadler).

From Ribnitz-Damgarten the road goes via Ostseebad Dierhagen to Ostseebad **Wustrow**, where the many thatched-roof cottages go a long way to preserving the charm of this small resort. Before exploring the village however it is worth climbing the tower of the church as it offers excellent views over the Saaler Bodden (*Bodden* is a Low German term for an irregularly shaped coastal inlet) and the Baltic Sea.

Ostseebad **Ahrenshoop** is only a short distance further north and has long been a favourite retreat for artists. Paintings by local artists

Relaxing on the beautiful sandy beach at Prerow

are on exhibition in the 'Bunte Stube' and 'Kunstkate'. In the local church model sailing boats are reminders of the fact that the resort was first settled by fishermen and seafarers. Just to the north of town is the Naturschutzgebiet Ahrenshooper Holz which is particularly interesting because of the large stands of holly.

After Ahrenshoop the road leaves Fischland and enters what used to be the island of Darß. The west coast of Darß has been left for the most part in its natural state and gives some idea of what the Baltic Coast was like before it was discovered by tourism. Typical of the vegetation here are the pine-trees which have been twisted into bizarre shapes by the prevailing west wind. When such a wind is blowing there is a reasonable chance of finding amber washed up on shore.

The villages of **Born** and **Wiek** also make a pleasant enough impression with their thatched-roof cottages and serve as pictur-esque stepping-stones to Ostseebad **Prerow**. Protected as it is from westerly winds by an area of primeval forest known as Darßer Wald and because of its fine beach Prerow has developed into a popular resort. Relics of the town's old seafaring tradition are the so-called *Seemannshäuser* (seafarer's homes) with their beautifully decorated doors and the eighteenth century *Seemannskirche* (Seafarer's Church) with its collection of votive ships. In the Darß-Museum there are displays about the peninsula's flora and fauna as well as its history.

One of the many beautifully decorated doors in the seaside resort of Prerow

A number of walking trails lead from Prerow into the Darßer Wald. One walk (the Leuchtturmweg) of 5km (3 miles) goes through a very scenic stretch of forest to the hundred-year-old lighthouse at Darßer Ort. The path is marked with a horizontal red line. It is also possible to simply walk along the beach which adds about 1km (⅔ mile) to the walk.

East of Prerow and marking the start of what used to be the island of Zingst is Ostseebad **Zingst**. Swimming and sun-bathing on the sandy beach are of course the main activities here but there are also some quaint old seafarers' houses in town to have a look at. As around Prerow there are plenty of interesting walking trails leading into the surrounding countryside. The bird sanctuary at the eastern tip of Zingst is of great importance because it is the largest resting place for migratory cranes in Europe.

The peninsula is left on the road going south from Zingst to **Barth**. Not much is left of the town's medieval fortifications except for an impressive town gate known as the Dammtor (fourteenth century) and a tower called the Fangelturm (sixteenth century). The tower of the Gothic Marienkirche has long been used as an orientation point by sailors and it can be climbed for panoramic views over the Barther Bodden. Inside the church it is possible to view a rare copy of the Barther Bibel, a sixteenth-century bible that was printed in Barth in the Low German dialect. At the south end of town is a memorial to those who died in the prisoner of war camp that was set up here during World War II.

The imposing interior of the Marienkirche, Stralsund

Somewhat over 30km (19 miles) to the east of Barth is the Hanseatic town of **Stralsund**. Adding much to the charm of the picturesque *Altstadt*, which is studded with architectural gems, is the fact that it is almost completely surrounded by water. This fact is best appreciated from the tower of the Gothic Marienkirche, though bear in mind that it is not only the view but also the climb that is breathtaking!

A highlight of the *Altstadt* is the *Alter Markt* with its impressive Gothic *Rathaus* and some fine-looking burgher houses. Nearby the Gothic Nikolaikirche has a magnificently furnished interior. Within the large monastery complex of the Katharinenkloster, further south of the Alter Markt, are two excellent museums. The *Kulturhistorisches Museum* (Museum of Cultural History) has exhibits relating to the region's prehistory and early history, including a display of Viking gold. Among the drawing cards of the *Meeresmuseum* (Marine Museum) are a large aquarium for tropical fish and the 16m (52ft) long skeleton of a whale. On top of all this Stralsund also has a number of good fish restaurants and a pleasant beach promenade (*Sundpromenade*) with views across to Rügen.

Rügen

Rügen is Germany's largest and many would say most beautiful island. It is *the* major attraction of the Baltic coast and draws thousands of visitors every year. Rügen's main attractions are mostly located along the island's eastern coastline and include the biggest and most popular beach resorts and the famous Stubbenkammer, a stretch of spectacular chalk cliffs falling steeply to the sea. Covering as it does an area of 926sq km (575 square miles) with some 600km (372 miles) of coastline it is not all that surprising to find that the rest of the island is comparatively free of tourist crowds. This description concerns itself almost entirely with those sights lying outside the island's main tourist centres.

Rügen is linked to the mainland and Stralsund by a combination of road embankment and bridge. After leaving the bridge it is worth stopping a moment in Altefähr because of the view from the beach of Stralsund's impressive skyline. Otherwise take the scenic secondary road via **Gustow**, with a pretty village church, and Poseritz to Garz.

Garz is the oldest town on Rügen however it has never really developed beyond the stage of a large village. The ravages of time have left little of historical interest except for a late Gothic church and the remains of an ancient Slavonic fortress. Not far from the fortress is the Ernst-Moritz-Arndt-Museum. Arndt was a nineteenth century writer of patriotic prose who was born only a few kilometres away in Groß Schoritz. Located on the *Halbinsel* (peninsula) Zudar to the south of Garz are a couple of less frequented beaches and a small camping ground.

Putbus is about 10km (6 miles) north-east of Garz. The town was planned in the nineteenth century by Prince Malte von Putbus as a residency in classical style. Good examples of classical architecture include the *Theater* in the *Markt* and those buildings to be found around the *Circus* (a circular public place) and in the *Schlosspark*. In spite of the name do not expect to find a *Schloss* in the park as it was torn down in 1962. Laid out in the English manner the park is a pleasant place to stroll with lots of beautiful old trees offering shade. One section has been set aside as a deer enclosure.

A magnificent avenue of lime-trees leads from Putbus to the harbour town of **Lauterbach**. A short distance outside of town, at the edge of an area of beech forest, is *Badehaus* (bathhouse) Goor. This impressive, white building in classical style was built in 1818 for Prince Malte. Because of the prudery of the times (they would have thought of it as the 'decency of the times') one did not simply jump into the sea, but instead, the salt water was pumped into a marble bath within the discreet confines of a *Badehaus*. The *Badehaus* is not open to the public but a walk in the neighbouring woods which fringe the coast here is quite pleasant.

From Lauterbach it is possible to take a boat across to the island of **Vilm**. This island used to be the private holiday retreat of some of the top officials in East Germany's former communist government, including the party boss Erich Honecker. In order to protect the island's virtually unspoiled natural environment access is strictly limited and it can only be visited by prior arrangement. The address to contact is: Touristenbüro Putbus, 18581 Putbus, ☎ (038301) 60513. Visitors to the island are taken on a guided tour of about three hours duration. These tours take place only once a day, starting from Lauterbach at 1pm, and the group may not exceed 30 persons. In summer it is advisable to book a tour as far ahead as possible.

A steam locomotive known as *Rasender Roland* brings tourists from Putbus to the popular seaside resorts of **Binz**, **Sellin**, and **Göhren**. This narrow gauge railway was opened in 1895 and operates in winter as well as summer. On the way to Göhren the train stops near Jagdschloss Granitz (1837-46). With its four corner towers and a massive central tower the building seems more like a castle than a mere hunting seat. The central tower can be climbed and offers some of the best views on the island.

Badehaus Goor, a fine example of classical architecture, near Lauterbach on the island of Rügen

The stretch of land from Ostseebad Binz to Thiessow on the Mönchgut peninsula is one of the prettiest parts of the island. Because the peninsula is quite narrow the feeling of being on an island is much stronger here than elsewhere on Rügen. The old-world charm of resorts like Sellin and Göhren, together with the abundant natural attractions (some beautiful beaches) of the landscape makes a visit here a must for first-time visitors. However so much beauty draws the crowds and many will find it quieter, and cheaper, to stay somewhere else on the island (near Lauterbach for instance) and to come here just for the day.

Bergen lies a few kilometres to the north of Putbus. Because of its central location the town serves much of Rügen as a place to shop or do business. Of interest for tourists are the late Romanesque Marienkirche and the Ernst-Moritz-Arndt-Turm (1870-77). This lookout tower stands amidst the remains of a Slavonic fortress and offers tremendous panoramic views over Rügen.

The village of **Ralswiek** is not far north of Bergen and is prettily situated on the Grosser Jasmunder Bodden (an irregularly shaped coastal inlet). The little café near the marina is a nice spot for a break from sightseeing and the park surrounding Ralswiek's *Schloss* (not open to the public) is a good place to stretch the legs afterwards. Shortly before town is a pretty wooden church.

From Bergen the B96 crosses a narrow neck of land separating the Grosser Jasmunder Bodden from the Kleiner Jasmunder Bodden and arrives at **Sagard** on Jasmund peninsula. Near the entrance to town is the Dobberworth, the largest Bronze Age tumulus in northern Germany. Other Bronze Age tumuli (the Fürstengräber) can be found near Quolitz a little further north. A map showing the numerous prehistoric graves on Rügen can be obtained from one of the island's tourist offices.

Those who wish to visit the famous Stubbenkammer cliffs with the Königsstuhl (a very picturesque section of cliff made famous in a painting by C. D. Friedrich) should continue from Sagard to Sassnitz. From here it is a 12km (7 miles) walk (the Hochuferweg) north through a beautiful area of beech forest within the recently created Nationalpark Jasmund. It is also possible to drive to a car park located much closer to the cliffs. A much less visited stretch of coast to walk along is to the north of Quolitz, between Lohme and Ruschvitz. It is about a 6km (4 mile) hike from the beach at Lohme to the Königsstuhl.

Yet another narrow neck of land, the Schaabe, links Jasmund to Wittow peninsula. The Schaabe is basically one long sandy beach and is accordingly popular in summer. Roughly in the middle of the peninsula, which would be an island were it not for the Schaabe, is the village of **Altenkirchen** with its pretty *Dorfkirche* (village church). At the very northern tip of Wittow, near Putgarten, are the lighthouses at Kap Arkona. Near the two lighthouses (only the taller of the two is still in use) is the Jaromarsburg. All that is left of this Slavonic fortress are the imposing 13m (42ft) high earthen walls. It was destroyed by the Danes in 1168 who were then able to establish Christianity on the island and end the period of Slavonic rule. At the end of a road leading south from Putgarten is the fishing village of **Vitt**, hidden in a kind of gully and described by some as the loveliest village on Rügen. Because of its uniquely original state of preservation Vitt has been placed on Unesco's list of 'World Heritage Sites'.

Unless visitors go back the way they came the only way to get back to central Rügen is to go south via **Wiek** (with a nice church) and to take the car ferry (Wittower Fähre). This small ferry only takes up to five cars and runs between 5.50am and 7.50pm, so that in summer there can be a rather long wait before your car can board. A boat also goes to the island of Hiddensee from here.

The west of Rügen is the least visited part of the island. After leaving the ferry the first place of any significance is **Trent**. Here a fifteenth-century brick church is of special interest. To the west of

Trent **Schaprode** is the main departure point for the boat to Hiddensee. There is also a very old church here and a number of nice thatched cottages.

The small island of Hiddensee has long been a popular tourist destination and on warm weekends in summer it can easily get overrun with visitors. Fortunately no cars are allowed on the island so it is a paradise for hikers and cyclists — cycles can be hired on the island. A lovely, unspoiled landscape and the pretty village of **Kloster** are the main attractions that Hiddensee has to offer. As accommodation is very limited on the island it is best visited on a day trip from Rügen or Stralsund on the mainland.

The shore and hinterland of the Großer Jasmunder Bodden between Neuenkirchen and Ralswiek is virtually untouched by tourism. This region of farmland is dotted with Bronze Age barrows, some of the most impressive are near Woorke (Woorker Berge). One of Rügen's most secluded camping grounds is located at Groß Banzelvitz, near Rappin. Visitor's should note, however, that the roads here can be very poor.

Gingst lies to the south of Trent. Deserving of attention here are the church and an interesting little *Handwerkermuseum* (Craftsman Museum). From Gingst it is not far, in a westerly direction, to the island of Ummanz.

Ummanz is reached via a bridge which leads to **Waase**, the only settlement of any size on the island. In the village church is a magnificent carved altar. It was made in Antwerp in 1520 and came to Waase (for reasons as yet unexplained) via Stralsund in 1708. There is nothing spectacular about the island as such, which is completely flat and mainly covered by fields. However it is the scene of a spectacular natural phenomenon, when, with the approach of winter, vast flocks of migratory birds rest here on their way south. Particularly numerous are the flocks of cranes and grey lag geese. The southern tip of Ummanz is an important nesting-place for seabirds and is protected as a bird sanctuary. The island is quiet at any time of the year and there are some nice stretches of beach and even a small camping ground near **Suhrendorf**.

The secondary road from Gingst joins the B96 at Samtens, from where it is not far to Stralsund on the mainland. Continuing south along the coast it is only another 30km (18 ½ miles) or so to Greifswald.

The old Hanseatic town of **Greifswald** is well worth visiting because of its nicely preserved *Altstadt*. Particularly attractive is the *Markt* with its medieval *Rathaus* and some old burgher houses with magnificent gabled fronts. Towering above these buildings is the 100m (328ft) high tower of the Gothic St Nikolai cathedral. Inside the cathedral the medieval frescoes and some late Gothic paintings are worth special attention. Also of note is the fourteenth-century Marienkirche which stands out because of its vast interior dimensions. In the *Museum der Stadt* (Town Museum) are some paintings by the Romantic artist Caspar David Friedrich who was born here.

East of Greifswald at **Wieck** is an old wooden bascule bridge (1887) that is still in working order. Right next to the bridge is the harbour where it is possible to observe the fishing boats bringing in their catch. In the *Dorfkirche* is a superbly crafted votive ship. Not far away, on the road to Lubmin are the romantic ruins of the *Zisterzienserkloster* (Cistercian monastery) at **Eldena**. These ruins were made famous in a painting by Caspar David Friedrich.

If the secondary road via Kemnitz and Wusterhausen is taken to Wolgast it is possible to make detours to the beaches near **Ludwigsburg**, **Loissin** and **Lubmin**. Close to Lubmin is what used to be the largest nuclear power-station in East Germany. It has since been shut down.

Wolgast was rather neglected in the old days of communist East Germany and many find that the town gives a somewhat dilapidated impression. However in the next few years a bit of paint and lots of restoration work might do wonders for the place. Hard to miss is the massive bulk of the fourteenth century St Petrikirche. Within the church is a cycle of *danse macabre* paintings (1700) and the tomb of the dukes of Pommern-Wolgast. In the Kreismuseum are exhibits relating to the early Romantic painter Philipp Otto Runge (1777-1810), who was born here, and to the development of the V-2 rocket at nearby Peenemünde. Near the bridge to the island of Usedom is a half-timbered building that was erected in 1835 for the storage of grain. Note that the bridge is raised to let boats through at the following times: 5.30-5.45am, 8.40-8.55am, 12.10-12.25pm, 3-3.15pm, 6.30-6.45pm and 9-9.15pm.

Usedom

Usedom's beautiful sandy beaches cause most people to overlook the large areas of unspoiled countryside that go to make up the greater part of the island. The huge aurochs, or wild ox, that once roamed Usedom's dense forests is unfortunately long since extinct, but the island's numerous nature reserves still provide a refuge for a number of rare birds like the white-tailed eagle and black stork. On top of all this Usedom is one of the few places in Germany where

The beaches on the island of Usedom are not yet overrun by tourists

otters are still to be found. The island's south-eastern tip with the resort of Swinoujscie (Swinemünde) belongs to Poland.

The north-western section of Usedom is relatively ignored by most tourists. There is a beach at **Trassenheide** and also at **Karlshagen**. However visitors should be very careful on that stretch of beach between Karlshagen and Peenemünde. This area was long used as a military testing ground and what looks like amber on the beach may in fact be clumps of phosphorus from incendiary bombs. Do not touch them on any account! They burn very easily and stick to the skin like napalm. The woods north of Karlshagen are classified as a prohibited area (*Sperrgebiet*). This is because there are still unexploded bombs left from the time of the Allied air attack on the rocket station at Peenemünde.

On 3 October 1942 the first V-2 was able to leave the earth's atmosphere and fly a distance of 192km (119 miles) before plunging into the sea. A short time later the V-2 was able to manage an even longer distance and brought death and destruction to far-off England. The space age had arrived but so had the age of inter-continental ballistic missiles.

Much of the research on the V-1 and V-2 rockets was carried out by Wernher von Braun and his team of top scientists at **Peenemünde**. The 'V' stands for *Vergeltungswaffe* (retaliatory weapon) and was the name given to the rockets by the Nazis. Due to heavy bombing in

World War II not much remains from the once gigantic experimental station. However a museum dealing with the development of the V-1 and V-2 rockets has recently been set up in the old coal-fired power station that belonged to the complex.

It has been rightly criticised that the museum tends to glorify the V-2 as a milestone in the development of space technology without paying sufficient attention to the grim background of its production. Thousands of prisoners were forced to do work connected with the rocket and many died under the inhuman conditions. Although work on the V-1 and V-2 contributed to the development of the Saturn 5 rockets that put man on the moon, they were first and foremost a weapon of destruction. Hopefully the museum will endeavour to present a more balanced picture of what they have chosen to call 'the cradle of astronautics'.

A perfect place for those seeking peace and quiet is the area south of Wolgaster Fähre and Krummin known as Wolgaster Ort. From the village of **Krummin** it is possible to go for enjoyable walks along the coast without fear of bumping into tourists at every turn. A similarly peaceful corner of Usedom is the tongue of land, known as the Gnitz, on the opposite side of the bay from Krummin. Accessible by road from Ostseebad Zinnowitz the landscape of the Gnitz is a pleasant mixture of hills, fields and woods. There are good views over the surroundings from the elevation of the Weißer Berg (32m/105ft) at the southern tip of the peninsula. Located within the beautiful nature reserve (Naturschutzgebiet Mövenort) that surrounds the Weißer Berg is a camping ground. A bit further east the village of **Lütow** has a pretty location just outside the reserve.

All the most popular seaside resorts are to be found in the stretch of coast between Ostseebad Zinnowitz and Seebad Ahlbeck. In summer it can get very busy along here, but the old resort towns with their splendid turn-of-the-century architecture are well worth visiting. Among the more interesting resorts in this respect are Zinnowitz, Bansin, Heringsdorf and Ahlbeck. **Ahlbeck** is the only resort that has been able to preserve its charming old pier (*Seebrücke*) of 1892 with a restaurant.

Just east of Zinnowitz is the small resort of **Zempin**. Near here at **Lüttenort** — the sign is hard to see but it is just before the turn-off to Koserow on the right-hand side of the road — is the Otto-Niemeyer-Holstein-Gedenkatelier. Niemeyer was a well-known East German artist and when he died he left his house, atelier and garden to the state. A guided tour of the memorial museum is worth the effort for those with an interest in contemporary German art.

Occupying the hinterland to the south of Bansin is the so-called Usedomer Schweiz. This unspectacular yet attractive area of hills and lakes is ideally suited for walking and cycling tours away from the crowds. Of interest in **Benz**, a small town at the centre of the Usedomer Schweiz, is a nicely restored windmill on a hill above town. The views along the road going from Bansin via Sallenthin to Benz are quite good, but the best overall view of the lakes is from the modest heights of the Kückelsberg (58m/190ft) to the south of Benz.

Korswandt is only a short drive south of Ahlbeck and might make a good alternative place to stay for those seeking cheaper accommodation. Right next to the village is the pretty little Wolgastsee, a lake surrounded by woods. Further south the road from Zirchow to Garz leads to a little visited corner of Usedom close to the Polish border. **Garz** itself has a number of picturesque old houses and a fifteenth-century church. A bit further on the fishing village of **Kamminke** is located near the Naturschutzgebiet Golm. Within this nature reserve are the scanty remains of a Bronze Age fortress and a large war cemetery. Buried here are the 20,000 victims of the battle that took place in 1945 near Swinemünde. One of Usedom's more secluded camping grounds is near Kamminke.

Another isolated corner of Usedom is the Lieper Winkel. This peninsula juts out into the body of water known as the Achter Wasser. Once again it is a place best explored on foot or by bicycle. The only road to speak of is the one going from Suckow via Rankwitz to Warthe. As the other villages can only be reached along roads in rather poor condition it is probably a good idea to leave the car in either Liepe or Warthe. It remains to be seen how long this haven from the noise and stress of modern civilisation (and tourism) will survive as it is.

The last stop on Usedom before returning to the mainland is the town of **Usedom**. Of note here is the Anklamer Tor, a town gate from the fifteenth century, and the beautiful doors on some of the houses. At the edge of town, near Usedomer See, are the remains of a Slavonic fortress. A white cross serves as a reminder that the christianization of Pomerania began here in 1128.

The bridge to the mainland at Zecherin (Zecheriner Brücke) is raised at the same times as the Wolgaster Brücke.

To reach **Anklam** from Usedom take the B110 east, then the B109 south. Although much of historic interest in this old Hanseatic town was destroyed in World War II it is still worth at least a brief stop. Of interest is the fourteenth-century Steintor (town gate) and the fine

Gothic frescoes in the thirteenth-century Marienkirche. The *Heimatmuseum* 'Otto Lilienthal' deals mainly with the life and work of the aeronautical engineer Otto Lilienthal (1848-96), who was born here. Lilienthal did pioneering work in the construction of gliders and completed many successful flights until fate caught up with him and he was killed in a crash near Berlin.

Ueckermünde, the last stop on this tour of the Baltic coast, lies to the south-east of Anklam near a lagoon known as the Oderhaff. The town as a whole makes a quite pleasant impression, though there is not a great deal of historical interest to see. Worth visiting is the eighteenth-century Marienkirche because of its elaborate rococo altar with pulpit (1775). All that is left of the Renaissance *Schloss* is the south wing; the small Haffmuseum is to be found here. There are a number of beaches, for instance at Grambin, in the vicinity of Ueckermünde and the town is also a starting point for boat trips on the lagoon. The extensive forests of the Landschaftsschutzgebiet Ueckermünder Heide invite exploration either on foot or by bicycle. All in all the little visited stretch of coast near Ueckermünde is an ideal place to spend a quiet holiday.

Further Information
— The Baltic Coast —

Boat Trips
Details of the following and other boat trips are available from the tourist offices.

Weiße Flotte (White Fleet)
Fährstrasse 16,
D(O)-2300 Stralsund,
☎ (03831)692371:
Wismar to the island of Poel
Stralsund to the island of Hiddensee
Zingst/Darß to island of Hiddensee

Rügen and Usedom: cruises to a number of destinations along the Baltic coast from Rügen and Usedom. Ferries to Sweden leave from Sassnitz/Rügen (TS-Line).

Fishing trips (Angelfahrten)
From a number of towns along the coast for instance Sassnitz/Rügen:
Fischereigenossenschaft 'Sassnitz', Am Hafen, ☎ (038392) 22496

Cycle Hire
Bicycles can be hired at many resorts along the coast.

Places to Visit

Ahrenshoop
Kunstkate
Strandweg
Open: daily 10am-12.30pm, 1.30-5pm

Anklam
Otto-Lilienthal-Museum
Ellbogenstrasse 1a
Open: Wednesday-Friday 9am-4pm, Saturday/Sunday 2-5pm. Closed Monday/Tuesday
☎ (03971) 5500

Benz/Usedom
Holländermühle (windmill)
Open: Guided tours by prior arrangement. Contact Gemeindeverwaltung Benz
☎ (038379) 226 and 227

Bergen/Rügen
Ernst-Moritz-Arndt-Turm
Open: April-August daily 10am-6pm,
September-March daily 10am-4pm

Garz/Rügen
Ernst-Moritz-Arndt-Museum
An den Anlagen 1
Open: May-September Tuesday-
Sunday 10am-12noon and 2-5pm.
October-April Monday-Friday 10am-
12noon and 1-4pm
☎ (038304) 211

Gingst/Rügen
Handwerkermuseum
Open: 1 May-31 October Tuesday-
Sunday 10am-6pm, 1 November-April
Monday-Friday 10am-4pm
☎ (038305) 304

Greifswald
Museum Greifswald
Theodor-Pyl-Strasse 1/2
Open: July/August Monday-Tuesday
1-6pm, Wednesday-Sunday 10am-6pm
☎ (03834) 2647

Jagdschloss Granitz
(South of Binz/Rügen)
Open: 1 April-31 October daily 9am-
5pm, 1 November-31 March Tuesday-
Sunday 9am-4.30pm
☎ (038393) 2263

Kirchdorf/Poel
Inselmuseum
Open: during the summer months
Tuesday-Friday 9am-12noon and 2-
4pm, Saturday/Sunday 9.30-11.30am.
September-May only Tuesday,
Wednesday and Saturday.

Klockenhagen
Freilichtmuseum
Open: April-October daily 9am-5pm
☎ 2775

Lüttenort/Usedom
Otto-Niemeyer-Holstein-Gedenkatelier
Open: Guided tours Tuesday, Wednesday, Thursday and Sunday at 10am,
11am, 2pm and 3pm. Saturdays 2pm

and 3pm
☎ (038375) 213

Neubukow
Schliemanngedenkstätte
Mühlenstrasse 7
Open: Monday 10am-12noon and 1-
5pm, Tuesday and Thursday 1-5pm,
Fridays 10am-12noon

Peenemünde/Usedom
Informationszentrum des Raumfahrt-
   zentrums
Bahnhofstrasse 28
Open: daily except Mondays 9am-5pm

Prerow/Darß
Darß-Museum
Waldstrasse 48
Open: May-October daily 9am-5pm
☎ (038233) 233

Ribnitz-Damgarten
Bernsteinmuseum
Im Kloster 1/2
Open: May-September daily 9.30am-
5.30pm
☎ (03821) 2931

Rostock
Schiffahrtsmuseum
August-Bebel-Strasse 1
Open: Saturday-Thursday 9am-5pm
Tel: (0381) 22697

Schiffbaumuseum
Rostock-Schmarl
Open: Tuesday-Sunday 9am-5pm

Stove (Stowe)
Windmill
Open: Tuesday-Sunday 10am-1pm, 2-4.30pm

Stralsund
Kulturhistorisches Museum
Mönchstrasse 25-27
Open: daily 10am-5pm
☎ (03831) 2180

Meeresmuseum
Katharinenberg 14-17
Open: June, September, October daily
10am-5pm, July, August daily 9am-6pm
☎ (03831) 295135

Ueckermünde
Haffmuseum (in Schloss)
Am Rathaus 3
Open: May-September Tuesday 9am-
12noon and 12.30-5pm, Wednesday/
Thursday 9am-12noon, 12.30-4pm,
Friday 9am-12noon and 12.30-3pm,
Saturday/Sunday 10am-12noon, 1-5pm
☎ (039771) 501
Local history, history of ship-building
and fishing industries.

Warnemünde
Heimatmuseum
Theodor-Körner-Strasse 1
Open: July/August Tuesday-Sunday
9am-12.30pm and 2-5pm
☎ (0381) 52667

Wismar
Stadtmuseum (in Schabbellhaus)
Schweinsbrücke 8
Open: Tuesday-Sunday 10am-4pm
☎ (03841) 4964

Wolgast
Kreismuseum
Karl-Liebknecht-Strasse 6
Open: Tuesday 10am-12noon and 1-
6pm, Wednesday-Friday 10am-12noon
and 1-5pm. July/August also Saturdays 9am-12noon
☎ (03836) 3041

Tourist Information Offices

Regional
Landesfremdenverkehrs-
    verband
Mecklenburg-
    Vorpommern
Hermann-Duncker-Platz 2
18055 Rostock

*Regionaler Fremden-
    verkehrsverband*
Mecklenburgische
    Ostseeküste
Marktstrasse 1
18209 Bad Doberan
☎ (038203) 2120

Local
(These are known as
Kurverwaltung unless
listed otherwise)

Ahlbeck
Dünenstrasse 45
17419 Ahlbeck
☎ (039775) 8228

Ahrenshoop
Kirchnersgang 2
18347 Ahrenshoop
☎ (038220) 234

Anklam
Anklam-Information
Am Steintor/Kleiner
    Wall 11
17389 Anklam
☎ (03971) 2541

Bad Doberan
Goethestrasse 1
18209 Bad Doberan
☎ (038203) 3001

Bansin
Seestrasse 64
17429 Bansin
☎ (038378) 9433 or 9301

Barth
Barth-Information
Ernst-Thälmann-Strasse 51
18356 Barth
☎ (038231) 2464

Bergen/Rügen
Stadt-Information
Am Markt
18528 Bergen
☎ (03838) 21129

Binz/Rügen
Fremdenverkehrsverein
Bahnhofstrasse 38
18609 Binz
☎ (038393) 2215

Boltenhagen
Ernst-Thälmann-Strasse
    66
23946 Boltenhagen
☎ (038825) 9284 or 9263

Born/Darß
Fremdenverkehrsamt
Chausseestrasse 75
18375 Born
☎ (038234) 208

Graal-Müritz
Rosa-Luxemburg-Strasse
    11
18181 Graal-Müritz
☎ (038206) 224

Greifswald
Stadtinformation
Schuhhagen
17489 Greifswald
☎ (03834) 3460

Heringsdorf/Usedom
Seestrasse 13
17424 Seebad
Heringsdorf
☎ (038378) 32017

Kirchdorf
Fremdenverkehrsamt Insel
Poel
Wismarsche Strasse 22a
23999 Kirchdorf
☎ (038425) 347

Kloster/Hiddensee
Fremdenverkehrsverein
Hiddensee
Gaststätte 'Zum
Enddorn'
18565 Kloster
☎ (038300) 304

Kühlungsborn
18225 Kühlungsborn
☎ (038293) 6620

Prerow/Darß
18375 Prerow
☎ (038233)551

Putbus/Rügen
In the Orangerie
Alleestrasse
18581 Putbus
☎ (038301) 431

Rerik
18230 Rerik
☎ (038296) 214/219

Ribnitz-Damgarten
Stadtinformation
Markt 1
18311 Ribnitz-
Damgarten
☎ (03821) 5701

Rostock
Rostock-Information
Schnickmannstrasse 13-14
18055 Rostock
☎ (0381) 25260

Stralsund
Stadtinformation
Rathaus
Alter Markt
18439 Stralsund
☎ (03831) 252251

Ueckermünde
Ueckermünde-Information
Schulstrasse 18
17373 Ueckermünde
☎ (039771) 3159

Usedom
Usedom-Information
Markt 1
17406 Usedom
☎ (038372) 226

Warnemünde
Kuramt Warnemünde
Gästeservice
Heinrich-Heine-Strasse 17
18119 Rostock
☎ (0381) 5311

Wismar
Wismar-Information
Stadthaus Am Markt
23966 Wismar
☎ (03841) 4251

Wolgast
Wolgast-Information
Lange Strasse 15
17438 Wolgast
☎ (03836) 600118

Wustrow
Fremdenverkehrsverein
Strandstrasse 11
18347 Wustrow
☎ (038220) 251

Zingst
Klosterstrasse
18374 Zingst a Darß
☎ (038232) 633 or 638

Zinnowitz/Usedom
Fremdenverkehrsverband
Insel Usedom
Dünenstrasse 11
17454 Zinnowitz
☎ (038377) 2884

13 • The Uckermark

Tucked in between Berlin and the Baltic coast, in a thinly populated corner of Brandenburg bordering Poland, is the Uckermark.
Formed by glacial action during the last Ice Age it is a fascinating
region of gently undulating hills concealing literally hundreds of
small lakes. The western Uckermark is especially beautiful as one
string of lakes is followed by another around places like Lychen,
Templin and Boitzenburg. In the north much of the land is used
agriculturally, whereas in the south larger areas are cloaked in forest
and provide a habitat for many species of animals and plants now
rare in Germany.

The southern edge of the Uckermark at Eberswalde-Finow is
quickly reached from Berlin on the A11 motorway. Prenzlau in the
north of the Uckermark can be reached from Berlin along the A11 and
(from Hohengüstow) B198. The slower but more scenic way of
getting from Berlin to Prenzlau is to take the B109.

To say that history has not always been kind to **Prenzlau** is
somewhat of an understatement. After having achieved a good
measure of prosperity in the Middle Ages one war after the other
descended on the town. The Thirty Years' War (1618-48) brought the
first wave of destruction and this was followed by the Seven Years'
War (1756-63), the Franco-Prussian War (1870-71) and of course the
last two World Wars. Towards the end of World War II the town was
almost completely destroyed, but what remains, amid the rows of
anonymous apartment houses, gives an impression of what Prenzlau
must once have been like.

In view of what has been said it would have been almost a miracle
if the magnificent Marienkirche had survived the centuries unscathed since it was built. In fact it was completely gutted by fire in
World War II and had to be largely rebuilt. It is a beautiful example
of a brick Gothic church and has an ornate gable decorating the
eastern wall. At the time of writing work on the interior had not yet
been finished, but it is planned to use the church as a museum. Set in

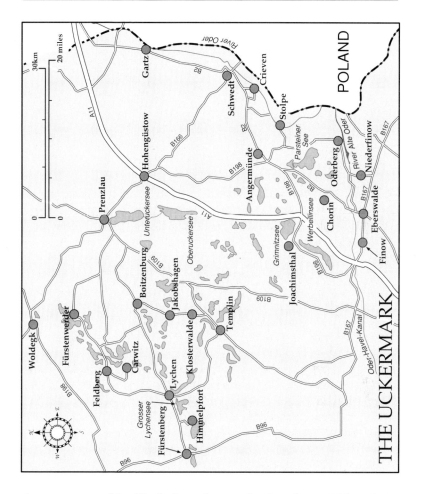

the pavement of the Kirchplatz, close to the church, is a *Richtstein*. In the Middle Ages all the executions that took place in Prenzlau were carried out on this stone.

Other interesting churches include the Dreifaltigkeitskirche and Sabinenkirche. The former Dominican monastery (*Dominikanerkloster*) now houses the *Kulturhistorisches Museum* (Museum of Cultural History). Among the exhibits are works by the artists Jakob Philipp Hackert (1737-1807) and Leo Wiese (1888-1982). In the old refectory some frescoes dating from 1516 have been preserved.

Still remaining from the town walls are three town gates and a few towers. The *Hexenturm* (Witch's Tower) at the edge of the town park was once used as a prison complete with dungeon. It got its name because the last woman who was tried as a witch in Prenzlau was

Feldberg, in an idyllic setting by one of Uckermark's many lakes

somehow forgotten (purposely?) and died of hunger in the tower. The most photogenic of the former town gates is the formidable looking Mitteltorturm. It is only a stone's throw away from the Marienkirche and if the sun is in the right place photographers will be able to include both. There are good views over town from the thirteenth-century Steintorturm, only a short distance away from the monastery.

Prenzlau gains a lot in attraction from its position at the north end of the pretty Unteruckersee. A lovely lakeshore promenade starts from the *Stadtpark* and a trip on the steamer *Uckerschwan* is also to be recommended. There is a camping ground near Warnitz on the shores of the Oberuckersee, which is linked to the Unteruckersee by a canal. Both lakes are home to a large variety of waterfowl and with luck it might even be possible to spot a sea-eagle or osprey.

Fürstenwerder is situated to the north-west of Prenzlau. The most attractive thing about this quiet little town is its idyllic location between two small lakes, though there is also an old church and remains of a town wall to be seen. A short distance north **Woldegk** is worth visiting because of its windmills. One of the five windmills is used as a *Mühlenmuseum*.

Moving south from Fürstenwerder the next place of interest is **Feldberg**. Surrounded by lakes and forest the town is in one of the loveliest parts of Mecklenburg, just outside the boundaries of the

One of the three lakes that surround the village of Himmelpfort

Uckermark. It makes an excellent base for those who are keen on boating, walking and swimming. There are a number of boarding-houses (*Pension*) and a youth hostel in the town, as well as several camping grounds around the lakes. The best views in the area are from the Reiherberg (142m/466ft) to the north of Feldberg and the Hauptmannsberg, a few kilometres further south near Carwitz.

A secondary road continues south from Feldberg through several tiny hamlets to **Lychen**. Also surrounded by lakes Lychen started developing as a holiday resort around the turn of the twentieth century. In those days a new railway connection brought innumerable day-trippers from Berlin, who relished the peace and unspoiled scenery of this thinly populated region. To cater for wealthier visitors who came by car eight filling stations were opened in town at a time when there were only three cars in Lychen itself!

After heavy bombing in 1945 not much was left of the old town except for the early Gothic parish church and a few remnants of the medieval walls. A pretty part of town is the so-called *Malerwinkel* (Painter's Corner) where there are lovely views over the lake. In spring and summer passenger launches offer trips on the Grosser Lychensee and along the Woblitz and Havel rivers.

Between Lychen and Fürstenberg is the pretty little village of **Himmelpfort**. The village is squeezed in between three lakes and there is also a ruined Cistercian monastery to look at. Just outside

The town hall at Templin

Fürstenberg, at **Ravensbrück**, is the site of a former Nazi concentration camp. It is now used as a museum documenting the atrocities that took place there. Further west the countryside is studded with the lakes of the large Mecklenburg lake plateau (Mecklenburger Seenplatte), an exceptionally beautiful region belonging to the federal state of Mecklenburg-Vorpommern.

Known as the 'Pearl of the Uckermark' **Templin** is situated 19km (12 miles) to the south-east of Lychen. The surrounding lakes and forests are not only a paradise for holiday-makers but also for many species of birds such as storks, herons and nightingales. In town itself the main interest concentrates on the superbly preserved town wall with its gates and towers. The *Volkskundemuseum* (Ethnological Museum) located in the Prenzlauer Tor offers an insight into how the people of the Uckermark lived in the past.

Among the various excursions that can be made from Templin is the following circular tour. Take the road a few kilometres north-east in the direction of Petznick, then turn left at the far end of Templiner See and drive via Klosterwalde and Jakobshagen to Boitzenburg. From here the road is taken south-west to Lychen and from there back to Templin. This route goes through some very pretty countryside and in summer visitors should keep their eyes open for locals selling fresh honey (*Honig*).

Boitzenburg has a lovely location in the midst of hilly, forested

The ruins of the Cistercian monastery at Boitzenburg

A typical village church in the Uckermark

scenery and is worth a longer stop. In the town itself are a few nice old houses and an interesting, if rather dilapidated, stone church from the thirteenth century. The still imposing *Schloss* is set in a park at the edge of town but is not open to the public. Just out of town, in the direction of Prenzlau, are the very picturesque ruins of a Cistercian monastery (founded in 1269), next to which is a water mill that is now used as a museum (*Produktionsmuseum Klostermühle*). It is worth visiting the museum just to see the impressive collection of old wooden wall clocks in the ticket office! A visit to the museum could be followed by a walk in the surrounding woods where there are oak trees that are supposed to be up to 500 years old. The reasonably priced café near the museum is a good place to take a well-deserved break.

Spreading out to the east and south-east of Templin is the Biosphere Reservation at Schorfheide-Chorin. This nature reserve with its extensive forests and myriads of small lakes was established in 1990 with the support of UNESCO and covers a large chunk of the Uckermark (830sq km, 515 square miles). Among the animals that can be found here are beavers, badgers, martens, deer and a wide variety of aquatic birds including the very rare black stork. There are plenty of walking trails going through the reserve though some shorter walks starting from car parks lining the B109 may be handy for motorists.

For many centuries the forests of the Schorfheide were the private hunting domain of margraves, kings and emperors. In the sixteenth century a 70km (43 miles) long fence was erected to stop deer wandering into the fields of the northern Uckermark and remained standing until 1730. However the barriers for the common folk were not to fall before the Berlin Wall. The last lord of the Schorfheide was communist party chief Erich Honecker who enjoyed the Schorfheide as his exclusive hunting ground along with other prominent members of the former East German government. Ironically it was this long isolation from the general public that allowed the Schorfheide's flora and fauna to survive relatively undisturbed up to the present day.

Joachimsthal is a holiday resort situated at the centre of the Schorfheide between Werbellinsee and Grimnitzsee. Of these two lakes it is Werbellinsee that is most attractive and a particularly nice drive is to follow its western shore south — the road going down the eastern side of the lake is not in terribly good condition. Being one of the cleanest and clearest lakes in eastern Germany Werbellinsee is well stocked with fish such as pike, eels, perch and bream. Pleasure cruises start from the Joachimsthal end of the lake.

Chorin is reached by taking the secondary road south from Joachimstal via Golzow, then the B2 north. Kloster Chorin, a magnificent example of North German brick Gothic architecture, was founded in 1273 by Cistercian monks. During the Middle Ages more than 400 monks lived and worked in the monastery and some twenty-five villages fell under the monastery's sphere of influence. Perhaps the most impressive feature of the complex, which has been extensively restored, is the gabled exterior wall of the west wing. The monastery ruins of Chorin are beautifully situated next to a small lake and well marked paths lead into the surrounding woods. In summer the popular 'Choriner Musiksommer' (performances of classical music) are held amid the ruins.

South of Chorin the large town of **Eberswalde-Finow** (Finow and Eberswalde used to be two separate towns) stretches for some 10km (6 miles) along both banks of the Finowkanal. Places of interest include the early Gothic parish church of Maria Magdalena, the Forstbotanischer Garten (botanical gardens featuring over 1,000 different species of trees) and the *Tierpark*, a pleasant zoo covering an area of about 20 hectares. However the town is most interesting as a starting point for boat trips to various destinations in the Uckermark such as Werbellinsee and Oderberg.

Not far north-east, near **Niederfinow**, is the impressive *Schiffs-*

*The brick -built
monastery at Chorin*

hebewerk (boat-lift). This amazing piece of machinery was built during 1927-34 to overcome the 36m (118ft) difference in height between the Oder-Havel canal and Oder valley. Boats weighing up to 1,200 tonnes can be carried up or down in only 5 minutes. The trough which carries the boats is huge; when filled with water it weighs 4,300 tonnes. Attached to the trough are 256 steel hawsers with counterweights whose combined weight is as much as the trough itself. This counterweighting means that the trough plus boat can be raised by just four 75hp motors. Anybody who is even faintly interested in technology should not miss a look at this remarkable feat of engineering. Boat trips which include a ride in the lift start from Eberswalde-Finow and Oderberg.

A pleasant drive east of Niederfinow is to **Oderberg**, near the Polish border. There are a lot of nice old houses in town but it is mainly the beautiful location near the River Alte Oder that gives the town its special charm. Oderberg has a couple of hotels and would

*The boat lift near
Niederfinow*

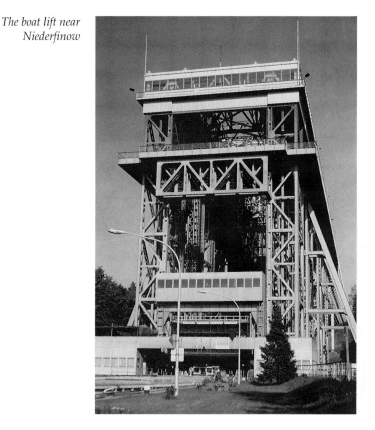

be a nice 'out of the way' base for people who want to explore the surrounding countryside with its forests and lakes. Parsteiner See, only a few kilometres further north of Oderberg, is renowned for the clarity and purity of its water — a fact bathers will appreciate. There is a camping ground with modernised facilities directly on the shores of the lake, near the village of **Parstein**.

Angermünde can be reached on the B2 going north from Chorin. In spite of years of neglect the town still has a reasonable amount to show from its long and sometimes prosperous past. Apart from a large number of half-timbered houses lining quaint, cobbled streets it is the former Franciscan monastery church (*Klosterkirche*) and the parish church of St Marien that attract most attention. Both are Gothic buildings but the former can claim the distinction of having been probably built to plans by the same architect who worked on the famous monastery in Chorin. The most impressive remnant of the once massive town wall is the *Pulverturm* (Gunpowder Tower),

Barge on the River Alte Oder near Oderberg

which is now used by the *Kreisheimatmuseum* (district museum) for exhibitions. The area around the *Marktplatz* is the best preserved part of town with the simple but well proportioned *Rathaus* providing a focal point. Finally it might be added for those with a slightly macabre turn of mind that the local executioner once lived opposite the small St Martinskirche in the Marienplatz. The old half-timbered house still stands and was known simply as the *Scharfrichterei* (Hangman's House).

From Angermünde the B198 leads back to the start of this tour at Prenzlau. However before finally leaving the Uckermark it is worth mentioning a couple of places lying close to the Polish border, which is defined here by the River Oder.

Roughly 8km (5 miles) south-east of Angermünde, on an arm of the River Oder, is the small settlement of **Stolpe**. Situated on a range of hills behind town is a still formidable looking stronghold known locally as the 'Grützpott'. It was built in the second half of the twelfth century with walls that are up to 6m (20ft) thick. There are good views over the pretty Oder valley from the hill where the tower is perched.

Schwedt can be reached on the B2 from Angermünde. There is not much to recommend this modern industrial town with its dreary 'socialist' architecture except for the fact that boat trips on the River Oder start from here. South of town the spacious *Schlosspark* in the village of **Criewen** is worth visiting, though the *Schloss* itself is not open to the public. Of interest in **Gartz**, to the north of Schwedt, is the town gate, remnants of the medieval walls and a late Gothic brick church.

For those who like to leave their cars behind the *Uckermärkischer Rundweg* is an excellent long distance walk taking in much of this chapter. This circular walk (total length of 134km and waymarked by a red dot on a white ground) is also suitable for cyclists. The towns along the way are well served by public transport so it should be possible to pick out a shorter stretch and to return to the starting point with either the bus or train. Local tourist offices should be able to help with maps. The route is: Angermünde-Ringenwalde-Templin-Boitzenburg-Prenzlau-Warnitz-Angermünde, and will take at least six days

Further Information
— The Uckermark —

Angling
Information as to where to obtain fishing permits (*Angelkarten*) can be obtained from the various tourist offices. Permits can be valid for a day, week, month or year.

Boat Trips (*Dampferfahrten*)
Pleasure cruises are offered on many of the larger lakes and also along the canals. Further information and departure times are available from the local tourist offices.
Eberswalde-Finow
From Eberswalde Stadtschleuse (lock) to the Schiffshebewerk Niederfinow, to Oderberg and to Werbellinsee.
Joachimsthal: On Werbellinsee
Lychen: On Stadtsee
Prenzlau: On Unteruckersee
Templin: On Templiner See

Canoeing
Like the Mecklenburger Seenplatte of which it forms the easterly extension the Uckermark offers plenty of opportunities for canoeists. Lakes are often linked by rivers and canals, thus allowing water tours lasting several days. Rowing boats may be hired at many of the lakes, and sometimes even yachts, but the most interesting possibilities are for those with their own kayak or collapsible canoe. A recommended map for planning a canoe/kayak trip is: Wasserwanderatlas 1:100,000 published by Tourist Verlag/Kümmerly + Frey, ISBN 3-350-00159-9.

Cycle Hire (*Fahrradverleih*)
Bicycles can be hired in Angermünde, Eberswalde-Finow, Joachimsthal, Lychen, Prenzlau, Schwedt and a number of other towns in the Uckermark. For addresses contact the local tourist offices.

Festivals

Angermünde
The '*Uckermärkische Tage*':
Annually in June with plays, cabaret, music and dancing events.

Chorin
Choriner Musiksommer (June-August)
Performances of classical music.

Places to Visit

Angermünde
Kreisheimatmuseum
Brüderstraße 18
Open: At the time of writing closed, but guided tours of the Pulverturm are possible by prior arrangement.
☎ (03331) 32249

Boitzenburg
Produktionsmuseum Klostermühle
Open: Tuesday-Sunday 9-11.30am and 1.30-5pm

Chorin
Kloster Chorin
Open: Tuesday-Sunday 9am-12noon, 1-4pm

Eberswalde-Finow
Tierpark Eberswalde (Zoo)
Rudolf-Breitscheid-Straße
Open: daily 9am-dusk.
☎ (03334) 22733

Forstbotanischer Garten
Open: daily 9am-6pm
☎ (03334) 22193

Oderberg
Oderberger Museum
Next to the bridge over the Alte Oder.

History of inland shipping and fresh-water fishing industry. Exhibits include model boats and the paddle-steamer *Riesa* moored nearby.
Open: 1 April-31 October Tuesday-Friday 9am-4.30pm, Saturday-Sunday 9am-5pm. 1 November-31 March Tuesday-Sunday 9am-4pm.

Prenzlau
Kulturhistorisches Museum
(In the Dominikanerkloster)
Uckerwieck 813
Open: Tuesday-Sunday 10am-12noon & 2-4pm, Wednesday until 6pm, Saturday/Sunday until 5pm

Ravensbrück
Konzentrationslager
(Concentration camp)
Open: 8am-5pm. Closed Monday.

Templin
Volkskundemuseum
(In the Prenzlauer Tor)
Open: Monday-Friday 9am-12noon , 1.30-5pm; Saturday & Sunday 1.30-5pm.

Woldegk
Mühlenmuseum
Open: 10am-12noon, 1-4pm; Saturday & Sunday 2-5pm. Closed Monday.

Tourist Information Offices

Regional
Angermünde
Fremdenverkehrsverband Uckermark eV
Schwedter Strasse 20
16278 Angermünde
☎ (03331) 33491

Potsdam
Landesfremdenverkehrs-verband Brandenburg
Friedrich-Ebert-Strasse 115
14467 Potsdam
☎ (0331) 42221

Local
Angermünde
Angermünde-Information
Rosenstraße 15
16278 Angermünde
☎ (03331) 32268

Boitzenburg
Gemeindeverwaltung
Templiner Strasse 8/9
17268 Boitzenburg
☎ (039889) 235

Chorin
Dorfstraße 19
16230 Chorin
☎ (033366) 336

Eberswalde-Finow
Stadtinformation
Pavillon am Markt
16225 Eberswalde-Finow
☎ (03334) 22645

Fürstenwerder
Stadtverwaltung
Ernst-Thälmann-Str 33d
17291 Fürstenwerder
☎ (039859)202

Joachimsthal
Stadtverwaltung
Joachimsplatz 3
16247 Joachimsthal
☎ (033361)216

Lychen
Kurverwaltung der Stadt
(In the Rathaus)
Markt 1
17279 Lychen
☎ (039888)284

Oderberg
Fremdenverkehrsamt
Berliner Strasse 89
16248 Oderberg
☎ (033369)202

Prenzlau
Uckermark-Information
Langer Markt 12
17291 Prenzlau
☎ (03984)2791

Schwedt
Schwedt-Info
Platz der Befreiung 6
16303 Schwedt/Oder
☎ (03332)23456

or contact
Stadtverwaltung Schwedt
Lindenallee 25-29
☎ (03332)29397

Templin
Stadtinformation
Am Markt 13
17268 Templin
☎ (03987)2631

14 • The Altmark

The Altmark is an area of lowlands bounded by the Mittelland-Kanal in the south and the River Elbe in the north. Today's travellers tend to pass it by, as do the major roads, on their way to more important destinations like Hanover, Hamburg, Magdeburg or Berlin. Left forgotten, in between, are wonderful old medieval towns like Salzwedel, Gardelegen and Stendal; places that were also of note, once upon a time, but which have now retired to a kind of provincial slumber.

The Hanseatic town of **Salzwedel** first appeared in the historic records in the twelfth century when Kaiser Heinrich V (1081-1125) laid siege to the castle here. Though the town has managed to preserve much of its medieval character not much remains of the *Burg* itself except for a large brick tower and remnants of the *Burgkapelle*. Still remaining from the town fortifications are a couple of gates and a tower known as the *Karlsturm*.

Some of Salzwedel's loveliest old buildings are to be found in the vicinity of the Marienkirche. Especially worth noting are the beautifully carved portals at Salzstrasse 7 and Schmiedestrasse 27, the Hochständerhaus (an early type of half-timbered building, dating from about 1520) at Schmiedestrasse 30 and the former *Propstei* (provost's residence). Other old half-timbered buildings are to be found grouped near the Katharinenkirche and along Reichestrasse and Burgstrasse. The so-called Bürgermeisterhof at Burgstrasse 18 is a quaint little courtyard formed by crooked-looking houses dating from the sixteenth century. A café in one of the buildings makes a pleasant spot for a break. Giving just that extra touch of charm to this old quarter of town is the River Jeetze, which flows parallel to Reichestrasse and Burgstrasse.

One of the most interesting churches in Salzwedel is the Marienkirche. Originally late Romanesque in style it was redesigned and extended in late Gothic style between 1450 and 1468. In the gloom of the cool, sombre interior the smell of damp, ancient stone

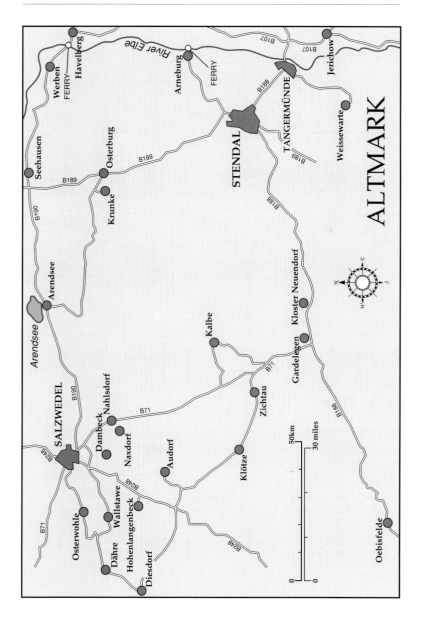

conjures up more vividly than the pages of any book the atmosphere of the Middle Ages. A magnificently carved altar, choir stalls, stained glass windows and a fifteenth-century pulpit belong to the medieval treasures of this church.

Half-timbered buildings near the Marienkirche, Salzwedel

Other churches worth visiting are the Mönchskirche (fifteenth century), the Lorenzkirche (thirteenth century), and the late Gothic Katharinenkirche. The last-mentioned is interesting not only for its fifteenth-century stained-glass windows but also for some peculiar circular indentations on one of the exterior walls. These thumb-sized depressions were worn into the brick of the church over the centuries by people rubbing against the wall with the bare flesh of their fingers or thumbs. They probably did this as an act of self-sacrifice which added weight to their prayers in times of dire need —when the town was visited by plague for instance. Exactly why the practice started and why only at this church is unknown. A possible answer to the mystery was lost when the town records were destroyed by fire in 1896. By World War I the practice had died out.

Under the former communist regime Salzwedel's main claim to fame was as the place where Jenny von Westfalen (1814-81) was born. She later became the wife of Karl Marx and in the house where she was born a museum has been set up that deals with the Marx family. Not far away the Friedrich-Danneil-Museum (housed in the former *Propstei*, see above) concerns itself with the prehistory of the Altmark.

Visitor's strolling around town will have noticed the many cafés and *Konditoreien* (confectioneries) selling a local speciality known as a *Baumkuchen* (pyramid cake). The baking of *Baumkuchen* in Salzwedel

The cakes known as Baumkuchen are a speciality in Salzwedel

has over 150 years of tradition and this is the place where they are supposed to taste the best. Baked, or rather roasted, on a long spit over a beech-wood fire (often gas flame today) the cakes are covered with either sugar or chocolate-icing before being cut into more manageable slices. By first inquiring at the tourist office it may be possible to visit one of the several *Baumkuchen* bakeries in town.

The Altmark is a veritable treasure trove as far as quaint old village churches are concerned. There are about 500 Romanesque and Gothic churches in the Altmark as a whole, with around 70 of them in the vicinity of Salzwedel. Many of these churches were built of field-stones (in the towns brick was used), and this gives them much of their simple, rustical charm. Perhaps the most outstanding of all these village churches is to the west of Salzwedel, in **Osterwohle**. Its superbly carved and surprisingly lavish Renaissance furnishings are what one might expect of a richly endowed cathedral, not an obscure rural church. Choir-stalls, pulpit, coffered ceiling and rood screen combine harmoniously to give the effect of a single, wonderfully elaborate carving hewn from oak and lime. Other churches of

Havelberg

special interest near Salzwedel are in Dambeck, Mahlsdorf, Maxdorf, Hohenlangenbeck and Audorf.

To get to the village of **Diesdorf**, 28km (17 miles) to the south-west of Salzwedel, it is best to take the road via Wallstawe and Dähre. Located here is not only one of the most beautifully preserved late Romanesque churches in the Altmark but also one of Germany's oldest open-air museums (1911), the Freilichtmuseum der Altmark, where it is possible to see traditional farm buildings as well as exhibits concerning local folk traditions.

The B190 provides a quick link to *Luftkurort* (climatic health resort) **Arendsee**, 24km (15 miles) to the east of Salzwedel. Most people are drawn to this small town because of the beautiful lake of the same name. There is a very pretty walk circling the lake but those who simply want to sit and relax can seek out one of the cafés or restaurants directly on the lake shore. Fishing, swimming, sailing or a boat trip on the steamer *Queen Arendsee* are the main activities for visitors here. However not only the culturally-minded will find Arendsee's Romanesque *Klosterkirche* (monastery church) and the picturesque ruins of the monastery itself of great interest. The church has a late Gothic carved altar and a rare thirteenth-century oak crucifix among its prized possessions. Next to the church and ruins is a *Heimatmuseum* (local history).

A treat for bird-watchers is in October/November when large

flocks of grey lag geese visit Arendsee. According to one local this natural spectacle resembles a scene from Hitchcock's *The Birds*!

A short drive east of Arendsee is **Seehausen**. Of interest here is the impressive parish church (Pfarrkirche St Peter und Paul) and a fifteenth-century town gate known as the Beuster Tor. A very worth-while detour further east from Seehausen can be made to **Werben**, an idyllic little village close to the River Elbe. Many half-timbered houses and a late Gothic church with a beautiful interior add to Werben's unspoiled charm.

Once in Werben the temptation is to continue this detour along a lovely tree-lined road to **Havelberg**, on the River Havel — the River Elbe is crossed on a small car-ferry (ferry runs from 5.30am-9.30pm) as there are no bridges along this part of the Elbe. The *Altstadt* is situated on an island in the river and rising majestically above all else, on a hill, is the huge Mariendom. This cathedral was built by Premonstratensian monks in the middle of the twelfth century in Romanesque style, but was altered in the Gothic manner after a fire in 1279. Of especial note in the richly furnished interior are the late Gothic stained glass windows, the choir stalls and coloured reliefs portraying the sufferings of Christ on the Cross. Located in the former cloisters (*Kreuzgang*) is the very interesting Prignitz-Museum (Havelberg actually lies just outside the Altmark in a region known as the Prignitz). Its subjects range from the region's earliest history to the building history of the cathedral.

Of interest in the *Altstadt* are some old half-timbered buildings, the Stadtkirche St Laurentius and the octagonally shaped St-Anna-Kapelle. One of the oldest festivals in this part of Germany — the *Pferdemarkt* (Horse Market) — takes place in Havelberg on the first weekend in September. Its beginnings go back possibly to the consecration of the cathedral in 1170. Up until the end of World War I it was the most important of all the cattle-markets that took place in Germany. From 1920 on the fun-fair aspect of the market with side-shows and so forth started to dominate. However hundreds of horses are still brought here for sale, so the *Pferdemarkt* has remained a big attraction for horse lovers from all over Germany.

Osterburg lies south of Seehausen and, after the excursion to Havelberg in the Prignitz, we are back again in the Altmark. Worth seeing are remnants of the town walls, the Nikolaikirche and a number of pretty half-timbered houses. In **Krumke**, a short distance west of Osterburg, is a neo-Gothic *Schloss* (not open to the public) set in a beautiful, romantically overgrown park. There was a large restaurant here but it now stands derelict, its place being taken at

A ferry across the River Elbe

present by a modest snack stall. In any case the park makes a good place to stop and stretch the legs before continuing south to Stendal.

Once a member of the Hanse **Stendal** is now the largest town in the Altmark with a population of 52,000, and is one of the economic centres of the region. However in the fifteenth and sixteenth centuries it enjoyed far more importance as the largest and richest town in the entire Mark Brandenburg, a former state that once occupied a large chunk of central East Germany and parts of western Poland. Stendal's trading connections once stretched from the city-states along the North and Baltic seas, to Flanders and deep into the south of Germany. The Thirty Years' War brought an end to the years of prosperity and it was only the slow onset of industrialisation in the nineteenth century that finally brought Stendal a measure of prosperity again. The town was lucky enough to have escaped the worst destruction that World War II brought to so many other German towns and there are still many fine buildings in predominantly brick Gothic style left to be seen.

Standing in the *Markt* is the Gothic *Rathaus* with its beautiful gabled front. The statue of Roland in front of the *Rathaus* is a copy of an original from 1525 that was destroyed in a storm. These 'Roland' statues are characteristic of many North German cities (the most famous one is in Bremen) and were seen as symbols of independence and freedom from feudal law. Nearby and hard to miss with its two

A stained glass window in the Katherinenkirche, Salzwedel, in the Altmark

A late summer evening on the shores of the Arendsee, Altmark

Neustädter Rathaus (town hall) at Salzwedel, in the Altmark

imposing towers is the Pfarrkirche St Marien. Inside the church is a valuable altar covered with gold from 1471 and visitors should also note the magnificent sixteenth-century astronomical clock. Seen as a whole the ensemble of *Rathaus* and church combine to make this one of the most impressive medieval marketplaces in North Germany.

From the *Markt* follow Hallstrasse south in order to get to the cathedral (*Dom*) St Nikolaus. Along with the Pfarrkirche St Marien it is an outstanding example of German brick Gothic architecture. It was built between 1423-67 and the interior is remarkable, above all, for the twenty-three very impressive fifteenth-century stained-glass windows depicting legends of the saints and scenes from the life of Christ.

Remaining from what must once have been a quite formidable wall surrounding the town are two town gates: the Tangermünder Tor and the Uenglinger Tor. The latter is considered to be one of the finest examples of a brick town gate in this part of Germany and it really does seem to embody in the sheer grandeur of its size all the wealth and above all the power of a medieval Hanseatic town. It is possible to climb the gate-tower for views over the old quarter.

Stendal was the birthplace of the renowned archaeologist and art historian Johann Joachim Winckelmann (1717-68). He pioneered modern art historiography and the house where he was born has now been set up as a museum devoted to his life and work. An interesting fact is that the French writer Henri Beyle (1783-1842) adopted the pseudonym 'Stendhal' because he was an admirer of Winckelmann's work. Another museum that may be of interest is the Altmärkisches Museum. It is housed in a building that once formed part of the Katharinenkloster (a monastery) and deals mainly with the early history of the area.

About 14km (9 miles) to the north-east of Stendal is the sleepy little town of **Arneburg** on the River Elbe. Marking the centre of town is the *Markt* with its imposing half-timbered houses and *Rathaus*. The most important building is, however, the *Stadtkirche* St Georg. It dates back to around 1200 and is therefore one of the oldest churches still to be found in the Altmark. There are good views over the Elbe valley from the ruins of a tenth-century castle that once protected the town against the attacks of neighbouring Slavonic tribes.

Tangermünde, to the south-east of Stendal, is also situated on the banks of the River Elbe and was, like Stendal, a member of the Hanse. The town has a beautifully preserved *Altstadt* with brick Gothic and half-timbered buildings combining to give a genuinely medieval atmosphere. As the old quarter of town is relatively small all the

The Neustädter Tor, the most impressive of Tangermünde's town gates

A superbly decorated door in Kirchstrasse, Tangermünde

main sights can easily be found in the course of a casual stroll.

As though to protect it against the incursions of the modern world the *Altstadt* is enclosed by an almost perfectly preserved town wall. Of the town gates it is the Neustädter Tor (1450) that is most impressive though the Hühnerdorfer Torturm and Wassertor are also worthy of attention. Lange Strasse leads from the Neustädter Tor to the *Rathaus* (1430), in which the *Heimatmuseum* (local history) is also housed. It is one of Tangemünde's finest brick Gothic buildings. The splendid façade is 24m (79ft) high and gives the *Rathaus* the appearance of a small castle or church. By continuing from the *Rathaus* along Kirchstrasse, a street running parallel to Lange Strasse, it is not far to the Pfarrkirche St Stephan. This late Gothic brick church was built over the Romanesque foundations of an earlier building. From the 94m (308ft) high tower the view extends as far as Magdeburg in clear weather.

Adding much to the character of the *Altstadt* are the many half-timbered houses, some of which have superbly decorated doors. The best examples are to be found along Lange Strasse (house No 42) and Kirchstrasse (house No 23) but the so-called Buhnenkopf at Marktstrasse 13 is also of interest. It is only the width of a window and has similarities to the half-timbered house at Finkenherd 1 in Quedlinburg (see the Harz). An explanation for such unusually small houses is that space was obviously limited in fortified medieval towns.

Just outside the town wall is what remains of the castle of Kaiser Karl IV (1316-78). Surviving from the Middle Ages are parts of the outer walls, the keep (1376), the *Burgtor* or castle gate (1480) and the fourteenth-century *Kanzlei* (chancellery). From the castle it is only a short stroll down to the River Elbe. At anchor here is a boat that has been converted into a restaurant (*Schiffsrestaurant Störtebeker*).

A treat for the children might be an excursion to Wildpark Weissewarte, a deer park near the small town of **Weissewarte** (drive south in the direction of Tangerhütte). Apart from a large herd of white fallow deer and other native animals there is also a children's playground and a restaurant here. The mixed forests (many old oaks and alders) surrounding the park make for pleasant walking or cycling.

On the other side of the Elbe, about 9km (5½ miles) to the south-east of Tangermünde, is the small town of **Jerichow** (the name has Slavonic origins, not biblical). The main reason for coming here is to see the famous Premonstratensian *Klosterkirche*, a late Romanesque brick building. Apart from the church itself there are also remnants of the medieval monastery to be seen. There is now a museum in the building where the monk's once had their cells.

Gardelegen is situated 36km (22 miles) to the south-west of Stendal and can be reached along the B188. Shortly before town a short pause could be made in **Kloster Neuendorf** in order to see the monastery church. Inside this Romanesque building are some very beautiful stained glass windows from the fourteenth and fifteenth centuries.

The name Gardelegen is associated in some people's minds with a particularly barbaric act that took place towards the end of Word War II. On 13 April 1945, just outside the town gates, 1,016 prisoners from the concentration camp 'Mittelbau Dora' were herded into a barn and burnt alive by the SS. Only a day later and they would have been freed by American troops. The memorial marking the spot is 1km outside of town coming from the direction of Stendal. It is signposted Gedenkstätte 'Isenschnibber Feldscheune'.

Gardelegen itself has a well preserved medieval *Altstadt* to ex-

The simple interior of Kloster Neuendorf, near Gardelegen

plore. Because parts of it have been turned into a pedestrian zone it is a very pleasant place to wander about in. Of particular note are the numerous half-timbered houses, the *Rathaus* (1526-52), the richly furnished Marienkirche (1200) and the odd-looking, though very imposing Salzwedeler Tor. The hotel Deutsches Haus in the *Rathausplatz* is one of the nicest half-timbered buildings in the town. A great time for keen beer-drinkers to visit Gardelegen is during the 'Bockbieranstich' in November. The town's history has long been associated with the art of brewing beer and in the sixteenth century over 250 breweries were registered as being established here. 'Garley-Bräu' has been brewed in Gardelegen since 1600 and is highly regarded by 'connoisseurs'. Naturally it tastes best fresh from the tap (*frisch vom Faß*).

Oebisfelde lies 39km (24 miles) south-west of Gardelegen. Of interest in this old town are the *Burg* with its 27m (88ft) high keep, the Gothic Pfarrkirche St Katharina and a few medieval half-timbered houses. Not far from town is the Naturpark Drömling, a large patch of protected moorland. Visitors are attracted here not only because of the uniquely beautiful scenery but also because the nature park serves as a refuge for a large variety of wildlife. With a bit of luck it might be possible to spot curlews, cranes, kingfishers and perhaps even rare black storks.

Those who wish to continue back to the start of this tour can take the B71 north to Salzwedel. On the way it might be worth stopping to explore the pretty countryside around **Zichtau** or, further west, around **Klötze**. North-east of Zichtau in **Kalbe** is a ruined castle and a twelfth-century church. The church library is known for its large collection of books dating from the sixteenth century.

Further Information
— The Altmark —

Festivals

Gardelegen
Bockbieranstich
Beer festival in November

Havelberg
Pferdemarkt (Horse Market)
1st weekend in September

Places to Visit

Diesdorf
Freilichtmuseum der Altmark
(Altmärkisches Bauernhaus-Museum)
Open: April-September Tuesday-
Sunday 9am-6pm. October-March
10am to dusk. Closed Mondays.
☎ (03902) 450

Havelberg
Prignitz-Museum
(In the Dom)
Domplatz 1
Open: Wednesday-Sunday 10am-
12noon and 1-6pm (in winter until
5pm).

Jerichow
Klosterkirche
Klostermuseum
Open: April-October daily 10am-5pm,
November-March Tuesday-Friday
10am-12noon and 1-5pm
☎ (039343) 285

Salzwedel
Geburtshaus 'Jenny Marx'
Jenny-Marx-Strasse 20
Open: Tuesday-Friday 10am-12noon
and 1-5pm, Saturday and Sunday
11am-5pm. Closed Mondays.

Johann-Friedrich-Danneil-Museum
(Kreisheimatmuseum)
An der Marienkirche 3
Open: Tuesday-Friday 10am-4.30pm,
Saturday and Sunday 11am-4.30pm
☎ (03901) 23380

Stendal
Altmärkisches Museum
Schadewachten 48
Open: Tuesday-Friday 10am-12noon
and 2-5pm, Saturday and Sunday 1-
5pm
☎ (03931) 212415

Uenglinger Tor
Open: Sundays 9.30am-12.30pm

Winckelmann-Museum
Winckelmannstrasse 36
Open: Tuesday-Sunday 9am-12noon
and 2-5pm
☎ (03931) 212026

Tourist Information Offices

Regional

Landesfremdenverkehrs-
  verband Sachsen-
  Anhalt eV
Geschäftsstelle
Trothaer-Strasse 9h
06118 Halle
☎ (0345) 340086/29887

Fremdenverkehrsverband
  Altmark eV
Arneburger Strasse 94
39590 Tangermünde
☎ (039322) 3216

Local

Arendsee
Stadtinformation Arendsee
Am Strand
Lindenstrasse 19a
39619 Arendsee
☎ (039384) 406

Gardelegen
Stadtverwaltung
Rathausplatz 1
39638 Gardelegen
☎ (03907) 5031

Havelberg
Tourist-Information
Markt 1
39539 Havelberg
☎ (039387) 224 or 225

Osterburg
Stadtinformation
Kleiner Markt 7
39606 Osterburg
☎ (03937) 561

Salzwedel
Salzwedel-Information
Strasse der Jugend 32
29410 Salzwedel
☎ (03901) 22438

Stendal
Landratsamt Stendal
  Bereich Fremdenverkehr
Hospitalstrasse 1-2
39576 Stendal
☎ (03931) 2616

Tangermünde
Fremdenverkehrsamt
(Stadtverwaltung)
Lange Strasse 61
39590 Tangermünde
☎ (039322) 2971

15 • The Harz

Though the Harz Mountains only rise to modest heights above the
North German lowlands they have many of the ingredients that
go to make up a romantic German landscape: dark forests clinging
to the sides of rugged mountain slopes, cool mountain lakes nestled
in long winding valleys, time-worn castles with tidy medieval towns
clustered below and, as a final touch, the legend of a mist-shrouded
peak where witches meet to celebrate their sabbath.

The present geographical division of the Harz between Oberharz
(Upper Harz) and Unterharz (Lower Harz) once reflected the political division between East and West Germany, as the Unterharz once
belonged to the former East German state. Now the Harz is shared
by the three federal states of Lower Saxony, Saxony-Anhalt and
Thuringia. Although this region has long been popular with German
holiday-makers, as far as foreign tourists are concerned it is mainly
the Dutch who have discovered the charms of this North German
answer to Bavaria and the Black Forest. Most of the Oberharz has
been declared a nature park while the area around the Brocken (the
highest elevation in the Harz) comes under even stricter protection
as the Nationalpark Hochharz.

The Harz as a whole is ideal walking country and there are plenty
of marked trails criss-crossing the entire region, while it is the
Oberharz that has the best winter sports facilities. Some of the more
important winter resorts include Lautenthal, Hahnenklee,
Wildemann, Altenau, St Andreasberg and Bad Lauterberg. There are
hundreds of kilometres of prepared cross-country ski trails and even
downhill skiing is possible on the Wurmberg (972m/3,188ft),
Sonneberg (850m/2,788ft) and Ravensberg (660m/2,164ft). There
are also ski slopes at St Andreasberg and Hohegeiss. In general
accommodation is better in the western Harz (Oberharz) than in the
eastern Harz (Unterharz), though this situation is certain to improve
in the not too distant future.

A good place to start a tour of the Harz is **Goslar** in the Oberharz.

This beautiful medieval town, which has recently been added to UNESCO's list of World Heritage Sites, is one of the region's major attractions and there is a wide range of accommodation as well as plenty to see and do. It is a good idea to visit the tourist office in the *Marktplatz* where it should be possible to pick up an English language brochure describing several tours around the *Altstadt*. Though not exactly off the beaten track Goslar is certainly worth a thorough look before setting off to discover other, less frequented places.

There are a number of interesting buildings around the attractive *Marktplatz* but the most impressive is the *Rathaus* with its magnificent Huldigungssaal (Hall of Homage). Especially worth noting are the late Gothic paintings on the walls and ceiling. Near the *Rathaus* is the late Romanesque Marktkirche opposite which is a very pretty burgher house known as the 'Brusttuch' (1526). Located in Münzstrasse, a street going north from the Marktkirche, is the Zinnfiguren-museum (Tin Soldier Museum). Several other museums in Goslar ensure that there is plenty to do even on those rainy days which are,

Marktplatz, Goslar

unfortunately, not uncommon in this part of the Harz. They include the Goslarer Museum with its exhibits on town history and the flora and fauna of the Harz, the Mönchehaus-Museum für moderne Kunst (Museum for Modern Art) and the Museum im Zwinger with its collection of medieval weapons and instruments of torture.

The most famous of Goslar's many ancient buildings is the Kaiserpfalz to the south of the *Marktplatz*. It is the largest palace to have survived from the Romanesque period in Germany. The Kaiser-pfalz was built at a time when Germany's emperor's lead a nomadic existence, moving from one palace to the next in order to keep a hold on their wide-flung and unstable empire. The Reichssaal (Imperial Hall), which occupies the whole of the upper floor, contains murals depicting episodes from Germany's imperial history. Attached to the main building is the chapel of St Ulrich, a masterpiece of Roman-esque architecture.

Goslar's massive town wall was erected around 1500, mainly to protect the town from being ravaged by the Dukes of Braunschweig-Wolfenbüttel. A good indication of just how formidable an obstacle these fortifications must have been is offered by the mighty Breites Tor (Broad Gate) of 1505 at the north-eastern edge of the *Altstadt*.

Anybody with an interest in mining should make sure they visit the mining museum (*Bergbaumuseum*) which has been set up in a shaft (the Roeder-Stollen) belonging to the Rammelsberg mine to the

Goslar's massive town wall, erected about 1500

south of town. The mining of silver and copper on the Rammelsberg first began in the early Middle Ages and continued up until a few years ago. The museum is in the process of being expanded and tours can be booked at the tourist office in the *Marktplatz*.

West of Goslar Innerste-Stausee is an artificial lake set amid picturesque forested surroundings. It is possible to go swimming here and boats can be hired at Hotel Berghof on the lake's eastern shore. Granestausee is closer to town, but because it is used as a drinking water reservoir swimming is not permitted. There is, however, some nice walking in the general area.

From Goslar the B241 winds its way south through beautiful forest scenery towards Clausthal-Zellerfeld. On the way a detour could be made to **Hahnenklee** where there is a pretty Norwegian-style stave church (1908). For those who prefer breathtaking views a cable railway ascends the nearby Bocksberg (727m/2,385ft), at the top of which there is a restaurant.

The Oberharzer Bergwerksmuseum in **Clausthal-Zellerfeld** deals with the history of mining in the Harz. The inhabitants of Clausthal-Zellerfeld, like those in many other towns in the Harz, once depended on ore mining for their livelihoods, but it is now tourism on which they pin their futures. Also of interest in town is the Marktkirche zum Heiligengeist (1642), which is the largest wooden church in Germany, and the large mineral rock collection (*Mineraliensammlung*) belonging to the Technische Universität. Anybody looking for souvenirs or gifts might like to try their luck at the Kunsthandwerkerhof 'Alte Zellerfelder Münze'. Among the handicraft-artists working there are glass-blowers, goldsmiths and potters.

West of Clausthal-Zellerfeld, near **Bad Grund**, is the Iberger Tropfsteinhöhle (stalactite cave). The cave was discovered over 450 years ago in the course of a search for new ore deposits. Also of interest in Bad Grund is the *Bergbaumuseum* (Mining Museum) 'Rohstoffquelle Harz'.

Osterode is only another 12km (7½ miles) further south of Clausthal-Zellerfeld. A disastrous fire destroyed many of the towns half-timbered houses in 1545 so that much of the beautifully preserved medieval *Altstadt* dates from the period following. The most interesting buildings within the *Altstadt* are the parish church of St Ägidii (1545), the old *Rathaus* (1552), the richly decorated Ratswaage (1553) and the Ritterhaus (1610). The Harzkornmagazin (now used as the *Rathaus*) in Eisensteinstrasse was built in the early eighteenth century for the storage of grain. It had a capacity of up to 40,000 tons and was supposed to ensure that the local miners could be supplied with grain even during periods of economic hardship. Just to the north-east of town the Söse river has been dammed to create a reservoir.

The B243 runs south-east from Osterode to **Herzberg**. This pretty little town has also retained something of its medieval atmosphere; especially around the picturesque Marktplatz. High on a hill above town is the *Schloss* (1510) where Duke Ernst August I (1629-98), the first elector of Hanover, was born. By marrying Sophia (1630-1714), the granddaughter of James I of England, Ernst August established a link to the British throne which eventually lead to the founding of the royal House of Hanover. His son Elector George Louis inherited the title King George I of Great Britain in 1714. Within the *Schloss* is a Forestry Museum and Zinnfigurenmuseum (Tin Soldier Museum).

A very pretty circular drive from Herzberg is to take the second-ary road north via Sieber to St Andreasberg, from where the B27 is joined at Oderhaus, and then to follow the B27 south via Bad Lauterberg back to Herzberg. **St Andreasberg** attracts many visitors in winter because of its ski slopes, but there is also good walking in the area and a silver mine (Silberschacht 'Samson') that can be visited. The Oder Stausee north of Bad Lauterberg is popular with anglers and those keen on water sports. There are a couple of camping grounds near the lake with pleasant forest settings.

Bad Sachsa lies to the south-east of Herzberg. This spa town also has its share of pretty half-timbered buildings and there are excellent views from the nearby summit of the Ravensberg (660m/2,164ft). East of the town the ruins of the Cistercian monastery at **Walkenried** are worth visiting. The monastery was founded in 1129 and became one of the richest in Germany. Even as a ruin the church has quite imposing dimensions. The other monastery buildings have survived largely intact and the Gothic cloisters are deserving of especial note. Concerts are held here from June to October.

From Walkenried a secondary road runs in an easterly direction to **Niedersachswerfen**. From here it is possible to either visit the Schaubergwerk 'Rabensteiner Stollen' (a coal mine near Netzkater railway station to the north of town), or to make a short detour south to Nordhausen.

Nordhausen was devastated in World War II and much that might have been of interest went up in flames. There are still a few interesting buildings to be seen such as the *Rathaus* (1360) and the late Gothic *Dom* but the real reason for stopping here is to catch a ride on the famous Harzquerbahn, a steam train that traverses the Harz between Nordhausen and Wernigerode. The most picturesque part of the trip is from Benneckenstein to Wernigerode and it is possible to board the train there.

Back in the direction of Niedersachswerfen, near **Krimderode**, is a memorial to the thousands who died in the Mittelbau-Dora concentration camp (Gedenkstätte 'Lager Dora'). Around 60,000 prisoners were forced to do work here concerning the infamous V-1 and V-2 rockets. The former crematorium now houses a museum dealing with the camp's gruesome history.

To the west and south-west of Nordhausen is an attractive landscape of forest and gently undulating hill-country known as the Eichsfeld. This region is scarcely visited by German holiday-makers, let alone foreign tourists, and is a real haven for those seeking peace and quiet, as well as a bit of relatively undisturbed nature off the beaten track. The scenery is particularly attractive in the hills of the Ohmgebirge, Bleicheroder Berge and Dün and also to the south of Heiligenstadt in the Naturpark Eichsfeld-Werratal. Places of interest include the beautiful medieval town of **Duderstadt, Heilbad Heiligenstadt** and at the southern edge of the Eichsfeld the historic town of **Mühlhausen**. Visitors should note that in this thinly populated region accommodation can be hard to find outside the larger towns.

From Niedersachswerfen continue east via **Neustadt**, where the impressive ruins of Burg Hohnstein are well worth inspecting, to Rottleberode. From here it is not far to Stolberg. However those who wish could first turn south and visit a large gypsum cave known as the Heimkehle, near **Uftrungen**.

Stolberg, dominated by its Renaissance *Schloss*, is picturesquely situated at the intersection of three narrow valleys and must be one of the loveliest towns in this part of the Harz. Whole streets are lined with unbroken rows of wonderfully preserved half-timbered buildings. It is a place to wander about and savour at leisure. Good overall views of the town can be obtained from paths skirting the surrounding hillsides. The views are especially good from the look-out point Lutherbuche. A popular excursion is to the Grosser Auerberg (579m/ 1,899ft), about 5km (3 miles) east of the town. Here there is a look-out tower that has been built in the form of a cross, as well as a restaurant.

From the historical point of view Stolberg is interesting as the birthplace of Thomas Müntzer (1489-1525). Müntzer was the leader of the peasant uprisings against the church and nobility that broke out in 1525. Although the peasants were at first successful the princes were finally able to organise themselves under the leadership of Duke Georg von Sachsen who prepared them for the decisive battle. This took place near Frankenhausen and ended with the death of

Stolberg is one of the prettiest towns in the Harz

over 5,000 of the peasant soldiers. A wave of executions followed and Thomas Müntzer himself was finally caught and executed on 27 May 1525 at Mühlhausen. For the former East German government he was a revolutionary hero and initiator of the first great revolutionary movement on German soil. It was for this reason that they added the honorary title 'Thomas- Müntzer-Stadt' to the names of towns that were associated with him and the peasant uprisings. Stolberg of course bore this title and part of the *Heimatmuseum* has been set aside as a memorial to the rebel leader.

About 20km (12 miles) north-east of Stolberg is **Harzgerode**. Lead and zinc mining used to be important here but now tourism is the main industry. Of interest is the Renaissance *Schloss* of 1550, the half-timbered *Rathaus* and the baroque parish church. A little to the west of town is the pretty village of Alexisbad.

Ballenstedt lies 13km (8 miles) to the north of Harzgerode and was once the residence of the princes of Anhalt-Bernburg. These days the baroque *Schloss* serves as a school for students of forestry but it is possible to stroll in the park with its impressive fountains and to visit the *Heimatmuseum* which is housed in one of the palace buildings. The *Altstadt* has a number of old half-timbered houses and there are also the remains of the sixteenth-century town wall to be seen.

North-west of town a worthwhile excursion can be made to the Roseburg. This *Schloss* was built in the early part of this century by Bernhard Sehring, a wealthy Berlin architect. His hobby was collecting valuable antiques and he decided that they needed a suitably palatial setting. The Roseburg with its small park was gradually extended over a period of nearly twenty years and cost Sehring over 13 million Marks. After Sehring died the *Schloss* was expropriated by the East German state which promptly demonstrated its determination to make the former playgrounds of the rich serve the common folk by first using it as a school for poultry farmers. The blackboards charting the growth rate of chickens were removed in 1968 when the *Schloss* was opened to the general public. Part of the Roseburg is now used as a small hotel with a restaurant.

Another excursion from Ballenstedt is to Burg Falkenstein, to the south-east of the town near **Meisdorf**. Within the *Burg* , which is one of the most impressive castles in the entire Harz, is a museum dealing with its history and also hunting. It was here that the thirteenth-century scholar Eike von Repkow wrote the *Sachsenspiegel*, the oldest German book of law. About 14km (9 miles) north-east of Ballenstedt the medieval town of **Aschersleben** is worth visiting because of its beautifully preserved town wall.

Only a short distance west of Ballenstedt is **Gernrode**. Running between here and Hasselfelde is a narrow-gauge railway known as the Selketalbahn. The carriages are pulled by a steam locomotive built in 1897 and for the most part the tracks wind their way along the romantic Selke valley. Those who happened to miss the train can at least visit the magnificent Stiftskirche St Cyriakus. Inside this Romanesque church special attention should be given to the Heiliges Grab, an eleventh-century copy of the Holy Sepulchre in Jerusalem, and the late Gothic tomb of Margrave Gero.

Quedlinburg lies directly north of Gernrode and has all that might be considered essential to a good medieval town: *Schloss*, half-timbered houses (over 1,000 of them) and Gothic churches. As the tourist brochures proudly proclaim, Quedlinburg is a step back into the Middle Ages, into nearly a 1,000 years of history.

Like in almost every other old German town the best place for visitors to start looking around is the *Markt*, which is dominated by the stately Renaissance *Rathaus* (1616-19). From here it is only a few steps to Breite Strasse, a street with some of Quedlinburg's oldest and finest half-timbered buildings. Other interesting half-timbered houses

Quedlinburg in the Harz has retained much of its medieval character

Berg Oybin, in the Oberlausitz

A Baroque doorway at Jonsdorf, in the Oberlausitz

The Renaissance town hall at Quedlinburg

from various historical periods are to be found in Marktstrasse, Kornmarkt, Hölle, Stieg (all near the *Marktplatz*), Finkenherd and Lange Gasse (near the *Schloss*). At Wordgasse 3 a Fachwerkmuseum has been arranged in the town's oldest half-timbered building, a so-called *Hochständerbau* from the fourteenth century. Here it is possible to see how the half-timbered style of architecture developed over the centuries.

The Renaissance *Schloss* is set upon a hill south-west of the *Markt* and Fachwerkmuseum. Rooms like the Thronsaal and Fürstensaal received their lavish decoration and furnishings in the eighteenth century. The *Schlossmuseum* is in buildings that once belonged to the neighbouring Stiftskirche St Servatius. This Romanesque church contains an interesting crypt and a valuable *Domschatz* (cathedral treasury) in the vestry.

Below the *Schloss* and St Servatius is the imposing Klopstockhaus. It was here that the poet Friedrich Gottlieb Klopstock (1724-1803) was born and the house is now a museum devoted to his life and work. Klopstock's most famous work is *Der Messias* ('The Messiah') which was inspired by Milton's *Paradise Lost*. Not far away is the Feininger-Galerie with a collection of works by the Cubist artist Lyonel Feininger (1871-1956).

Apart from St Servatius other churches worth visiting are St Benedikti (late Gothic), St Nikolai (Gothic) and above all St Wiperti,

The beautiful Bode valley

a Romanesque basilica probably dating from the tenth century. Under the choir is the Wiperti-Krypta, a crypt that dates from the Carolingian period — churches were often built over the crypt of an older church.

Some 14km (9 miles) north-west of Quedlinburg, in **Halberstadt**, it is well worth visiting the Gothic *Dom* of St Stephanus, a very impressive cathedral with a richly endowed treasury. Next door is the almost equally impressive Romanesque Liebfrauenkirche.

Also in the vicinity of Gernrode and Quedlinburg is **Thale**. Here it is nature rather than art that gets its due as Thale serves as the main gateway to the beautiful Bodetal (Bode valley). Flanking the Bode river just south of town are the Rosstrappe cliff (403m/1,321ft) and the Hexentanzplatz (Witches' Dancing-Ground, 451m/1,479ft), a relatively flat area of rock fringed by steeply falling cliffs from where there are spectacular views over the rugged scenery of the Bodetal. The Rosstrappe can be reached from Thale by chair-lift (*Sessellift*) and the Hexentanzplatz by cable railway (*Schwebebahn*). For the energetic there are walking trails leading to both attractions from Thale, but it is also possible to drive; at the Hexentanzplatz there is a large car park for which there is a charge.

Visitor's are warned that weekends are not the best time to visit the above sights. The Hexentanzplatz, especially, has been highly commercialised over the years, and though the crowds cannot detract from the beauty of the scenery, it certainly cannot be described as 'unspoiled'. There is a hotel with restaurant here and a number of other attractions to satisfy the tourist's desire for entertainment. They include the Harzer Bergtheater (an open-air stage), the Museum Walpurgishalle with its collection of paintings inspired by the legend of Faust and a *Tierpark* (animal enclosure).

According to legend the Hexentanzplatz is the place where witches gather on 1 May (Walpurgis Night) before flying off on their broomsticks to celebrate a witches' sabbath on the bare granite peak of the Brocken. Whether or not they make use of the hotel and car park is difficult to say, in any case there seems to be no charge for parking a broomstick!

The 10km (6 miles) stretch of the Bode valley between Treseburg and Thale is protected as the Naturschutzgebiet Bodetal. Within the reserve it is still possible to find some magnificent specimens of yew tree, a species of tree quite rare in Germany. The yew can reach a fantastic age and one of the trees within the reserve is supposed to be between 2,000 to 3,000 years old. A beautiful walk through the reserve runs close to the river and goes through thickly wooded, often quite wild scenery. It takes about 5 hours in one direction (there is a bus service between both towns) and is highly recommended as one of the nicest walks in the Harz.

Though the direct route to Blankenburg is via Timmenrode a very scenic, if much more roundabout alternative, is to first go south from Thale via Friedrichsbrunn to Allrode, then north via **Treseburg** and **Altenbrak**. The last two villages are in the Bode valley and are quite picturesque. There is accommodation (*Gasthaus/Pension*) in both villages and they make excellent bases from which to tour the Harz away from the main centres. Because of the large stands of deciduous trees this route is especially pretty in autumn.

Blankenburg has a baroque *Schloss*, now used as a school, and a respectable number of half-timbered dwellings to attract the eye of the visitor. The oldest of these dwellings are to be found in Bäuersche Strasse. Attached to the *Kleines Schloss* (Small Palace), which is situated below the main *Schloss*, is a very pretty baroque garden. The former monastery of Michaelstein is located to the north-west of the town. Not only is there a collection of old musical instruments to be seen here but the music that was once played on them can be heard during one of the regular concerts given by the Telemann-Kammerorchester.

The ruins of Burg Regenstein (dating from the twelfth-fourteenth centuries) are a few kilometres north of Blankenburg. Enough is left of the castle to give a reasonable impression of what it must once have looked like, though it is worth coming here for the wonderful views alone. The castle was once home to a clan of robber-barons who did their best to make the surrounding countryside an unsafe place to live. Gravestones belonging to members of this family can be seen in the Bartholomäuskirche in Blankenburg.

In the direction of Timmenrode is an unusual formation of sandstone rocks known as the Teufelsmauer (Devil's Wall). These rocky outcrops extend for a distance of some 4km (2½ miles) and are within a nature reserve. There is a car park near the Teufelsmauer from where it is possible to wander about the area along marked trails.

The B6 provides the quickest connection to Wernigerode from Blankenburg but the B27 south has the advantage of going through **Rübeland** where some impressive stalactite caves — the Baumannshöhle and Hermannshöhle — can be visited. Evidence indicates that both cave systems were known to man at least as far back as the early Stone Age. Of the two cave systems it is the Baumannshöhle that has the more interesting stalactite and stalagmite formations, though the Hermannshöhle has even larger caverns and the Crystal Chamber as a special attraction. Every year close to half a million people visit the caves and particularly on weekends it can get unpleasantly crowded — parking in Rübeland is very difficult in summer.

A short distance south-east of Rübeland is the Rappbodetalsperre, a dam that has created a long narrow lake in the Rappbode valley. There are excellent views from the dam and though no water sports are allowed on the Rappbodestausee it is possible to hire boats on the lake formed by the adjacent Wendefurth-Talsperre. From Rübeland it is only 15km (9 miles) via Elbingerode on the B244 to Wernigerode.

Wernigerode is another of those Harz towns where words like 'medieval' and 'half-timbered' apply. It is the most famous of all the historic towns in the eastern Harz and has an *Altstadt* so beautifully preserved that it is almost like being able to step into the canvas of a medieval painter. Among the most outstanding half-timbered buildings are Krummelsches Haus (1674) with its magnificently carved

Wernigerode has many preserved half-timbered buildings

façade at Breite Strasse 72, Gothisches Haus (1544) in the *Marktplatz* and Gadenstedtsches Haus (1582) at Oberpfarrkirchhof 13. Kleinstes Haus at Kochstrasse 43 is the smallest house in town (only 3m/10ft wide!) and Ältestes Haus (1400) at Hinterstrasse 48 is the oldest.

If there is one building that manages to outshine all others then it must be the *Rathaus*. It dominates the *Marktplatz* and many locals will assert (not without some justification) that it is the most beautiful in Germany. The building dates from 1277, though it was enlarged in late Gothic style between 1492-7. Before it became the town hall it was used by the counts of Wernigerode as both a court-house and dance hall — they obviously had the knack of combining business with pleasure. Not far away at Klint 10 is the Harzmuseum with its collection of old costumes from the northern Harz and documents concerning the history of half-timbered architecture.

On a hill to the south-east of the *Altstadt* is the *Schloss*. With its many turrets and towers it has something of a fairy-tale castle about

The Café Wien is housed in one of Wernigerode's finest Renaissance buildings

Schloss Wernigerode now houses a regional history museum

it and this was no doubt the intent of the extensive changes made in the nineteenth century. The oldest parts of the *Schloss* date from the twelfth century and it was the seat of the counts of Stolberg-Wernigerode until 1930, when they had to give it up after going bankrupt. It is now used as a regional history museum.

The Harzquerbahn (steam railway) runs from Wernigerode south to Nordhausen (see Nordhausen), a distance of 60km (37 miles). It is linked to the Selketalbahn (see Gernrode) which can be joined at Eisfelder Talmühle station. A combined journey on both steam trains is a great experience not only for railway enthusiasts but also the romantic at heart.

To the west of Wernigerode the small towns of **Drübeck** and **Ilsenburg** have a few interesting churches worth visiting. Further north-west, in the Harz Borderlands (Harzvorland), **Osterwieck** is highly recommended because of its outstanding half-timbered buildings.

There are two ways of getting from Wernigerode to the Brocken. The first route is to take the secondary road via Hasserode and Drei Annen Hohne and the second is to follow first the B244, then the B27 south to Elend, from where a secondary road climbs up to the tourist resort of Schierke and the Brocken. The first alternative has the advantage of following the tracks of the Harzquerbahn quite closely and allows photographers plenty of chances to get snapshots of the old steam train running along this route. The other alternative is also picturesque and allows a detour to Rübeland (see above).

Schierke is the main starting point for walks on and around the Brocken. The village is prettily situated and has plenty of nice old hotels to cater for the throngs of visitors who come here every year. In the surrounding forest are a number of odd looking rock formations known locally as *Klint* or *Klippen*. One of them is hidden in woods quite close to the railway station and is known as the Feuersteinklippen. This particular rock has given its name to a bittersweet herb liqueur called 'Schierker Feuerstein'. It can be bought virtually everywhere in the town and makes a handy souvenir to take home.

For many months of the year, blanketed in snow and often scarcely visible under a veil of mist, the Brocken is a mountain woven in legend and seems to hold a peculiar fascination for the Germans who have been visiting it in numbers since the middle of the sixteenth century. Reasons for this popularity are no doubt the fact that it is the highest mountain (1,142m/3,745ft) in this part of Germany, that the views from the summit are simply magnificent (at least on those rare days when it is fine) and that the centuries-old myth that the Brocken peak is the scene of a witches' sabbath excites the romantical imagination of a people who have been nourished on the sagas of the Nibelungen and Faust.

Another thing that draws people to the Brocken summit is a phenomenon that can sometimes be observed here known as the 'Brockengespenst' (Brocken spectre). These are huge shadows of the people and buildings standing on the summit which are cast against a 'wall' of rising mist.

The Brocken was on the eastern side of the border that once divided Germany and when it was made accessible again (for years the peak was within a prohibited zone) after the collapse of communist East Germany people rushed to climb it in their thousands. There are excellent views towards the Brocken from Torfhaus on the B4 between Bad Harzburg and Braunlage. However when seen from the distance it looks quite unremarkable, distinguishable from the surrounding mountains only by its bare granite peak and the monitoring station which was used to eavesdrop on West Germany.

The Harzquerbahn includes Schierke on its route and since June 1992 the train goes right to the top of the Brocken. This stretch of track is known as the Brockenbahn and has caused a great deal of controversy. Environmentalists claim that the fragile eco-system that has managed to survive relatively unscathed on the Brocken during its years of isolation will not be able to cope with the additional onslaught of tourists that the train will bring. Even those people who prefer the healthier alternative of walking up the mountain are causing damage because of their sheer numbers. Visitors who wish to climb the Brocken (11km/7 miles to the top from Schierke) should make sure they have warm clothes, as even in summer the summit can be very windy and cold. Weekends in summer should be avoided because of the crowds and it should also be noted that the Brockenstrasse (the road to the top from Schierke) is closed to cars.

South-west of the Brocken in the western Harz (Oberharz) is the fashionable tourist resort of **Braunlage**. The resort makes a rather over-commercialised appearance but then it offers all the facilities that a tourist could want. A cable railway goes up the nearby Wurmberg (972m/3,188ft), a mountain popular with skiers. The best route back to Goslar from here is to follow the B242 north-west and then join the B498 north in the direction of Altenau and the Okertal (Oker valley).

Altenau is a pleasant resort with a pretty wooden church dating from 1670. Just north of town is Okerstausee, another of the Harz's many artificial lakes. There is a camping ground at the southern end of the lake and lots of beautiful walking in the vicinity. Further north the Romkerhalle waterfall is located right next to the road and directly opposite a hotel. This is the prettiest part of the Okertal and from here it is only a few kilometres more to Goslar.

Further Information
— The Harz —

Festivals

Walpurgisfeier (Walpurgis Night)
1 May on the Brocken and Hexentanzplatz near Thale but also in many other places in the Harz.

Buntenbock

(south of Clausthal-Zellerfeld)
Fuhrherren-Diploms
Summer competition including whip cracking, yodelling and milking a cow. Information from *Kurverwaltung*.

Thale and Hohegeiß

Finkenmanöver
At Whitsuntide. A competition to decide whose chaffinch can sing best.

Places to Visit
Bad Grund
Bergbaumuseum 'Rohstoffquelle Harz'
Am Knesebeck-Schacht
Open: Guided tours May-October daily except Mondays,10am, 11am, 12noon, 2pm, 3pm and 4pm. November-April Thursdays and Sundays 10am, 11am, 12noon, 2pm and 3pm. 25 December-6 January daily 10am, 11am, 12noon, 2pm and 3pm.
☎ (05327) 2021

Iberger Tropfsteinhöhle
(Stalactite Cave)
On the B242 (large car park)
Open: April-October daily 9am-4.30pm.

November, February and March
Tuesday-Sunday 10am-3.30pm, closed
Monday. December and January
Thursday and Sunday 10am-3.30pm. 25
December-6 January daily 10am-
3.30pm.
☎ (05327) 2021

Ballenstedt
Heimatmuseum
Allee 37
Open: May-September Tuesday-
Saturday 9am-12noon and 2-5pm,
Sunday 9am-12noon. October-April
Tuesday-Saturday 9am-12noon and 2-
4pm, Sunday 9am-12noon
☎ 8866

Roseburg
Open: daily 10am-dusk

Burg Falkenstein
(south-east near Meisdorf)
Museum für Kulturgeschichte
Open: Tuesday-Friday 9am-5pm,
Saturday and Sunday 9am-6pm
☎ 8135

Blankenburg
Heimatmuseum Kleines Schloss
Schnappelberg 6
Open: January-December, Tuesday-
Saturday 10am-5pm, Sunday 2-5pm,
July-August daily
☎ 2658

Kloster Michaelstein
Musikinstrumente-Museum
Open: Tuesday-Sunday 2-5pm
☎ 2795

Clausthal-Zellerfeld
Kunsthandwerkerhof 'Alte Zellerfelder
Münze'
(Arts and Crafts Workshop)
Bornhardtstrasse 11
☎ (05323) 81024-25 (*Kurverwaltung*)

Oberharzer Bergwerksmuseum
Bornhardtstrasse 16
Open: 9am-5pm
☎ (05323) 82705

Mineraliensammlung
Technische Universität
Adolf-Römer-Strasse 2A
Open: Monday 2-5pm, Tuesday-Friday
9am-12noon

Goslar
Kaiserpfalz
Kaiserbleek 6
Open: April-October 10am-5pm,
November-March 10am-4pm
☎ (05321) 704-358

Rammelsberger Bergbaumuseum
Bergtal 19
Open: daily 9.30am-6pm (last admission 4.30pm). For safety reasons
children under the age of 6 are not
allowed into the mine.
☎ (05321) 2891

Rathaus
(Huldigungssaal)
Marktplatz
Open: April-October 10am-5pm,
November-March 10am-4pm
☎ (05321) 704-241

Zinnfigurenmuseum
Münzstrasse 11
Open: daily 10am-5pm
☎ (05321) 25889

Goslarer Museum
Königstrasse 1
Open: April-October 10am-5pm,
November-March 10am-4pm
☎ (05321) 704-359

Mönchehaus-Museum für moderne Kunst
Mönchestrasse 3
Open: Tuesday-Saturday 10am-1pm
and 3-5pm, Sunday 10am-1pm, closed
Monday

Museum im Zwinger
Thomasstrasse 2
Open: Sunday-Friday 9am-5pm, closed
Saturday. Closed November.
☎ (05321) 43140

Harzgerode
Schloss
Schlossplatz
Open: guided tours by prior arrangement
☎ 2324

Herzberg
Schloss (Welfenschloss)
Zinnfiguren- und Forstmuseum
Open: April-October Tuesday-Friday
10am-1pm, 2-5pm, Saturday and
Sunday 9.45am-1pm, 2-6pm. November-March Tuesday-Friday 11am-1pm,
2-4pm, Saturday and Sunday 11am-
1pm, 2-5pm
☎ (05521) 4799

Ilfeld
Rabensteiner Stollen Schaubergwerk
(near Netzkater station)
Open: Wednesday and Thursday 1-
5pm, Saturday and Sunday 10am-5pm
☎ 302

Krimderode (near Nordhausen)
Gedenkstätte 'Lager Dora'
Open: 1 April-30 September daily
10am-6pm. 1 October-31 March daily
10am-4pm.

Quedlinburg
Schlossmuseum
Schlossberg 1
Open: May-September, Tuesday-
Sunday 10am-6pm, October-April
10am-5pm
☎ 2730

Fachwerkmuseum
Wordgasse 3
Open: May-September 10am-5pm,
closed Thursdays

Klopstockmuseum
Schlossberg 12
Open: May-September, Wednesday-
Sunday 10am-6pm, October-April,
Wednesday-Sunday 10am-5pm
☎ 2610

Feininger-Galerie
Finkenherd 5a
Open: April-September, Tuesday-
Sunday 10am-12noon, 1-6pm, October-
May, Tuesday-Sunday 10am-12noon, 1-
5pm
☎ 2238

Rübeland
Hermannshöhle (cave system)
Hasselfelder Strasse 2
Open: May-September, Monday-
Sunday 9.45am-5.15pm, September-
May, Monday-Sunday 9.15am-4.15pm,
Monday & Friday only one cave open.
☎ 9110

Baumannshöhle
Blankenburger Strasse 36
Open: as above
☎ 9208

St Andreasberg
Silberschacht 'Samson' ('Grube Samson')
Open: Guided tours daily except
Sunday 11am and 2.30pm
☎ (05582) 1249

Stolberg
Heimatmuseum
Niedergasse 19
Open: Tuesday-Sunday 9.30-11.30am,
1-4pm
☎ 416 or 454

Thale
Walpurgishalle
Hexentanzplatz
Open: April-September 10am-5pm

Tierpark (animal enclosure)
Hexentanzplatz
Open: daily 8am until dusk.
☎ 2880

Uftrungen
Heimkehle (gypsum cave)
Open: daily (guided tours by prior
arrangement) 10am; 11am; 1.30pm;
2.30pm; 3.30pm
☎ 305

Walkenried
Zisterzienserkloster Walkenried
Steinweg
Open: 10am-12noon and 2-5pm
☎ (05525) 1354

Wernigerode
Schloss/Schlossmuseum
Open: Tuesday-Sunday 10am-6pm
☎ 32095

Harzmuseum
Klint 10
Open: Monday-Friday 9am-4pm,
Saturday 9-12noon. Closed Sunday

Cycle Hire
(*Fahrradverleih*)
For further addresses contact local
tourist offices

Altenau
Armin Leipholz
Rothenberger Strasse
☎ (05328) 365

Braunlage
Hans Wickenhagen
Herzog-Wilhelm-Strasse 4
☎ (05520) 431

Clausthal-Zellerfeld
Fa Langer
Zellbach 75
☎ (05323) 1496

Goslar
Harz-Bike (mountain-bikes)
Bornhardtstrasse 3-5
Open: Monday-Friday 9.30am-6pm and
Saturday 9.30am-2pm
☎ (05321) 82011

Bad Sachsa
Kurverwaltung
(also mountain-bikes)
Am Kurpark 6
☎ (05523) 30090

Walkenried
Kurverwaltung
Steinweg 4
☎ (05525) 357

Ski Hire
(*Ski-Verleih*)
The following list is not exhaustive.
Further information and addresses
from the local tourist offices.

Altenau
Sporthaus Biegholt & Just
Kleine Oker 1a
☎ (05328) 1200

Braunlage
Sporthaus Kohlrusch
Harzburger Strasse 1
☎ (05520) 444

Clausthal-Zellerfeld
H. Menzel
Spiegeltaler Strasse 23
☎ (05323) 81225

Hohegeiss
Sporthaus Schönekäs
Klippenstrasse 3
☎ (05583) 809

Bad Sachsa
Heinz Schildknecht
Goethestrasse 1
☎ (05523) 8800

St Andreasberg
K. Neuendorf
Schützenstrasse 30
☎ (05582) 1288

Stolberg
At the Museum
Niedergasse 19
☎ 416

Tourist Information Offices

Regional	*Local*	**Altenbrak**
Harzer Verkehrsverband	**Altenau**	*Kurverwaltung Altenbrak*
Marktstrasse 45	Schultal 5	Sankt Ritter 17
38640 Goslar	38707 Altenau	38889 Altenbrak
☎ (05321) 20031	☎ (05328) 80222	☎ (039456) 205

Aschersleben
Stadtinformation
Taubenstrasse
06449 Aschersleben
☎ (03473) 3711 or 53335

Bad Grund
Kurverwaltung
Clausthaler Strasse 38
37539 Bad Grund
☎ (05327) 2021

Bad Sachsa
Am Kurpark 6
37441 Bad Sachsa
☎ (05523) 30090

Ballenstedt
Ballenstedt-Information
Allee 50
06493 Ballenstedt
☎ (039483) 8636

Blankenburg
Kurverwaltung
  Blankenburg
Am Markt
38889 Blankenburg
☎ (03944) 2898

Braunlage
Elbingeröder Strasse 17
38700 Braunlage
☎ (05520) 1054

Buntenbock
Kurverwaltung
  Buntenbock
Alte Fuhrherren Strasse
38678 Clausthal-Zellerfeld
☎ (05232) 3583

Clausthal-Zellerfeld
Bahnhofstraße 5a
38678 Clausthal-Zellerfeld
☎ (05323) 81024

Duderstadt
(in the Eichsfeld)
Marktstrasse 66
37115 Duderstadt
☎ (05527) 841200

Gernrode
Tourist-Information
Clara-Zetkin-Strasse 28
06507 Gernrode
☎ (039485) 478 287

Goslar
Markt 7
38640 Goslar
☎ (05321) 2846 or 2847

Harzgerode
Tourist-Information
Am Markt
06493 Harzgerode
☎ (039484) 2301

Heilbad Heiligenstadt
(In the Eichsfeld)
Heiligenstadt-Information
Wilhelmstrasse 68
37308 Heiligenstadt
☎ (03606) 2063

Herzberg
Stadt Herzberg am Harz
  Fremdenverkehrsabteilung
Marktplatz 30-32
37412 Herzberg am Harz
☎ (05521) 85256

Ilsenburg
Kurverwaltung Ilsenburg
Vogelsang
38871 Ilsenburg
☎ (039452) 8112

Mühlhausen
(in the Eichsfeld)
Fremdenverkehrsamt
Ratsstrasse 20
99974 Mühlhausen
☎ (03601) 2912/523 16-21

Nordhausen
Tourist-Information
Töpferstrasse 42
99734 Nordhausen
☎ (03631) 8433

Osterode
Verkehrs- und Reisebüro
Dörgestrasse 40
37520 Osterode am Harz
☎ (05522) 6855

Quedlinburg
Fremdenverkehrsamt
Markt 12
06484 Quedlinburg
☎ (03946) 2866

Schierke
Kurverwaltung Schierke
Brockenstrasse 5
38879 Schierke
☎ (039455) 310

Stolberg
Stolberg-Information
Markt 5
06547 Stolberg
☎ (034654) 454

Thale
Tourist-Information
Rathausstrasse 1
06502 Thale
☎ (03947) 2597

Uftrungen
Gemeindeverwaltung
  Uftrungen
Hauptstrasse 20
06548 Uftrungen
☎ (034653) 625

Walkenried
Steinweg 4
37445 Walkenried
☎ (05525) 357

Wernigerode
Fremdenverkehrsamt
  Wernigerode
Friedrichstrasse 154
38855 Wernigerode
☎ (03943) 32837/32040

16 • The Oberlausitz

The Oberlausitz and the Niederlausitz together form the Lausitz, an area that stretches from Cottbus in the north to Zittau in the south. This description concerns itself with the Oberlausitz, an area roughly defined by Bischofswerda to the west, Görlitz to the east, Kamenz in a line with Niesky to the north and Zittau to the south. Of the two regions comprising the Lausitz it is the Oberlausitz with its hilly to mountainous character that is scenically most attractive.

One thing that makes the Lausitz as a whole so interesting is that it is home to one of the few ethnic minorities living in Germany. These people are known in German as *Sorben* (Wends or Sorbs in English) and are descendants of the Slavonic tribes that came to this part of Europe during the period of the great migrations in the sixth century. The Wends have retained their own language and customs up to present times in spite of repression on the part of the German speaking majority in the past. It was only after World War II (1948) that the rights of the Wends were actually guaranteed under (East) German law and they were officially encouraged to cultivate their own distinct cultural identity. Today there are about 60,000 Wends living in the area of the Spreewald and Lausitz. Visitors will notice that street names in places like Bautzen are written in both German and Wendish. In the following text the Wendish name for the more important towns is in brackets.

A good time to come to the Oberlausitz for those who have an interest in old (Wendish) customs and festivals is in winter or spring. On the 25 January the Vogelhochzeit (Bird's Wedding) takes place. This festival has its origins in pre-Christian beliefs as do many Wendish customs. During this festival the children dress up in bird costumes or in clothes that are traditionally worn at Wendish wedding ceremonies. At Easter the Easter eggs are beautifully decorated with traditional patterns and this is also the time of the colourful Osterreiten (Easter horse parades). Another festival is the Hexenbrennen (Burning of the Witches) on the evening before the 1 May.

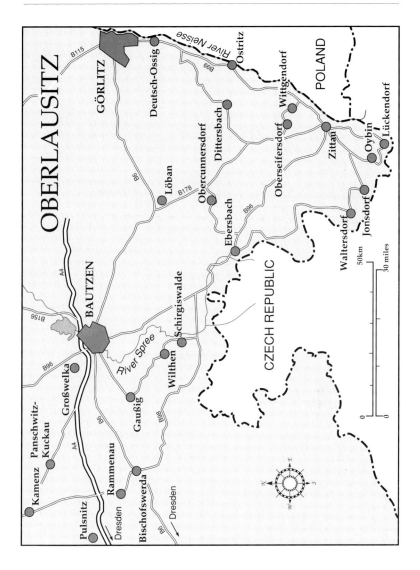

Bautzen (Budysin) is easily reached from Dresden along the B6. The town is not only a centre of Wendish cultural life but also a magnificently preserved medieval town with over 1,000 years of history behind it. Unfortunately recent history has done little to improve the town's image as place worth visiting. Under both Nazi and communist rule the town had a particularly unpleasant ring in the ears of those who dared to oppose or criticise the government, as it was home to an infamous jail for political prisoners. Today the only

The Alte Wasserkunst (left) seen from the Friedensbrücke, Bautzen

really unpleasant things about the town are the odd examples of utilitarian socialist architecture and the shoddy state of some fine old buildings.

The traditional centre of Bautzen is the *Hauptmarkt*. It is surrounded by a number of impressive old buildings among which is the three-storied Baroque *Rathaus*. Those who leave the *Hauptmarkt* in an easterly direction along Reichenstrasse pass along an almost unbroken row of beautifully preserved Baroque burgher houses and eventually come to the Reichenturm (1490-2), a tower with look-out platform that has a lean of around 1.44m (5ft) from the vertical. Not far south in the Kornmarkt is the Museum für Stadtgeschichte (Municipal Museum). Another fifteenth-century tower is to be found in Innere Lauenstrasse, which leaves the *Hauptmarkt* in a southerly direction and is also lined with buildings from the Baroque period.

Joining the *Hauptmarkt* to the north is the Fleischmarkt. Towering above this marketplace is the Petridom, a cathedral that dates from the thirteenth century. The cathedral is unusual in that it serves both Catholics and Protestants as a place of worship. In the Catholic section the ornate high-altar (1722-4) is of especial interest whereas in the Protestant section it is the seventeenth-century Fürstenloge (Prince's Pew) that catches most attention.

Not far west of the cathedral (follow the streets An der Petrikirche and Schloßstrasse) is the Ortenburg. Especially worth seeing inside the main building of this *Schloss* is the magnificent stucco ceiling in the Audienzsaal (Audience Chamber). It depicts the most significant events in the history of the Lausitz and was created by Italian artists in 1662. In an attached building is the Museum für sorbische Geschichte und Kultur (Museum of Wendish History and Culture). Among the various items on display here are traditional costumes, handicrafts and paintings.

The Ortenburg lies along the line of the old town walls and a little further south, directly above the River Spree is a stone tower known as the Alte Wasserkunst. This tower, now used as a technical museum, not only served the purpose of defence but also incorporated a bucket elevator that was used to distribute water throughout the medieval town. The best views of the Alte Wasserkunst and *Altstadt* are from the Friedensbrücke, a bridge over the Spree.

Just to the north of town — take the B156 — is an artificial lake, the eastern side of which has been developed as a recreational area. Swimming is allowed here but the western shore has been set aside as a bird sanctuary. Nudists have their own 'FKK' stretch of beach.

The Saurierpark Kleinwelka, between **Kleinwelka** and **Groß-welka**, is only a short excursion north-west of Bautzen along the B96. This highly original 'zoo' was created by the artist Franz Gruß who started modelling life-size dinosaurs as a hobby in his garden. It was not long before Gruß's work became known in scientific circles and the experts were surprised to find that the artist really knew what he was doing and encouraged him in his work. The garden was soon too small and the town council, realizing that they had a major tourist attraction on their doorstep, put the adjoining park at Mr Gruß's disposal. Children will love the 'dinosaur park' but adults will not be disappointed either.

A longer excursion from Bautzen is to the town of **Kamenz**, which lies about 30km (19 miles) north-west. Kamenz has an interesting *Altstadt* and was also the birthplace of the German dramatist Gotthold Ephraim Lessing. There is a Lessingmuseum in town which offers a good insight into the life and work of this great writer of the Enlightenment. Another museum of special interest is the Museum der Westlausitz which concerns itself with pre- and early history as well as the local geology. Those who take the secondary road to Kamenz via **Panschwitz-Kuckau** can visit the Cistercian Kloster Marienstern. This convent is also starting point for the Osterreiten (Easter horse parade), a very old Wendish custom that takes place on Easter Sunday.

The B6 leads south-east from Bautzen to **Löbau** (Lubij). Because of its central position the town makes a good base for excursions to many points of interest in the Oberlausitz, including the mountains known as the Zittauer Gebirge in the south. The nicest aspect of town is the *Marktplatz* with its Baroque *Rathaus*. However the Johanniskirche and Hauptkirche St Nikolai are also of interest, as is the *Alter Friedhof* (Old Cemetery) to the south of the *Altstadt* where the eighteenth-century tomb (Lückesche Gruft) of the merchant M. Lücke is especially outstanding. On Löbauer Berg (447m/1,466ft), just east of town, is a magnificent, elaborately constructed cast-iron look-out tower dating from 1854.

Further east on the B6 is **Görlitz** (Zhorjelc). The town lies right next to the Polish border and since World War II that section of the town on the left bank of the River Neisse has belonged to Poland. Görlitz is in some ways an even more fascinating town than Bautzen and it is definitely worth taking time here to explore the various sights at leisure.

The rectangular Obermarkt not only offers good parking (especially on weekends) but its north side is also lined by a number of splendid baroque house façades. Especially nice is number 29, the so-called Napoleonhaus, which also houses the Görlitz-Information office. Roughly opposite is the Gothic Dreifaltigkeitskirche. The church has a beautiful interior and contains some valuable furnishings from the late Gothic period. A little further on from the church the narrow Brüderstrasse forms a link to the Untermarkt, the medieval centre of Görlitz. Brüderstrasse itself is lined with some impressive buildings dating from the Renaissance and Baroque periods. Marking the end of the street, at number 8, is the Schönhof, the oldest Renaissance dwelling (1526) in Germany.

Buildings from the late Gothic, Renaissance and Baroque periods give the Untermarkt its special character and charm. The *Rathaus*, directly opposite the Schönhof, is easily identifiable by its tower with the two clocks and the elaborate external staircase (1537). Houses 1-5 in the Untermarkt are linked to the Schönhof and together they form a late Gothic arcade known as the Lange Laube. Among the houses worth noting along the northern side of the marketplace are the Ratsapotheke with its two sundials and the house at number 22, where the late Gothic portal is noted for its acoustic effects. It is known locally as the 'Flüsterbogen' ('Whispering Arch') because when you whisper at one end you can be heard by a person with their ear pressed to a groove at the other.

Just off the Untermarkt, to the east, in Neißstraße, is the Museum der Städtischen Kunstsammlungen (Municipal Art Gallery) and the

The medieval Untermarkt, Görlitz, with the twin spires of the Gothic Peterskirche in the background

Renaissance Biblisches Haus (1570), which gets its name from the fact that the façade is decorated with biblical reliefs.

The late Gothic church of St Peter and Paul (Peterskirche) is reached by following Peterstrasse north from the Untermarkt. The brightly painted interior is superb and is dominated by a magnificent organ that dates from the early eighteenth century. Another highlight of the church is the hall crypt of St Georg which is considered to have the most beautiful late Gothic interior in the Oberlausitz. A little further north-west of the Peterskirche is the Nikolaikirche (1452-1520). The surrounding cemetery with its numerous Baroque tombs and gravestones must be one of the prettiest in Germany.

At the south-west end of the Obermarkt is the Demianiplatz. The main points of interest here are the Reichenbacher Turm and the Kaisertrutz, a massive circular building from 1490 that once served as part of the town defences. Both buildings contain departments of the Städtische Kunstsammlungen (see above). At the south-eastern end of Demianiplatz, next to the Frauenkirche, is the Warenhaus

'Centrum' (1912-13). The impressive interior of this department store is well worth a look.

The B99 runs south from Görlitz, closely following the Polish border all the way to Zittau. On the way it passes through **Deutsch-Ossig** where there is a Baroque church that justifies a brief stop and **Ostritz**, where the Cistercian Kloster Mariental is of interest. This convent was founded in 1234 but what remains today dates mainly from the seventeenth and eighteenth centuries.

An alternative, if somewhat longer route to Zittau, is to branch off the B99 at Hagenwerder and to follow the secondary road until the turn-off to Kiesdorf. From here continue through the villages of Dittersbach, Schlegel and Oberseifersdorf to Zittau.

Dittersbach, Oberseifersdorf and nearby **Wittgendorf** have many superb examples of a traditional type of building known as the *Umgebindehaus*. It is a mixture of half-timbered and log-cabin construction techniques and manages to combine the advantages of both in one building. Though the walls of log-cabins have good insulating qualities they are not able to support the weight of a second or third storey. This problem was overcome by supporting the simple half-timbered construction of the upper-storey independently of the log-cabin which formed the ground floor. The supporting construction of vertical beams linked by arched struts more or less straddles the log-cabin and is therefore clearly visible from outside. The insulating qualities of the 'log-cabin' were so valued by the locals because many of them earned their livings by weaving and linen fibres are very sensitive to changes in temperature. It is for this reason that the *Umgebindehaus* is widespread in those villages where this cottage industry was practiced.

Zittau (Zitawa) lies close to both the Polish and Czech borders. Centre of the old quarter of the town is the *Markt*. The most imposing building here is the *Rathaus* (1840-5) which was built in the style of the Italian Renaissance according to plans by the famous architect Karl Friedrich Schinkel. Most of the other buildings here are in Baroque style and include the former Gasthof Zur Sonne (No 9), Noacksches Haus (No 4) and the Altes Amtsgericht (No 24). A little further north of the *Markt* is the classicist Johanniskirche (1837) which, like the *Rathaus*, was built according to plans by Schinkel. It is possible to climb the church tower for views over town and the surrounding countryside.

Circling the old town centre is a green belt in which there are a few churches worth visiting. They are the Gothic Weberkirche with its interesting old cemetery, the Gothic Kreuzkirche and on the edge of

'Umgebinde' houses are typical of the Oberlausitz

the green belt, to the north-east of the Johanniskirche, the Franciscan Klosterkirche St Petri und Pauli. Located in the former Franciscan monastery buildings is the town museum where there are exhibits of local arts and crafts as well as a collection of prettily painted traditional furniture from the outlying rural areas.

Running between Zittau and Oybin is a romantic old steam railway known as the Zittauer Bimmelbahn. The locomotive takes 50 minutes for the 13km (8 miles) it has to travel! Departure times are obtainable at the railway stations in Zittau or Oybin and at tourist offices.

Oybin is a nicely located holiday resort to the south of Zittau in the Zittauer Gebirge. What immediately impresses visitors here is the unusually shaped Berg Oybin (513m/1,682ft), a monolithic protrusion of sandstone that conceals an impressive ruined castle and monastery church on its forested summit. Part of the ruined castle is now used as a museum. Near the Bergfriedhof (cemetery) with its sixteenth-century gravestones is a restaurant with magnificent views over the rugged scenery. A circular path goes from the restaurant to the best look-out points. At the foot of Berg Oybin is the Bergkirche, a small Baroque church with a magnificently painted interior — the ascent to the castle begins by the church.

In the vicinity of Oybin are a number of picturesque mountain villages that have also developed into popular tourist resorts in

The Zittauer Bimmelbahn runs regularly between Zittau and Oybin

recent years without, however, losing any of their intrinsic charm. **Lückendorf** is best reached on the road going south from Oybin and has a very interesting little Baroque church to visit. Something to look out for in **Jonsdorf** are the Baroque door-frames hewn from local sandstone. **Waltersdorf** lies at the foot of the Lausche (793m/ 2,601ft), the highest peak in the Zittauer Gebirge. Surrounded by forest and meadows the village is an important winter sports resort and has around sixty *Umgebinde* houses with ornamented sandstone door-frames. Also of interest is the church and the Volkskunde- und Mühlenmuseum (Ethnological and Mill Museum). A lovely old hotel in which to stay is the Pension und Gaststätte 'Zur Lausche'. Here the rooms are as large as the prices are modest.

A characteristic of the Zittauer Gebirge are the many bizarre rock formations and in this respect they are similar to the more famous Elbsandsteingebirge further west. Just out of Oybin, on the road to Lückendorf, are a few good examples of strangely eroded sandstone rocks and near Jonsdorf the Nonnenfelsen (537m/1,761ft) are of interest. The Mühlsteinbrüche (a former quarry) near Jonsdorf is popular with rock climbers, as is the region as a whole. Plenty of walking trails criss-cross the Zittau ranges and any of the above-mentioned villages serves as a good starting-point for a hiking tour.

From Zittau the B96 goes north-west to **Ebersbach**. There are many fine *Umgebinde* houses here, for instance in Steinstrasse and

The Zittau Ranges near Oybin

Oststrasse. The Baroque Pfarrkirche is interesting for its painted wooden tunnel vault. North-east of Ebersbach, in **Obercunnersdorf**, are some 280 *Umgebinde* houses, all of which are classified as historical monuments.

From Ebersbach continue via Neusalza-Spremberg, Wehrsdorf (a very picturesque town) and Neukirch to **Bischofswerda**. The town was burned to the ground by plundering French troops in 1813 so very little is left from earlier times. Following the fashion of the day Bischofswerda was rebuilt in classical style and this can best be seen in the *Marktplatz* with its burgher houses and *Rathaus*. Near the *Marktplatz* the Christuskirche is also in classical style.

A short distance north of Bischofswerda, at **Rammenau**, is one of the most beautiful Baroque palaces in the state of Saxony. Set in an English-style park Schloss Rammenau houses a restaurant and a museum devoted to the great German philosopher Johann Gottlieb Fichte (1762-1814), who was born in Rammenau. Among the splendidly furnished rooms that can be visited are the Hall of Mirrors and the Chinese Room.

Pulsnitz lies to the north-west of Rammenau and those with a sweet-tooth will find the place a must to visit as the town is famed in eastern Germany as the *'Pfefferkuchenstadt'* (Gingerbread Town). Gingerbread has been baked here since 1558 and the tradition is still going strong. Another old trade that is still practiced here is indigo

*Baroque doorways
are a feature of many
traditional houses in
the Zittau Ranges*

printing (Blaudruckerei), a traditional method of printing patterns on linen or cotton cloth. The indigo printing workshop at Bachstrasse 7 is the last of its kind in the state of Saxony.

From Bischofswerda it is not far on the B6 back to Bautzen or, by taking the B6 south-west, to Dresden. However those who have succumbed to the quiet charms of the Lausitz might like to set off along the secondary roads to discover for themselves the many picturesque villages and towns that could not be mentioned here. Places like Gaußig with its *Schloss* or Wilthen and Schirgiswalde with their traditional *Umgebinde* houses might serve as orientation points in a search for the kind of 'unspoiled charm' that only remains so as long as it is left unmentioned in tourist brochures or by authors like ourselves.

Further Information
— The Oberlausitz —

Festivals

Regional
'Hexenbrennen' (Evening before 1 May)
'Burning of the Witches'

Osterreiten (Easter Sunday)
Easter horse parades. In some catholic
parishes: Panschwitz-Kuckau,
Wittichenau, Nebelschütz and Storcha.

Vogelhochzeit (25 January):
Bird's Wedding. (See text)

Bautzen
Puppenfest (last weekend in August)
Puppet Festival

Places to Visit

Bautzen
*Museum für Sorbische Geschichte und
    Kultur*
Ortenburg 3
Open: daily 10.00am-12.30pm and 1.00-
4pm
☎ 42403

Museum für Stadtgeschichte
Kornmarkt 1
Open: Wednesday-Sunday 10am-
12noon and 1-5pm
☎ 44446

Alte Wasserkunst Technisches Museum
Am Wendischen Kirchhof
Open: April-October daily 9am-12noon
and 1-5pm

Reichenturm
Open: April-October daily 10am-5pm

Görlitz
*Museum der Städtischen Kunstsamm-
    lungen*
Neißstrasse 30
Open: Tuesday-Wednesday 10am-1pm
and 2-6pm, Thursday-Sunday 10am-
1pm and 2-4pm

Kaisertrutz
Demianiplatz 1
Open: April-October Tuesday-
Wednesday 10am-1pm and 2-6pm,
Thursday-Sunday 10am-1pm and 2-
4pm. Closed in winter.
History of Görlitz and picture-gallery.

Reichenbacher Turm
Open: same times as Kaisertrutz

Großschönau (north of Waltersdorf)
Damast- und Heimatmuseum
Schenaustrasse 3
Open: mid-April to October Monday-
Saturday and every first Sunday of the
month. From November-mid-April
only Tuesday and Friday.
This museum deals with the produc-
tion of damask which used to be an
important industry in Großschönau.

Großwelka
Saurierpark Kleinwelka (Urzoo)
(Situated in a park between
Kleinwelka and Großwelka)
Open: February-March 9am-5pm,
April-September 8am-6pm, 1October-
November 9am-4pm, December-
January 9am-3pm .

Kamenz
Lessingmuseum
Lessingplatz 1-3
Open: Monday-Thursday 9am-12noon
and 1-4pm, Saturday/Sunday 1-4pm
☎ (03578) 5551

Museum der Westlausitz
Pulsnitzer Strasse 16
Open: Tuesday, Thursday, Saturday
9am-12noon and 1.30-3.30pm, Sundays
9am-12noon.
☎ (03578) 6237

Oybin
Burg/Oybin-Museum
Open: mid-February-late October 9am-
4pm, during summer until 6pm.

Rammenau
Schloss Rammenau and Museum
Open: daily
☎ (03594) 3559

Waltersdorf
Volkskunde- und Mühlenmuseum
Open: Monday-Saturday

Zittau
Stadtmuseum
Klosterstrasse 3
Open: Tuesday, Thursday 10am-
12noon and 1-4pm; Wednesday 10am-
12noon and 1-6pm; Friday 10am-1pm;
Sunday 10am-12noon and 2-5pm.

Tourist Information Offices

Regional
Fremdenverkehrrsverband
  Oberlausitz/Nieder-
  schlesien
Ernst-Thälmann-Strasse 9
Postfach 764
02625 Bautzen
☎ (03591) 573290

Fremdenverkehrsgemein-
  schaft Dreiländereck-
  Zittauer Gebirge eV
Landratsamt Zittau
Marschnerstrasse 3
02763 Zittau
☎ (03583) 85453/452

Local

Bautzen
Bautzen-Information
Fleischmarkt 2/4
02625 Bautzen
☎ (03591) 42016

Bischofswerda
Stadtverwaltung
Altmarkt 1
01877 Bischofswerda
☎ (03594) 860

Görlitz
Görlitz-Information
Obermarkt 29
02826 Görlitz
☎ (03581) 406999/402977

Jonsdorf
Fremdenverkehrsamt
Auf der Heide 1
02796 Jonsdorf
☎ (035844) 627

Kamenz
Stadtverwaltung
Platz der Befreiung 1
01917 Kamenz
☎ (03578) 8041

Löbau
Löbau-Information
Rittergasse 2
02708 Löbau
☎ (03585) 3333

Lückendorf
Fremdenverkehrsbüro
Kammstrasse 34
02797 Lückendorf
☎ (035844) 812

Oybin
Fremdenverkehrsamt
Freiligrathstrasse 8
02797 Oybin
☎ (035844) 346

Pulsnitz
Stadtverwaltung
Platz der Befreiung 1
01896 Pulsnitz
☎ (035955) 641

Waltersdorf
Fremdenverkehrsbüro
Dorfstrasse 97
02799 Waltersdorf
☎ (035841) 2354

Zittau
Zittau-Information
Rathausplatz 6
02763 Zittau
☎ (03583) 512631

Index

A

Abtei 65
Affeln 36
Ahlbeck 278
Ahrensburg 17
Ahrenshoop 267
Aicha vorm Wald 147
Altmark 298-297
Alt Schönau 157–158
Altbeuern 216–217
Altena 37
Altenau 329
Altenbrak 323
Altenhellefeld 44
Altenkirchen 274
Amerang 223–224
Angermünde 293
Anklam 279
Annweiler 91–93
Archshofen 126, 127
Arendsee 302
Arnbruck 177
Arneburg 305
Arnsberg 43–44
Arrach 173
Aschaffenburg 101
Aschau im Chiemgau
   216
Aschersleben 320
Assingshausen 48
Attendorn 33
Aub 125

B

Bad Bergzabern 94–95
Bad Doberan 266
Bad Dürkheim 87
Bad Grund 316
Bad Mergentheim 118–
   120

Bad Reichenhall 231
Bad Sachsa 317
Bad Segeberg 18
Bad Tölz 203–205
Bad Wiessee 205–206
Ballenstedt 319–320
Baltrum 26
Balve 37
Baltic Coast 259-283
Bamberg 107
Bansin 278, 279
Banz 109
Barth 269
Bautzen 335–337
Bavarian Alps 184-238
Bayerisch Eisenstein 170
Bayerische Wald 132-183
Bayreuth 110
Bayrischzell 214
Beckingen 70
Benediktbeuern 198–201
Benz 279
Berchtesgaden 232–233
Berchtesgadenerland
   230
Berg 195–196
Bergen 225–226, 273
Berghausen 52
Bernau 218
Bernried 197–198
Berus 74–75
Besseringen 67
Bestwig 47
Beuron 243–245
Bieberehren 122
Biggesee 32
Bilstein 53
Binz 272
Bischmisheim 78
Bischofswerda 343

Blankenburg 323–324
Blieskastel 79
Bockenheim 86
Bödefeld 52
Bodenmais 177–178
Bodetal 322–323
Bogen 144
Boitzenburg 288
Boltenhagen 261
Borkum 25
Born 268
Braunlage 329
Breckerfeld 36
Breitenberg 154
Brilon 48
Brocken 328–329
Bronnbach 115
Bruchhausen 48
Bübingen 79
Buchelberg 147
Büchlberg 153
Budysin. See Bautzen
Burgerroth 125
Burgstall 127

C

Castell 107
Cham 177
Chiemgau 214
Chieming 225
Chiemsee 218–223
Chorin 290, 291
Clausthal-Zellerfeld 316
Cloef 66
Coburg 109
Creglingen 123–125
Criewen 295

D

Dahn 93

Danube, Upper 239-253
Danube Valley 245–247
Darß 267, 268–269
Degerndorf 214
Deggendorf 144–145
Deidesheim 88
Detwang 127
Deutsch-Ossig 340
Diedrichshäger Berg 264
Diemelsee 49
Diesdorf 302
Dillingen 70
Dittersbach 340
Donaustauf 142
Dörnschlade 53
Dörrenbach 96
Dörzbach 120
Drübeck 327
Druggelte 42
Duderstadt 318
Düren 73
Dürnbach 211

E
Ebbegebirge 32, 35
Ebersbach 342
Ebersberg 146
Eberswalde-Finow 291
Edenkoben 91
Eggstätt 222
Eging am See 165
Eichsfeld 318
Eiringhausen 35
Eldena 276
Elspe 53
Endorf 223
Enkenbach 86
Ennepetal 40
Eppenbrunn 93
Erlenbach 95
Eslohe 52
Ettal 189–190

F
Falkenstein 142
Feldafing 196–197
Feldberg 286
Felsberg 73
Finnentrop 34
Finsterau 158
Fischland 267, 268
Förchensee 228

Franconia 101-111
Frauenau 160
Fraueninsel 221–222
Frauental 125
Fredeburg 52
Freudenberg 66
Freyung 155–156
Friesland 21-29
Frickenhausen 106
Froschsee 230
Fürstenwerder 286
Furth im Wald 174–176

G
Gamburg 116
Gardelegen 308
Garmisch-Partenkirchen 190
Gartz 295
Garz 271, 279
Gaußig 344
Gelterswoog 87
Gernrode 320
Gingst 275
Gmund 211
Gnitz 278
Göhren 272
Görlitz 338–340
Goslar 312–316
Gothmund 16
Graal-Müritz 266
Grabenstätt 226
Grafenau 161–162
Grafschaft 51
Grainau 190
Greifswald 275
Grevenstein 44
Grimnitzsee 291
Grosser Arber 170–171
Grosser Auerberg 318
Grosser Lychensee 287
Grosshemmersdorf 71
Großwelka 337
Grünstadt 86
Güdingen 78
Gustow 271

H
Hagen 38–40
Hahnenklee 316
Haibach 180
Haibühl 173

Haidmühle 156
Halberstadt 322
Hallenberg 50
Halver 36
Hamburg 9–14
  Hagenbeck Zoo 13
  Hansa Theatre 13
  Jenisch-Haus 12
  Kunsthalle 10
  Museum für Kunst
    und Gewerbe 12
Harz 312-333
Harzgerode 319
Haus im Wald 162
Hauzenberg 153
Havelberg 303
Heigenbrücken 103
Heilbad Heiligenstadt 318
Heiligendamm 264–266
Hellefeld 44
Hemmersdorf 71
Heringsdorf 278
Herrenchiemsee 222
Herscheid 35
Herzberg 317
Hesborn 51
Hexentanzplatz 322–323
Hiddensee 267, 275
Himmelpfort 287
Hintersee 231
Hirschberg 45
Hoben 261
Hofkirchen 146
Hohenzollern Castle 248
Homburg 106
Hönnetal 38
Hüinghausen 35
Hüsten 44
Hutthurm 152

I
Ihn 71
Ilsenburg 327
Inzell 230
Iphofen 107
Iserlohn 38
Ising 225
Itzbach 71

J
Jasmund 274

Jerichow 308
Joachimsthal 291
Jonsdorf 342
Juist 25

K
Kaiserslautern 86
Kaitersberg 178
Kalbe 310
Kallenhardt 46
Kallstadt 87
Kamenz 337
Kamminke 279
Karlshagen 277
Karlsruhe 97
Karlstadt 106
Kassel 49
Kastel-Staadt 65
Kehlstein 232
Kelheim 141
Kellberg-Thyrnau 151
Kiel 16
Kierspe 36
Kirchdorf 263
Kirchdorf im Wald 160
Kitzingen 107
Kleinwelka 337
Klingen 123
Klockenhagen 266
Kloster 275
Kloster Neuendorf 308
Klötze 310
Kochel am See 201
Kochelsee 202
Köllerbachtal 75
Königsee 233
Konz 63
Körbecke 42
Korswandt 279
Kötzting 178
Kreuth 207
Krimderode 318
Krumke 303
Krummin 278
Kühlungsborn 264
Küstelberg 50

L
Laboe 16
Lalling 160–161
Lam 172
Landau in der Pfalz 91

Langeoog 27
Langscheid 44
Laudenbach 121
Lauterbach 272
Leidingen 74
Lemberg 93
Lendringsen 40
Lenggries 203
Lennestadt 52
Lieper Winkel 279
Löbau 337
Lodensee 228
Lohberg 171
Loissin 276
Losheim 69
Lübeck 14–16, 18
Lubij. *See* Löbau
Lubmin 276
Lückendorf 342
Lüdenscheid 35
Ludwigsburg 276
Lütow 278
Lüttenort 278
Lychen 287

M
Maikammer 91
Marquartstein 226–227
Marsberg 48
Medebach 50
Meinerzhagen 35
Meisdorf 320
Menden 40
Merzalben 94
Merzig 67–69
Meschede 45
Meschendorf 264
Mespelbrunn 112
Metten 144
Mettlach 66–67
Miesbach 212
Mittagsstein 178
Mittenwald 191–193
Mittersee 228
Möhnesee 42
Molfsee 17
Mönchberg 103
Monsheim 85
Mühlhausen 318
Münster 126
Murnau 193
Museumsdorf 162–165

N
Neheim-Hüsten 44
Nennig 69
Neu Schönau 158
Neubeuern 216
Neubukow 263
Neuenrade 36
Neukirchen 166
Neukirchen beim
  Heiligen Blut 174
Neukloster 261
Neumünster 18
Neustadt 318
Neustadt an der
  Weinstrasse 88–89
Niedaltdorf 71
Niederfinow 291
Niedermarsberg 48
Niedersachswerfen 317
Niederstetten 125
Nierentrop 52
Norderney 26
Nordhausen 317
Nunkirchen 69

O
Oberlausitz 334-347
Oberammergau 188–189
Obercunnersdorf 343
Oberhundem 53
Oberkirchen 51
Obermarchtal 250
Obermarsberg 48–49
Obernzell 152
Oberseifersdorf 340
Oberuckersee 286
Oberwengern 39
Oberwössen 227
Oderberg 292
Oebisfelde 309
Offenbach 101
Okerstausee 329
Okertal 329
Olpe 32
Olsberg 47
Orscholz 66
Osterburg 303
Osterhofen 146
Osterode 316
Osterwald 52
Osterwieck 327
Osterwohle 301

Ostritz 340
Otterberg 86
Oybin 341

P
Palatinate Forest 84-100
Panker 18
Panschwitz-Kuckau 337
Parstein 293
Passau 148–151
   Cathedral 148
   Glass Museum 150
   Residenz 148
   Veste Oberhaus 148
Peenemünde 277–278
Pfälzer Wald 84-100
Pirmasens 93–94
Plattling 145
Plettenberg 34
Plön 17
Pöcking 194
Poel 263
Polling 194
Pommersfelden 109
Possenhofen 196
Prackenbach 179
Preetz 18
Prenzlau 284–286
Prerow 268
Prien 218–221
Pulsnitz 343
Pupplinger Au 198
Putbus 272

Q
Quedlinburg 308, 320–322

R
Ralswiek 273
Rammenau 343
Ramsau 232
Ramsbeck 47
Randersacker 106
Rappweiler 70
Rattenberg 179
Ravensberg 317
Ravensbrück 288
Regen 167–169
Regensburg 135–142
   Alte Kapelle 136
   Altes Rathaus 136–138

Befreiungshalle 140
Bischofshof 139
Cathedral 136
City Museum 140
Ducal Court 136
Haus zum Goldenen
   Kreuz 139
Kepler House 139
Marstallmuseum 140
Niedermünster 136
Roman Tower 136
Runtingerhaus 138
Schloss Thurn and
   Taxis 140
St Ulrich 136
Steinerne Brücke 138
Thon-Dittmar Palace
   139
Rehlingen 71
Reichholzheim 115
Reiste 52
Reit im Winkl 227–228
Rerik 264
Ribnitz-Damgarten 266
Ried 177
Riedlhütte 158–159
Riedlingen 250
Rimberg 52
Rimsting 223
Rinchnach 160
Rodalben 94
Römershagen 53
Rönsahl 36
Rosen Insel 196
Rosenheim 215–216
Rosstrappe 322
Rostock 266
Rothenburg 128
Rottach-Egern 207–210
Röttingen 122
Rübeland 324
Rügen 271–275
Ruhpolding 228–230
Rumbach 93
Rüthen 46

S
Saalachsee 231
Saalhausen 53
Saarbrücken 76–78
Saarburg 63–65
Saarlouis 72

Saar Valley 60-83
Sagard 274
Salzwedel 298–302
Salzweg 152
Sauerland 30-59
Schaprode 275
Scheuereck 169
Schierke 328
Schirgiswalde 344
Schledorf 201
Schliersee 212–213
Schmallenberg 51
Schön 126
Schönberg 161
Schorfheide 290, 291
Schwedt 294
Schweigen-Rechtenbach
   97
Seebruck 224–225
Seehausen 303
Seeon 224
Seeshaupt 198
Sellin 272
Serrig 66
Sierksdorf 17
Siersburg 71
Sigmaringen 240–243
Soest 41–42
Sonnen 153
Sorpesee 38
Spessart 101–103
Spiegelau 159
Spiekeroog 27
Spitzingsee 213
St Andreasberg 317
St Englmar 180
St Oswald 158
Staffelsee 193
Starnberg 195
Starnbergersee 194, 195–198
Steigerwald 107
Steinbruch 176
Steingaden 187
Stendal 304–305
Stolberg 318–319
Stolpe 294
Stove 263
Stralsund 271
Straubing 143–144
Stuppach 120
Suhrendorf 275

Sulzfeld 106
Sundern 44
Swabian Alb 248–253

T
Tangermünde 305–308
Tauberbischofsheim
116–118
Tauberrettersheim 122
Taubertal 112-131
Tegernsee 205, 210–211
Templin 288
Teufelsmauer 324
Thale 322
Tieringen 248
Timmenrode 324
Tittling 162
Trassenheide 277
Traunstein 225
Travemünde 16
Trent 274
Treseburg 323
Trippstadt 87
Trittau 17
Tuttlingen 245–247
Tutzing 197

U
Übersee-Feldwies 226
Uckermark 284-297
Ueckermünde 280
Uftrungen 318
Ummanz 275
Unteruckersee 286
Unterwössen 227
Usedom 276–279, 279

V
Veitshöchheim 105

Veringenstadt 249
Viechtach 178–179
Vierzehnheiligen 109
Vilm 272
Vilshofen 146
Vitt 274
Volkach 107
Vorderriss 202

W
Waase 275
Wachenheim 87
Wadgassen 75
Walchensee 202
Waldfischbach-
Burgalben 94
Waldhäuser 157
Waldkirchen 154–155
Waldmannshofen 125
Waldmünchen 176–177
Walkenried 317
Wallerfangen 71
Waltersdorf 342
Wangerooge 27
Wariner See 261
Warnemünde 266
Warstein 45–46
Weikersheim 120–122
Weilheim 194
Weiskirchen 69–70
Weissenhäuser Strand
17
Weissewarte 308
Weitsee 228
Weltenburg 141
Wenden 53
Wendorf 261
Werbellinsee 291
Werben 303

Werdohl 36
Werl 41
Wernigerode 324–327
Wertheim 113–115
Wieck 276
Wiek 268, 274
Wies 187
Wildewiese 44
Willingen 49
Wilthen 344
Windorf 146
Winterberg 50
Wismar 259–261
Wittgendorf 340
Woldegk 286
Wolfratshausen 198
Wolgast 276
Wolgastsee 279
Wormbach 52
Wössnersee 227
Wuppertal 40
Wurmberg 329
Würzburg 103–105
Wustrow 267

Z
Zempin 278
Zhorjelc. *See* Görlitz
Zichtau 310
Zingst 267, 269
Zinnowitz 278
Zitawa. *See* Zittau
Zittau 340–341
Zittauer Gebirge 341–
342
Zugspitze 191
Zwiefalten 250–252
Zwiesel 168–170

ACCOMMODATION AND EATING OUT

G eneral notes on the conditions to be found by visitors to the eastern part of Germany (the former German Democratic Republic) can be found in Chapter 11 'Eastern Germany: An Introduction'.

A booklet listing some 300 typical German hotels is published by the German National Tourist Office. Lists containing a wider variety of accommodation such as camping grounds (*Camping-plätze*) and the many privately run small hotels or inns (*Gasthöfe*) can be obtained in Germany from regional or local tourist offices. Many local tourist offices will reserve rooms but not every office will do this over the telephone.

Accommodation in the east is generally not up to the standard of the west and prices are lower, but standards are rising and so are prices!

Camping

A free list of camp sites is available from the German National Tourist Office. The two most well-known books listing camping sites are put out by the German Automobile Club (ADAC) and the Deutscher Camping Club. Both are available in larger bookshops and are updated annually, as is *ECC, Europa Camping and Caravanning* (published by 3 Brunnen Verlag, Stuttgart), which has the most important information in English.

Most camping grounds are open only between April to October, though near major cities or resorts with summer and winter seasons they remain open throughout the year. It is advisable to reserve places during the summer season.

Camping rough has been made illegal in the interests of protecting the environment.

Campsites are widespread in eastern Germany, though many are still lacking in adequate sanitary facilities. Charges are much lower than in the west.

For further information on camping in Germany contact:

ADAC
Am Westpark 8
81373 Munich
☎ (089) 7676-0

Deutscher Camping-Club
Mandlstrasse 28
80802 Munich
☎ (089) 334021

Hotels

The German Hotel Reservation System (ADZ) run by the German National Tourist Board (DZT) will book accommodation in all hotels, inns and boarding-houses. Contact:

DZT-Serviceabteilung ADZ
Corneliusstrasse 34
60325 Frankfurt am Main
☎ (069) 740767

Youth Hostels

German Youth Hostels are listed in the International Youth Hostels *Guide to Budget Accommodation Handbook, Volume 1, Europe and the Mediterranean.* Hostels in Germany are identified by a green triangle with the letters DJH. For information contact:

Deutsches Jugendherbergswerk (DJH)
Hauptverband
Bismarckstrasse 8
Postfach 1455
32756 Detmold
☎ 05231/7401-0

Currency and Credit Cards

The German unit of currency is the Deutsche Mark (DM). 100 Pfennigs (Pf) = 1DM. It is freely convertible ie, it can be exchanged for any foreign currency at any time at the going rate. You can bring as much currency as you wish into Germany.

The Deutsche Mark comes in **notes** of DM10, DM20, DM50, DM100, DM200, DM500 and DM1,000; **coins** of DM0.01 (one pfennig), DM0.02, DM0.05, DM0.10, DM0.20, DM0.50, DM1, DM2 and DM5.

Because some credit cards are not so widely accepted in Germany travellers should get a list of those banks accepting their credit cards before leaving home. Money may be withdrawn using credit cards from the following banks:

Visa ☎ (069) 792010: Citibank, Deutsche Verkehrs-Bank and the Sparkasse (not every Sparkasse accepts Visa). The booklet *Automated Teller Machines in Germany* from Visa gives further information.

Diners Club ☎ (069) 26030: Citibank, Deutsche Verkehrs-Bank (DVB, usually located at railway stations).

Eurocard/Mastercard ☎ (069) 79330: Commerzbank, Dresdner Bank, Sparkasse, Deutsche Bank. Eurocard is the most widely accepted card in Germany.

American Express ☎ (069) 720016: Deutsche Verkehrs-Bank (DVB), Amex Offices.

All banks exchange traveller's cheques. If the cheques are in Deutschmarks the full face value will be given. If they are in a foreign currency the bank will make a service charge of around 2 per cent.

Eurocheques, together with a cheque card, are used like ordinary domestic cheques and must be made out in the local currency. Eurocheques can be used for all business transactions but petrol stations make a small additional charge. They can only be cashed up to a value of 400DM per transaction. Scottish bank notes and foreign coins are not accepted for exchange.

Bureaux de change: at airports, main railway stations and border crossings. Open: usually 6am-10pm.

The Deutsche Verkehrsbank (see Banks) will give a cash advance against major credit cards (DM100 minimum).

Telephones

In the main post offices you can use the direct phone service. Ask at the counter marked *Ferngespräche* for a phone booth. You pay at the counter when you have finished your phone call. This is much more convenient than queuing for a pay phone and saves having to find change.

Every telephone booth has a local directory. Phone books covering all Germany are found in the post offices. Local and national calls may be made from all post offices and coin/card-operated phone booths. Unit fees for calls from hotels are about twice as expensive as the standard call units. International calls can be made from post offices and phone booths with a phone marked *Auslandsgespräche*.

Coins that can be used in a phone booth are: 10 Pfennig, 1DM, 5DM. A much more comfortable way of telephoning is with a Telefonkarte. These cards are available at post offices and obviously solve the problem of small change. Telephone booths which accept these cards are usually marked *Kartentelefon* — they are becoming more widespread but may not yet exist in smaller towns or villages.

You can only reverse charges (*R-Gespräch*, ring collect) to the USA. To do this look up the number of the international *Fernamt* under the heading *Telefon-Sonderdienste* in the telephone book. This number is usually 0010 but it can vary from region to region. The person at reception will then give further details. You cannot ring collect within Germany.

Instructions on using payphones are in English in phone booths for international calls. Otherwise lift up the receiver, insert the coins and dial. A meter shows how much credit is left.

International directory inquiries dial 0 01 18. This number will also help if with language difficulties in finding a number in an emergency.

Emergency Numbers
Police and accidents 110, Fire brigade 112
National directory inquiries dial 11 88 or 0 11 88.
Main international direct dialling codes are:
Australia 00 61
Britain 0044
Irish Republic 00 353
New Zealand 00 64
USA and Canada 00 1

Telephone call rates are cheaper after 8pm and at weekends. This does not apply to calls outside Germany.

When dialling from Germany remember after dialling the national code to omit the first zero of the number you are ringing.

In the east the telephone system is still rather antiquated and not all houses or hotels have a telephone, but there may be a public phone booth nearby, some of which take the modern phone cards. If telephoning within eastern Germany it is advisable to check the number and code locally whenever possible.

Tipping

Not a must but usual for good service. Small sums are rounded up, sums over 100DM might include a tip of around 2DM.

Tourist Offices

The main German National Tourist Offices are:

Australia
Lufthansa House
12th Floor
143 Macquarie Street
Sydney 2000
☎ (02) 221 1008

Canada
175 Bloor Street East
North Tower, 6th Floor
Toronto
Ontario M4 W3R8
☎ (416) 968-1570

Germany
Deutsche Zentrale für Tourismus
  eV (DZT)
Beethovenstrasse 69
60325 Frankfurt am Main
☎ (069) 7572-0
(general information)

Deutsche Fremdenverkehrsverband
Niebuhrstrasse 16b
53113 Bonn
☎ (0228) 214071-72
(general information)

USA
444 South Flower Street
Suite 2230
Los Angeles CA 90071
☎ (213) 688-73 32

747 Third Avenue
33rd Floor
New York, NY 10017
☎ (212) 308-3300

UK
Nightingale House
65 Curzon Street
London W1Y 7PE
☎ (071) 4953990 or 91

Accommodation and Eating Out

***   Expensive
**   Moderate
*   Inexpensive

These three grades are
approximately:
above DM160, DM90-160
and less than DM90
repectively for a double
room

Chapter 1•
The Hanseatic Towns

Accommodation

Hamburg
Pension Remstal *
Steintorweg 2
☎ (040) 244560

Hotel Popp *
Kirchenallee 53
☎ (040) 246045

Hotel Eggers **
Rahlstedter Strasse 78
☎ (040) 6774011

SAS Plaza Hotel ***
Marseiller Strasse 2
☎ (040) 35020

Kiel
Schweriner Hof *
Königsweg 13
☎ (0431) 61416

Hotel Astor **
Holstenplatz 1
☎ (0431) 93017

Avance Hotel Conti-Hansa
***
Schlossgarten 7
☎ (0431) 51150

Kiel-Elmschenhagen
Gasthaus Reimers *
Dorf 2
☎ (0431) 783108

Lübeck
Hotel Zur Burgtreppe *
Hinter der Burg 15
☎ (0451) 73479

Hotel Astoria *
Fackenburger-Allee 68
☎ (0451) 46763

Park Hotel **
Lindenplatz 2
☎ (0451) 84644 & 84760

Alter Speicher ***
Beckergrube 91
☎ (0451) 71045

Eating Out

Hamburg-Eimsbüttel
Bistrot Vienna *
Fettstrasse 2
☎ (040) 4399182

Hamburg-Eppendorf
Mario Ganzoni Traiteur *
Eppendorfer Landstrasse
61
☎ (040) 473855

Hamburg
Brasserie Belle Epoque **
Grosse Bleichen 35
☎ (040) 3508419

Dominique **
(Altstadt)
Karl-Muck-Platz 11
☎ (040) 344511

Fischküche **
Kajen 12
☎ (040) 365631

Cölln's Austernstuben ***
Brodschrangen 1-5
☎ (040) 326059

Kiel
Schwerinerhof e *
Königsweg 13
☎ (0431) 61416

Damperhof **
Damperhofstrasse 5
☎ (0431) 92324

Lübeck
Zur Burgtreppe *
Hinter der Burg 15
☎ (0451) 73479

Hotel Schönwald *
Chasot 25
☎ (0451) 64169

Das kleine Restaurant **
An der Untertrave 39
☎ (0451) 705959

Wullenwever ***
Beckergrube 71
☎ (0451) 704333

Chapter 2 •
The East Friesland
Islands

Accommodation

Baltrum
Haus Westfalia *
☎ (04939) 227

Hotel-Pension Seehof **
☎ (04939) 249

Strandhotel Wietjes ***
☎ (04939) 237 or 283

Borkum
Villa Ems *
Georg-Schütte-Platz 9
☎ (04922) 795

Hotel 'Zum Hanseaten' **
Deichstrasse 35
☎ (04922) 615

Hotel Miramar ***
Am Westkaap 20
☎ (04922) 891 or 892

Juist
Haus Agnes ✳
Billstrasse 33
☎ (04935) 1618

Hotel-Pension Angelika ✳✳
Mittelstrasse 7
☎ (04935) 1004 or 1592

Hotel Achterdiek ✳✳✳
Wilhelmstrasse 36
☎ (04935) 8040

Langeoog
Pension Wilma Bents ✳
Otzumer Weg 5
☎ (04972) 506

Hotel-Pension Kolb ✳✳
Barkhausenstrasse 32
☎ (04972) 404

Hotel Flörke ✳✳✳
Hauptstrasse 17
☎ (04972) 6097

Norderney
Haus Sturmvogel ✳
Am Alten Schirrhof
☎ (04932) 2190

Strand- und Kurhotel ✳✳
Haus Wasserkant
Kaiserstrasse 9
☎ (04932) 777

Inselhotel König ✳✳✳
Bülowallee 8
☎ (04932) 8010

Spiekeroog
Haus Sonnenblick ✳
Bi d' Utkiek 7
☎ (04976) 1424

Müller's Inselhotel ✳✳
Noorderpad 6
☎ (04976) 263

Inselfriede ✳✳✳
Süderloog 12
☎ (04976) 233

Wangerooge
Haus Bläubaum ✳
Nikolausstrasse 3
☎ (04469) 321

Hotel Hansa-Haus ✳✳
Dorfplatz 16
☎ (04469) 237

Strandhotel Upstalsboom
✳✳✳
Strandpromenade 21
☎ (04469) 8760

Eating Out

Borkum
Graf Waldersee ✳
Bahnhofstrasse 6
☎ (04922) 1094

Juist
Hotel Worch ✳
Friesenstrasse 11 + 28
☎ (04935) 1048

Villa Seestern ✳
Friesenstrasse 16
☎ (04935) 210

Pabst-Freesenkroog ✳✳
Strandstrasse 15
☎ (04935) 8050

Juist
Achterdiek-Die gute Stube
✳✳✳
Wilhelmstrasse 36
☎ (04935) 8040

Langeoog
Strandeck-Strandrose ✳✳✳
Kavalierpad 2
☎ (04972) 755

Norderney
Strandvilla an der
Kaiserwiese ✳
Kaiser 6
☎ (04932) 1485

See Villa Miramar ✳
Kaiser 5
☎ (04932) 526

Restaurant Lenz ✳✳
Benekestrasse 3
☎ (04932) 2203

Chapter 3 •
The Sauerland

Accommodation

Arnsberg
Zur Linde ✳
Ruhr Strasse 41
☎ (02931) 3402

Zum Landsberger Hof ✳✳
Alter Markt 18
☎ (02931) 3318

Attendorn
Zum Ritter ✳
Kölner Strasse 33
☎ (02722) 2249

Hotel Rauch ✳✳
Wasserstrasse 6
☎ (02722) 2048 or 2049

Burg Schnellenberg ✳✳✳
(2km east in direction of
Helden)
☎ (02722) 6940

Hagen
Hotel Harnau ✳
Eppenhäuser 53
☎ (02331) 53798

Haus Wortmann ✳
Zur Heide 31
☎ (02331) 83893

Hotel Central ✳✳
Dahlenkampstrasse 2
☎ (02331) 16302

Hagen-Haspe
Hotel Union ✳✳✳
Kölner Strasse 25
☎ (02331) 49091

Soest
Zum Amtsgericht ✳
Nötten 31
☎ (02921) 13303

Haus Gellermann ✳
Konrad-Stecke-Weg 8
☎ (02921) 73167

Pilgrim-Haus ✳✳
Jakobistrasse 75
☎ (02921) 1828

Eating Out

Arnsberg
Tanneck ✳
Sundernerstrasse 25
☎ (02931) 10457

Menge ✳✳
Ruhrstrasse 60
☎ (02931) 4044

Arnsberg-Neheim
Haus Risse ✳✳
Neheimer Markt 2
☎ (02931) 29889

Attendorn
Zur Post ✳
Niederste Strasse 7
☎ (02722) 2465

Attendorn-Neulisternohl
Le Paté ✳✳
Alte Handelsstrasse 15
☎ (02722) 7542

Hagen
Deutsches Haus ✳
Bahnhofstrasse 35
☎ (02331) 21051

Targan ✳
Hugo-Preuss-Strasse 5
☎ (02331) 16883

Hagen-Haspe
Union ✳✳✳
Kölner Strasse 25
☎ (02331) 49091

Hagen-Rummenohl
Dresel ✳✳
Rummenohler Strasse 31
☎ (02337) 1318

Soest
Drei Kronen ✳
Jakobistrasse 39
☎ (02921) 13665

Biermann's Bistro ✳✳
Thomästrasse 47
☎ (02921) 13310

Biermann's Restaurant
✳✳✳
Thomästrasse 47
☎ (02921) 13310

Chapter 4 •
The Saar Valley

Accommodation

Dillingen
Meilchen ✳✳
Hüttenwerkstrasse 31
☎ (06831) 77066

Konz
Alt Konz ✳✳
Gartenstrasse 8
☎ (06501) 3012

Merzig
Zur Annaburg ✳
Wilhelmstrasse 51
☎ (06861) 4095

Mettlach
Zur Spitz ✳
Heinert Strasse 5
☎ (06864) 581

Zum Schwan ✳✳
Freiherr-von-Stein-
Strasse 34
☎ (06864) 7279

Mettlach-Orscholz
Zur Saarschleife ✳✳
Cloefstrasse 44
☎ (06865) 1790

Saarbrücken
St Johanner Hof ✳
Mainzer Strasse 3
☎ (0681) 34902

Bayrischer Hof ✳
St. Ingberter Strasse 46
☎ (0681) 62545

Parkhotel ✳✳
Am Deutsch-
Französischen Garten
☎ (0681) 581033

Am Triller ✳✳✳
Trillerweg 57
☎ (0681) 580000

Saarburg
Haus Brizin ✳
Kruterberg 14
☎ (06581) 2133

Weiskirchen
Sporthotel ✳✳✳
In the Kurzentrum
☎ (06876) 7080

Eating Out

Dillingen-Diefflen
*Bawelsberger Hof — Ma
Cuisine* ✳✳
Dillinger Strasse 5a
☎ (06831) 703993

Merzig
Zum Römer ✳
Schankstrasse 2
☎ (06861) 2645

Mettlach
Zur Post ✳
Heinert Strasse 17
☎ (06864) 557

Saarbrücken
Kaiserhof ✳
Mainzer Strasse 78
☎ (0681) 66426

Bitburger Residenz ✳✳
Dudweiler Strasse 56
☎ (0681) 372312

C'est Ça & chez l'ami Fips
✳✳
Mainzer Strasse 3
☎ (0681) 399576

Saarbrücken-St Arnual

Gasthaus Felsen ✳✳✳
Feldstrasse 17
☎ (0681) 851931

Saarburg
Wagners Restaurant ✳
Brücken Strasse 5
☎ (06581) 3616

Zunftstube ✳
Am Markt 11
☎ (06581) 3696

Burg-Restaurant ✳✳
Schlossberg 12
☎ (06581) 2622

Saarlouis-Beaumarais
Altes Pfarrhaus Beaumarais
✳✳✳
Hauptstrasse 6
☎ (06831) 60848

Weiskirchen-Rappweiler
La Provence ✳✳
Merzigerstrasse 25
☎ (06872) 4326

Chapter 5 •
The Palatinate
Forest Nature Park

Accommodation

Bad Bergzabern
Haus Rita ✳
Petronella Strasse 4
☎ (06343) 8202

Petronella ✳✳
Kurtalstrasse 47
☎ (06343) 1075

Bad Dürkheim
Schillerstube ✳
Schillerstrasse 8
☎ (06322) 63269

Bad Dürkheim-Seebach
Landhaus Fluch ✳✳
Seebacher Strasse 95
☎ (06322) 2488

Dahn
Haus Burgenland ✳
Am Griesböhl 13
☎ (06391) 5641

Pfalzblick ✳✳✳
Goethestrasse 1
☎ (06391) 4040

Kaiserslautern
Zum Deutschen Michel ✳
Richard-Wagner-Strasse
47
☎ (0631) 61890

Pfälzer Hof ✳
Fruchthall 15
☎ (0631) 61922

City Hotel ✳✳
Rosenstrasse 28
☎ (0631) 13025 or 13026

Dorint Hotel ✳✳✳
St-Quentin-Ring 1
Auf dem Betzenberg
☎ (0631) 20150

Landau
Parkhotel ✳✳✳
Mahlastrasse 1
☎ (06341) 32387

**Neustadt an der
Weinstrasse**
Hotel Kurfürst ✳✳
Mussbacher Landstrasse
2
☎ (06321) 7441

Eating Out

Bad Bergzabern
Zur Linde ✳
Schlitt Strasse 1
☎ (06343) 2048

Haus Waldmühle ✳
Kurtal Strasse 59
☎ (06343) 7090

Bad Dürkheim
Hotel Boller ✳
Kurgarten Strasse 19
☎ (06322) 1428

Fronmühle ✳✳
Salinenstrasse 15
☎ (06322) 68081

Weinrefugium ✳✳
Schlachthausstrasse 1a
☎ (06322) 68974

Dahn
Pfalzblick — Schlemmer-
stübchen ✳✳
Goethestrasse 1
☎ (06391) 404-0

Deidesheim
Deidesheimer Hof —
Schwarzer Hahn ✳✳✳
Marktplatz 1
☎ (06326) 1811

Kaiserslautern
Reitz ✳
Pfaffplatz 1
☎ (0631) 13048

BBK-Stammhaus ✳✳
Pirmasenser Strasse 27
☎ (0631) 26426

Uwe's Tomate ✳✳✳
Schillerplatz 4
☎ (0631) 93406

**Neustadt an der
Weinstrasse**
Bayerischer Hof ✳
Landauer Strasse 25-27
☎ (06321) 2202

Mandelhof ✳✳
Mandelring 11
☎ (06321) 88220

Chapter 6 •
Franconia

Accommodation

Bamberg
Hospiz ✳
Promenade 3
☎ (0951) 200011

Hotel Berliner Ring ✳✳
Pödeldorfer Strasse 146
☎ (0951) 131050

Residenzschloss ✳✳✳
Untere Sandstrasse 30-32
☎ (0951) 60910

Bayreuth
Zum Brandenburger ✳
St Georgenstrasse 9
☎ (0921) 20570

Goldener Anker ✳✳
Opernstrasse 6
☎ (0921) 65051

Coburg
Hotel Blankenburg ✳✳
Rosenauer Strasse 30
☎ (09561) 75005

Festungshof ✳✳✳
Festungsberg 1
☎ (09561) 75077

Iphofen
Zum Hirschen ✳
Lange Gasse 25
☎ (09323) 3326

Randersacker
Zur Alten Fähre ✳
Ochsenfurterstrasse 2
☎ (0931) 708200

Würzburg
Hotel Groene ✳
Scheffel 2
☎ (0931) 74449

Hotel Strauss ✳✳
Juliuspromenade 5
☎ (0931) 30570

Hotel Rebstock ✳✳✳
Neubaustrasse 7
☎ (0931) 30930

Eating Out

Bamberg
Die Alte Post ✳
Heiliggrab Strasse 1
☎ (0951) 27848

Residenzschloss Bamberg
✳✳
Untere Sandstrasse 32
☎ (0951) 60910

Bayreuth
Goldener Löwe ✳
Kulmbacher Strasse 30
☎ (0921) 41046

Coburg
Münchner Hofbräu ✳
Johannisgasse 8
☎ (09561) 75049

Kräutergarten ✳✳
Rosenauer Strasse 30
☎ (09561) 75005

Dettelbach
Grüner Baum ✳
Falter Strasse 2
☎ (09324) 1493

Iphofen
Zur Iphöfer Kammer ✳✳
Marktplatz 24
☎ (09323) 6907

Würzburg
Goldener Hahn ✳
Marktgasse 7
☎ (0931) 51941

Rebstock ✳✳
Neubaustrasse 7
☎ (0931) 3093-0

Stefan's Stuben auf dem Nikolaushof ✳✳
Am Käppele
☎ (0931) 81810

Bernardo ✳✳✳
Dompassage
☎ (0931) 18090

Maritim — Palais Restaurant ✳✳✳
Pleichertorstrasse 5
☎ (0931) 3053-0

Chapter 7 •
The Tauber Valley

Accommodation

Bad Mergentheim
Alte Jagdstube ✳
Wachbacher Strasse 1
☎ (07931) 2526

Bocksbeutelstuben ✳
Schlossgarten 23
☎ (07931) 2339

Central am Markt ✳✳
Hans-Heinrich-Ehler-
Platz 40
☎ (07931) 6101

Hotel Victoria ✳✳✳
Poststrasse 2
☎ (07931) 5930

Creglingen
Grüner Baum ✳
Torstrasse 20
☎ (07933) 618

Lauda-Königshofen
Ratskeller ✳✳
Josef-Schmitt-Strasse 17
☎ (09343) 957 or 958

Tauberbischofsheim
Weisses Ross ✳
Hauptstrasse 13
☎ (09341) 2338

Adlerhof ✳✳
Bahnhofstrasse 18
☎ (09341) 2336

Am Brenner ✳✳
Goethestrasse 10
☎ (09341) 3091

Weikersheim
Krone ✳
Hauptstrasse
☎ (07934) 8314

Laurentius ✳✳
Marktplatz 5
☎ (07934) 7272

Wertheim-Bettingen
Schweizer Stuben ✳✳✳
Geiselbrunnweg
☎ (09342) 3070

Eating Out

Bad Mergentheim
Gästehaus Kippes ✳
Erlenbachweg 14
☎ (07931) 7214

Zum Wilden Mann ✳
Reichengässle
☎ (07931) 7638

Haus Bundschu ✳✳
Cronbergstrasse 15
☎ (07931) 3043-45

Victoria — Zirbelstuben
✳✳
Poststrasse 2
☎ (07931) 5930

Creglingen
Krone ✳
Hauptstrasse 12
☎ (07933) 558

Tauberbischofsheim
Am Schloss ✳
Hauptstrasse 56
☎ (09341) 3271

Weikersheim
Deutschherren Stuben ✳
Marktplatz
☎ (07934) 8376

Grüner Hof ✳
(At entrance to Schloss)
☎ (07934) 252

Laurentius ✳✳
Marktplatz 5
☎ (07934) 7007

Wertheim-Bettingen
Schober Landgasthof ✳✳
Geiselbrunnweg 11
☎ (09342) 3070

Schweizer Stuben ✳✳✳
Geiselbrunnweg 11
☎ (09342) 3070

Taverna La Vigna ✳✳✳
Geiselbrunnweg 11
☎ (09342) 3070

Chapter 8 •
The Bayerischer
Wald

Accommodation

Bayerisch Eisenstein
Waldschmidt ✳
Waldschmidt Strasse 9
☎ (09925) 288

Bernried
Reiterhof Koller ✳
Böbrach Strasse 21
☎ (09905) 265

Bodenmais
Hofbräuhaus ✳✳
Marktplatz 5
☎ (09924) 7770

Cham
Randsberger Hof ✳✳
Randsberger-Hof-Strasse
15
☎ (09971) 1266

Grafenau
Bucher-Bräu ✳
Freyungerstrasse 7
☎ (08552) 1602

Säumerhof ✳✳
Steinberg 32
☎ (08552) 2401

Passau
Dreiflüssehof ✳✳
Danziger Strasse 42
☎ (0851) 72040

Passauer Wolf ✳✳✳
Rindermarkt 6
☎ (0851) 34046

Regensburg
Spitalgarten ✳
St.-Katharinen-Platz 1
☎ (0941) 84774

Stadlerbräu ✳
Stadtamhof 15
☎ (0941) 85682

Kaiserhof am Dom ✳✳
Kramgasse 10
☎ (0941) 54027 or 54028

Regensburg
Parkhotel Maximilian ✳✳✳
Maximilianstrasse 28
☎ (0941) 51042

Eating Out

Bayerisch Eisenstein
Waldspitze ✳
Hauptstrasse 4
☎ (09925) 308

Bernried
Sagstetter ✳
Böbrach Strasse 41
☎ (09905) 326

Bischofsmais
Wastlsäge — Wastlstube
✳✳
Lina-Müller-Weg
☎ (09920) 170

Grafenau
Postwirt ✳
Rosenau Strasse 48
☎ (08552) 1018

Steigenberger Sonnenhof —
Hobelspan ✳✳
Sonnenstrasse 12
☎ (08552) 2033

Passau
Blauer Bock ✳
Fritz-Schäfer-Promenade
☎ (0851) 34637

Heilig-Geist-Stift-Schenke
und Stiftskeller ✳✳
Heilig-Geist-Gasse 4
☎ (0851) 2607 & 35387

Wilder Mann ✳✳✳
Am Rathausplatz
☎ (0851) 35075

Regensburg
Peterhof ✳
Fröhliche-Türken-Str 12
☎ (0941) 57514

Bischofshof ✳✳
Krauterermarkt 3
☎ (0941) 59086

Regensburg
Historisches Eck ✳✳✳
Watmarkt 6
☎ (0941) 58920

Viechtach
Schmaus ✳✳
Stadtplatz 5
☎ (09942) 1627

Chapter 9 •
The Bavarian Alps

Accommodation

Aschau/Chiemgau
Café Pauli ✳
Höhenberg 3
☎ (08052) 1466

Burghotel ✳✳
Kampenwandstrasse 94
☎ (08052) 392

Bad Reichenhall
Villa Luitpold ✳
Luitpold 6
☎ (08651) 2494

Hofwirt ✳✳
Salzburger Strasse 21
☎ (08651) 62021 or 62022

Kurhotel Luisenbad ✳✳✳
Ludwigstrasse 33
☎ (08651) 6040

Bad Tölz
Pension Marianne ✳
Schützenstrasse 2
☎ (08041) 4851

Bayrischzell
Alpenrose ✳
Schlierseer 6
☎ (08023) 620

Die Meindelei ✳✳
Michael-Meindl-Strasse
13
☎ (08023) 318

Garmisch-Partenkirchen
Sanktjohanser ✳
Samweberstrasse 3
☎ (08821) 56375

Brunnthaler ✳✳
Klammstrasse 31
☎ (08821) 58066 or 58067

Reit im Winkl
Bichlhof ✳✳
Alte Grenzstrasse 1-3
☎ (08640) 1073

Unterwirt ✳✳✳
Kirchplatz 2
☎ (08640) 8010

Eating Out

Bernau/Chiemsee
Alter Wirt ✳
Kirchplatz 9
☎ (08051) 89014

Bad Reichenhall
Hansi ✳
Rinck Strasse 3
☎ (08651) 3108

Hofwirt ✳✳
Salzburger Strasse 21
☎ (08651) 62021

Neu-Meran ✳✳
Nonn 94
☎ (08651) 4078

Bad Reichenhall-
Kirchberg
Kirchberg-Schlößl —
Schweizer Stuben ✳✳✳
Thumseestrasse 11
☎ (08651) 2760

Bad Tölz
Lindenhof ✳
Königsdorfer Strasse 24
☎ (08041) 9668

Mittenwald
Bavaria ✳
Mühlenweg 44-46
☎ (08823) 1484

Arnspitze ✳✳
Innsbrucker Strasse 68
☎ (08823) 2425

Garmisch-Partenkirchen
Alpengruß ✳
Gehfeld Strasse 10
☎ (08821) 2616

Alpenhof ✳✳
Bahnhofstrasse 74
☎ (08821) 59055

Posthotel Partenkirchen ✳✳
Ludwigstrasse 49
☎ (08821) 51067

Sonnenbichl — Blauer
Salon ✳✳✳
Burgstrasse 97
☎ (08821) 7020

Chapter 10 •
The Upper Danube

Accommodation

Beuron
St Gregoriushaus ✳
Wolterstrasse 9
☎ (07466) 202

Hechingen
Bären ✳
Gutleuthausstrasse
☎ (07471) 2414

Klaiber ✳✳
Obertorplatz 11
☎ (07471) 2257

Brielhof ✳✳✳
On B27 at foot of Burg
Hohenzollern
☎ (07471) 2324 or 4097

Riedlingen
Brücke ✳✳
Hindenburgstrasse 4
☎ (07371) 12266

Sigmaringen
Zum Alten Fritz ✳
Zimmerackerstrasse 9
☎ (07571) 12059

Pfauen ✳
Mühlberg 1
☎ (07571) 13222

Fürstenhof ✳✳
Zeppelinstrasse 12
☎ (07571) 72060

Tuttlingen
Rosengarten ✳
Königstrasse 17
☎ (07461) 5104

Alter Römer ✳
Bahnhofstrasse 39
☎ (07461) 2766

Hotel Schlack ✳✳
Bahnhofstrasse 59
☎ (07461) 72081

Stadt Tuttlingen ✳✳✳
Donaustrasse 30
☎ (07461) 17040

Eating Out

Beuron-Hausen
Steinhaus ✳
Schwenninger Strasse 2
☎ (07579) 556

Gammertingen
Post - Posthalterei ✳✳
Sigmaringer Strasse 4
☎ (07574) 876

Hechingen
Mohren ✳
Schloss Strasse 18
☎ (07471) 2393

Brielhof ✳✳
(On the B27)
☎ (07471) 2324 & 4097

Hechingen-Beuren
Dreifürstenstein ✳
Bismarck Strasse 18
☎ (07477) 704

Sigmaringen
Traube ✳
Fürst-Wilhelm-Strasse 19
☎ (07571) 12227

Tuttlingen
Rößle ✳
Hornberg Strasse 8
☎ (07461) 2913

Chapter 12 •
The Baltic Coast

Accommodation

Ahlbeck/Usedom
Hotel Ahlbeck ✳
Dünenstrasse 1
☎ (039775) 8123

Ahrenshoop/Fischland
Travel Hotel ✳✳
Kurhaus
Dorfstrasse 45
☎ (038220) 206/8

Binz/Rügen
Kurhaus Binz ✳✳
Strandpromenade 27
☎ (038393) 5131

Heiligendamm
Ostsee-Bungalowsiedlung ✳
Seedeichstrasse 18
☎ (038203) 2996

Heringsdorf/Usedom
Hotel Weisses Schloss ✳✳
Rudolf-Breitscheid-Str 3
☎ (038378) 414

Kühlungsborn
Travel Hotel Arendsee ✳✳✳
Strasse des Friedens 30
☎ (038293) 446

Prerow/Darß
Pension Linde ✳
Waldstrasse 33
☎ (038233) 327

Putbus/Rügen
Hotel Pommernstübchen ✳
Bahnhofstrasse 7
☎ (038301) 278

Ueckermünde
*Hotelschiff MS 'Burg
Landshut'* ✳
Altes Bollwerk 1
☎ (039771) 2735

Warnemünde
Hanse-Hotel ✳✳✳
Parkstrasse 51
☎ (0381) 5011

Hotel Neptun ✳✳✳
Seestrasse 19
☎ (0381) 5460

Wismar
Altes Brauhaus ✳✳
Lübsche Strasse 95
☎ (03841) 3223

Eating Out

Binz/Rügen
Poseidon ✳✳
Lottumstrasse 1
☎ (038393) 2669

Göhren/Rügen
Nordperd ✳✳
Nordperdstrasse 11
☎ (038308) 70

Graal-Müritz
Restaurant 'Waldperle' ✳
Clara-Zetkin-Strasse 10
☎ (038206) 234

Kühlungsborn
Brunshöver Möhl ✳✳
An der Mühle 3
☎ (038293) 937

Stralsund
Zur Kogge ✳
Triebseerstrasse 26
☎ (03831) 3846

Scheele-Haus ✳✳
(impressive interior)
Fährstrasse 23/24
☎ (03831) 292987

Ueckermünde
Pommer'scher Hof ✳
Ueckerstrasse 74
☎ (039771) 2443

Usedom
Deutsches Haus ✳
Swinemünder Strasse 25
☎ (038372) 201

Warnemünde
Spezialitäten-Restaurants
✳✳✳
Am Hotel Neptun
Schillerstrasse 14
☎ (0381) 5371

Wieck
Zur Fähre ✳✳
Fährstrasse 1
☎ (03834) 2490

Wismar
Seehase ✳
Altböterstrasse 6
☎ (03841) 2134

Alter Schwede ✳✳
Am Markt 20
☎ (03841) 3552

Chapter 13 •
The Uckermark

Accommodation

Eberswalde-Finow
Gasthaus Am Walde ✳✳
Brunnenstrasse 6
☎ (03334) 65218

Feldberg
Waldrestaurant und
Pension ✳✳
Stieglitz
Klinkecken 7
☎ (039831) 420

Fürstenwerder
Ferien- und Schulungs-
zentrum ✳
Fibigershof
☎ (039859) 458

Himmelpfort
Gaststätte Zur Sonne ✳
Fürstenberger Strasse 1
☎ (033089) 366

Joachimsthal
Haus am Werbellinsee ✳✳
Seerandstrasse 10
☎ (033361) 227

Hotel am Grimnitzsee ✳✳✳
Angermünder Strasse 18
☎ (033361) 728

Lychen
Ferienhotel Sängerslust ✳
Sängerlust
☎(039888) 277

Ferienpension Waldesruh ✳
Springstrasse 9
☎ (039888) 697

Oderberg
Hotel Goldener Löwe ✳
Berliner Strasse 3
☎ (033369) 246

Prenzlau
Parkhotel ✳
Grabowstrasse 14
☎ (03984) 2219

Stolpe
Hotel-Restaurant Stolper
Turm ✳✳
☎ (033338) 540

Templin
Ferienhotel am Lübbesee ✳✳
Am Lübbesee 1
☎ (03987) 45120

Eating Out

Angermünde
Schwedter Tor ✳✳
Schwedter Strasse 29
☎ (03331) 33015

Boitzenburg
Klostercafé ✳
(next to Mühlenmuseum)

Chorin
Alte Klosterschänke ✳✳
Am Amt 9
☎ (033366) 433

Eberswalde-Finow
Gasthaus 'Am Walde' ✳
Brunnenstrasse 6
☎ (03334) 65218

Ratskeller Eberswalde ✳✳
Strasse der Jugend 44
☎ (03334) 22590

Himmelpfort
Haus Daheim ✳
Klosterstrasse 12
☎ (033089) 210

Joachimsthal
Speisegaststätte 'Zur Krim' ✳
Marktstrasse 11
☎ (033361) 460

Dorfkrug 'Alt Grimnitz' ✳
Hövelstrasse 1
☎ (033361) 420

Lychen
Stadttor Pizzeria ✳
Stargarder Strasse 16

Prenzlau
Tommy's Igel ✳✳
Robert-Schulz-Ring 37b
☎ (03984) 4352

Templin
Stadt Templin ✳
Mühlenstrasse
☎ (03987) 2708

Treff Nr 1 ✳✳
Ernst-Thälmann-Strasse 19
☎ (03987) 2327

Chapter 14 •
The Altmark

Accommodation

Arendsee
Heuhotel Klaus Ziems ✳
Koloniestrasse 17
☎ (039384) 347

Gasthaus Cordes ✳
Friedensstrasse 88
☎ (039384) 330

Hotel Deutsches Haus ✳✳
Friedensstrasse 91
☎ (039384) 500 and 7294

Hotel Stadt Arendsee ✳✳
Friedensstrasse 113
☎ (039384) 234

Hotel Waldheim ✳✳
Lüchower Strasse
☎ (039384) 237 and 238

Gardelegen
Hotel Deutsches Haus ✳
Rathausplatz 1
☎ (03907) 2281

Salzwedel
Bahnhofshotel ✳
Bahnhof 10

Hotel Union ✳✳
Goethestrasse 11
☎ (03901) 22097

Stendal
Stadtsee-Herberge ✳
Arthur-Becker-Strasse 27
☎ (03931) 412039

Hotel Schwarzer Adler ✳✳
Kornmarkt 5/7
☎ (03931) 212265

Gästehaus I und II ✳✳
Heersener Strasse
☎ (03931) 2513301

Hotel Stadt Stendal ✳✳✳
Bahnhofstrasse 15
☎ (03931) 212403-04

Eating Out

Arendsee
*Binnenfischerei zum
Maränenhof* ✳
(on the lake near Zießau)

Gaststätte Seglerheim ✳
Lindenstrasse 15

Altmärker Hof ✳✳
Seehäuser Strasse 30
☎ (039384) 369

Steakhouse & Hotel ✳✳
Stadt Arendsee
Friedensstrasse 113
☎ (039384) 234

Gardelegen
Café am Rathaus ✳
Rathausplatz
☎ (03907) 2829

'Quickbox' ✳
Marktstrasse 2
☎ (03907) 2327

Steak House ✳✳
Stendaler Strasse 106
☎ (03907) 41137

Salzwedel
Café Baumkuchen ✳
Holzmarktstrasse 4
☎ (03901) 22107

'Alte Stadtwache' ✳
Breite Strasse 51
☎ (03901) 26240

Restaurant 'Athen' ✳✳
Arendseer Strasse 25
☎ (03901) 22344
Closed Monday

Stendal
Ratskeller ✳✳
Kornmarkt
☎ (03931) 212665

Tangermünde
Störtebeker ✳✳
Am Hafen
☎ (039322) 901

Chapter 15 • The Harz

Accommodation

Altenbrak
Pension Haus Bodetal ✳
Ludwigshütte 9
☎ (039456) 207

Blankenburg
Pension Klaus ✳
Lindenstrasse 12
☎ (03944) 2423

Clausthal-Zellerfeld
Hotel Kronprinz ✳✳
Goslarsche Strasse 20
☎ (05323) 81088

Goslar
Hotel Schwarzer Adler ✳✳
Rosentorstrasse 25
☎ (05321) 24001

Kaiserworth ✳✳✳
Markt 3
☎ (05321) 21111

Harzgerode
Hotel Harzquell ✳
Hauptstrasse 10
☎ (039484) 2346

Quedlinburg
Motel Quedlinburg ✳✳
Wipertistrasse 9
☎ (03946) 2855/6

Schierke
Schierker Baude ✳
Barenberg 18
☎ (039455) 422

Hotel Heinrich Heine ✳✳
Ernst-Thälmann-Strasse 1
☎ (039455) 354/6

Stolberg
Pension Hahnemann ✳
Niedergasse 101
☎ (034654) 458/320

Wenigerode
Hotel Stadt Wernigerode
✳✳
(Just south-west in
Hasserode)
Langer Stieg 62
☎ (03943) 36216

Gothisches Haus ✳✳✳
Am Markt
☎ (03943) 3750

Eating Out

Altenau
Gebirgshotel ✳✳
Kleine Oker 17
☎ (05328) 218

Bad Sachsa
*Romantischer Winkel-Die
Galerie* ✳✳✳
Bismarckstrasse 23
☎ (05523) 1005

Blankenburg
Kurhotel Blankenburg ✳✳
Mauerstrasse 9
☎ (03944) 2683

Braunlage
Zum Jermerstein ✳✳
Harzburger Strasse 19
☎ (05520) 560

Braunlage
Zur Tanne ✳✳✳
Herzog-Wilhelm-Strasse 8
☎ (05520) 1034-35

Clausthal-Zellerfeld
Museums-Gaststätte ✳
(Next to Oberharzer
Bergwerksmuseum)
☎ (05323) 82261

Goslar
Rigoletto ✳
Marktstrasse 38
☎ (05321) 23705

*Hotel-Restaurant 'Das
Brusttuch'* ✳✳
Hoher Weg 1
☎ (05321) 21081

Nordhausen
Goldener Hahn ✳
Freiherr-vom-Stein-
Strasse 4
☎ (03631) 4537

Quedlinburg
Buntes Lamm ✳✳
Schmale Strasse 1a
☎ (03946) 2641

Schierke
Heinrich Heine ✳
Thälmannstrasse 1
☎ (039455) 354-56

Wernigerode
Ratskeller ✳✳
Markt 1
☎ (03943) 32704

Chapter 16 •
The Oberlausitz

Accommodation

Bautzen
Hotel Lubin ✳✳
Wendischer Graben 20
☎ (03591) 511114

Bischofswerda
Pension Gürena ✳
Kamenzer Strasse 24
☎ (03594) 6949

Pension Felsenkeller ✳✳
Neustädter Strasse 10
☎ (03594) 3346

Görlitz
Pension Schellergrund ✳
Martin-Opitz-Strasse 2
☎ (03581) 401687

Hotel Hansa ✳✳
Berliner Strasse 33/34
☎ (03581) 406301

Jonsdorf
Gasthof Lindengarten ✳
Großschönauer Strasse 21
☎ (035844) 654

Löbau
Hotel Stadt Löbau ✳
Elisenstrasse 1
☎ (03585) 521/3621/3622

Lückendorf
Hotel Hochwaldblick ✳✳
Kammstrasse 13
☎ (035844) 835

Obercunnersdorf
*Hotel und Gaststätte Zum
Bahnhof* ✳
Hintere Dorfstrasse 11
☎ (035875) 224

Oybin
Pension 'Kammbaude' ✳
Grenzstrasse 7 / Hain
☎ (035844) 477

Oybiner Hof ✳✳
Hauptstrasse 5
☎ (035844) 297 or 298

Waltersdorf
*Pension und Gaststätte
'Zur Lausche'* ✳
Hauptstrasse 60
☎ (035841) 2476

Eating Out

Bautzen
Kaniga ✳✳
Kurt-Pchalek-Strasse 1
☎ (03591) 47913

Ratskeller ✳✳
Innere Lauenstrasse 1
☎ (03591) 42474

Görlitz
Bürgerstübl ✳✳
Neißstrasse 27
☎ (03581) 24722

Goldener Baum ✳✳
Untermarkt 4/5
☎ (03581) 6268·

Kamenz
Altertumsschänke ✳
Pulsnitzer Strasse 74
☎ (03578) 6424

Stadt Dresden ✳✳
Weststrasse 10
☎ (03578) 5304

Obercunnersdorf
Hotel Altes Schützenhaus ✳
Am Ferienheim 9
☎ (035875) 372

Oybin
Burgkeller ✳
Hauptstrasse 26
☎ (035844) 454

Rammenau
Barockschloss Rammenau ✳✳
Am Schloss 4
☎ (03594) 3065

Zittau
Pizza-Buffet ✳
Johannistrasse 1
☎ (03583) 3651

Hotel 'Schwarzer Bär' ✳✳
Ottokarplatz 12
☎ (03583) 2366

Dresdner Hof ✳✳
Äußere Oybiner Strasse 9
☎ (03583) 3919

A Note To The Reader

The accommodation and eating out lists in this book are based upon the authors' own experiences and therefore may contain an element of subjective opinion. The contents of this book are believed correct at the time of publication but details given may change. We welcome any information to ensure accuracy in this guide book and to help keep it up-to-date.

Please write to The Editor, Moorland Publishing Co Ltd, Moor Farm Road, Airfield Estate, Ashbourne, Derbyshire, DE6 1HD, England.

American and Canadian readers please write to The Editor, The Globe Pequot Press, 6 Business Park Road, PO Box 833, Old Saybrook, Connecticut 06475, USA.

M P C

The Globe Pequot press

EXPLORE THE UNEXPLORED

with

OFF THE BEATEN TRACK

With the *Off the Beaten Track* series you will explore the unexplored and absorb the essential flavour of the countries you visit.

An *Off the Beaten Track* book is the only companion you will need on your travels.

The series includes the following titles which are or will shortly be available:

Off the Beaten Track: Austria
Off the Beaten Track: Britain
Off the Beaten Track: Northern France
Off the Beaten Track: Southern France
Off the Beaten Track: Germany
Off the Beaten Track: Greece
Off the Beaten Track: Ireland
Off the Beaten Track: Italy
Off the Beaten Track: Portugal
Off the Beaten Track: Scandinavia
Off the Beaten Track: Spain
Off the Beaten Track: Switzerland

These books are on sale in all good bookshops or can be ordered directly from the publishers.

SIMPLY THE BEST